Chicago Public Library

W9-BNA-973

A cry unheard : new insights into t

DISCARD

A Cry Unheard

New Insights into the Medical Consequences of Loneliness

By James J. Lynch

ALSO BY JAMES J. LYNCH

THE BROKEN HEART:

THE MEDICAL CONSEQUENCES OF LONELINESS

LANGUAGE OF THE HEART:

THE BODY'S RESPONSE TO HUMAN DIALOGUE

To the children of

Joe and Camille, Jim and Francesca, Francis and Kathleen,

With a prayer that the exquisite love of Eileen,

Wife, mother, and grandmother

Who inspired this book and nurtures our lives,

Will flow ever outward, ever expanding

From the children of your generation

To all the children of generations yet to come.

A Cry Unheard

New Insights into the Medical Consequences of Loneliness

Published by Bancroft Press ("Books that enlighten")
P.O. Box 65360, Baltimore, MD 21209
800-637-7377
410-764-1967 (fax)
bruceb@bancroftpress.com
www.bancroftpress.com

ISBN 1-890862-11-8
Printed in the United States of America

First Edition

1 3 5 7 9 10 8 6 4 2

Distributed to the trade by National Book Network (NBN), Lanham, MD

PREFACE

The *Broken Heart: The Medical Consequences of Loneliness* was completed in 1976—the bicentennial anniversary of the United States of America—and *A Cry Unheard* in 1999 as our nation prepares to enter the new millennium. I mention these dates for two reasons. First, these two books present many facts and figures about social and educational life and their links to health in the United States of 1976 and 1999 that are not particularly complimentary. While the implications of all the health data and trends are universal—companionship, communication, social isolation, school failure, and loneliness are by no means idiosyncratic American problems—the statistics on which they are based were largely drawn from the United States. These occasionally unflattering health statistics are nevertheless presented with a deep love of this country, its people, and its ideals.

Second, both 1976 and 1999 were important years for another reason that is far more personal—in March of 1976, my father died, and in June of 1999, my mother died. Both of my parents died six months before the publication of these respective books. My parents were peasant immigrants from the Inishowen Peninsula of Northern County Donegal in Ireland, and the social, emotional, and spiritual ethic that pervades these books owes much to them. Their ideals were clear—the love of God, love of family, and love of neighbors. For their ideals and their love, I thank them.

TABLE OF CONTENTS

ACKNOWLEDGEMENTS

Aristotle was once asked how to define a "friend." His answer, according to Diogenes Laetrus, writing in the year 200 A.D., was, "One soul abiding in two bodies." While they are in no way responsible for any errors of omission or commission contained in the pages of this book, I believe that the many friends who have helped me over the years do indeed share my soul, my spirit, and my heart. I am profoundly grateful for their friendship and their support.

In 1962, as a young graduate student, I had the good fortune to meet a professor and scientist at The Johns Hopkins Medical School who was to become the dominant intellectual influence of my life. My late, beloved teacher, W. Horsley Gantt, M.D., passed away in 1980, and three decades later I still deeply miss his intellectual curiosity, his originality, his love of research, and his zest for life. For more than a decade, I had the rare privilege of working in his laboratories, learning about his "Effect of Person," and witnessing first-hand the way human contact exerts such a powerful influence on the cardiovascular system.

During those formative years, Dr. Gantt introduced me to two remarkable individuals—one, a literary giant, John Dos Passos, and the other a pioneering medical investigator, Stewart Wolf, M.D. Few memories have remained more vividly etched in my heart than those wonderful Sunday evening dinners spent at Dr. Gantt's Baltimore home, where I sat in awe as Dos Passos, in his inimitable gentle style, spoke quietly of the foundations of American Democracy, and of Alexis de Tocqueville and Thomas Jefferson. Dos Passos brought these giants to life in a way that made me feel they were right there in the room, sharing dinner with us. My perspective on the socio-political and cultural context of human loneliness owes much to the inspiration I derived from this gentle literary figure and humble soul.

Dr. Stewart Wolf's pioneering work on "Life Stress and Essential Hypertension" at Cornell Medical School, as well as his remarkable studies of social cohesiveness and heart disease in the Pocono Mountain town of Roseto, Pennsylvania, similarly left a deep and lasting impression on me. Time and again in the intervening years, when I have been lulled into believing that I had stumbled across a new research discovery, or formulated a novel or important clinical insight, I have reread Dr. Wolf's research writings, only to discover that his footprints were there decades earlier. His friendship and teaching have inspired my work for the past three decades.

Paul Rosch, M.D., President of the American Institute of Stress in New York, and former student of Hans Selye, has been my collaborator and intellectual mentor for the past twenty-five years. His clinical wisdom, his intimate knowledge of the links between stress and disease, his "Yeshiva Bucher" scholarly temperament, his love for people, and, most importantly, his friendship have deeply enriched my life. I could never repay him for his generosity.

Three physicians at the University of Maryland Medical School played a vital role in all of my research endeavors. Eugene B. Brody, M.D., and Russell R. Monroe, M.D., both of whom were Chairman of Psychiatry, supported all of my research endeavors in every way possible for nearly two decades. Herbert S. Gross, M.D., the Medical Director of the Psychophysiological Clinics, brought to our collaborative research and clinical endeavors an in-depth analytic perspective that has been a constant beam of light for the past three decades.

Dozens of research colleagues at The Johns Hopkins Medical School, The University of Pennsylvania Medical School, and the University of Maryland Medical School also participated in numerous research studies linking companionship and human dialogue to cardiovascular health. While each of these colleagues contributed in his or her own unique way, Aaron H. Katcher, M.D., at the University of Pennsylvania, has been, for me, the living embodiment of "friend," as Aristotle defined it—"one soul abiding in two bodies." He helped form and shape virtually every core concept in this book, and our collective research efforts for the past thirty years have been a source of great personal satisfaction. His enduring friendship has been one of the sustaining forces of my life.

Three other very dear friends deserve special thanks. Diehl Snyder, M.D., Medical Director of the Philhaven Hospital in Mt. Gretna, Pennsylvania; Kenneth Gimbel, M.D., a cardiologist in Atlanta, Georgia; and Arnie Katz, a clinical psychologist in Seattle, Washington, have all provided invaluable support, wisdom, and love for the past three decades. They have been my teachers, as well as a source of unwavering support and comfort when it really counted. With a great deal of wit, Ken Gimbel also generously devoted a great deal of time trying to spare the readers of this book as much redundancy, ambiguity, and digression as my temperament would permit.

It has also been my very good fortune to work with the Mid-Atlantic Cardiovascular Group of Maryland, and in particular with Jeffrey Quartner,

M.D., Medical Director of Lifebridge Health, formerly known as Sinai-Wellbridge Cardiovascular Rehabilitation Center in Pikesville, Maryland. For over a decade, he has provided the wisdom, support, and friendship crucial to the development of our research and clinical endeavors. "We have to find better ways to help heart patients cope in the real world and in a real way" has been his untiring quest. To him and his marvelous "rehab staff," I owe a special debt of gratitude.

Francis Craig, Ph.D., a health psychologist at The State University of Pennsylvania at Mansfield, prepared the graphics for this book. While his tables and charts add considerably to an understanding of loneliness and its medical consequences, his knowledge of health psychology, as well as his editorial suggestions and research perspective, helped make the writing of this book an absolute joy.

I will always count it a privilege to have worked with Martin Kessler, my editor at Basic Books in New York, and the publisher of *The Broken Heart, and The Language of the Heart*. In his own gentle and inimitable style, Martin helped in a very substantial way to bring my message about the medical consequences of loneliness to the public's attention. His wisdom and understanding of the social and medical issues confronting our nation were crucial. His death several years ago left a real void in my life.

I am also deeply grateful to Bruce Bortz, my editor and publisher at Bancroft Press in Baltimore. He recognized the need to re-examine the links between loneliness and premature death, and was willing to assume the risks, as well as expend the time and energy, involved in bringing this book to fruition. His support and patience, as well as his wisdom and enthusiasm, are deeply appreciated.

Last but by no means least, it has been my privilege to serve and share in the lives of the many hundreds of patients who are the very heart and soul of this book. For thirty years, they have shared with me their pain and suffering, their loneliness and their love, indeed, their very heart beats so that I and others might understand. Their collective spirit is embodied in this book's central message: "Dialogue is the elixir of life." Dialogue with them has been, most assuredly, the elixir of *my* life, and I am both humbled and grateful for that gift. My hope is that the lessons they have taught me will enter the hearts of everyone who reads this book and help fill *their* lives with love.

Chapter One

AN OVERVIEW

"Thirty years ago, anyone blaming loneliness for physical illness would have been laughed at," the editors of *Newsweek* observed in a March 1998 cover story. That issue described the rapidly accumulating medical evidence linking the disruption of human relationships and loneliness to a sharply increased risk of disease and premature death in all post-industrialized nations. *Newsweek's* assessment was most assuredly correct. The medical consequences of loneliness *are* far better understood now by health professionals than they were when my first book, *The Broken Heart: The Medical Consequences of Loneliness,* was published in 1977. [1]

Although medical research on this topic began while I was still a boy running around in short pants, my own research journey in this area first began with a group of investigators at The Johns Hopkins Medical School in 1965. Since that time, there has been a veritable explosion in knowledge about the connections between social support and health, as well as an increased understanding of the links between human loneliness and the vulnerability to disease and premature death.

Slowly but surely over the past three decades, this growth in knowledge has led me to one inescapable conclusion: *Dialogue is the elixir of life and chronic loneliness its lethal poison.* Based on recent health trends, it is growing ever more apparent that New Age cultural forces that disturb, disrupt, and destroy human dialogue must be viewed with the same concern and alarm as has been brought to bear on other plagues, infectious diseases, viruses, bacteria, and cancers. For all of the recent health data suggest that if current trends persist, *communicative disease*, and its resultant loneliness, will equal *communicable disease* as a leading cause of premature death in all post-industrialized nations during the twenty-first century.

A wide variety of statistics suggest that large numbers of people fail to recognize the dangers, that they are unable to fully appreciate the potent health benefits derived from various forms of social support, including that provided by family, friends, neighbors, and loved ones. Signs of the disruption of human relationships and symptoms of human loneliness have grown ever more problematic in the past 35 years, indicating that attitudes about human relationships have changed, not only in America, but also throughout the rest of the Western World.

In 1900, for example, only 5 percent of American households consisted of one person living alone. By 1960, that figure had risen to 13 percent, and at the century's ebb it stood at 25 percent. Fifty percent of all marriages in America currently end in divorce, and over one million additional children annually are caught up in divorce. In addition, the number of children born to unmarried women rose 61 percent between 1980 and 1991—going from 18 percent of all live births in 1980 to 30 percent by 1991. The rate of increase has been particularly dramatic for white women, increasing over 94 percent in the last decade.[2]

Rapid increases in single parent households, high divorce rates, declining marriage rates, increasing numbers of people living alone, and the rapid increase in the number of children born into single parent households represent only one dimension of what has been a truly profound shift in attitudes. Widespread violence, rapidly growing numbers of men and women held in US jails, drug addiction and alcoholism, and an ever-increasing use of anti-anxiety and antidepressant medications are but a few additional signs of growing interpersonal and communicative problems within our society.

At times it seems as if our nation, having reached its high-water mark of prosperity, is simultaneously awash and drowning in a sea of narcotics and prescriptive medications to help deaden the pain. It is almost as if we have agreed to submit voluntarily to a national, chemically-induced frontal lobotomy to cope with the loneliness and disconnectedness of our age.

There are, as well, a variety of phenomena not usually associated with communicative disorders or the destruction of interpersonal relationships, social isolation, loneliness, and premature death. One such source can be found in school failure, which scars legions of children with the "Mark of Cain" for the rest of their life. Unable to relate to, or communicate with, their fellow man because of the shame of their "failure" in school, they wander in emotional exile, dying prematurely decades later, out of society's sight and broken-hearted.

Health experts inform us that if death rates for those white Americans with less than ten years of schooling were the same as those who graduate from college, at least 250,000 fewer people would die in the United States each year. They further inform us that this "excess" mortality has more to do with social isolation and loneliness than it does with economic stress. And I should note that these quarter-million white

Americans are casualties of a hidden plague that exacts a toll at least as lethal as any other medical problem facing our nation. The toll is equally devastating for Hispanic-Americans and African-Americans.[3]

In this book, I describe these varied phenomena and clarify what school failure and other socially isolating childhood experiences have in common with adult experiences such as being single, widowed, and divorced, and how they are all linked to an increased risk of premature death. I explain how these ostensibly disparate human experiences are particularly linked to an increased risk of heart disease. And I explain, perhaps most importantly, the mechanisms that contribute to the greatly increased risk of premature cardiac death.

I also suggest a variety of steps that can be taken to help solve these problems. For in one way or another, all of these situations share in the absence, the breakdown, or the failure of human dialogue, reflecting an increased struggle with a recently understood hidden type of *"communicative disease"* that exacerbates social isolation and loneliness. The resultant physiological stress can be unbearable, and even break the human heart.

A NEW PERSPECTIVE: A CRY UNHEARD

Shortly after *The Broken Heart* was published in 1977, I had the good fortune to be among the first to come across a significant technological advance—one that revealed a dimension of the human cardiovascular system that had previously escaped attention. With the aid of what was then brand new computerized technology, I was able to monitor blood pressure automatically while continuing to engage patients in conversation.

This major technical advance permitted me and my colleagues to observe that a mode of human interaction previously considered "mental" in nature—*ordinary, everyday human dialogue*—could have profound effects on the human heart. Prior to the development of this technology, blood pressure was typically monitored with a stethoscope and mercury manometer. Since the physician had to listen with his stethoscope to the pulsation of the heart beat in the brachial artery, neither the doctor nor patient could talk during the measurement process. Silence was built-in.

With the new computerized technology, however, it was easy to engage patients in dialogue while their blood pressure was measured automatically. And that one simple procedural change in the measurement of blood pressure opened up an entirely new vista, completely altering my understanding of human dialogue and its links to loneliness and heart disease. My colleagues and I began to observe what we would come to call the "vascular see-saw" and "vascular rhythm" of all human dialogue. It was the predictable rise of blood pressure whenever a person began to talk, and then, just as predictable, its fall whenever a person became quiet and listened to others, or attended to the external environment. Thus produced were dramatic new insights into the links between human dialogue, loneliness, disease, and premature death.[4]

For the first time, I was able to appreciate the devastating health consequences of varied life experiences, including school failure, which made human dialogue either difficult or impossible. In those situations, the normal rhythm of the "vascular see-saw" could be disrupted. In its place were rapid, marked surges in blood pressure, reflecting the hidden "vascular cries" of shame, anxiety, anger, and fear that had previously gone unrecognized, undetected, and unheard.

It also became easier to observe the potent health consequences of talk between and among adults who used language not to reach, understand, and share with each other, but to hurt, manipulate, control, and offend. These communicative problems, and the accompanying vascular cries, frequently occurred outside of the person's awareness. From all external appearances, patients were calm, cool, and collected, while internally their bodies were reacting in terrible distress.

Communicative difficulties of this sort frequently could be traced back to earlier training and traumatic experiences with parental use of language in childhood. Outside of their own conscious awareness, parents far too often instilled this type of dysfunctional and abusive rhetoric in their own children, who then carried it into adulthood, and passed it along to their own unwitting offspring.

The repetitive and cumulative exposure to language used to hurt, manipulate, control, and offend inexorably led to the serious wounding of self-esteem during childhood. If compounded by other traumatic developmental experiences such as school failure, the effects were both toxic and fatal. Irrespective of the original source of the wounding, however, the result was always the same—one that made it increasingly difficult for the victim to communicate with others without physiological distress. The greater the developmental damage, the greater the physiological distress whenever a person tried to communicate. Exposure to this "toxic talk" produced in its victims a hopelessness that language could be used in a constructive manner to reach others, and that, in turn, made human communication for them increasingly difficult and physiologically taxing. Exposure to such talk proved "toxic" precisely because it led to premature death.[5]

Eventually, I came to realize that it was the repetitive activation of one of two opposing bodily states during everyday dialogue that either enhanced health or conversely contributed to the premature development of disease and death. One bodily state I label the *physiology of inclusion,* and the other the *physiology of exclusion.*[6] In essence, dysfunctional dialogue, withdrawal from dialogue, or the type of dialogue that occurs in a social context where others are seen as a threat, triggers the repetitive activation of what scientists have long recognized as the "fight/flight response." It is this "wired-in" posture of *exclusion* towards others, one that is rooted in prior experience with toxic talk or linguistically-based injury, which activates the fight/flight response.

The "fight/flight response," regulated by the "autonomic nervous system," developed in higher level mammals over millions of years of evolution. It was designed to prepare the body for those emergency situations where physical activity was required for self-preservation. In the face of the proverbial "saber-tooth tigers and wooly mammoths" wandering about in the primeval forests, both human and non-human mammals alike had to have a way of reacting quickly to preserve their lives. They had to be able to respond to these threats in a way that would prepare them to either fight or flee.

The autonomic nervous system was designed to stimulate the cardiovascular system, which in turn was designed to deliver the energy needed to support the physical movements required in emergencies. In threatening situations, heart rate and blood pressure quickly increase, redistributing blood from the skin and various internal organs to the muscles involved in the physical activity. In addition, sugar and fat from bodily stores are released to provide energy for the movement, along with secretion of a highly active neurotransmitter, called catecholamines, that can affect almost any organ in the body and alter brain function. Various stress hormones, including adrenalin, also are released by the activation of this neurotransmitter from the cortex of the adrenal glands.

While the saber-tooth tigers, wooly mammoths, and primeval forests have long since disappeared from our lives, the autonomic nervous system still mobilizes in response to the perception of "symbolic saber- tooth tigers." Far too often, however, the perception of these dangers can be way out of proportion to the actual threat, leading to excessive emotional arousal, and fight/flight reactions in situations where there is no objective threat to life. Unfortunately, the repetitive mobilization of the cardiovascular system in a fight/flight response to situations not requiring either will eventually wear down and exhaust the human body.

It was the availability of the new blood pressure monitoring technology that first permitted us to observe the surprising frequency of fight/flight reactivity during everyday dialogue. It was surprising in part because words and dialogue are the stuff of human life, and it just did not seem possible that ordinary, everyday conversations could pose such a major threat to modern-day human beings. Because I was well aware that human loneliness was a major health risk, I first assumed, in a rather simplistic manner, that an increase in dialogue with others would be an obvious part of the solution.

Yet, the new technology helped to make it apparent that a chronic *exclusion* of others—an orientation where other human beings were seen as a threat, especially during everyday human dialogue—could trigger repetitive activation of the fight/flight response in situations where neither fight nor flight was necessary. These repetitive, undetected, maladaptive fight/flight reactions, frequently "wired-in" by exposure to toxic talk early in childhood, would inexorably lead to physiological exhaustion, creating a biologically-based need to withdraw from dialogue for one's "self-preservation." This *communicative reflex of exclusion,* in turn, would lead inexorably to an increased sense of loneliness and social alienation, and ultimately to disease and premature death.

By contrast, dialogue that included others—a dialogue that did not respond to others, or the living world around them, as a potential threat— would activate the *physiology of inclusion,* which I call a *state of enhanced relaxation.* This fosters precisely the opposite bodily state, one that produces health and longevity. It would help to draw people out of their own selves, and closer to others in dialogue, rather than exclude and seal them off. The new technology, at long last, gave us a way to help both children and adults to be more aware of these undetected and frequently unfelt physiological reactions to dialogue.

It also helped us teach them about these opposing reflexes, and guide them away from a "wired-in" communicative physiology of exclusion and toward one of communicative inclusion. The shift could help them embrace and touch others in dialogue in a way that at long last offered the hope of ending their communicative isolation, exile, and loneliness.

Understanding the paradoxical impact of human dialogue, one that could be physiologically inclusive or exclusive, provided an entirely new perspective on how to more effectively address and treat a variety of communicative diseases linked to human loneliness. It provided an entirely new perspective on school failure, too, and its links to premature cardiac death. It suggested new ways to help school children at risk. And the capacity to monitor blood pressure automatically also provided a new way to help couples communicate more effectively by permitting them to see the previously hidden, undetected, but heartfelt nature of their dialogue.

And most importantly, patients suffering from various cardiovascular disorders could utilize this new perspective to reduce the stress on their hearts, and increase their chances of living a longer and better life. Patients who literally had talked their way into heart disease could at long last be taught new ways to communicate in a less toxic manner, and to reduce the stress on their hearts.

Yet, even while my own perspective was undergoing fundamental change, it was easy to understand why the majority of people would have great difficulty grasping the vital links between everyday dialogue and physical health. In our age, each new dawn bears witness to yet another miraculous medical advance that boggles our imaginations. Heart transplants, and other organ transplants, coronary bypass surgery, genetically tailored medicines that offer the hope of eliminating cancer, and prescriptive remedies like Viagra that appear to guarantee erections into one's centennial years —these bear witness to the marvelous power of modern scientific medicine.

To the average reader, it seems far more likely that the elixir of life and the fountain of youth will be provided by a bottle of designer gene medicines and cloned self-images than in conversations with one's fellow man. In the midst of these advances, discussions of *"disembodied dialogue," "communicative disease,"* and *"human loneliness"* seem strangely out of place—outmoded romantic beliefs from an age that has long since passed us by. It is, unfortunately, a cruel perspective for those who suffer the most, and for those most at risk.

In addition, the triumphs of modern medicine have contributed to another widely held assumption that makes it difficult to grasp the vital role dialogue plays in our physical well-being. We are reminded, on a daily basis, that each human body is a separate and distinct biological machine, and that the human heart and circulation are part of a hydraulic pumping system. The routine availability of coronary bypass surgery, for example, has reinforced a belief in the mechanical nature of the heart. Heart transplant operations similarly reinforce these views, leading to the overarching assumption that the heart and its circulation are nothing more, and nothing less, than a hydraulic pumping and plumbing system. It has fostered the widely-held assumption that human beings are two entities—possessing a mind and a body that interact with one another.

Is it any wonder, then, that so many have come to assume that a child's body is little more than *a lunch box carrying a mind to the classroom*? The lunch box is exercised on the playground and in the gymnasium. The mind is exercised in the classroom. Is it any wonder that teachers have come to assume that *talking is mental*, and that it is their minds, not their hearts, that speak and relate to one another in the classroom? Is it any wonder that parents and teachers alike have great difficulty grasping that when they speak to a child, they literally touch their hearts as well?

In a world where couples have come to assume that the essential corporal relationship between human bodies is strictly sexual, and that dialogue is mental, is it any wonder that the majority of people in our society would find it very difficult to grasp that *real discourse is biologically more intimate than intercourse*; one leading to our genitals, the other leading into our hearts?

All of the recent medical and scientific advances serve to reinforce the widespread cultural assumption that the human body is a self-contained, biologically separate, genetically programmed machine designed for self-preservation. In the context of these assumptions, it appears almost heretical to suggest that "self-help" alone or designer gene medications will not suffice. Yet, that is the message of this book. We really *are* dependent on one another. We really *do* need human dialogue to stay alive. There *is* a "body-politic" and a "communal body" far greater than that which serves the needs of the individual. And that body politic *is* critically dependent on "real" communal dialogue for its very survival.

MY OWN JOURNEY

Events sometimes conspire in ways impossible to anticipate. October of 1998 had been a particularly difficult time in my own life. Early in that month, my youngest brother died quite unexpectedly at the age of 56. He was the fourth of my brothers to have died within the past decade, all before the age of 58. Those losses had brought me to a low point in my life, and it seemed for a while as if it would be impossible to ameliorate the pain that C.S. Lewis had asserted was "part of the deal," part of the price that one pays for love whenever it is lost.

Trapped in the despair of my own broken-heartedness, I was reminded once again about the redemptive nature of love and the healing power of friendship. My adult-children, my friends, and most of all my very dear wife were there beside me, determined to prevent me from becoming one of the medical statistics of my own books. With the power of their love and vigor of their indomitable spirits, they collectively lifted me up and encouraged me to go on. Without their help, I would never have written this book, which is my "part of the deal."

"Self-help" would hardly have worked to extract me from the grief felt by these personal losses. While there is much that an individual can do to cope with his or her own loneliness and grief, at times advice to solve such problems by self-help alone is little more than an oxymoron.

I suppose that everyone who has ever endured the loss of a loved one is struck one way or another by the fact that life goes on even in the midst of one's own private grief. In my own life, there were still patients who needed to be seen on a daily basis. Many were coping with life-threatening medical problems, including heart disease and cancer. Others were trying to cope with the overwhelming pain of their own personal losses, the emotional suffering of their own unhappy marriages, the suffering of their own children, or the loneliness in their own lives.

Other professional commitments—including the completion of this book—had to be honored as well. And so it was, several weeks after my brother's death, that I found myself travelling to the University of Pennsylvania in Philadelphia to fulfill a commitment I had made to Aaron Katcher, M.D., a very dear friend and longtime research colleague, to meet with a group of his graduate students taking a business course he was teaching on "Stress and Communication in the Workplace."

Several months earlier, I had begun what I perceived would be the revising, updating, and expanding of *The Broken Heart*. With the book no longer in print, Aaron complained to me that he was "tired of photocopying the entire book each semester for his graduate classes." He had urged me to revise the book, update the material, and add the insights and perspectives about loneliness and premature death that we had accumulated from our collaborative research over the past quarter century.

Most of Aaron's students that night were middle to upper level managers working in industrial, health, and high-tech settings. Aaron had asked his class to read *The Broken Heart*, examine it critically, prepare questions, and offer suggestions that they felt ought to be addressed in any revision. Perhaps my personal losses contributed to my mood that evening. Whatever the source, my encounter with his class evolved in ways that I had not anticipated.

These middle-aged men and women unanimously agreed that loneliness was a far more pervasive problem than when my book had been published in 1977. They were also unanimous that a number of sources were contributing to the increase in human loneliness that had not been addressed in that book. "Being unmarried is by no means the only source of loneliness in our society," one student reminded me, adding that she hoped that some of these other sources would be given more prominence in any revision.

Several students talked about the growing stress they felt in everyday face-to-face dialogue. One student speculated that perhaps this problem had something to do with the ever-increasing reliance on electronic modes of communication that had circumvented the need for face-to-face dialogue. Another pointed out that these newer modes of communication had greatly reduced, and in many instances had eliminated, the need for contact with other human beings. One older businessman noted that the problem had grown so serious that many people now considered public speaking every bit as stressful as being sent to jail. Several wondered aloud whether some sort of spa couldn't be developed along the lines of the physical fitness spas springing up across the United States, where people could be provided various exercises to help them communicate in ways that would facilitate face-to-face dialogue.

To emphasize the global nature of this problem, Aaron himself briefly described a recent National Public Radio news segment on the sad fate of French cafés. Thousands were closing each year, he reported, and in Paris they were attempting to bolster attendance by holding group therapy sessions in cafés so that people might be more willing to talk. A French person interviewed for the segment said people now had to be given permission to talk, whereas the French of the 1950s would have seized the opportunity to talk.

Aaron added two interesting statistics mentioned during the broadcast. The first noted that the number of prescriptions for mood elevating drugs was higher in France than anywhere else in the world. The second, according to the French National Bureau of Statistics, was that time spent in conversations had declined in France more than 20 percent in just the past ten years.

Aaron's remarks conjured up similar changes occurring in Great Britain—trends seen in virtually all the emergent post-industrial nations. A Reuters news story pointed out, for example, that within the next two decades, the majority of British adults would not be married. A statistician from the Government Actuary Service pointed out that "the number of married adults will fall to 48 percent in 2011, and 45 percent in 2021, from 55 percent in 1996. By 2021, the proportion of men who have never married is expected to rise to 41 percent," a figure 25 percent higher than in 1996.

In Iceland, the out-of-wedlock birthrate is now 65 percent, mirroring similar changes occurring throughout the post-industrialized world. In the United States, the Rutgers project on "The State of Our Unions" noted a similar trend, reporting that the likelihood of a person ever marrying in America had dropped by one-third between 1970 and 1990.

All of Aaron's students seemed to be quite familiar with the major sources contributing to the rise of loneliness in modern American life, including all-too-common dissolutions of marriages, and economic pressures exacerbating the stresses on relationships. They were well aware of the ever-growing number of single parent households in America, the rising number of children abandoned by their own parents, and the ever-growing number of older people isolated in assisted living and nursing homes, no longer living with their own children.

"We have no sense of our collective past, no familiarity or connection to previous generations, very little sense of history, and thus no sense of our own rootedness," one student remarked, adding, "without such rootedness, our society has lost a vital ingredient that binds people together."

Several students alluded to the increasing difficulty of long-term friendships, and the forces rupturing and fragmenting communal life in many parts of the United States. Others voiced familiarity with the rising number of school dropouts and that trend's contributions to social alienation, loneliness, and ultimately to premature death. Several businesswomen talked, as well, about the ever-increasing numbers of men and women incarcerated in prisons within the United States, and the senseless violence on many streets in urban America. "When strangers approach at night on our urban streets, the only sensible emotion you can have is fear," one female student said.

One young man wondered whether loneliness had become such an integral part of modern life that future medical statistics might no longer show its consequences. "Perhaps in much the same way that human beings have adapted to other problems, we will adapt to living in our own plastic bubbles, sealed off from one another! Perhaps we will somehow adapt to loneliness and be immunized from its consequences. Perhaps the Internet will become the primary mode not only of communication, but also of relationships, where even sex can be engaged in with anonymous people in the safety and privacy of chat rooms in cyber space! Perhaps we will develop pills to deaden the pain, and help us ignore the problem!"

There was one particular comment that evening that struck me as especially poignant. A senior executive asserted, with great certainty, that "loneliness was the great modern plague," adding his equal conviction that "no one will really argue with your statistics!" Pausing for a moment, as if lost in his own reflections, he asked: "But, after reading your book. what I would like to know is why love is so fragile? Why is it so elusive?"

Then, in a more subdued voice, he continued: "Everyone in this room would agree that love is one of the most precious gifts available to human beings. Why then does it seem to be so fragile and so difficult to sustain? Why do we withdraw from relationships, and so easily discard that which is most precious in our lives? As a society, we seem to be choosing social isolation and loneliness over companionship and love! Why do we succumb so easily to anger, hatred, and violence, or withdraw into complete indifference about the fate of our fellow man, when it is clear that love would be so preferable?"

"It's about power," "it's about control," "it's easier," "love requires a great deal of work," "love makes you vulnerable, and "getting rejected hurts too much"—those were but a few of the responses that poured forth from his classmates that night. Yet none of their answers seemed entirely satisfactory to me. As he asked his questions, I found myself wondering why I had to endure the terrible pain of my own brothers' deaths to be reminded over and over again what truly is precious in life? Indeed, why do we so easily get distracted from what is essential? Why do we so easily drift into loneliness, or give in to anger, when a commitment to try to love offers such an obvious healing alternative?

I returned to Baltimore that evening firmly committed to the importance of addressing these concerns. It was a commitment that gradually led me away from a simple revision of *The Broken Heart* to the writing of this book, *A Cry Unheard.* It includes not just health data and mortality statistics gathered from the type of marital statistics discussed in *The Broken Heart*, but evidence gathered from other sources of loneliness, including the premature mortality rates of those who fail in school.

For those who drop out of school confront a lifetime of communicative difficulties that lead to a devastating type of social isolation. Those who fail in school are every bit as isolated and lonely, and just as much at risk to die from a broken heart, as the single, widowed, and divorced. They, too, can become isolated from the "corpus majoris"—the friends, lovers, and community who could offer them so much. They, too, get cut off from the true elixir of life. And they, perhaps more than any other group, truly cry out in a way that goes unheard. Like so many other sources of loneliness, this major feeder stream of educational failure flows into the central river of social isolation and alienation now draining the health of our nation.

Yet, the very notion of multiple feeder streams supplying an ever-rising tide of loneliness in modern life makes it clear that solutions to this problem will not emerge from simplistic advice, or bland admonishments to seek "self-help." Advice "to get off one's duff and find a friend" belies the true complexity of the issues to be addressed. Although I do not mean to discourage such activities, attempting to solve the problem through self-help alone, at times, can be quite disconcerting when it comes to coping with loneliness.

Nor is the issue, as the *Chicago Tribune* once asserted in a review of *The Broken Heart*, as simple as "One is better off wed than dead." Neither the children who are isolated and lonely, nor those living with a sense of shattered self-esteem, nor the sick and the elderly cut off from their families, have the option of marrying to solve their problems.

Nor is there any magical potion in marriage itself, as the dissolution of so many marriages in America readily confirms. Help for the types of problems discussed in this book will have to be sought not just from one's marital partner and friends, but from the leaders of our society. Nor will superficial pop psychology solutions adequately address this problem. For loneliness has afflicted mankind since the dawn of creation, and many of the real solutions will involve a clearer recognition of time-honored approaches to this problem.

Our teachers, ministers, priests, rabbis, and mullahs, and those who share in the repository of historical wisdom, must play a central role. So, too, must our political leaders. And so must our cultural commentators in the media who do so much to shape public opinion. In addition, our health care professionals who daily see the casualties of loneliness on the frontlines of their health practices must join the battle to help turn the tide. The medical data in this book make it quite clear that we have no other choice. If the feeder streams of modern loneliness are not curtailed, then a floodtide of loneliness will eventually inundate and bankrupt our nation.

A SOLDIER'S STORY OF LOVE

Allyn Leavey happened to be the very first patient I saw the day after returning from Philadelphia. At 76 years of age, he had been through a great deal of pain and suffering in his life, as had his wife, Dot. Both had undergone triple bypass surgery several years ago. Since then, they had been coming to me once a month for follow-up treatments.

Like so many other patients with heart disease, Allyn, virtually his entire life, had experienced great difficulty talking about his own emotional struggles without triggering major increases in his blood pressure—a communicative problem that had caused him a great deal of difficulty throughout his life. Yet, he had done very well in my new form of therapy. His communicative blood pressure surges, as well as his resting blood pressure, were significantly lower than when we first met.

By instinct and inclination, Allyn was a philosopher, poet, and musician, and I thought that the questions raised the previous evening would be of special interest to him. After describing the general tenor of the class that evening and the graduate students' comments, I asked him why he thought love was so fragile and so elusive. A hallmark of his own life had been a deep appreciation for the love provided by his wife and his friends. And so I asked him why it seemed to be so difficult for so many to find love, or to maintain love in their lives.

His response at first completely bewildered me. It appeared to be utterly disconnected from the issues discussed the previous night. And, at first, he seemed to ramble, describing events that had occurred more than a half-century earlier. Yet, as he talked, the reality of those events was still there, etched indelibly in his heart. They were there in the rapid surge of his blood pressure as he talked. They were there in the tears that suddenly began to flow as he spoke about his 23rd birthday, on May 2, 1945, in the woodlands of Branau, Germany near the end of World War II. They were there when he spoke of his closest friend, Sergeant Frank Walankus.

In early May 1945, Allyn and 4,200 other American airmen then German prisoners-of-war were physically and emotionally exhausted. Eighteen days of relentless forced-marching over 281 miles from Stalag 17, located in Austria's Krems-Gneixendorf, to this remote woodland had brought the entire contingent to the brink of death. Dysentery, dehydration, starvation, along with uncontrollable retching and vomiting, echoed through the Branau forest on that spring evening.

For five days, the American prisoners had waited in the intermittent cold rain, with little food, hoping against hope that Patton's tanks would reach the junction of the Inn and Danube Rivers before it was too late. Unbeknownst to the Americans, their German captors, during a period of great chaos, were marching them away from the POW camps, so that they could surrender to the Americans rather than face the wrath of the Russians then storming the gates of Vienna.

Eighteen months earlier, in December 1943, a 21-year-old Allyn Leavey had been a waist gunner in a B-24 flying at 27,000 feet over Athens, Greece. It was a cold morning, with an air temperature 25 below zero. His squadron of two dozen B-24s had recently moved from Benghazi, Libya, and was now flying out of Brindisi, Italy. He was happy with that move, thinking it would be easier to safely get back to his air base in case of trouble. He and his fellow crewmen had survived the terrible losses suffered in the bombing runs against the Ploesti Oil Fields, and he was feeling a bit more reassured. Yet ack-ack fire from the mountains around Athens suddenly burst that illusion when his plane exploded and rapidly began to lose altitude.

"Six months earlier," he remarked with a smile that tried to obscure his tears, "I was a poor Jewish kid from Baltimore madly in love with American jazz and American life. There was no place in the world where you could hear better jazz music than in the pre-war Baltimore ghettoes along Pennsylvania Avenue. Count Bassie and Billie Eckstine were just a few of the artists who played on those wonderful summer evenings. God what an era! What an unbelievable era with so much talent!"

When his plane was hit, Allyn continued, his ankle was shattered by the shell-burst, the second time he had been wounded in the war. His right hand was also severely frost bitten. As his parachute opened high over the hills north of Athens, Allyn peered down for what seemed like an eternity on the homeland of Aristotle and Plato. The street kid from Baltimore, who had left his 18-year-old girlfriend, Dot, all alone, anxiously awaiting his return, was descending slowly, fearfully, and shivering with cold into a world he could scarcely imagine. Knowing that he might fall into enemy hands, and aware that his Jewish ancestry made it unwise for him to wear his dog tags, he had dressed only in his underwear and a thermal flight suit.

Now, two years later, as he shivered on the ground next to Frank Walankus in the darkness of the Branau forest, the two friends were preparing to die. They argued for several hours about which of them should eat their last piece of bread. Frank insisted that Allyn should live, while Allyn insisted that Frank had a better chance of surviving. And as they continued to argue, Allyn's mind drifted backward in time once more, back to the time when he was originally captured.

Seven of his fellow crewmen landed in a Greek partisan camp. He and two other airmen landed on the wrong side of the mountain, in an area where one of the regional senior intelligence officers was Kurt Waldheim, later to become Chancellor of Austria as well as head of the United

Nations. Badly wounded and unable to walk, Allyn was placed several times before a firing squad by captors identifying him as "Ein Amerikanishcher Juden," but each time he was spared. He was then put in solitary confinement for ten days, followed by a weeklong journey in a cattle train across Bulgaria and Romania. His captors constantly threatened to turn him over to the SS because of his Jewish background. He was saved, he said with a smile, because "I changed my name from Allyn Leavey to "Allyn LeVay." By the time he finally arrived at the relative safety of Stalag 17 in Krems-Gneixendorf, Austria, six weeks after he had first parachuted into Greece, his name had been changed to "Jose LeVay." He became the second American Jew to survive long enough to make it into the German POW camp.

It was there that "Jose LeVay" met Sergeant Frank Walankus, an American-born artist of Lithuanian ancestry from Pittsburgh. Frank had the bunk above Allyn's, and they formed a deep and enduring friendship.

"Although it was dangerous to be an American Jew without dog-tags or identification, Stalag 17 was like an open-air American university," explained Allyn, "with men from Harvard and Yale, and farm kids from Iowa. The brainpower in that camp was awesome. If it wasn't for those poor Russian men and women suffering across the barbed wire in an adjacent compound, it might have been a bit easier to forget the fear involved in being an American-Jewish prisoner of war."

The men in his compound hid a few Russians under their floor. "I knew that I would probably be killed by the Gestapo if they ever discovered it," Allyn recalled, "but it was the least we could do to help a few of those poor human beings."

In the Branau forest that desperate May evening, Frank and Allyn could not agree on who should eat their last piece of bread. And so they eventually agreed to divide it in half. Frank volunteered to leave the group and try to find help the next morning, a journey that put him at risk of being shot to death if he dared venture out onto the road. As the sun rose that next morning, Frank hugged his friend goodbye, and set out on the road.

At first, Allyn just watched, then he shouted to Frank to wait, insisting that "we may as well die together." Neither man knew when they set out that day, which happened to be Allyn's 23rd birthday, that the lead elements of Patton's army, with hundreds of tanks, were parked no more than a few thousand yards away, over the very next hill. The war was, in fact, over!

en had been far too willing to kill millions of human beings just
nk and Allyn.

e question from the previous evening continued to haunt me. Why
is love so fragile and so elusive? Why do we so easily yield to
hatred, violence, and destruction when the only real hope is love?
erein was an inherent and unsettling paradox. The very same
of love, and the elixir of life—human dialogue and human
ionship—if turned in on itself, can be the source of incalculable
ffering, and death. It is the essential paradox and ultimate dilemma
st be confronted in this book. Dialogue is the elixir of life, yet
lk can kill.

s Allyn spoke about love in the midst of his own tears, a feeling of
nd faith began to overwhelm me. Allyn, "ein Amerikanisher Juden"
altimore, had emerged alive from Hitler's hometown in the Branau
, destined to spend the next fifty-five years of his life in the warm
ving embrace of his beloved wife, Dot. Hitler, on the other hand,
isoned his mistress, Eva Braun, then bit down on a cyanide tablet,
t a bullet through his own brain, all alone in the isolation of his
ble concrete bunker in Berlin.

llyn's exodus from that forest had transformed the "terrible
ions" wreaked upon the world by that "rough beast from Branau"
more ancient truth, one that was unmistakably clear: against all
love had once again triumphed over hatred. It always does in the
hat is my deepest belief, bedrock faith, and most fervent hope. My
is that this book will help the forces of love to triumph over the
f loneliness and suffering described in these pages. And as a nation,
e we will again emerge into the warm, loving embrace that kept
Leavey and all of his comrades alive. We owe that victory to all of
who have fought against the forces of darkness and evil, as well as
who have suffered the consequences of such darkness and evil.

his book owes its very existence to hundreds upon hundreds of
ts like Allyn Leavey who have shared their lives, their pains and
vs, their loves, their triumphs, and all of their heartfelt memories, so
thers might understand. It has been a rare privilege to have met these
ts in dialogue. Some have emerged like ghosts from a time long
from the pits of despair—the last living human beings bearing
ss to places where human cries of suffering clearly went unheard,
3uchenwald, Auschwitz, Bergen-Belsen, and Dachau. Others have
successful businessmen, who have achieved great personal and
ial success.

Allyn abruptly returned to the question the
the previous evening, again apologizing for the
restrain his tears. Trembling with grief, he whis
Pausing to catch his breath, he continued, "There
keep us alive. Frank was willing to die for me. 1
That's something you can never know about unt
No one will ever really know but Dot. It is her lov
for the past 55 years...

"Please understand that I am no hero! There
were real heroes...so many who gave their lives. S
story as if I was a hero, for my contribution was
story for what it really was—a story about love;
love. It is hard to witness all the cruelty I have se
so many bastards, so many people who were an
another. And yet I am forced to recognize that it is
us alive. It is only love that will ultimately kee
other."

As Allyn continued to talk, I could not hel
days in the Branau woods at the end of World W
ironically, where Adolph Hitler had been born. M
and I thought momentarily about Yeats' poem,
and of his falcon spiraling ever upward, wider and
could not hold, and mere anarchy was loosed up
lacking all conviction, the worst filled with passic
rough beast slouched on slow thighs towards B
terrible revelation was about to be born!"

Yeats' spiraling falcon was quickly replac
flight, as I heard Vaughn Williams' marvelous
Ascending" in the back recesses of my mind. I be
could have been a lark in May of 1945, ascending
sky over the Branau woods, up into the far re
spiraling ever upward."

I would have been able to peer out over the
Europe, and see all of those concentration camps,
of France and Germany, and look eastward to
where so many millions upon millions of hum
needlessly. And I would have been able to peer c
Branau Woods and see the birthplace of Adolph H
of love shared in that dark forest by Frank Walar
They had been willing to die for each other,

Still others have struggled with loneliness, poverty, the shame of school failure, and despair for most of their lives. To all of these patients, and the staff of the Life Care Clinic and the Sinai Cardiac Rehabilitation Center who have cared so deeply for them, I owe a debt of gratitude that can never be repaid. I hope that this small effort will suffice to convey my profound gratitude for the privilege of sharing our lives together. And I pray that the lessons learned by heart might help a few more people to live their lives in love, escaping the loneliness and isolation that inexorably follow when our cries of suffering go unheard.

WHERE THIS BOOK IS GOING

To more fully examine the linkages between loneliness and premature death, and to clarify the biological power of human dialogue, this book is divided into four sections.

Section One explores the links between social isolation and increased incidence of premature death in adulthood. Emphasis is placed on the links between the conditions that exacerbate human loneliness and how they are connected to the increased risk of premature death from heart disease. Also discussed is evidence documenting the healing power of friendship and social support.

Section Two focuses on loneliness and social isolation in childhood, and how it contributes to a marked increased risk of premature death later in life. Special attention is devoted to school failure, along with an explanation of how this experience heightens social isolation and loneliness throughout a person's life and thus contributes to the far greater risk of premature death. Emphasis is placed on the links between school failure and the increased risk of heart disease. Evidence is marshaled proving that the excess increase in premature death from school failure is due far more to the destruction of a person's capacity to communicate with others than it is to economic problems later in life.

Section Three addresses issues of mechanisms that increase the risk of heart disease and premature death in those who are lonely. Two specific linkages are examined in detail:

1) The specific links between loneliness and heart disease common to both adulthood and childhood. Here, I describe both the power of

human touch, and the importance of physical contact, not just between human beings, but also with animals and the rest of the living world.

2) An explanation of the major, and previously unappreciated, links between talking, communication, and the cardiovascular system. This section shows how difficulties in communication trigger repetitive and, at times, marked surges in blood pressure. It also documents how these unfelt, repetitive, communicative-linked surges in blood pressure can lead either to the development of premature coronary heart disease, or exacerbate preexisting cardiovascular difficulties. Also described is the manner in which these undetected communicative stresses cause people to withdraw from contact with others, driving them into a viciously cycling series of events that lead to the increased risk of disease and premature death.

Section Four focuses on an understanding of "healing dialogue." It offers insights and ways to reduce loneliness, to enhance the physiology of inclusion and to diminish the physiology of exclusion in our communicative lives. It also describes steps that can be taken to lower the risk of developing premature heart disease, as well as help patients with heart disease to grasp that *communicative fitness* is every bit as important as physical fitness and diet in achieving optimal cardiovascular health.

Also described are remedial steps the educational system can take to help reduce the communicative stress experienced by high risk children— those who come to school already wired to react to dialogue with a physiological response-set of exclusion. Also described is how this "wired-in" response-set exacerbates the risk of school failure. Suggested are remedial steps that can be taken to alleviate this problem.

Finally, similar steps are outlined to help adults improve their communicative skills and thus alleviate the communicative stress that contributes to the interpersonal difficulties that frequently dominate their lives.

Section One

LONELINESS IN ADULTHOOD AND ITS LINKS TO PREMATURE DEATH

Chapter Two

INTIMACY: AMERICAN STYLE

"Man, you must be kidding about love! I think our young college kids have really latched onto something. Why get married when you can simply screw some young chick and nobody gets hurt? In the end, you owe her nothing and she owes you nothing."
—A 35-year-old Baltimore steelworker

"And in the naked light I saw / ten thousand people, maybe more. / People talking without speaking, / people hearing without listening, / people writing songs that voices never shared, / no one dared / disturb the sounds of silence."
—Paul Simon, Sounds of Silence

"Organized religion is a sham and a crutch for weak-minded people who need strength in numbers."
—Jesse "The Body" Ventura, Governor of Minnesota[7]

SPEAKING FROM NO-BODY TO NO-BODY

Kidding about love?
Kidding about human relationships?
Nobody gets hurt?
It's a sign of weakness to derive strength from a group?
Against the backdrop of widespread suffering and pain inflicted by the rising tide of human loneliness, such phrases must be viewed as utterly hollow. Yet, in spite of all the medical data to the contrary, they reflect attitudes that seem to be widely shared in our society—attitudes of a nation that seems to devalue human relationships, seems to devalue the importance of group relationships, and ridicules people who need the company of their fellow-man as "weak-minded," while cavalierly ignoring or dismissing the medical consequences of the loneliness now rising in our midst. The carnage is very real, however, and the rising toll exacted in premature death absolutely awesome.

It is a striking fact, for example, that mortality rates in the United States for all causes of death, and not just for heart disease, are consistently higher for divorced, single, and widowed individuals of both sexes and all races. Some of the increased death rates in unmarried individuals rise as high as ten times the rates for married individuals of comparable ages. In a similar manner, the premature death toll exacted by early developmental experiences such as school failure, which also isolate and consign human beings to a lifetime of communicative exile, is now one of the leading causes of premature death in America.

Yet, in spite of all the medical evidence to the contrary, there is a widespread belief in our modern culture that *love* is a word that has no meaning, that there are no medical consequences when "people talk without speaking, or hear without listening." An ever-growing number of people fail to recognize the medical dangers stemming from one of the more rapidly spreading communicative diseases of the modern age—the "sounds of silence" that emanate from what I call the "disembodied dialogue" endemic to modern life. It is a type of "unfelt" dialogue in which human speech has been extracted from our bodies, quite literally ripped from our hearts.

In today's world, telephones "talk" and radios "talk" and televisions "talk" and computers "talk" and there is "no-body" there. It is a world of image and digital rationality in which it is assumed that our flesh and blood is no longer a requisite part of human dialogue. It is a world in which people have come to believe that dialogue is "mental in character," and that they can literally speak from "no-place to no-body!" In an ironic sense, these electronic modes of communication at times mimic a serious problem well recognized by psychiatrists and psychologists and understood to be pathological in character.

They represent a state of affairs in which traumatized human beings similarly learn to speak from outside their own bodies, outside their own feelings, and outside their own hearts. In supplying such varied diagnostic labels as sociopath, paranoid, and narcissist, health professionals have long recognized these clinical conditions to be the result of a serious breakdown in the capacity to communicate in a heartfelt manner.

While certainly marvelous in many respects, our reliance on electronic means of communication has fostered and spread an entirely new set of problems within our midst. In an electronic age that appears to offer ever-expanding opportunities to communicate, it is seldom considered that these modes of interacting have drastically altered the very essence of human dialogue. While they have surely helped many lonely and isolated people communicate with each other, and transformed the global village, uniting the world through electronic commerce and reducing the dangers of nationalism, there are certain inherent problems with electronic communication that are seldom considered.

Human speech extracted from its own biological home within the human body—human speech extracted from its own heart and redefined as communication—has made it appear as if no human body is required to engage in dialogue. Unlike the experiences of our parents and grandparents, the physical presence of another human being in face-to-face dialogue is no longer deemed necessary for people to communicate with one another. In certain respects, it is compounding one of the central medical problems afflicting mankind since Adam first confronted his own loneliness in Paradise. Lulled into numbed complacency by the "company" of voices and sounds emanating from digital boxes, it seems as if we have become confused about the meaning of the Biblical admonition, "It is not good for man to be alone."

The electronic communicative media of our modern age do not require human flesh and blood to transmit their messages. Digital "images that speak" have come to be confused with the physical presence of human beings in face-to-face dialogue, fostering what I believe is an entirely new type of loneliness, one in which there is no shared "felt reality." "Virtual reality" has come to be ever increasingly confused with "real reality"! Indeed, the lines between what is "real" and what is "virtual" have become increasingly blurred.

In its most chilling form, we have been shocked by television images of lonely, socially isolated, and marginalized children taking machine guns into school, where they open fire on innocent classmates. Unable to relate to others, to use language to share their feelings with others, or to communicate their loneliness and anger, they seem unable to distinguish between video game murder and the real murder of their fellow students.

In 1998, for example, Kip Kinkel, a 15-year-old boy from Thurston High School in Springfield, Washington, killed both his mother and father, then drove to school, where he killed two classmates and wounded 25 others. A PBS *Frontline* documentary seeking to explain this gruesome tragedy noted that Kip Kinkel was kept back in the first grade because of an undiagnosed problem with dyslexia. Sensing that he would never be able to live up to his parents' academic expectations, he retreated inside himself, and developed an interest in computers, guns, and explosives.

Socially isolated and no longer able to communicate with anyone other than himself, Kip Kinkel wrote in his journal: "I sit here all alone. I don't know who I am. I want to be something I can never be. I try so hard every day. But in the end, I hate myself for what I've become." [8]

We live in a world in which scientific medicine continuously reinforces our cultural assumptions about the mechanical nature of the human body, and the disembodied nature of human feelings. Medical science informs us that the human heart is a pump, and that the human body is little more than a solitary, isolated, biological machine. Although it is usually implicitly assumed, rather than explicitly stated, this medical perspective makes it all the more difficult for people to grasp or understand the nature of heartfelt dialogue.

Adding to the traditional sources of loneliness faced by our ancestors, a new and highly insidious form of loneliness has crept into our midst. Yet, few perceive its medical dangers. Indeed, current medical assumptions about the mechanical nature of the human body have coalesced with electronic forms of communication to make it all the more difficult to grasp those dangers.

Many human beings, and particularly the children growing up in this new age, are lured into believing that they can communicate exclusively in digital form with other human beings in the privacy of chat rooms in cyber space. Some believe that they can even "have sex" with anonymous digital images in the isolated loneliness of cyber space, without any medical consequences. Virtual sex with digital images seems every bit as alluring as real sex with real human beings. Virtual pets and virtual nature seem just as attractive as the real McCoy.

Even many educators have now come to assume that children can learn more from computer-assisted instruction than they can from adult teachers. The vital human contact and potential dialogue offered by teachers is being replaced by the digitalized information and images provided by computers. Our politicians now speak about computers in the classroom as the great "educational equalizer," ironically committing our nation to deliver this technology to inner city children who are most at risk, and most in need of human contact and inclusive dialogue.

A whole generation of detached, independent, self-sufficient, non-committed individuals now agrees with the steelworker quoted above—that no one really needs to get hurt in modern human relationships. You can be "intimate" with someone and then leave, and nothing bad will happen. And equally large numbers agree with Governor Ventura that only "weak-minded" people need the company of their fellow man. "Intimacy, American Style" is how one nurse-patient described this new form of heartless dialogue and exploitative relatedness.

"It's like asking people to dance with death," observed one female lawyer-patient when I asked her why she thought the problem of human loneliness and its links to disease were so strongly denied in our society. "Everyone is afraid of their own loneliness," she added quietly, "and denial is the order of the day. We know that we will die, and we know that we are lonely. In response to these problems, we defend ourselves by becoming preoccupied with making money, keeping busy, and denying the problem. We fill the emptiness of our lives with sound and noise and frenetic activities, and at least on the surface, the loneliness seems to disappear...at least for a while."

Apart from the health toll exacted by the rising tide of human loneliness, its economic costs should give us all pause. For I am convinced that if we were to attack loneliness and its attendant symptoms of social isolation, and familial and communal disintegration, with the same dedication we have applied to the elimination of the physical aspects of AIDS, cancer, and heart disease, we could cut our national health expenditures by at least 50 percent. Those expenditures, which stood at 27 billion dollars in 1960, have risen 38 fold in the past three decades, up to 1,035 trillion dollars in 1996. Health expenditures consumed 5 percent of the gross domestic product of the United States in 1969. By 1996, they had risen to almost 14 percent. [9]

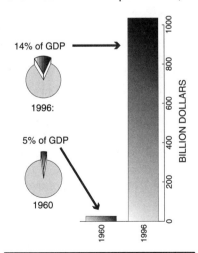

Relative and Absolute Change in U.S. Health Care Expenditures, 1960 & 1996

14% of GDP

1996:

5% of GDP

1960

BILLION DOLLARS

1960   1996

Compared to 1960, 1996 health care expenditures comprised *nearly 3 times* the portion of the gross domestic product (GDP) and was *38 times greater* in terms of dollars spent.

"ALL IS WELL, ALL IS WELL"

Everyone is familiar with road maps that show the major geographical features of a region, often down to the dirt roads of local jurisdictions. There are other maps, however, with which very few people are familiar. These depict disease rates and death rates in various parts of our country. They allow us to see, at a glance, in what part of the country diseases such as measles, mumps, polio, cancer, and cardiovascular disorders occur most frequently.

These maps show, for example, that certain diseases occur only in one section of the country, while other diseases occur more frequently in urban areas than in rural ones. Such maps not only give medical scientists clues about the causes of certain diseases, but they also suggest means for controlling them. Particularly germane to this book is the fact that certain patterns of disease in one area can be used to predict the future course of disease and death in the entire country.

Take, for example, a map originally drawn in 1965 for the President's Commission on Heart Disease as part of a detailed report called "A National Program to Conquer Heart Disease, Cancer and Stroke."[10] This particular map shows the annual death rate from major cardiovascular diseases for the period 1959-1961 for white males in the United States. While this map has many intriguing features, one aspect stands out immediately—Nevada was in 1960, as it remains in 1998, a unique state, and its uniqueness is not enviable.

In both epochs, Nevada ranked number one in the U.S. for the rate at which it terminated white people's lives in the United States, and not only from heart disease but from almost every other cause of death. In 1960, in the age range 25-64 (and indeed at all age ranges), Nevada had the second highest death rate in the United States, exceeded only by South Carolina. For white males and females between the ages of 25 and 64, Nevada had by far the highest death rates in the country. For females, no other state even ran a close second.

Yet, during that same period, Nevada had the second highest median level of income in the nation. Nevada also ranked about average in its number of physicians and hospitals and had one of the lowest population densities in the United States.

Average Annual Age-Adjusted Death Rates per 100,000
from Major Cardiovascular Diseases.
(White Males, United States 1959-61)

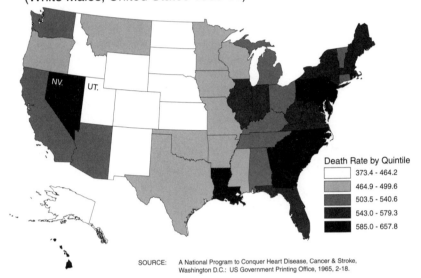

Death Rate by Quintile

	373.4 - 464.2
	464.9 - 499.6
	503.5 - 540.6
	543.0 - 579.3
	585.0 - 657.8

SOURCE: A National Program to Conquer Heart Disease, Cancer & Stroke,
Washington D.C.: US Government Printing Office, 1965, 2-18.

Now consider neighboring Utah, which had in 1960 one of the lowest death rates in the country, and in 1998 had *both* the absolute lowest incidence of cardiovascular disease, as well as the lowest overall mortality, in the United States. In 1960, the average per capita annual income in Utah was approximately $1,000 less than in Nevada (about 16-20 percent less). The number of people living in urban areas in these two adjacent states was practically identical.

So what could account for the startlingly different rates of heart disease and overall mortality in two adjacent states? Was the air different? Did people in Utah consume less fatty foods? Did they jog more? Were they thinner? Was their genetic vulnerability to heart disease different? None of these explanations seems likely to be accurate. Nor do these risk factors appear to account for the differences.

In his book *Who Shall Live*, Victor Fuchs pointed out some intriguing differences between these two states.[11] Utah is a deeply religious state, with the Mormon religion the dominant influence. Mormons neither drink nor smoke. They generally maintain very stable lives: marriages are generally secure, family ties remain strong, and most of the state's inhabitants stay in Utah. Nevada is quite the opposite. Both in 1960, as well as in 1998, Nevada was the divorce capital of the United States.

As Fuchs points out, "More than 20 percent of Nevada's males, ages 35-64, are single, widowed, divorced, or not living with their spouses. Of those who are married with spouse present, more than one-third had been previously widowed or divorced. In Utah, comparable figures in 1960 were half as large (p. 53)." Fuchs also notes that 9 out of every 10 middle-aged Nevadans were born someplace else, whereas 63 percent of Utah's residents over the age of 20 were born in that state. Nevada, it appears, may be a gambler's paradise, except for the odds on your life.

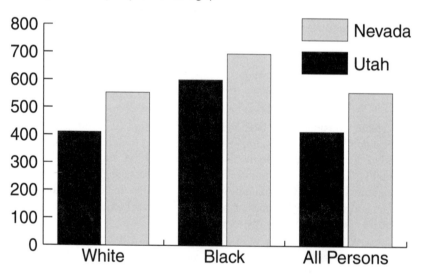

Death Rates: Nevada & Utah, 1994-96
(statistically adjusted for age)

SOURCE: Health, United States, 1998 with Socioeconomic Status and Health Chartbook, DHHS Publication number (PHS)98-1232.

Between 1960 and 1998, a great deal changed in the United States, yet certain life and death phenomena have remained constant. What was true a quarter century earlier remained true in 1998. For white Americans, in the period between 1994-1996, Utah still had the lowest death rate in the United States (410.4 per hundred thousand people), while Nevada still had the highest death rate (553.2), some 26 percent greater than Utah's. [12]

Unchanged, too, is the quality or quantity of the two states' health care. Utah averaged 19 physicians per ten thousand population in 1995, while virtually all of the New England and Middle Atlantic states averaged over 30 physicians per ten thousand population. In 1995, Utah also had the U.S.'s lowest length of days spent in the hospital by Medicare recipients—5.1 days per thousand population—50 percent lower than rates observed in New York and New Jersey. And according to both the American Heart Association and the National Center for Health Statistics, Utah in 1995 still had the lowest incidence of cardiovascular disease in the United States. It ranked number one in longevity, yet had one of the lowest per capita health expenditure figures in the United States!

One map, drawn by the National Institutes of Health in 1996, dramatically illustrates Utah's unique nature. [13] This particular chart depicts death rates for Chronic Obstructive Pulmonary Disease, and shows Utah shining like a lonely beacon among all its neighboring western states. Every state surrounding Utah ranked among the highest in the nation on this fourth leading cause of death, while Utah itself ranked among the lowest. Two factors contribute significantly to this disease—cigarette smoking and air pollution.

Average Age-Adjusted Death Rates from
Chronic Obstructive Pulmonary Disease (U.S., 1993-95)

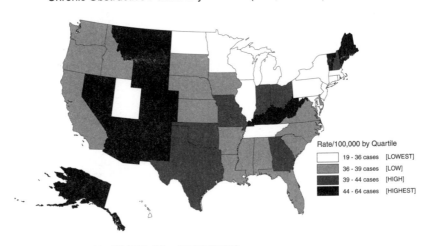

Rate/100,000 by Quartile

	19 - 36 cases	[LOWEST]
	36 - 39 cases	[LOW]
	39 - 44 cases	[HIGH]
	44 - 64 cases	[HIGHEST]

Source: adapted from NIH 1996 Morbidity and Mortality Chartbook

Yet, as the statistical data indicated in the early 1960s, the social trends observed in Nevada in the 1960s were a foretaste of what would eventually occur across the United States. Divorce, mobility, living alone, uprootedness, and births to unmarried women—these have now become acceptable middle-class norms throughout the United States. Nor do these basic demographic trends give us any reassurance that matters will improve in the near future. The Center for Disease Control points out that in both 1995 and 1996, Nevada had the highest rate of births to unmarried women in the United States, averaging almost 40 percent of all live births, while Utah had the lowest, at 15 percent.[14]

Percentage of Live Births to Unmarried Mothers 1995 and 1996

	1996	1995
NEVADA	39.5%	39.1%
UTAH	15.1%	14.8%
U.S. AVERAGE	25.7%	25.3%

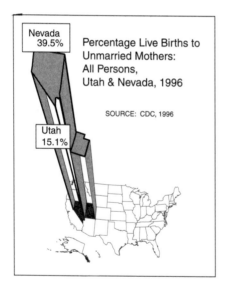

Nevada 39.5%
Utah 15.1%

Percentage Live Births to Unmarried Mothers: All Persons, Utah & Nevada, 1996

SOURCE: CDC, 1996

All of these statistics suggest that the health of our infants, young people, and aged will begin to look more and more like Nevada's and less and less like Utah's for decades to come. The mortality data for 1960, still unchanged in 1998, offered sufficient warnings about our future, but for a variety of reasons we have chosen to ignore them.

An entire generation has been raised to believe that dieting, exercise, inoculations, medications, increased health expenditures, and other forms of preventive and surgical care are the means par excellence to avoid disease and premature death. Strangely "unscientific" to our age is the idea that our physical well-being is also crucially influenced by our ability to live together and to maintain family and communal relationships; to sustain long-term friendships; and to share religious and spiritual values that have historically bound our communities together. It is clear that there will never be a social utopia, and that all societies have inherent human limitations and serious problems. Yet, the Mormon Church can perhaps feel justifiably reassured to proclaim in its hymn "Come, Come, Ye Saints," because, compared to the rest of the United States, in Utah indeed "All Is Well, All Is Well."

HUMAN COMPANIONSHIP IN THE NEW MILLENNIUM

Even the most cursory appraisal of social life in the United States indicates that something drastically altered many human relationships in the latter part of the twentieth century. Almost every segment of our society seemed to be deeply afflicted by one of the major diseases of our age—human loneliness. Yet, we do not seem to be waging any kind of effective battle against its lethal domination.

One reflection of the changes now taking place was discussed in an article in *Harper's Magazine* in 1999, entitled "Who Needs Men?" Addressing the prospects of a "matrilinear millennium," Lionel Tiger, The Charles Darwin Professor of Anthropology at Rutgers University, predicted that in the new millennium:

"More and more children will be born out of wedlock, as currently exists in the black community, and more and more women in the rest of society won't assume that they're going to marry. They will assume that they will live their lives themselves, or with their children or with other women or alone. The question still remains, What about the males? And here, I think, we will continue to see what we're currently seeing, which is a decline in male contribution to the labor force; that is, the number of hours men are working keeps going down, and they retire earlier and earlier.

Men will occupy their time with sports and pornography. Society will be very different when many people grow up without fathers around. The conviviality of kinship is likely to be much more alien in people's lives, and they will continue to have to create vigorous, vivid emotional experiences out of public experiences such as television and movies and the Internet.

Celebrities then become the surrogate family members. People will live more of their emotional lives in symbolic terms.

And as for private sexuality, one gets the impression that young people realize that sexuality is very, very demanding and can lead to a whole series of commitments that people are not ready to accept or understand very well. They find it difficult to contemplate a whole lifetime of doing something like raising children. So we may find, in that sense, a decline in long-term intimacy. Maybe we will see an increase in virtuoso intimacy for short periods of time, but not that kind of long-term commitment. In that sense, I guess as a citizen, I have a real question about what happens in such communities with few children. We end up a very wealthy society with a lot of people spending a lot of money flying to Key West." [15]

The institution of marriage itself is profoundly weakening in our nation. As noted in 1999 by investigators directing "The National Marriage Project" at Rutgers University:

As an institution, marriage has lost much of its legal, religious, and social meaning and authority. It has dwindled to a "couples relationship" mainly designed for the sexual and emotional gratification of each adult. Marriage is also quietly losing its place in the language. With the growing plurality of intimate relationships, people now tend to speak inclusively about "relationships" and "intimate partners," burying marriage within this general category. Moreover, some elites seem to believe that support for marriage is synonymous with far-right political or religious views, discrimination against single parents, and tolerance of domestic violence." [16]

On these rapid changes, Tom Smith, director of the General Social Survey from the National Opinion Research Center at the University of Chicago, commented: "We had the old system in place for hundreds of years. We have made the transition to the new system in 30 years." [17]

Examples of the disruption of, and shifting attitudes about, human relationships can be seen almost everywhere. As shown in the following figure provided by the Center for Disease Control in 1995, the divorce rate in the United States accelerated dramatically between 1965 and 1975, and remained virtually unchanged for the remainder of the twentieth century.

Before 1965, the divorce rate had remained relatively constant in the U.S., but then a profound shift in what had been traditional social patterns began to emerge. In 1975, more than one million marriages ended in divorce, an all-time record at that time. Allowing for the growth in population, the absolute divorce rate had doubled in the decade from 1964 to 1974. And as the Figure shows, there has been little change in this trend since 1975. According to the Center for Disease Control, there were

Children Under 18 Newly Involved in Divorce
(millions by year)

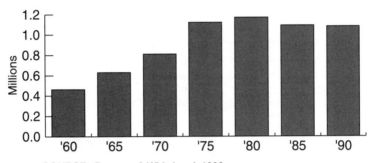

SOURCE: Popenoe & Whitehead, 1999

1,182,000 divorces in 1990, the highest since 1985. Little has changed since.[18]

The rapid rise in the divorce rate, however, is only one indicator of what has been an enormous shift in societal attitudes. The number of children under 18 years of age who now must endure the loss of a parent through divorce is growing commensurate to the divorce rate itself. Before 1955, almost 50 percent of all divorces occurred either among childless couples or among couples whose children had grown up and moved away.

The number of children caught in the middle of parental divorce more than tripled in the United States, from 330,000 children in 1953 to 1,075,000 children in 1990. When one considers the decline in the overall birthrate from 1953-1990, and the comparative absence of change since then, the increasing number of divorces involving children becomes even more striking. The reality is that children no longer serve as a restraint to keep couples married.[19]

Demographic data suggest that traditional family life in the United States is also changing fundamentally in other respects as well. While it is generally understood that the birthrate has fallen significantly in the last three decades, what is not so well known is that the numbers of children born to unmarried mothers has risen dramatically during the same period. As shown in the following Figure, this has led in the United States to a

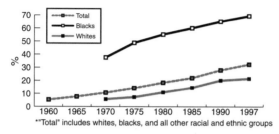

Increasing Births to Unmarried Women in U.S.
(percentage by race, by year, total population*)

*"Total" includes whites, blacks, and all other racial and ethnic groups

SOURCE: Vital Statistics of the United States, 1998

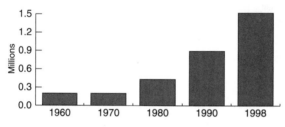

Unmarried Adult Couples Living with Children
(millions by year)

SOURCE: Popenoe & Whitehead, 1999

marked increase in the proportion of total live births of children without legal fathers.[20]

The Center for Disease Control commented on these trends in 1995 as follows:

"Because these increases occurred during a period of relatively stable fertility for all women, and declining fertility among married women, the proportion of all births to unmarried women rose from 18.4 percent in 1980, to 30.1 percent of all births in 1992." [21]

As is also shown, the rise in birth rates for unmarried women since 1980 has been due primarily to a sudden and very dramatic increase in births among white women. Since 1980, the unmarried birth rates for black women have increased 7 percent, while for white women the rates have increased 94 percent! [22]

The single most important factor correlated with this phenomenon is low educational attainment. As the Center for Disease Control noted:

"Unmarried mothers tend to be disproportionately poorly educated. Some of this disparity is linked to their generally younger age profile. Even when births to mothers aged 20 and older are examined separately, at least one-third of unmarried mothers were reported to have less than a high school education, compared with 13 percent of married mothers." [23]

Contrary to popular belief, the widespread availability of birth control and abortion services has not reduced the birthrate to unmarried women, although it has obviously acted to decrease the total birthrate in the United States. And though it is generally not recognized, children born to unmarried women are seen far more frequently by physicians than are children born to two-parent families. Such children also are at increased risk of failing in school, or performing in an academically unsatisfactory manner. Just this one shift in demographic trends is now costing billions upon billions of dollars annually, in both medical and educational expenditures in the United States. And those costs will continue to rise. History has made it abundantly clear that, once in place, this cycle tends to replicate itself.

The combination of high divorce rates and rapidly accelerating numbers of unmarried women having children has produced a very large rise in the total number of children living in single parent households in the United States. Based on census estimates, the number of children living in single-parent households in the United States increased from 8 million in 1968 to almost 20 million in 1998. An analysis of the figures shows that the number of single-parent households remained relatively stable between 1955 and 1965 (increasing from 2,100,000 to 2,727,000). It then began to accelerate rapidly to almost 5 million in 1975, reflecting the fact that the remarriage rate for divorced individuals was no longer keeping pace with the divorce rate. [24]

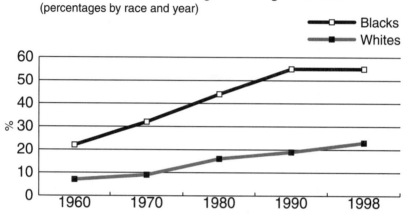

Children Under 18 Living with Single Parents
(percentages by race and year)

SOURCE: Popenoe & Whitehead, 1999

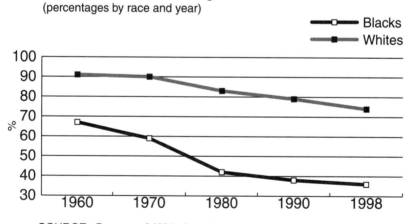

Children Under 18 Living with Two* Parents
(percentages by race and year)

SOURCE: Popenoe & Whitehead, 1999

*Includes persons living with a natural parent and a step-parent

In most single-parent situations today, the one parent (usually the woman) is forced to work for economic survival, and therefore must leave the children in the care of others. An ever-growing number of two-parent families also must leave their children in the care of others in order to survive economically. The economy has, in that sense, "adjusted" to the reality of women in the workplace. The majority of women have lost the economic freedom needed to make independent decisions about staying home to care for their own children.

All these demographic trends, once confined to states like Nevada, have spread across the entire United States. They are becoming the norm rather than the exception. The high divorce rates, the growing number of single-parent households, the slower re-entry of divorced individuals back into marriage, and proportional increases in the birth rate to unmarried women, suggest the possibility that in the near future two-parent families may be the exception rather than the rule.

The U.S. Census Bureau summarized these demographic trends in 1998. It described a nation that had changed drastically between mid-century and its close, and one that seemed far more vulnerable to social isolation and increased loneliness:[25]

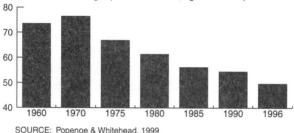

Declining Marriage Rates Among U.S. Women
(Number of marriages per 1000 women, Age 15 & older)

SOURCE: Popenoe & Whitehead, 1999

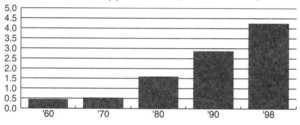

Increasing Number of Cohabitating, Unmarried Adults of the Opposite Sex (Number in millions)

SOURCE: Popenoe & Whitehead, 1999

- "In 1998, 110.6 million adults (56.0 percent of the adult population) were married and living with their spouse.
- Among people age 25 to 34 years old, 13.6 million had never been married, representing 34.7 percent of all people in the age group. For blacks in this age group, 53.4 percent had never been married.
- In 1998, 19.4 million adults were currently divorced, representing 9.8 percent of this population.
- Nearly half (45.2 percent) of all women 65 years old and over were widowed. Of the elderly widows, 70.1 percent lived alone.
- About 19.8 million children under 18 lived with one parent (27.7 percent of all children under 18).
- The majority of children who lived with a single parent in 1998 lived with their mother (84.1 percent).
- About 4 million children lived in households of their grandparents, representing 5.6 percent of all children under age

18. Of the children living with their grandparents, 1.4 million had neither parent present.

- The proportion of married couples who identified the woman as the householder has tripled since 1990, from 7.4 percent in 1990 to 22.9 percent in 1998."

In his book *The Pursuit of Loneliness*, Philip Slater suggests that the growth of social fragmentation is so severe in the United States that it is pushing our culture to the breaking point.[26] This book was written to document the fact that loneliness is not only pushing our culture to the breaking point. It is also pushing our physical health to the breaking point, and indeed, in many cases, has already pushed the human heart beyond that.

"HARDEN NOT YOUR HEARTS"

Ironically, all of these shifting demographic trends seem to fly in the face of both intuition and historical folk wisdom linking human relationships to the heart. Almost as soon as man discovered the existence and purpose of the heart, he recognized that human companionship and love had a profound effect on its functioning.

At one time or another, most of us have felt our hearts beating rapidly when close to those we love, or, occasionally, when others have offended or disappointed us. Many have felt our hearts sink, as if pressed by some crushing weight, after the loss of loved ones. In an endless variety of verbal and nonverbal dialogues with others, we have learned that human beings themselves have varied, and at times profound, effects on the cardiac systems of other human beings.

Long before scientists began to catalogue the various ways that human companionship could alter the heart, physicians were already well aware of its influence. Indeed, the very antiquity and ubiquity of this knowledge has, unfortunately, led many of us to take the medical benefits of companionship for granted. It has also served to obscure the fact that while we recognize the power of human contact, we are reluctant to explicitly acknowledge it. Still, it is now well known that a vast array of normal human interactions alter the heart in ways that range from barely detectable, transient reactions, to profound changes that are both life-enhancing and deadly.

In one sense, it would be remarkable if human contact did not influence our hearts—there are few conditions in life that do not involve some type of human contact. Like the air we breathe, it envelops every aspect of our lives. A simple visit to our doctor, arguments with a friend or loved one, reassurance and praise, sexual activity, social gatherings, competitive sports, the loss of a friend or loved one, jealousies, humiliations, triumphs, the cuddling of a child in our lap, the silent hand-holding between two lovers, the quiet comforting of a dying patient—all these affect the heart.

It is the very pervasiveness of human contact that makes it so hard to sort out the unique influence of human companionship from all other factors known to influence the heart: genetics, dietary habits, smoking, exercise, and so forth. The human interactions just described often involve these factors, as well as human companionship, the lack of love, the threatened loss of love, the fear of rejection, or indeed the real loss of love. How important is human companionship when compared, for example, with physical exercise and diet? Until very recently, most studies examining the effects of exercise, diet, smoking, and similar practices on the heart usually did not consider whether the lack of companionship or human love, or the general social milieu of the individual, might have influenced the results.

Incredibly complicated and expensive research projects have been carried out involving the entire populations of certain cities. But in many of these studies, the investigators seeking the "causes" of heart disease never even bothered to record whether their subjects lived alone, were married, or had companionship! Many examples of this peculiar state of affairs can be cited, but perhaps the most dramatic example of this type of scientific "benign neglect" is the failure to consider the effects of human love on the heart.

For while the symbolic linkage between love and the heart has been universally recognized, the one factor long neglected by scientists studying the heart is love. To my knowledge, when *The Broken Heart* was published in 1977, the word love was not indexed in any mainstream physiology textbook that dealt with the heart, nor did it appear in any physician's manual on the heart. Stress, pain, anxiety, fear, social support, and rage sometimes appeared in indexes of textbooks on the heart, but never love.

Take, for example, the *Index Medicus*, a scientific journal that annually provides the titles for and summaries of most medical research articles published in the world. In one four-year period (1970-1973) prior to *The Broken Heart*, the *Index Medicus* cited over 500,000 research articles. Only 15 of them dealt with the topic of love (all from a psychiatric point of view), and not a single one of those articles discussed any effects of love or lack of love on the heart.

By 1998, little had changed. Dr. Dean Ornish, who initially came to the public's attention because of his research documenting diet's use in reversing coronary heart disease, wrote a 1998 book, entitled *Love and Survival*, which supported the original thesis of *The Broken Heart*. He searched the National Library of Medicine's database from 1966 to 1997, and found just four articles that mentioned both love and heart disease together. So the publication of *The Broken Heart* might rightly claim some effect on medical scholarship and public attitudes. Twenty-two years later, four additional articles were published on love and Dr. Dean Ornish again pleaded with both the scientific and lay community to take love into account as a healing agent.[27]

Apparently a peculiar type of intellectual schizophrenia exists between common sense and scientific attitudes. Does common sense recognize something that scientists and physicians cannot see? Why do we continue to use phrases such as "broken heart," "heartbroken," "heartsick," "heartless," "sweetheart," "the language of the heart," and "harden not your heart"? Why do people persist in believing that fellow human beings die of broken hearts when no such diagnoses ever appear on twentieth and twenty-first century death certificates?

We live in a culture dominated by the power of science and scientific technology. One wonders, however, whether our increased understanding of the world "out there" has been accompanied by a similar growth in our understanding of our own private, interpersonal, and communicative worlds. An appreciation of the importance of human love, companionship, and face-to-face dialogue seems to be absent not only from our medical textbooks, but also from the newspapers and magazines that mirror our lives, indeed from the very cities that are our technical masterpieces. The price we pay for failing to understand our biological needs for love and human companionship may ultimately be exacted on our own hearts and blood vessels.

Chapter Three

IN SEARCH OF THE FOUNTAIN OF YOUTH

"The heart has reasons that reason knows not of:
do you love by reason?"
—Blaise Pascal, Pensees (1670)

PART ONE: THE GATES EAST OF EDEN

Pause for awhile at the small cemetery plots of rural America, particularly in those parts of our country settled a few hundred years ago, and you cannot help but be struck by the harsh existence our ancestors had to endure. There is one such small plot in a rural part of Maine, no different really from thousands of similar graveyards throughout the countryside, which remains a mute testimonial to the suffering these people experienced. No more than a hundred headstones marked the spot, but even in the warmth of a late summer's afternoon when I stopped by many years ago, you could still sense the pain and anguish of that era.

Here rests Sarah Ann, age 6, 1820, may she rest in peace
John, age 6 months, 1810
Mary Virginia, age 18, 1817
My beloved wife, Martha Reynolds, age 24, 1826
Our son, Mark, age 14, 1841, God's will be done
My beloved husband, John, age 39, 1850

More than half the tombs in this graveyard held the remains of people who died before they were 35 years old. Clearly, these settlers knew firsthand the uncertainty and terror of disease and death. Their children could be healthy, playing in the snow, one moment, then catch a cold and be dead in a week. Wives routinely died in childbirth or from mysterious fevers a few weeks later. A husband's cough could awaken the dread of pneumonia or tuberculosis in his wife's mind. Our forebears knew about disease and they knew about death. They were fully aware of their feelings of helplessness and hopelessness, products of the fact that they could not stop the ravages of diseases like pneumonia and tuberculosis. Death truly came like a thief in the night, disrupting their lives without warning.

As I lingered in this graveyard, I recalled how, as an adult, I had contracted pneumonia, but had quickly recovered with a few simple injections. To me, pneumonia was nothing more than a kind of curiosity. The legacy of fear and terror was behind us.

With few exceptions, medical science has eliminated most of the infectious and communicable diseases that once caused premature death. Yet, the medical triumphs of the twentieth century have not dispelled—and perhaps have encouraged—two persistent illusions. The rapidity with which disease has been conquered has contributed to the widespread illusion that, on average, we are now living significantly longer and longer lives. Rather, more people are surviving past infancy and childhood, and therefore more people are living to older ages. And with more people living to older age, the average bell-shaped curve of statistical variance means that more and more people will live into their 90s and even to one hundred years of age.

In fact, three-fourths of the entire statistical gain in our average life span has been due to the sharp reduction in infant mortality. The President's Commission on Heart Disease in 1965 noted that the average American lived 69.9 years.[28] By 1997, the average life expectancy had risen to 76.5 years—a gain of 6.6 years in the past 32 years. Yet, a closer analysis of the data reveals that this increase in life expectancy has been due in large measure to a gradual reduction in infant mortality, and perhaps secondarily to a significant reduction in the percentage of people who smoke.[29]

When one compares the overall gain in longevity from 1970 to 1996 with comparable gains made among people reaching the age of 65 during this same period, a far more modest picture emerges. During this period, the overall life span (from birth to death) increased from an average of 70.8 years to 76.1 years, or a statistical gain of 5.3 years. At that same time, the added life span for people who had already reached 65 years of age increased from 15.2 years to 17.5 years, a gain of 2.3 years in longevity. Thus, the overall gain in life span after 65 was 43 percent lower than the overall gain in longevity from birth. (*Health Statistics*, United States, 1998)

Increased Life Span for U.S. Population Since 1970:
Decreased Infant Mortality Masks Small
Changes for Adults

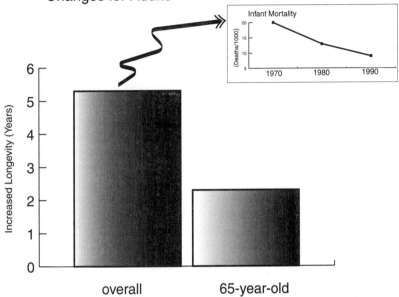

It is instructive, as well, to examine the modest gain in life span in the past thirty years against the increased amount of money that has been spent on health care in the United States during that same time period.

While overall health care expenditures have increased 39-fold in the last 30 years, and have made a difference in overall health, an intriguing economic picture emerges when one restricts the analysis to specific health problems, such as heart disease. According to a 1999 report of the American Heart Association, an estimated 1,241,000 cardiac catheterizations were performed in the United States in 1996, at an average cost of $10,880 per procedure. This represented a 315 percent increase since 1979. In addition, heart bypass procedures were performed on 367,000 patients in 1996 alone, at an average cost of $44,820 per procedure, a 424 percent increase in the occurrence of these surgical procedures since 1979. [30]

These economic facts are presented here not to question the value of these marvelous diagnostic and surgical advances, but to emphasize the economic costs involved. One does not need to see many patients in severe anginal (heart) pain, unable to walk or even catch their breath without extreme effort, to realize that bypass surgery can alleviate an enormous amount of human suffering. For many patients, this operation has meant the difference between life and death, as well as the difference between life as a cardiac cripple and a greatly improved quality of life. Still, an awareness of the costs involved might spur renewed national efforts to root out the causes of coronary heart disease in the first place.

To be totally effective, however, any programmatic efforts aimed at sorting out the causes of heart disease must include those risk factors stemming from the largely unappreciated sources that are this book.'s focus For ever-escalating health costs make it clear that more effective preventative measures must be developed if we are to successfully reduce reliance on these expensive remedies. If not, with a steadily aging population, far more difficult economic questions will be confronted in the very near future. One can only hope that ever-increasing health costs will not lead to the rationing of these life-saving procedures, especially in the later years of our lives.

In spite of the suffering that has been alleviated, and the modest gain in life expectancy that has been achieved in the past quarter century through these efforts, the average life span in the United States today is still remarkably close to the Psalmist's estimate of life expectancy four thousand years ago. "The days of our years are three score and ten, four score if we are strong"—in other words, 70 years on average, 80 if one was in particular good shape. That was the average four thousand years ago, and that seems to be the average today.

A second tenacious illusion, still held even by a few people within the medical profession, is the idea that disease is caused by factors outside of us, that we are helpless victims of malevolent forces in nature. To appreciate this perspective, one need only witness the public response in New York City in late 1999 to the appearance of the exotic-sounding "West-Nile-like encephalitis virus" transmitted by mosquitoes. Health departments throughout the city were swamped with calls from citizens concerned that six elderly New Yorkers had died of this disease as of October 10, 1999. At the same time, according to an article in *The New York Times* headlined, "*It's Infectious: Fear That's Out Of Proportion,*" an outbreak of whooping cough with 250 diagnosed cases in Chataqua County (New York) alone went completely unnoticed.[31] As the newspaper noted: "New York will certainly devote huge efforts to mosquito control next year even as vaccination programs for seemingly outdated causes are neglected."

The exotic, the new, and the rare diseases that "victimize" us are what captivate our attention, while medical problems bred by events such as human loneliness stemming from communal and interpersonal fragmentation or school failure are ignored. There's nothing exotic about school failure; nothing apparently infectious about loneliness; and certainly nothing to spray. The real threats to our communal health are simply denied and ignored.

Yet, as the "West Nile virus" helps to make clear, the legacy of suffering exacted by various infectious diseases in the recent past has left a deep imprint on our national psyche. Coupled with this historic experience is the belief that the human body is a solitary, genetically programmed machine, subject to certain capricious forces in nature that can destroy its efficiency. This belief, which haunts us like a ghost from our tortured past, in turn obscures the fact that many, if not most people who die prematurely today are not the victims of mysterious and malevolent forces "out there" in nature, but are instead the victims of human behavior.

In spite of the overarching mechanical perspective that dominates modern medical thinking, current mortality data make it abundantly clear that the "machine" body has great difficulty coping with its own loneliness, and indeed cannot tolerate its own isolation. The National Institute of Health's 1992 report on "Alternative Medicine" noted: "In study after study, the mortality of the surviving spouse during bereavement has been found to be 2 to 12 times that of married people of the same age." [32] Yet, such data are difficult to inject into the mainstream consciousness of a society hypnotized by the threats posed by such exotic diseases as the "West Nile Virus," or even more ominous sounding problems such as "E-Boli."

A TIME TO LIVE AND A TIME TO DIE

Before the dawn of the twentieth century, every generation was more or less preoccupied with the nitty-gritty details of day-to-day survival. The majority of people simply accepted the Biblical assertion that "there is a time to sow and a time to reap, a time to work and a time to play, a time to live and a time to die." Before the triumphs of mid-twentieth century medical science, the vast majority of people accepted premature death as an unpleasant but unavoidable part of life.

To them, the time to die was predetermined by forces far beyond individual control, and most people resigned themselves to their fate without question. Yet, by the twentieth century's ebb, advances in medical science prompted questions about life and death that previously had been taken for granted: When is disease really disease, and when is it simply part of the natural aging process? Is there really such a thing as a "time to die"? These questions have now erupted in public debate, and sometimes with bitter intensity in our courtrooms.

Is there a chronological time to die? Is the machinery of the body programmed to last for a fixed period of time and then to stop functioning? The concept of "premature death," which permeates modern medicine, ultimately has meaning only when guidelines can be established to determine what is meant by the proper chronological time to die! It is similar to the concept of "premature birth," a phenomenon that is intelligible only because we know that the normal gestation period is nine months.

But the forces that lead to death are not nearly so precisely understood as those that bring about life. While the life span of the average American is approximately 76.5 years, this average is the result of a kind of statistical lottery— a jumbling together of a large number of factors, totaling them up, and then looking at the bottom-line figure. The average may be 76.5 years in the United States, but there are important variations that should not go unnoticed.

On average, women live longer than men, the educated live far longer than the uneducated, the rich live longer than the poor, and the married live far longer than the non-married. The color of one's skin also seems to make a huge difference. In 1996, for example, white females lived 5.5 years longer than black females, while white males lived 7.8 years longer than black males. White Americans in general also had a longer life expectancy than Hispanic Americans or black Americans. [33]

While there may be a time to live and a time to die, there certainly are significant variations in the amount of time allotted to various racial and ethnic groups within the United States. There are, as well, huge differences in longevity depending upon where one lives within the borders of the United States, as in the Nevada-Utah comparison.

The obituary columns of American newspapers amply testify to the fact that many people still die long before age 76. They still die prematurely, although the causes of death today are very different from what they were 100 years ago. With the rise of effective antibiotics, the growth of immunization programs, and especially the rapid decline in infant mortality, the entire spectrum of forces that threaten our lives has changed.

For U.S. citizens over the age of 25, cardiovascular disease (including stroke) accounted for approximately 43 percent of all deaths in 1998, while cancer terminated the lives of another 24 percent. Since we all must die, and something must be listed as the "cause" of death, cancer and heart disease have emerged as the leading terminators of life. In the United States, these two diseases account for 67 percent of all deaths after age 25, and 80 percent of all mortality after the age of 65.

THE ENEMY WITHIN

In examining the statistics on premature death, it is easy to see that the way we live and behave has a great deal to do with our long-term survival. As shown in the following Table, the order of leading causes of premature death among U.S. adults between the ages of 24 and 65 did not change much between 1950 and the end of the century.[34]

Leading Causes of Premature Death in United States Adults (Ages 25-65)

1950	1980	1996
1. Heart Disease	1. Heart Disease	1. Heart Disease
2. Cancer*	2. Cancer	2. Cancer
3. Cirrhosis of the liver	3. Cerebrovascular Disease	3. Cerebrovascular Disease
4. Accidents	4. Unintentional Injuries	4. Chronic Pulmonary Disease
5. Influenza/Pneumonia	5. Chronic Pulmonary Disease	5. Unintentional Injuries
6. Motor Vehicle Accidents	6. Pneumonia/Influenza	6. Pneumonia/Influenza
7. Suicide	7. Diabetes	7. Diabetes
8. Homocide	8. Chronic Liver Disease	8. AIDS
	9. Atherosclerosis	9. Suicide
	10. Suicide	10. Chronic Liver Disease

*Lung cancer most common in males

The influence of human behavior on premature death becomes even more obvious if one examines the causes of death between the ages of 25-44.

Leading Causes of Death Ages 25-44, 1997
1. AIDS
2. Accidents
3. Cancer
4. Heart disease
5. Suicide
6. Homicide

Between 1950 and the end of the century, there has been very little change in the major sources of mortality and premature death in the United States. And most people would agree that, with the exception of influenza, pneumonia, cancer, and heart disease, these leading causes of premature death are, in many cases, totally avoidable. They are due to the way people behave. By 1999, some of the leading epidemiologists in the United States were beginning to openly recognize this fact. For example, Dr. Jeremiah Stamler, a professor at Northwestern University, estimated that if citizens in the United States could change poor health behaviors, they could add anywhere from 6-10 years to their lives.[35] And this is true, he said, not only for the obvious cases of premature death, but for heart disease and cancer as well.

A NATION AT RISK

Of all the health problems in the United States, heart disease is by far the leading cause of death, and has ranked as the number one crippling agent for people between the ages of 25 and 64 since 1919. In the twentieth century, there has been a sharp increase in the percentage of individuals dying in the United States from heart disease. In 1900, about 20 percent of all deaths were caused by heart disease. That percentage increased steadily until 1950, when heart disease accounted for fifty-five percent of all deaths.

Since that time, there has been a slow but steady reduction in the overall mortality, due in large part to the development of more effective medications, surgical advances in coronary bypass surgery and angioplasty, and changes in various health behaviors. The sharp increase in cardiac-caused mortality in the first half of the century was due in large part to the reduction in infant and young adult deaths from infectious and communicable diseases, which resulted in a progressive aging of the population.[36]

By 1995, various forms of cardiovascular disease terminated the lives of 960,000 Americans annually, claiming as many lives as the next seven leading causes of death combined. By 1999, the American Heart Association estimated that nearly 59 million Americans, more than one in every five, were living with some form of cardiovascular disease. In 1998, various forms of cardiovascular disease terminated the lives of 154,000 Americans *under* the age of 65. Cardiovascular disease also disabled a larger proportion of the U.S. population than any other disease.

Deaths from Heart Disease in the United States*
(1900-1996)

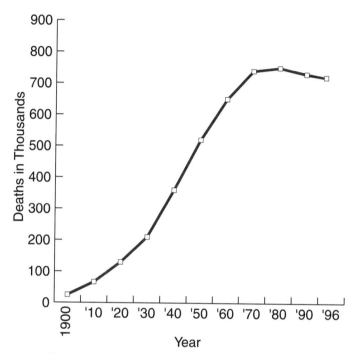

*Note: this chart include only coronary heart disease (CHD), not all
cardiovascular disease (CVD) deaths which exceed 1 million deaths annually

SOURCE: AHA Heart & Stroke Statistical Update, 1998

Premature death rates were similarly high for heart disease. Thirty-five percent of all heart attacks occur in Americans under the age of 65, while nearly 7 million Americans under the age of 60 live with the disabling effects of a heart attack or angina. Overall in 1998, almost 14 million Americans were living with various disabling effects of a heart attack or angina. [37]

An additional 600,000 Americans suffered a stroke in 1995, and one-third of them died a few months later. The residual effects for stroke survivors are equally disturbing. There are currently 4 million stroke survivors in the United States, and most are permanently disabled. And while these various forms of cardiovascular disease exact their heaviest toll on individuals over 65 years of age, 50 percent of all disabling cardiovascular conditions occur in people under 65 years of age.

The American Heart Association listed the following as the most important cardiovascular diseases, along with the numbers of people afflicted in 1999:

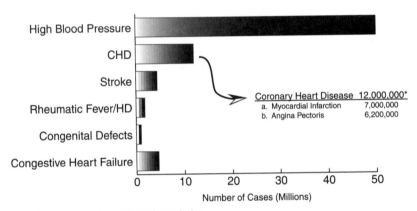

Prevalence of Major Forms of Cardiovascular Disease in the United States, 1995

Coronary Heart Disease 12,000,000*
a. Myocardial Infarction 7,000,000
b. Angina Pectoris 6,200,000

Number of Cases (Millions)

Source: American Heart Association

*Frequently patients are treated for multiple forms of CVD. As might be expected, many heart patients suffer from both MI and Angina Pectoris

While there are important differences in vulnerability to these diseases according to one's sex, race, and age, there is nevertheless widespread misunderstanding about the relative health threats these problems pose within the United States.

For instance, 33 percent of all men, and ten percent of all women, will develop some form of serious heart disease before the age of 60. After age 60, vulnerability according to sex changes dramatically. Since 1984, heart disease has actually terminated the lives of more women than men. Furthermore, while the incidence of heart disease has been reduced in men during the past two decades, death rates for females have remained virtually unchanged.

The picture is far more serious for women than is commonly understood. Since 1984, cardiovascular disease has killed more women than men, terminating the lives of 505,000 women in 1998. These mortality rates are more than the next 16 causes of death combined. While breast cancer now terminates the lives of 1 in 26 females, cardiovascular disease terminates the lives of 1 out of every 2 females in the United States.[38]

Cardiovascular Disease Mortality Trends for Males and Females (United States 1979-1996)

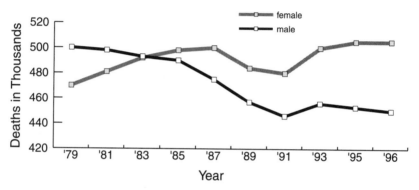

SOURCE: American Heart Association
Heart & Stroke Statistical Update, 1998

There are, as well, significant racial and ethnic differences in the incidence of heart disease within the United States. In 1997, age-specific death rates for heart disease and stroke were 67 percent higher in African-American women than in white women, while the rates for African-American men were 50 percent higher than for white American men. African-Americans were also 2.5 times more likely to die from stroke than white Americans. In addition, more than 60 percent of Hispanic-Americans ages 60 and older were found in 1997 to have high blood pressure.

HEALTH EXPENDITURES AND THE COST/BENEFIT RATIO

The American Heart Association estimates that in 1999 cardiovascular disease will cost over 274 billion dollars in medical expenditures and lost productivity in the United States alone. Heart disease, in fact, *now amounts to four-fifths of all hospital costs for insurance payers in the United States.* In addition, the National Institutes of Health spent almost three billion dollars searching for the causes and prevention of heart disease in 1998, with increased expenditures allocated for future federal budgets.

These substantial expenditures for cardiovascular disease, coupled with all of the clinical advances that have been made, particularly in medications, cardiovascular surgery, and cardiac care, prompt several obvious questions: Why does the United States still rank 16th among the industrialized countries in cardiovascular mortality for its male citizens, and 12th for women? Why does it rank 22nd in overall life expectancy after the age of 65? Why is the mortality rate for males under age 55 double that of Norway, Sweden, and Denmark, and six times higher than Japan?

The coronary death rate for Japanese men between the ages of 35 and 64, for example, is 64 deaths per 100,000 population, while in the United States comparable death rates are 400 per 100,000 population. Even more perplexing is the relative changes over the last decade. The NIH recently reported that fifteen countries have had greater declines in cardiovascular mortality for men than the United States. [39]

These differences have occurred in spite of the fact that Japan spent two-thirds less per capita on health care than the United States in 1991. Yet, its premature heart disease rates were six times lower. Equally revealing is the fact that twenty-two nations had a significantly higher life expectancy after the age of 65 than the United States. And this was achieved in spite of the fact that the United States spent more than double the amount of money per capita on health care than any other nation on earth!

What is it about life in the United States that leads to our high mortality rates? What is it about life in Japan, Sweden, Greece, Switzerland, Australia, Israel, Canada, the Netherlands, Norway, Italy, England, France, Spain, Singapore, Austria, New Zealand, Germany, Finland, Denmark, and Ireland that permits its citizens to live longer than in the United States?

Are we simply not getting the proper bang per buck for our vast health expenditures? Are our technologically sophisticated medical centers, with their superb diagnostic and treatment programs, insufficient to turn the tide? Or are there other unique social and familial forces at work in the United States operating to counterbalance and negate improvement in health statistics that one might reasonably expect from this vast expenditure of our national treasury?

DIET AND EXERCISE BUT NEVER LONELINESS

Intriguingly, the differences in coronary mortality among the various countries have been used in different ways to support divergent theories about the causes of heart disease. The very low premature coronary death rate in Japanese men has been generally "explained away" with the suggestion that their diets contain far less cholesterol than typical American diets. Little reference is made to the fact that the divorce rate, school dropout rate, and unmarried birth rate in Japan are also far lower than in the United States, and that social cohesiveness, family ties, and social stability are hallmarks of Japanese culture, albeit gradually "catching up" to the ways of the West.

Drs. Marmot, Syme, and Kagan explored low Japanese coronary disease rates by examining 11,900 Japanese men who lived in Japan, and then comparing them to Japanese men who had emigrated to Honolulu and San Francisco. They found that the closer the Japanese men got to mainland America, the higher their incidence of premature coronary heart disease. Yet, the differences in disease rates could not be explained by any measurable differences in blood pressure, diet, or serum cholesterol levels. Paradoxically, the one difference the researchers did find was in the incidence of cigarette smoking. It was far higher among Japanese men living in Japan than in either Honolulu or San Francisco![40]

What did make a difference was adherence to traditions and maintenance of communal and family ties. Those Japanese men living in either Honolulu or San Francisco who maintained family and communal ties had three to five times less heart disease than those who had become "Americanized," and who had lost their sense of rootedness. Those who maintained close ties while living in America had the very same heart disease rates as those in Japan.

Similarly, a series of studies compared the coronary death rates of Irishmen who emigrated to America to those remaining in Ireland. These studies were originally undertaken because the male coronary death rate in America was observed to be four times higher than that in Ireland. A large number of Irishmen living in Boston who still had at least one brother in Ireland were identified and examined.

After exhaustive analysis, it was found that the brothers who stayed in Ireland had anywhere from two to six times fewer signs of coronary heart disease (depending on the measures used) than those who had emigrated to America. What made these studies even more interesting was the fact that the brothers who remained in Ireland not only consumed at least 500 more calories per day than their Bostonian siblings, but they also seemed to pick menus far richer in saturated fats. In short, the Irish diets were not the type of fare recommended by either gourmet cooks or cardiologists. [41]

Why then the startlingly lower heart disease rate in Ireland? The investigators concluded that it must have been due to differences in amounts of physical exercise. The Irish who remained in Ireland were apparently less sedentary than their American brothers.

Once again, this explanation was presented with minimal descriptions of the relative differences in social environments. Little recognition was given to the social and familial cohesiveness in Ireland versus Boston, and little attention was paid to the stresses involved in leaving one's family and homeland to come to a new country. No data at all were gathered on the marital status of the relative populations. So we are left to conclude that it is diet in Japan (with some strange immunity to cigarette smoking) but exercise in Ireland that prevents heart disease.

By no means do I intend to belittle the importance of diet and exercise. These factors have been repeatedly linked to increased risk of heart disease, and should be taken seriously by every reader of this book. Nevertheless, it is important to recognize the types of premises that have dominated most medical perceptions of the causes of heart disease. And equally important is an appreciation for how these perceptions first came to light—in the town of Framingham, Massachusetts beginning in 1948.

PART TWO: LIFE AND DEATH IN "ANY TOWN U.S.A."—FRAMINGHAM HEART STUDIES

The public's general perceptions and attitudes about the causes of heart disease can perhaps best be seen in any cardiac rehabilitation clinic in the United States. For in these settings it is easy to meet heart patients who talk with religious-like zeal about the importance of their "blood pressure" readings the last time they visited their doctor's office. Similarly, they recite their most recent cholesterol readings, even knowing the difference between their so-called "good cholesterol and bad cholesterol" readings, as if somehow these numbers determined the amount of time left for them here on this earth. They also know about the importance of maintaining their weight, and they readily acknowledge the health benefits of exercise. They know these factors to be important because physicians and the media in general have repeatedly informed them that these are the major risk factors for heart disease.

In these same settings, however, most heart patients react with a sense of unease when informed that depression is a major risk factor for heart disease, and that their interpersonal life and social relationships have a major impact on their cardiovascular health. When shown that their own blood pressure can rise rapidly when they speak in spite of the medications they are taking, and told that in fact peak blood pressure increases are far higher when they talk than when they exercise to their maximum capacity, they respond to such information as if some alien from another planet was delivering the message.

In order to more fully appreciate why certain information is readily accepted by heart patients, while other information appears to be coming from some alien planet, it would be helpful to trace out the original underpinnings of our current perceptions about the causes of heart disease, and why our interpersonal, communicative, educational, social, and communal existence appears to be far less important to cardiovascular health than the conventionally accepted risk factors.

Questions about the causes of heart disease are not new. They have preoccupied the attention of U.S. health policy makers since the end of World War II. Indeed, it was shortly after war's end that the growing problem of heart disease first prompted the U.S. government to undertake massive and comprehensive studies into the causes. Long after other major diseases had been conquered, heart disease still appeared to come like a thief in the night, terminating people's lives prematurely and without warning. The mandate to medical science in the post-war period was simple and straightforward: find the cause of heart disease, especially premature heart disease, and seek out ways to eradicate it as a national problem.

In many ways, the post-war period was a turning point for modern medical science. For the first time, the U.S. government began to move into the health field, especially the research aspects of health, in a really big way. Given the conquest of other diseases, it seemed only a matter of time before medical scientists would eliminate the last pocket of resistance barring our way to unbridled good health. Cardiac disease, it was clear, had to go, and would go.

It was in this spirit of scientific optimism that a small army of medical scientists descended on the town of Framingham, Massachusetts, in 1948 to begin to seek out the causes of heart disease. Fifty years after this venture began, Dr. Michael DeBakey, a renowned heart surgeon, and Professor of Surgery at Baylor College of Medicine in Houston, would hail these pioneering research investigations as "the model in epidemiology...one of the great studies of this century." [42]

To this day, I still remember Framingham in 1948. It was a small, beautiful, and peaceful town of 28,000 working people, some 20 miles or so from my own city of birth—Boston. In many ways, it seemed to be an ideal place for research. In its ethnic, social, and economic mixes, it appeared to be mainstream America, a model city, so to speak, for medical research. Its population was largely of Irish, Italian, and English ancestry. Poverty was minimal. And its population was almost fully employed.

It was here that the U.S. government joined forces with medical science to try something never tried before, a kind of Manhattan Project for health. Framingham was chosen as the testing ground because it seemed such an average American community: hardworking, mostly white, mostly middle class, and very stable. In 1948, people didn't move around very much in Framingham, and the scientists hoped that, as a result, it would be relatively easy to keep track of the study volunteers. The mission was clear: find out what predisposes a person to develop heart disease, so that medical scientists could develop more effective means to block the development of this dreadful disease.

By 1948, physicians were already well aware of how the healthy human heart functioned. They were also very familiar with the events that immediately preceded and followed a heart attack. They knew that the coronary arteries were vitally important to the healthy functioning of the heart muscle, and that a process called atherosclerosis, especially coronary atherosclerosis, put a person at high risk for having a myocardial infarction, or what is commonly called a heart attack.

At that time, however, as the Framingham investigators noted in 1999, "little was known about the general causes of heart disease and stroke, but the rates for cardiovascular disease had been increasing steadily since the beginning of the century and had become an American epidemic" (*See Framingham web site*).

It was believed at that time that atherosclerosis was caused by a gradual narrowing of the inner walls of the arteries, which were thickened by soft, fatty deposits called atheromas or atheromatous plaques. It was known that this process increased the likelihood that the blood supply (via the coronary arteries) to various portions of the heart muscle (or brain, via the carotid arteries) could be temporarily or permanently cut off, leading to a heart attack or stroke.

Before 1948, autopsies performed on heart attack victims had shown that their coronary arteries had lost their normal elasticity, becoming quite rigid and clogged. What was unclear in 1948, however, was what caused atherosclerosis: how did it first develop, what about it led to fatal heart attacks, why did it develop at such different rates in different people, and what could be done to ameliorate this condition?

To help answer these questions, the medical scientists selected 2,336 men and 2,873 women from Framingham who were then free of heart disease. The 5,209 volunteers were distributed between the ages of 30 and 62. The medical investigators asked them to participate in a study planned to last the rest of their lives. [43] Each of these volunteers was then given a physical examination, including blood tests, electrocardiograms, X-rays, and blood pressure readings. A history of all participants' previous medical problems was also taken and documented.

The study's initial phase involved mammoth amounts of work, but after that, it was just a matter of wait and see: who would remain healthy and who would develop heart disease or other physical problems? Who would be the first to die? At regular two-year intervals, all the participants were called back for reexamination. Between intervals, their family doctors, who were requested to report major physical problems to the research team, followed the participants' health. When any of the volunteers died, a post-mortem conference conducted by three physicians was convened in order to determine the precise cause of death.

During the 50 years this study has been in existence, the computers have churned out mountains of medical data about risk factors for heart disease discovered in Framingham. Gradually, certain, especially important, factors were statistically connected with the eventual development of coronary heart disease:[44]

1. Elevated blood pressure;
2. Elevated serum cholesterol;
3. Cigarette smoking;
4. Electrocardiographic abnormalities;
5. Glucose intolerance (diabetes);
6. Enlarged left ventricle;
7. Lack of exercise;
8. Obesity.

These were identified as the "risk factors" for heart disease. In a sense, they were like warning flags signaling the impending approach of a storm, except that these cautioning signs were hoisted long before the storm arrived, even years in advance. All the risk factors seemed to be connected with the eventual development of heart disease, and if you had various combinations of these risk factors, then your chances of developing heart disease and dying prematurely increased significantly.

As the data poured in, the studies began to have an ever-increasing influence on medical attitudes, first in the United States, and then around the world. Framingham began to dominate medical assumptions about the cause of cardiovascular disease in much the same way that Rome, Jerusalem, and Mecca might dominate religious attitudes. From Framingham, the original repository for information, came alarms that sounded around the world, first in the medical literature and then in thousands of articles in the various news media.

The investigators themselves characterized the significance of these studies in their 1999 web site as follows: "In the past fifty years, the (Framingham) study has produced approximately 1,000 articles in leading medical journals. The concept of cardiovascular disease risk factors (developed in Framingham) has become an integral part of modern medical curriculum and has led to the development of effective treatment and preventative strategies in clinical practice."

There is no doubt that the medical investigators are quite right in that assessment. The impact of the Framingham studies cannot be overestimated. Americans may not have known exactly what cholesterol is, but they came to learn that it was in their diets and that it was linked to the hardening of their coronary arteries. They also came to understand that they needed to keep their blood pressure low. Foods were (and still are) advertised on television specifically because they were low in saturated fats. From this and other research studies, Americans also got the message that they had better start exercising to keep in shape, or else increase their risk for heart disease.

A CLOSER LOOK AT FRAMINGHAM

Over the years, there were to be many other studies similar to the Framingham investigations, but it was the prototype, and it remains to this day the most famous. Indeed, the fiftieth anniversary of these studies in 1998 led to major news stories and front-page headlines in virtually all of the national media in the United States. Because it has had such a profound impact on the medical community, it is vitally important to look more closely at many of the fundamental premises and findings of this pioneering work.

For it turns out in retrospect that the Framingham Heart studies may one day become far more famous for their implicit findings about the origins of human health than their discoveries of risk factors linked to heart disease. They may indeed become every bit as famous for unwittingly uncovering the social and interpersonal factors conducive to good health and longevity as for helping us understand the causes of heart disease. In that regard, it could prove to be a double blessing, helping to alter opinions among health policy makers and average citizens alike about the essential risks to our nation's health.

Yet, to arrive at an understanding of this hidden blessing, several questions must first be asked. Among them, perhaps none is more fundamental than whether the risk factors identified in Framingham are the main causes of premature heart disease? By raising this question, I do not mean to imply that the risk factors identified there are not important. Yet, are the risk factors discovered at Framingham the *primary* causes for the development of premature heart disease? Or are there other hidden risk factors, what I call the *risks behind the risks,* that have a far greater impact on the development of premature heart disease, and on virtually every other cause of premature death?

Can the lack of love, chronic loneliness, social isolation, low self-esteem, dysfunctional patterns of communication, sudden blood pressure surges while talking, interpersonal stresses, communal disintegration, and educational failure pose far greater risks for the development of heart disease? Or perhaps, even more to the point, do these latter "risk" factors significantly compound or exacerbate the types of risks discovered at Framingham?

These questions first came to my attention when other studies began to reveal powerful links between loneliness, marital status, school failure, and heart disease. It naturally led to the question of why these health problems were not identified at Framingham. That issue soon led to an even more fundamental question: Was Framingham really a representative town in which to study cardiovascular disease in the first place? Would the research team have discovered different relationships if, instead of Framingham, Massachusetts they had chosen in 1948 the boomtowns of Reno or Las Vegas, Nevada, or even Harlem, New York?

Yet, almost as quickly as the question could be framed in this manner, other problems became equally obvious. Conducting a fifty-year prospective study in Reno or Las Vegas, or even Harlem, would have been a far tougher research assignment, maybe even impossible, because people didn't seem to stick around those communities for very long. Conducting a long-term study in Reno or Las Vegas would have been an especially messy assignment, what with all those people coming and getting divorced, drinking, and gambling their lives away—hardly the types likely to come back every two years for a medical checkup. Many citizens of Reno, Las Vegas, or Harlem would have been mighty hard to find after two years, let alone track for over 50 years.

Framingham, by contrast, was one of the more socially stable communities in the United States in 1948. Its residents were religious, churchgoing, non-divorcing, and relatively well-educated. They were an ideal research population precisely because their community was, on the whole, so dependable and so well integrated socially.

This fact was not ignored by the original investigators, for they wrote of Framingham: "As is true of New England towns, it included not only built-up business and residential areas, but also the outlying rural areas within the town limit. Framingham has the town-meeting form of government and the people were accustomed to and well versed in the group approach to their problems." For the first 30 years of study, the scientists were able to keep track of almost 80 percent of the original population of volunteers who were still alive, a truly remarkable record of reliability.[45]

If the entire United States were like Framingham, then the health data discovered there might be more applicable to the whole country. Yet, by 1976 (when I first examined the Framingham studies), certain social realities seemed to make the Framingham of 1948 very different from mainstream America. I suspect that very few people who lived in Framingham in 1948 had come from broken homes. I believe very few had experienced childhood deprivation, were raised in single-parent households, or were mired in poverty. I think the majority of these volunteers were reasonably well-educated.

I suspect, I feel, I think, I believe all of these things, but the simple fact is that I do not know them. Nor does anyone else. The fact is that while blood pressure, weight, diet, and a host of other physical factors were painstakingly determined, the original researchers did not analyze these basic indices of human life. In 1948, social stability in the United States was more or less taken for granted.

Not only did the Framingham studies initially neglect social, educational, interpersonal, and psychological risk factors that might contribute to heart disease, but they inadvertently caused the public to minimize the importance of such factors in heart disease. Indeed, the Framingham investigators even began to assert that emotional stress, and specifically the stress involved in divorce, were not related at all to coronary heart disease. In 1966, one circular, entitled "The Framingham Heart Study: Habits and Coronary Disease," emphatically stated that marital status to lower the incidence of heart disease and

e one chosen to support the assertion of no relationship
ital status and death had a total of only six cases! No Las
er in his right mind would have ever given you any odds on
of that statement! What should have been clear even in 1966

the Framingham Data on
rce and Mortality a Valid Tool
J.S. Population Comparison?
s of Divorce and Separation,
d States & Framingham (1966)

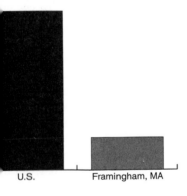

U.S.   Framingham, MA

se investigators did not have sufficient evidence to make any
out the relationship between marital status and death rates in

was something else about the figures in this Table that
caught my eye. It was obvious that very few people in the
study were getting divorced! According to the study's own
percent of their research population was either separated or
statistic that could hardly be matched anywhere else in the
s.

marital status was not related to coronary h
distributed to thousands of physicians acr
seen by a large number of ordinary citizens

"Marital status was unrelated to risk
though changes in marital status through
would be regarded by many as evidenc
upheaval."

Adjacent to the graphic display sh
relationship between marital status and he
This one, relating family size and heart dis
point:

"Family size appeared unrelated to ri
disease. Some married couples with no chil
might be construed as living under stressful

The message was clear: marital and f
heart disease were unrelated.

Accompanying these assertions was a
and marital status. It showed data labeled i
This ratio was based on the idea that th
widowed, divorced (or separated), and mar
population who died should be equivalen
such people in their total sample. The rese
the following data:

FRAMINGHAM

	EXPECTED TO HAVE DIED	OBSERVED
Married	328	322
Single	26	31
Widowed	19	23
Divorced	8	6

Of the researchers' claim that mari
coronary heart disease, what is most interes
observed cases of death in divorced or sepa
had been expected! Two other categorie
actually had relatively higher incidences
individuals had slightly fewer deaths than
other words, the three largest groups did s

all sho
death.
Y
betweer
Vegas
the reli

12
10
8
6
4
2
0

Percent of Population

was that
statemer
Framing
The
immedia
Framing
data, onl
divorced,
United S

LEGACIES FROM THE PAST

These studies have generated controversies that have raged in the medical community for decades. Elevations in serum cholesterol have been shown to be linked not only to diet, but to educational failure and emotional stress. People who are more stressed psychologically have significantly higher levels of serum cholesterol.[47] Elevated blood pressure,[48] and smoking and obesity,[49] also have been linked to emotional stress and loneliness, as have been marital status, educational failure, and, most importantly, dysfunctional patterns of communication.

Entirely new questions began to emerge. Could the same dietary intake of cholesterol be absorbed differently, depending on your level of anxiety or your sense of self-esteem? Does food digested in a stable marriage, or with friends, or within a relatively tranquil community like Framingham, have the same effect as food digested in Reno or Las Vegas, or in a solitary environment?

In the 1960s, Dr. Stewart Wolf, an internist, and former dean of the University of Oklahoma Medical School, began to write up the results from his long-term heart studies in Roseto, Pennsylvania, a town in the foothills of the Pocono Mountains about 60 miles from New York City. At that time, Roseto's population was largely made up of Italian immigrants, who came there initially to work in the local quarries. They seemed to eat many things that would cause cardiologists to worry. Their daily caloric intake was above the national average. Strangely, while they had only one-third as many heart attacks as surrounding communities, their blood cholesterol levels were about the same as those of people in neighboring towns. Why?

Dr. Wolf gave his opinion: "The most striking feature of Roseto was its social structure.... Study revealed that unlike most American towns, Roseto is cohesive and mutually supportive, with strong family and community ties. Because of the concern of the inhabitants for their neighbors, there is in Roseto no poverty and little crime. The family was found to be the focus of life in Roseto.... Few men over the age of 25 were unmarried." [50]

Observations similar to those made in Roseto have been subsequently corroborated by an ever-growing list of studies, and the suspicion is now gaining credence among medical scientists that social and interpersonal factors may not only significantly influence the course of heart disease. They may be the most important risk factors of all!

HEALTH AND SOCIAL STABILITY

By 1998, fifty years after this study began, there was little doubt. The risk factors discovered in Framingham had been confirmed by hundreds of other studies. But the greatest irony may yet turn out to be that the town was really another Roseto all along, disguised under miles upon miles of computerized medical data. This reality about Framingham may prove much more important than all of the risk factors that have been linked thus far to heart disease. For the focus in Framingham has been so strongly oriented toward heart disease that a far more obvious fact has escaped general attention—the town was a very healthy place to live. Evidence supporting this assertion has been there almost since the beginning, but it was taken for granted.

From the very beginning of the studies, the incidence of coronary heart disease in Framingham has been far below what the experts had originally estimated it would be. They based their original estimates on the national incidence of coronary heart disease in similar populations. At the start, they pondered what the likely incidence of cardiovascular disorders would be in 5,000 randomly chosen people initially free of the disease. Basing their estimates on health trends at that time, they wrote:

"For the 13 years between 1953 and 1966, 1,017 Framingham participants were expected to have died (based on national death rates for these age ranges). The number of deaths that actually occurred was 883— about 15 percent fewer deaths than predicted."

Far more intriguing is the fact that nowhere near the expected number of people developed cardiovascular disorders. Twenty years after the study began, the figures simply didn't add up. In 1968, some 3,785 of the original 5,127 volunteers were still completely free of heart disease. Even throwing in the extra 209 people (the difference between 5,000 and the actual number of 5,209), only 1,342 people had developed any form of cardiovascular disease. That was 808 fewer people than the 2,150 the experts had originally estimated would have some form of heart disease after 20 years. Framingham had at least one-third fewer heart problems than had been originally predicted.

Of all the statistics emerging out of Framingham, the longevity of the population is itself the most revealing of all phenomena. By 1976, 28 years after the study was initiated, 73.2 percent of the original participants were still alive. The youngest members of the sample were approaching their 60s, while the oldest members were reaching 90.

In February 1976, 3,754 of the original group of volunteers were still alive. Comparing that against the national survival rates for a similar race-sex-age range, the number of people expected to live for 28 years was 3,116. Thus, at least 638 people (or 17 percent more people) were still alive in Framingham who would have been dead in other parts of the United States. Using far more conservative figures, the life expectancy of people in Framingham could be compared to the life expectancy of whites covered by life insurance by the 15 largest insurers in the country. These people are the "good risks"—that is, they are screened carefully for health (otherwise, the companies that gamble on their health would lose money).

Again, using the mortality figures of insured whites in the United States, one would have expected 3,438 people to have survived 28 years until 1976. By this criterion, at least 316 people were still alive in Framingham who would have been dead anywhere else in the United States according to the very conservative figures of the life insurance companies. More people in Framingham were actually living longer than the estimates of insurance companies for their very best risks! Why so many people were still alive and so healthy in Framingham was, I believe, far more interesting than why 26.8 percent had died.[51]

Was this simply a statistical fluke? Or did the fact that they were coming back for continuous medical checkups make the people of Framingham so health conscious that they took unusually good care of their bodies? Or was the social milieu of Framingham in 1948 similar to that of Roseto in the 1960s? Did the investigators inadvertently stumble upon, or select, a population that experienced such a low degree of interpersonal, emotional, or social stress that the only risk factors likely to emerge from the medical data would have been physical in nature?

Mortality and Heart Disease in Framingham:
Healthier than "Anytown, USA"

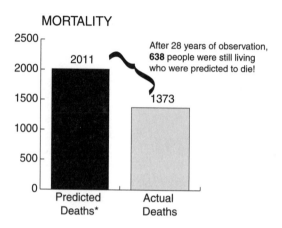

MORTALITY

After 28 years of observation, **638** people were still living who were predicted to die!

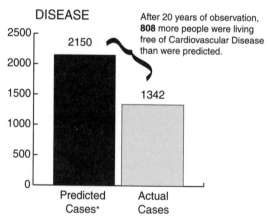

DISEASE

After 20 years of observation, **808** more people were living free of Cardiovascular Disease than were predicted.

*Predicted cases & deaths based on
U.S. population averages

THE GOLDEN ANNIVERSARY

1998 marked the fiftieth year of continual existence of the Framingham Heart Studies. The original cohort of volunteers had witnessed fifty years of medical history, and I suppose for those still alive, it had gone by in a flash. There were 1,095 volunteers still alive, and the youngest were now at least 80 years of age. The figures on survival provided by the Framingham web site were as follows:

ALIVE AS OF FEBRUARY 1998

AGE	79-89	90-99	100+	TOTALS
MEN	318	34	1	353
WOMEN	624	114	4	742
TOTAL	942	148	5	1095

Twenty-one percent of the entire population was still alive, with the youngest now being 80 years of age! According to the Center for Disease Control and the Office of Vital Statistics (1998), these survival rates exceed the upper limits for the average life span of Americans born between 1910 and 1931 (the original birth years of the volunteers) by anywhere from 20 to 40 percent!

In 1998, a research article gave details on premature mortality in Framingham up to 1988. The investigators noted that only 36 people had died before the age of 45, and that thirty percent had died before the age of 75. That is, only 30 percent of the Framingham participants had died before reaching the average life span in the United States! An additional 1,125 participants had died over the age of 75 (22 percent of the population), while the remaining 2,490 volunteers (48 percent) were still alive.

One need only recall the original predictions of the Framingham scientists: "2,150 people would have heart disease after 20 years of study." Yet, in twice that period, after 40 years, only 2,719 people had died! By the time the average person in the United States would have perished, almost 70 percent of this population was either still alive, or had lived past 75 years of age.[52]

One final fact confirms that Framingham may not really represent "Anytown USA." Of the 1,594 deaths under the age of 75, only 496 were from coronary heart disease. That is, only 9.5 percent of the entire population died of premature coronary heart disease. Such findings are at marked variance with the American Heart Association's 1999 findings that 35 percent of all heart attacks occur before the age of 65. In only 31 percent of the total number of deaths before the age of 75 was coronary heart disease listed as the certifiable cause of death. Thus, not only was the incidence of premature death remarkably low in Framingham, but so, too, was the contribution of coronary heart disease to mortality.

A POSTSCRIPT

By 1970, the population of Framingham had reached almost 65,000, or more than double its 1948 size. The Massachusetts Turnpike passing nearby had overshadowed the Boston and Maine train station that had once connected the town to Boston. The birthrate to unmarried women in 1970 was 3 percent. There were no deaths by homicide. And only four suicides were recorded. In Massachusetts, divorce records are not kept by individual towns like Framingham, but are instead maintained by counties. In Middlesex County, of which Framingham is a part, the 1970 population was 1,400,000. In 1970, the county had 1,400 divorces, far below the national average.

Between 1970 and 1975, however, social patterns in the area began to shift rapidly. Cultural tides from regions like Nevada began to affect these New England communities. "Framingham is changing very fast now," a town clerk (and lifelong resident) told me at that time. "It wasn't too long ago that when you walked down the street, you knew everyone. Now, there seem to be so many strangers." She thought the birthrate to unmarried women of 3 percent was "shockingly high," and she refused to believe that it was still ten to twenty times lower than the average of many American cities.

Between 1970 and 1974, the number of divorces granted in Middlesex County tripled. All the signs pointed to the fact that Framingham was well on its way to "catching up" with the life-style of mainstream America. By 1990, the town had in many ways "caught up" with the rest of the United States. While the median income of $45,378 in Middlesex County was well above that of the rest of the United States, some 9.5 percent of the adult population was now listed as divorced, slowly catching up with the rest of "mainstream America."

Although the investigators have now launched second-generation studies at Framingham, it would be very difficult to begin an investigation in 1998 that compares with the original study begun in 1948. Yet, one cannot help but wonder if its citizens will be as healthy in 2048 as they were in 1948 when the U.S. government first moved in to wipe out heart disease, and help create a model town for health. Was the Fountain of Youth already in existence in Framingham in 1948? And is that fountain slowly being drained away by more lethal social trends already growing within the body-politic of our nation?

HEALTH AND THE BODY-POLITIC:
THE JOURNEY FROM NOD BACK TO EDEN

At this point, you may well be wondering why I have chosen to spend so much time reviewing a study of healthy people who lived in a relatively tranquil and socially stable town where the majority lived long lives. The point, after all, is not to prove that longevity in Framingham more closely approximates that of people living in Osaka, Japan, than Reno, Nevada. Nor is the point to suggest that Framingham in 1948 was some sort of American Utopia.

Clearly, human beings who lived there had their own share of psychological, social, and interpersonal struggles. And it is not unreasonable to wonder whether those who struggled more with these sorts of issues were also more vulnerable to heart disease and premature death. What did not exist in that town, however, was the kind of acute interpersonal chaos, family and communal fragmentation, and social turmoil so prevalent in other communities in the United States.

Recent data make it clear that if the investigators had chosen a more socially unstable town, they would have had a field day with their "risk factors." In that sense, they ironically stacked the deck against themselves. Yet, it is clearly not fair to criticize these medical pioneers for choosing a town of this sort to conduct a long-term study. They had little choice if they hoped to follow people for more than a half-century.

And most assuredly their efforts have not been wasted. Quite the contrary. We owe much to the generations of dedicated medical scientists who spent their lives helping us understand some of the important factors that increase the risk of developing premature heart disease. Indeed, the risk factors discovered at Framingham may turn out to be far more important for reasons that have not yet been recognized.

For the Framingham studies tell us a great deal about the links between health, longevity, and social cohesiveness. The types of cardiac risk factors discovered in Framingham appear far more frequently and far more acutely in other, more socially dysfunctional communities. Every one of the risk factors discovered at Framingham, for example, occurs far more frequently and far more acutely in individuals who fail to finish high school. That relationship is directly linear, and quite remarkable. As educational level goes down, virtually every one of the risk factors found in Framingham dramatically goes up. The same is true for other socially isolated and lonely human beings.

And that simple fact brings us to the central point of this chapter. There is, in the final analysis, nothing mystical, magical, or mysterious about the links between loneliness and the increased risk of heart disease. Nor is the notion of a" broken heart" mere poetry. Chronically lonely and socially isolated people die prematurely from heart disease for reasons that are quite intelligible. They suffer from all the risk factors uncovered in Framingham, plus others not noticed in that town. They also suffer to a far greater extent from those very same risk factors.

Yet, certain far-reaching questions must be asked precisely because these studies are so important and have had such a profound impact on medical attitudes around the world. For Dr. Michael DeBakey is quite right when he asserted that these studies are widely viewed as "the model in epidemiology—one of the great studies of this century."

Ironically, it is the very word "epidemiology" that raises basic questions not usually associated with the Framingham Heart Studies. Derived from the Greek word "epidemios," the word literally means to be "among the people." Yet, the question must be asked: Did the Framingham investigators focus on the hearts of human beings living their lives "among the people"?

From the very outset, their focus was on heart disease, and the risk factors that contributed to it. Rooted as it originally was in an infectious disease model, there was something about the way these risk factors were assessed in Framingham that I believe was inadvertently misleading. High blood pressure, elevated serum cholesterol, diabetes, sedentary life style, cigarette smoking, electrocardiographic abnormalities, etc, all seemed to emerge as if they were solitary problems within an individual, and not problems that stemmed from the "epidemios," or "life lived among the people." They did not appear to be risk factors that arose from any particular social, interpersonal, communicative, or communal struggles within that town.

I believe the infectious disease model that dominated these studies may have unconsciously led the original investigators to think of human relationships in Framingham more as a source of communicable disease than as a source of vitality. In addition, by focusing on cardiovascular illness, these studies ironically diverted attention away from the vital life-sustaining power derived by its citizens precisely because they lived their lives "among the people."

There were, as well, certain unconscious biases and philosophical assumptions about the human body built into these studies that further compounded this problem. In its all-encompassing mechanistic and objective approach, buttressed by infectious disease models of health and illness, the Framingham studies, I believe, were but one small part of a far deeper medical-philosophical movement that began to take root in post-war American society.

This perspective served to lull physicians, health policy makers, and average U.S. citizens alike into a sense of benign neglect regarding the crucial health importance of our interpersonal lives. Scientific assumptions that the heart is solely a pump, and that the human body is a genetically wired, biological machine quite literally have been drummed into our national consciousness. Pumps and machines have no interpersonal or communal life. Cholesterol and high blood pressure are likewise perceived to be merely part of the inner biochemical workings of the body-machine, and thus seemingly impervious to the exigencies of our intimate, or felt, relationships.

In addition to these assumptions, I believe these studies were but one small part of a post-war medical zeitgeist that coalesced with several other powerful American attitudes and beliefs. Like a mighty river that emerges out of the confluence of numerous small tributaries, these beliefs came together in a way destined to have far-reaching consequences on the health consciousness of our nation.

Operating with these entrenched assumptions, the post-war period was to witness the rise of a widely shared health perspective destined to influence several generations of Americans. It unwittingly led people even further astray, lulling them to uncritically assume that their "epidemios," their "life among people," their interpersonal, communicative, and communal lives, had little to do with their cardiovascular health. Average citizens were directed, instead, to look elsewhere. They were told that if they jogged, exercised, and ate the right foods, if they lowered their blood pressure and lowered their cholesterol, then they would be guaranteed good health.

This confluence of beliefs and interests, flowing together in what would become a cultural floodtide, does not mean that the findings at Framingham were invalid, or that the health perspective used to promote an "attack" on these risk factors was not highly effective. To the contrary, these combined efforts have yielded an enormous amount of good. They have developed approaches that help address some of the more troubling medical problems of our society in ways that are, at times, absolutely brilliant.

Indeed, if I was experiencing anginal pain, I can assure you that I would be the first in line for a bypass operation, in order to give the plumbing of my arteries a second chance. And if my blood pressure was seriously elevated, or my serum cholesterol abnormally high, then, without hesitation, I would take the medications designed to help ameliorate these problems.

Yet, the fact is that a whole host of national and international pharmaceutical companies, food industries, and medical technology companies have a vested interest in spreading the word about the types of physical risk factors discovered in Framingham. With over fifty million Americans identified as having high blood pressure, and 98 million estimated to have total blood cholesterol levels of 200 milligrams per deciliter, both according to the American Heart Association in 1999, medications designed to "treat" these problems have emerged as multi-billion dollar industrial enterprises. And these medications, and the technological and advertising efforts expended to attack these problems, have helped.

Yet, these very same companies do not have an equal economic interest in fostering the "epidemios," the idea that all of us live our lives among the people. While not intending to imply cynical motivations or any grand conspiracy, the simple fact is that there is far less corporate profit to be earned from fostering an alternative health consciousness in our nation.

Thus, while our nation spends billions upon billions of dollars attending to the "solitary risk factors" linked to heart disease, other major risk factors are ignored. Issues of love and loneliness, marital relationships, self-esteem, community life, school failure, poverty, and most importantly everyday human dialogue have been relegated to the backburners of our national health consciousness. With the total cooperation of bio-medical industries that "beat the drums," Framingham, and thousands of similar epidemiological and laboratory studies, have insinuated themselves into our national health consciousness. It is, we are frequently reminded, cholesterol, diabetes, obesity, sedentary life styles, and cigarette smoking that are our primary nemeses.

I do not mean to imply that there has been any form of conscious or even unconscious collusion between medical investigators and corporations that helped shape the type of risk factors discovered at Framingham. That would be both offensive and absurd. Much to their credit, the Framingham investigators were among the first to take on the tobacco industry when they saw a problem. What is at issue here, however, is the process and manner by which information about health risks comes to the attention of the average citizen in our country.

Even more important is the impact that such findings have on the body politic of our nation. For just as the human body has been viewed and "understood" ever more exclusively in mechanistic terms, so too the "body-politic" of our nation has grown more isolated and mechanistic in nature. The American "epidemios" and its "body-politic" have tended to grow ever more fractured, alienated, and lonely, unable to fully appreciate the philosophical winds now blowing with unparalleled ferocity through our culture.

The casualties of the new mechanical-social order—the legions of the modern medically "disappeared"—show up in our shock trauma units and inner city emergency rooms. Or they simply die prematurely, and quietly out of sight, from premature coronary heart disease, cancer, and a host of other risk factors not noticed in Framingham.

We owe to our Greek forefathers certain of the bedrock principles of our American democracy. Aristotle long ago noted that man was far more than a "social animal," that man was unique among all the animals because man alone was "political." "A man wholly solitary," he warned us, "would either be a God or a brute." Aristotle's "polis," the root derivation of the very word "politics," was literally intended to convey an understanding that "man was one among many men."

According to Aristotle, it was in the very nature of man to be political, to communicate and debate and live among one's fellow man. Man and man alone used language to communicate essential ideas. The "agora" or marketplace of Aristotle's Greek politics was a living, breathing, vibrant community where one "pressed the flesh" of one's fellow man on a daily basis. To Aristotle, the very derivation of the phrase "the body-politic" would imply a life lived both with and among one's fellow man. And to Aristotle, dialogue was key to that life.

Thus, when we speak in modern times about the health of the nation's "body-politic," we are in a very real sense speaking about those health problems that arise precisely because we are both "social beings" as well as "political beings." It includes those health problems that arise precisely because we live in dialogue among and with our fellow man. Yet, medicine's evolution, which eventually turned into a post-war cultural revolution about the human body, left us with little more than a solitary, independent, self-sufficient biological machine. Life among one's fellow man could be understood as a potential source of infectious and communicable disease, but no longer as a source of health and vitality.

In that sense, the medical and cultural philosophies that permeate modern life have extracted the human body from the body politic of our nation. They have extracted language from the human body, and quite literally wrenched human speech from the human heart. They did so unwittingly at Framingham, and they do so in our hospitals, medical schools, and research laboratories throughout our nation. With the human body extracted from the body politic, and the human heart reduced to a mere pump, is it any wonder that both medical science, as well as the average citizen in our nation, might have great difficulty fully understanding one of the major health threats of the twenty-first century?

To reiterate the point one final time, I believe that in this new millennium *communicative disease* will emerge as every bit as important a health threat as *communicable disease*! Yet, at present, these two major sources of disease operate like two massive tectonic plates grinding against each other. The machine body and the communicative body are moving in opposite directions, threatening to break into pieces, fragmenting and rupturing the communal and physical health of our nation. Even now, modern medicine, with all of its brilliant technologies, appears to be feverishly racing to cure problems stemming in large part from the "social diseases" and communicative diseases of a "heartless body-politic" that it inadvertently helped to foster.

Chapter Four

LIVING TOGETHER, DYING ALONE

"No animal or plant lives alone or is self-sustaining. All live in communities including other members of their own species, and also a number, usually a large variety, of other sorts of animals and plants. The quest to be alone is indeed a futile one, never successfully followed in the history of life."
—George Gaylord Simpson, evolutionary biologist, 1994[53]

"The best combinations of the standard 'risk factors' fail to identify most new cases of [coronary] disease.... And, whereas simultaneous presence of two or more risk factors is associated with extremely high risk of coronary disease, such situations only predict a small minority of cases.... A broad array of recent research studies ... point with ever increasing certainty to the position that certain psychological, social, and behavior conditions do put persons at higher risk of clinically manifest coronary disease."
—C. David Jenkins, *The New England Journal of Medicine*, 1976[54]

AN APOLOGY

I have repeatedly asserted, so far without any direct proof, that loneliness, while largely overlooked, ranks as one the most lethal risk factors determining who will live and who will die prematurely in modern industrialized nations.

I have introduced several additional concepts as well, so far without detailed explanation. I have suggested, for example, that many sources of loneliness in modern life have a common denominator in what I have labeled "communicative disease." It is this disease, reflected in such autonomic activity as marked blood pressure surges when a person begins to speak, that plays a major role in a whole host of health problems leading to premature death.

I have also stated that not only can communicative disease strike down people in the prime of their adult life, but also that these problems can be frequently traced back to childhood experiences that disrupted and destroyed their capacity to engage fellow human beings in dialogue. The most obvious source of this problem is the parental use of what I have labeled "toxic talk"—abusive language that, in effect, was taught to children through its very use.

Equally devastating, however, is school failure, which is linked to a marked increased risk of premature death. Such failure frequently compounds a child's prior experiences with toxic talk at home, forcing many into a lifetime of communicative isolation, social withdrawal, increased depression, and hopelessness, all of which ultimately increase the risk of developing a variety of medical problems that ultimately break the human heart.

The following chapters move beyond rhetorical assertions about these phenomena to the medical data itself. An array of health data is marshaled to help illustrate both the many faces of loneliness, as well as its lethality. Yet, an apology of sorts, or at the very least a warning, is in order. The following three chapters move sequentially. They start with a general overview of the links between factors that potentially exacerbate social isolation and increase the risk from all causes of death. Then they move to a detailed analysis of the specific impact that those isolating forces exert on the incidence of heart disease, both in adulthood and childhood.

While every effort has been made to summarize these studies in the briefest manner possible, the medical and statistical data themselves pose a real challenge. For statistical data, no matter how they are presented, tend to leave readers a bit bleary eyed and bored. To aid in this process, a significant portion of the research studies and statistics have been placed on my web site (www.lifecarehealth.com) for readers who wish to examine these additional studies in more detail.

To help begin forging these linkages, perhaps a few clinical vignettes, all dealing with sudden death from heart disease and cancer, would be helpful. These vignettes are presented to help illustrate both the unique, as well as the complex, aspects of our individual lives, as well as hint at the powerful impact that human relationships and the sudden loss or absence of such relationships can exert on physical health.

MOON SHOTS AND LOVE

Every once in a while, an image flashes across the television screen that captures in a particularly poignant way mankind's indomitable spirit. Huge, powerful rockets blasting space shuttles into orbit, and the earth trembling in response, are one example. Alan Shepard's moon-shot is yet another.

For it was Alan's mighty golf shot with his trusted "six iron," made to demonstrate to children on earth the nature of gravitational forces on the moon that captured mankind's imagination. Seemingly oblivious to his cumbersome space suit and bulky life support equipment, Alan blasted two golf balls into lunar orbit. In the powdery dust of the moon, devoid of life and vegetation, he made history. Years earlier, he had been the first American to be launched into space, and now he was the first to tee-off on the 19th "green" of the moon. It was a moon-shot of beauty not to be matched by the greatest professional hole-in-one ever made on the azalea-framed greens of Augusta's Master's Tournament.

Alan's lunar golf caper helps provide a glimpse into the marvelous character of the man his wife, Louise, had married so many years earlier. He died on July 21, 1998 at the age of 74, after a prolonged struggle with leukemia. Before his death in 1998, Alan and Louise had spent their leisure time touring various golf courses around the globe, delighting fans everywhere with stories about his moon shot. It was obvious to those who saw them that Louise and Alan delighted in each other's company.

The end of their love story appeared several weeks later in the obituary section of our nation's newspapers. On August 27, 1998, the item noted: "Louise Shepard died of a heart attack while flying home from visiting one of her three daughters. She was 74 years of age. It had been four weeks since her husband, Alan, had died."

THE DEAL OF LOVE

First-hand knowledge sometimes makes "coincidences" of this sort somewhat easier to understand, at least on the surface. Shortly after Louise Shepard's death, I met my colleague, Dr. Jeffrey Quartner, a cardiologist and Medical Director of the Sinai-Wellbridge Cardiac Rehabilitation Center in Baltimore. He was, at that time, both stunned and deeply grieved about the sudden death of his mother, at age 74. Similar to Mrs. Shepard, she too had died without warning, in her case just three months after her husband's death.

Dr. Quartner's father had been bedridden with a series of dreadful medical problems for over twenty years, and for the last seven years of his life he could not even speak. For those twenty years, Dr. Quartner's mother faithfully took care of her husband. She endured the terrible stress involved in watching helplessly as someone so dearly loved suffered continuously and without hope of recovery. She had accepted her fate with dignity and without complaint. Dr. Quartner knew that his mother had heart disease. She had been diagnosed years earlier, and was under excellent medical care.

And then, shortly after her husband's demise, death came "like a thief in the night." She died of a cardiac arrhythmia, at a point where the "objective stress" and "terrible burden" of caring for her very sick husband had finally been lifted from her shoulders. Death came at a moment when one might have thought she could finally find some relief. Some call a death of this sort, "God's kiss," a form of blessing imparted to those who have suffered more than the human heart can endure.

Knowledge that Dr. Quartner's mother suffered from pre-existing heart disease helps to understand the "coincidental timing" of her death. But why, three months after the death of her husband? Why not years earlier, when the terrible stress involved in caring for him would seemingly have put her at far greater risk? "It was a love story," I murmured reflexively while trying to share his grief. "It's part of the deal—as C.S. Lewis had asserted, the price human beings frequently pay when love is lost."

Deaths of this sort are mentioned almost daily in our newspapers. Usually they go unnoticed. For the most part, we do not know the circumstances nor do we understand the details. Often, it is impossible to discern what really happened. "A committed bachelor all of his life" was the phrase the local newspaper recently used to describe the sudden cardiac death of one particular 62-year-old man. Yet, one had to wonder: Why did he die so young? Had he been lonely most of his life? Did he smoke? Or drink? Was genetic bad luck in play? Or was it all just coincidence?

CLOCKWORK AND LONELINESS

One such notice appeared in the February 26, 1999 edition of *The New York Times*. It described the death of Winthrop K. Edey, an internationally known expert on antique clocks. He died of Hodgkin's disease, his family reported, at the age of 61. He was the grandson of Morris W. Kellogg, a noted engineer who made his fortune building oil refineries, as well as our nation's atomic bomb plants. That inheritance left Winthrop Edey free to pursue his interest in antique clocks, a passion that began when he was six-years-old! When he died, he left his collection, estimated to be worth millions, to the Frick Gallery in New York.

Certain details in the *Times'* obituary gave some oblique hints about his interpersonal sensitivity. In addition to his interest in clocks, Mr. Edey began writing a diary at age six, which he kept faithfully until his death. Commenting on this diary, the *Times* obituary writer noted: "Proustian in its sweep and attention to details (Mr. Edey could devote several pages to the ramifications of a friend's failure to return a phone call), the multivolume diary, some of his friends are convinced, will someday be regarded as an important social document of New York life." The obituary described Mr. Edey as somewhat "eccentric," yet having what appeared to be an active social life. He apparently remained a bachelor all of his life. A brother and two sisters survived him.

Again the same questions arise: Why did he die so young? What factors predisposed him to Hodgkin's disease? Simple fate? Genetic bad luck? Unknown, or undisclosed, environmental conditions? Or had he been lonely since his childhood, perhaps escaping into the whirling mechanical world of antique clocks to escape whatever might have pained him? Most children do not begin writing diaries at age six, or maintain that mode of communication throughout their lives. Yet, one can never be certain, or even hope to find answers to questions of this sort in a newspaper obituary. It is factually clear, however, that Mr. Edey died at age sixty-one, that he was single, that he loved antique clocks, that he kept a diary that he began when he was six years old, and that he was far too young to die.

WHEN THE MIRROR IMAGE DIES

Linkages between the loss of a loved one and sudden death are frequently reported in the medical literature. One of the more unusual cases described the simultaneous deaths of two 32-year-old schizophrenic sisters.[55] The circumstances surrounding their deaths in a North Carolina psychiatric hospital are intriguing. Neither twin was ever married, nor were the sisters ever separated from each other for any prolonged period. At about age 21, both began to deteriorate psychologically, with a progressive flattening of their emotional expressions, loss of social interest, and disturbances of sleep and appetite.

This was accompanied by growing suspiciousness and delusions, until they were simultaneously institutionalized, at the age of 31. They were discharged twice from this hospital under pressure from their parents, but in neither instance could they function adequately outside the institution. After their final readmission the following year, they refused to eat, withdrew from all social contact, and gave only minimal answers to questions. When their refusal to eat grew serious, it was decided to separate the twins into different wards, since the staff felt they were reinforcing each other with negative attitudes. The description of events following their first evening of separation was as follows:

Statements by the nursing and attendant staff showed that during the evening they had been under constant observation. Both patients were ambulatory and went to bed as usual. At 10:20 p.m., 11:30 p.m. and 12:00 midnight, both patients were observed in routine checks. Both were sleeping and examination of their respiratory movements showed nothing unusual. At 12:45 a.m. on April 12, twin A was found dead. An immediate investigation was made as to the condition of her twin and she was also found to have died. It was considered from immediate examination of the bodies that death in both cases was recent. Twin A's death was unobserved, but another patient shared the room with twin B. Apparently a short time before their deaths were discovered, twin B had stood looking out of the window of her dormitory, looking up at the window where her sister was a patient. She then sank to the floor and her body was found in this position. The patient who shared her room was accustomed to peculiar behavior in other patients and felt that there was no cause for alarm in this unusual incident *(pp. 378-379)*.

DEPRESSION THAT BREAKS YOUR HEART

In the cases involving heart disease just cited, there are some general clinical hunches or hypotheses that can be made about sudden death in the wake of human loss. Though in the individual cases just described they remain only hunches and speculative hypotheses at best, investigators nevertheless have been able recently to use case studies of this sort to isolate a major new risk factor for heart disease. Fifty years after the Framingham Studies were first initiated, sufficient medical data has been gathered to add a potent new risk factor to the conventional list linked to heart disease.

In late 1999, the National Institute of Mental Health sent out a medical bulletin entitled "Depression Can Break Your Heart."[56] (In a personal sense, I felt a twinge of satisfaction that at long last the very title of my first book was beginning to enter mainstream medical thinking.) Citing a variety of recent medical findings, including research in Baltimore and Montreal, the National Institute of Mental Health alerted physicians to be more cognizant of the fact that depression is a major risk factor for heart disease, and must be considered just as important as other risk factors, such as hypertension and elevated serum cholesterol.

Investigators from The Johns Hopkins Hospital conducted the Baltimore study. They described 1,551 people who were originally free of all signs and symptoms of heart disease. Yet, when they followed them over the next fourteen years, those who were depressed were *four times* more likely to develop heart disease than those who were not depressed. In Montreal, a companion study observed a correlative finding in patients with pre-existing heart disease. They discovered that those people who were depressed were *four times* more likely to die in the next six months than those who were not depressed. [57]

In 1996, Dr. Susan Everson and her colleagues also described similar findings from 942 middle-aged men in Kuopio, Finland. They observed that those who reported feelings of hopelessness developed 20 percent more coronary atherosclerosis within a four-year period than those who reported feeling more hopeful about their present and future situations. The investigators asserted "this is the same magnitude of increased risk that one sees in comparing a pack-a-day smoker to a non-smoker."[58]

Several major reviews have also linked depression to an increased risk of heart disease and sudden death. Investigators at Emory University and The University of Pennsylvania have described a large number of studies indicating that depression is a major contributor to the development of coronary heart disease, as well as a significant factor contributing to cardiac arrhythmias (electrical instability of the heart) and sudden cardiac death.[59]

In a similar manner, Dr. Brenda Penninx and her colleagues at the National Institute of Aging recently reported that older people who are chronically depressed had an 88 percent higher risk of developing cancer. In an article published in the *Journal of the National Cancer Institute*, they speculated that depression may suppress the immune system, which then fails to fight cancerous cells. They based their findings on information gathered on 4,800 men and women over the age of 70 from Massachusetts, Connecticut, and Iowa.

All were interviewed on three separate occasions in 1982, 1985, and 1988, and none had cancer at the time. All participants were tested for depression using standard assessment tests when interviewed. In 1992, the investigators went back, examined the records, and found that 146 members of the group had been chronically depressed, and they had an 88 percent higher rate of cancer than the remainder of the group interviewed.[60]

Depression is almost always accompanied by a tendency to withdraw from others, to reduce engagement with others, difficulties communicating, and with increased feelings of loneliness and abandonment. These are themes one routinely hears from depressed patients. William Styron wrote a particularly gripping autobiographical account of these tendencies when he described his own struggles with depression. In *Darkness Visible,* he captures the dreadful sense of loneliness and social isolation felt in the depths of depression. He also describes with eloquence the power of the loving support he received from his wife, a love that ultimately kept him from destroying himself.

Several decades before these recent research studies, however, a number of pioneering investigators already had described the links between depression, social isolation, loss, loneliness, and sudden death.

VOODOO DEATH AND SOCIAL ISOLATION

Walter Cannon, a renowned professor of physiology at Harvard University (and the scientist who first outlined the physiology of the "fight/flight response"), wrote extensively about the phenomenon of "voodoo death."[61] He was intrigued by reports of sudden deaths among primitive peoples in Brazil, Africa, New Zealand, Australia, the Hawaiian Islands, Haiti, and the former British Guyana. Examining these reports, Cannon concluded that the deaths were commonly preceded by alienation, intense loneliness, social isolation, and the total lack of any social support for the doomed victim. Death was the only escape from the oppressive social climate. Cannon concluded:

"The social environment as a support to morale is probably much more important and impressive among primitive people because of their profound ignorance and insecurity in a haunted world than among educated people living in a civilized and well protected community."

He also surmised that without the social support of the tribe, fear ran wild, leading to massive physiological changes that could abruptly terminate life.

THE LOSS OF LOVE AND SUDDEN DEATH

Subsequent data, however, persuasively argued against Cannon's assertion that modern man is less vulnerable to sudden voodoo-like deaths. Dr. George Engel at the Rochester University Medical School described a large number of sudden deaths reminiscent of the voodoo-like deaths described by Cannon. During a six-year period, he collected 170 newspaper reports, many from the Rochester press, of sudden deaths in which he could rule out suicide as a cause of death and in which the circumstances surrounding the sudden death could be reconstructed.[62]

In 59 percent of these cases, Dr. Engel was able to document that the specific life events that preceded the sudden death involved some type of interpersonal loss. These sudden deaths occurred:

(1) After the collapse or death of a close person—36 people
(2) During a period of acute grief (within 16 days)—35 people
(3) Threat of the loss of a close person—16 people
(4) After loss of status or self-esteem—9 people
(5) During mourning or the anniversary of some event—5 people

Many of the incidents documented by Dr. Engel are truly remarkable. He cites the cases of two teenagers who died abruptly after being told of the death of someone close to them. In another case, a 14-year-old girl died after being told that her 17-year-old brother had died suddenly. In a third case, an 18-year-old girl died upon being told of the death of a grandfather who had helped to raise her.

In a case similar to that of the schizophrenic twins, Dr. Engel noted that a pair of 39-year-old twins who had been closely attached to each other died within a week of each other, with no cause of death being mentioned.

Among other cases cited by Dr. Engel were the following:

(1) "A 52-year-old man had been in close contact with his physician during his wife's terminal illness with lung cancer. Examination, including electrocardiogram, six months before her death showed no evidence of coronary disease. He died suddenly of a massive myocardial infarction the day after his wife's funeral" (p. 774).

(2) "A 40-year-old father slumped dead as he cushioned the head of his son lying injured in the street beside his motorcycle" (p. 775).

(3) "A 17-year-old boy collapsed and died at 6 a.m., June 4, 1970. His older brother had died at 5:12 a.m., June 4, 1969, of multiple injuries incurred in an auto accident several hours earlier. The cause of the younger boy's death was massive sub-arachnoid hemorrhage caused by a ruptured anterior communicating artery aneurysm" (p. 775).

(4) "A 55-year-old man died when he met his 88-year-old father after a 20-year separation. The father then dropped dead" (p. 775).

(5) "A 70-year-old man died six hours after his wife came home from the hospital, presumably recovered from a heart attack. She herself then had another attack and died 13 hours later" (p. 777).

The "coincidence" of grief and human loss in so many of these sudden deaths prompted Dr. William Greene and his colleagues to reexamine the psychosocial circumstances surrounding sudden coronary deaths. [63]They interviewed the surviving next of kin (usually wives) of 26 male patients who died suddenly while employed by the Eastman Kodak Company in Rochester, an industrial population of 44,000 employees. They found that, in most instances, the sudden death was preceded by a combination of circumstances that included both feelings of depression and increased work.

Common to at least 50 percent of the sudden deaths "was the departure of the last or only child in the family for college or marriage, in response to which the patient had been depressed." They also observed that a large number of patients who had a heart attack but survived to reach the hospital also mentioned that a child had recently left home. Dr. Greene concluded: "There is some wisdom in the lore which Engel has read into the reports in the newspapers."

At the University of Oklahoma Medical School, Dr. Stewart Wolf reported on 65 patients who had documented myocardial infarctions, and 65 matched control subjects who were physically healthy. All 130 of these individuals were interviewed monthly and given a battery of psychological tests to determine their levels of depression and social frustration. After a series of interviews, predictions were made as to which 10 subjects would most likely have a recurrent heart attack and die—the prediction being based solely on the level of depression and social frustration, without any knowledge of who, in fact, even had had a heart attack.

All 10 patients selected by purely psychological criteria were among the first 23 who died within the four-year period after these predictions were made. Dr. Wolf adds that all 10 had failed to find meaningful satisfaction in their social and leisure activities.[64]

IN THE STILL OF THE NIGHT

Sometimes knowing more intimate details of a person's life heightens one's suspicion about the premature appearance of life-threatening illness. Margaret was fifty years of age when she returned to see me in therapy after an eight-year hiatus. A review of her clinical charts quickly brought back to mind the interpersonal pain she had endured for most of her life. "Reactive depression" was the original psychological diagnosis the computer had churned out eight years earlier. It was a shorthand diagnostic way of saying that she was essentially normal, except for a series of dreadful life circumstances which made it difficult for her to cope and which triggered her depression.

An attractive, bright, and professionally accomplished woman, she had raised two children successfully on her own. There had been, unfortunately, one notable change since we last met. Her eyes spoke volumes about the medical problems that now threatened her life.

"I have advanced stage non-Hodgkin's lymphoma," she blurted out almost as soon as she sat down in my office, "and my oncologist tells me that I will need a bone marrow transplant in order to have a chance of surviving." As she continued, she apologized for the fact that she could not control her crying: "I cannot endure the thought of going through this alone and so I thought it might help to come back to see you. It frightens me to go through these medical procedures all by myself."

After pausing for a moment, she continued, "How could I have wasted so many years of my life? What was I thinking? I must have had a hole in my head to live with a man who did not love me! How could I have been so stupid?"

The guilt and self-recrimination that characterized so much of her life, and which contributed to her depressive feelings, had not changed since we had last met. She still blamed herself without mercy for the outcome of her decisions, even though she now faced the most difficult challenge of her life. Feelings of guilt and self-recrimination had been there since her childhood. Her early life had been consumed with fear and far too much responsibility. She described her father as a strict, cold, and emotionally aloof man. She also recalled his occasional violence, which had frightened her deeply. She remembered her mother as a very warm and kind woman who had been intimidated by her husband.

Even as a young child, she recalled being a "caretaker," someone who "tried to make everything okay." Early in her twenties, she endured two failed marriages, both of which she tried in every way possible to preserve in spite of her mates' emotional abuse and excessive drinking. After her second divorce, she spent a number of years alone before living with "a man who did not love me." The pain she felt in that relationship had brought her to therapy eight years ago.

When it became clear that the person she was living with was emotionally distant and psychologically unavailable, and was unwilling to come to therapy for help, she was advised to break off that relationship. Unfortunately, she said felt trapped and lacking the strength to leave. Unlike other cases of this sort, however, her decision to stay in a dysfunctional relationship was not based on economic necessity. Her professional life had guaranteed her some modicum of financial independence.

Instead, she was frightened by the thought of living a life of unbearable loneliness, even though she was reminded several times that her life with him was itself lonely. She reported her hope against hope that somehow he would change, if only she worked hard enough. She terminated therapy at that time, unable to confront the loneliness involved in ending that relationship. Seven years later, she finally could not take it any more, and left him. She then moved to Florida to take care of her mother, who was, at that time, seriously ill. Her mother and two children, she added, had been a source of great joy, but even their love was not sufficient to fill the void she felt in her personal life.

After her mother's death, escalating feelings of loneliness and isolation overwhelmed Margaret. Having left her friends in Maryland to be near her mother, she now felt completely alone and abandoned in Florida. Her loneliness became so unbearable that one Friday evening she found herself crying out loud, wishing that she could just die. Three months later, exhausted and emotionally drained, she felt a mass in her lower abdominal region. Several months later, still physically depleted and emotionally exhausted, she detected a second mass in her neck. She returned to Baltimore, where an oncologist at The Johns Hopkins Hospital informed her that she was suffering from an advanced stage of non-Hodgkin's lymphoma.

"Strange," she added almost stoically, "how your body seems to grant what you wish for. Funny how it can be so obliging." Pausing momentarily, as if lost in her own thoughts, she then admonished me with a smile: "Be careful what you wish for!" She then asked me directly, "Do you think that the loneliness collapsed my immune system, and made me more vulnerable to cancer after my mother's death? Do you think I just got totally depressed, and my immune system and my resistance simply collapsed?"

"You can never be certain," I commented, trying to not add to her depressive feelings of self-blame. I did not discuss the fact that, according to the National Cancer Institute, the incidence of non-Hodgkin's lymphoma had doubled in the last two decades (1973-1993), and other than the increase caused by the AIDS epidemic, the reasons for the increase were poorly understood. And while I did not discuss any specific research findings with her, I thought of The Johns Hopkins Medical School studies that had linked increased vulnerability to cancer to types of childhood and adult experiences similar to hers.

THE JOHNS HOPKINS PRECURSOR STUDIES

Dr. Caroline Thomas and Karen Duszynski followed 1,185 medical students who had attended The Johns Hopkins Medical School between the years of 1948 and 1964. When the studies first began, all of the medical students were relatively young and in good health. While still in medical school, they were asked a series of standardized questions geared to assessing various aspects of their lives. In the ensuing years, some of these Hopkins-trained physicians began to develop serious health problems, and some died prematurely. The investigators then went back to their original questions and found that medical students who developed various cancers prematurely later in life were statistically far more likely to have originally described their parents as cold and aloof.

They found that the physicians who went on to develop cancer were far more likely to have described the lack of close family relationships, particularly with their fathers, early in their lives. These physicians also described themselves as suffering far more from loneliness, as well as experiencing far more frequent disruptions of close relationships throughout their professional lives.[65]

HARVARD STUDIES:
PARENTAL CLOSENESS AND HEALTH

In a similar study, Drs. Russek, Schwartz, King and their colleagues randomly chose 125 men from the Harvard classes of 1952-1954, and asked them to rank their parents on a four-point scale as to the degree of their emotional closeness. The division was as follows:

(1) Very close
(2) Warm and friendly
(3) Tolerant
(4) Strained and cold

Thirty-five years later, they examined the medical histories of these volunteers, and found that those who had ranked their relations with parents as strained and cold experienced significant increases of poor health. An astounding 91 percent of those who had reported that they did not have a close relationship with their mothers suffered serious medical crises by mid-life, including coronary heart disease, hypertension, duodenal ulcer, and alcoholism. This was in contrast to the 45 percent of such illnesses in those who reported that they had warm relationships with their mothers. Even more remarkable was the fact that 100 percent of those who reported that *both* their parents were cold and aloof had serious medical problems by mid-life. By contrast, only 47 percent of those who had ranked themselves as close to both their parents had serious medical problems by mid-life.[66]

THE ALAMEDA COUNTY STUDIES

Dr. Lisa Berkman and her colleagues uncovered similar links to cancer and other life-threatening diseases in a research project known as the Alameda County Studies. In Alameda County, near San Francisco, they examined the health conditions of almost seven thousand adult men and women.

They reported in 1979 that those who lacked close social and community ties were 1.9 to 3.1 times more likely to die during a nine-year period that extended from 1965-1974. Those who lacked close ties were at sharply increased risk of dying from coronary heart disease, stroke, cancer, and a variety of other causes. Women who reported being socially isolated or feeling lonely had a significantly increased risk of dying from a variety of cancers. In both sexes, the absence of close personal ties and the lack of perceived sources of emotional support were associated with a significantly increased risk of cancer. In women, this appeared especially true for the increased risk of developing breast cancer.[67]

Pursuing this finding further, Dr. Reynolds and his colleagues then studied a second cohort of almost one thousand women in Alameda County recently diagnosed with breast cancer. As was true in the earlier studies, those women reporting a lack of close personal ties and lack of emotional support had almost twice the death rate from breast cancer in the following five years after the diagnosis was first made.[68]

In 1990, Drs. Marshall and Funch reported on the effects of social support for an even longer period of time in the Alameda population. They studied 283 women who had been diagnosed with breast cancer twenty years earlier. Again, the data indicated that those women who were more socially active and involved with others had longer to live, and were less likely to develop recurrent metastatic problems.[69]

Social Networks, Age, and Mortality:
Findings from the Alameda County, CA Study

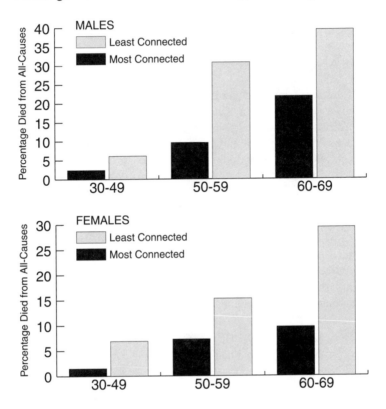

SOURCE: Berkman & Syme, 1979

I did not discuss these studies with Margaret, in part because they were similar to the type of chronic loneliness and isolation she had suffered for most of her life. Instead, I summarized these studies by focusing on what was positive. "We do know that depression can suppress immune system functioning and lower resistance," I told her. "That's the bad news. The good news is that it works both ways. You can also enlist the help of your immune system to fight this disease."

I then asked her if there was any time when she felt particularly vulnerable and depressed, and she replied: "It's 11 o'clock at night, when I go to bed, and there is no one there to hold you—not yesterday, not today, and not tomorrow. And I lay awake in the stillness of the night with a cancerous tumor the size of an orange in my lower abdominal region. It's an unbearable and terrifying feeling." Then, pausing momentarily, she added: "I intend to fill my house with life. Tomorrow, I am getting a puppy, and then I will get a cat and some fish and even some plants. My house has been silent and empty long enough. I need to let life back in."

PETS AND FRIENDS IN THE STILLNESS OF THE NIGHT

I quickly reinforced her decision to get some pets by informing her that my colleague Aaron Katcher, M.D. and I were among the first to demonstrate how pets helped heart patients recover from heart attacks. When we initiated these studies, it did not seem likely that something as ordinary as a pet-companion would make a difference in long-term survival.

Yet, when we followed a large number of heart patients after their release from a university coronary care unit, the data could scarcely be ignored. Those patients with pet-companions had a significantly greater chance of living during a one-year follow-up period than those who did not have pets. Even when we controlled for every other variable that could affect such an outcome, the results were the same. Pets appeared to alleviate the cardiac patients' sense of isolation and loneliness in a way that substantially enhanced their chances for long-term survival.[70]

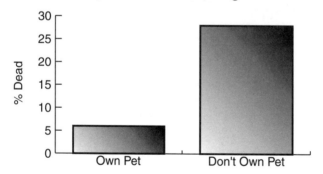

Pet Ownership and One-Year Survival After Coronary Care Unit Discharge

SOURCE: Public Health Report (1980). Vol. 95 (4) 307-311

I also reinforced Margaret's decision to join a church group and gave her the name of a woman who belonged to a local church with strong outreach programs, and which was close to her family's religious traditions. I knew this woman would be delighted to help. She would gladly introduce her to the members of her local church community and help her feel the power of that communal love.

I also suggested that she read Dr. Bernie Siegel's book, *Love, Medicine and Miracles*. A Yale University cancer specialist, Dr. Siegel has written eloquently about the links between hope, social support, and surviving cancer. [71]There were, I added, a variety of Internet web sites where she could discuss her struggles with various support groups, including patients who had survived her specific disease. [72]

Also recommended to her was Dr. David Spiegel's recent book, *Living Beyond Limits: New Hope and Help for Facing Life-Threatening Illnesses*. [73] Dr. Spiegel's research was first published in the prestigious British medical journal, *Lancet*. Ironically, he had set out to prove that psychosocial support would not significantly help women survive breast cancer. He was scarcely prepared for the results, and says that the findings shocked him. He divided patients with breast cancer into two groups. Both were given the exact same medical treatments. One group was given the additional experience of participating in group therapy once a week for the first year after surgery. Five years later, the results showed that women who participated in group therapy survived twice as long as those who did not have this type of therapeutic experience.

Dr. F.I. Fawzy and his colleagues at the University of California Medical School observed similar results. They studied the survival rates from malignant melanoma in two groups of patients. Like the previous study, all these cancer patients had the same medical treatments, but half were assigned the additional experience of participating in a six-week group therapy. Five years later, they discovered—much to their amazement—that three times as many individuals died who did not have the six-week session, compared to those who were able to talk with others about their struggles. A mere six weeks of therapy made a statistical difference five years later! [74]

AN INTERIM ANALYSIS

The clinical cases and the prospective studies discussed thus far help one formulate hypotheses that can be tested. It is not unreasonable, for example, to hypothesize that people who are single, widowed, and divorced would struggle more with loneliness. By no means, however, should the formulation of such an elemental hypothesis be misconstrued to imply that many married people don't have miserable relationships, and aren't just as lonely as, or lonelier than, those who are not married.

Certainly, Margaret's case is prima facie evidence that there are awful marital relationships that can be both very depressing and terribly destructive to one's physical health. Equally obvious is the fact that many single, widowed, and divorced individuals lead highly satisfying lives and are quite content with the social accommodations they have made in their respective life situations.

In addition, there are a variety of life situations where individuals are listed in mortality statistics as "single," but where census classifications belie the true nature of their living conditions. Priests, monks, and nuns are but one example of individuals listed as single on mortality tables, whereas in reality they frequently live in communal situations.

Homosexuals and lesbians are also listed on mortality statistics as "single." Yet, many of these individuals form long-standing relationships that are deeply gratifying and very meaningful. Many homosexuals and lesbians, however, do face the terrible problem inherent in confronting the conscious or even unconscious rejection of their own parents, families, neighbors, and communities because of their sexual preferences. A number of patients have described these struggles to me in therapy as extremely painful. They find themselves driven into a harsh and bitter type of social exile that is sometimes impossible to bear. In its worst form, this appears as a cruel form of "gay-bashing."

In its more subtle forms, these individuals are simply made to "disappear from decent society," and driven into their "own communities," where their "life-style" is more acceptable. Unfortunately, this form of exile, with all of its resultant exacerbation of human loneliness, has not been studied scientifically, nor measured in mortality statistics, and is thus difficult to gauge accurately. But it is not difficult to assume that this type of forced exile and alienation from one's family and neighborhood acquaintances exacts a particularly cruel and lethal medical toll.

All of these complexities, however, are precisely what makes an examination of marital statistics, and their potential linkages to long-term survival, a highly useful approach. For while the "statistical noise" in marital statistics could easily obscure the medical consequences of loneliness, any consistent effects that did appear would suggest something powerful at work and deserving closer scrutiny.

One could go further and reasonably hypothesize that the effects of human loneliness would appear in far starker terms if the statistics could be "cleaned up," and these specific effects isolated and identified. That is, if loneliness is hypothesized to be a lethal and toxic agent, and dialogue the supposed elixir of life, then the acid test would be to compare happily married people with divorced, single, and widowed individuals unhappy with that particular state of life.

Or one could even contrast people who are happily married against those who are unhappily married and ascertain whether there are any medical differences. In a similar manner, one could theoretically examine homosexuals and lesbians who have formed deep and long-lasting relationships, and contrast their health with those who have suffered from feelings of loneliness and isolation all of their lives. Unfortunately, neither census gatherers nor coroners ask such questions, and so we must begin with the medical statistics that are at hand.

And these data, in spite of all the "statistical noise," are quite revealing. They help create a mosaic in which it is apparent that loneliness is a lethal force with the power to break the human heart.

LIVING TOGETHER, DYING ALONE

It is a striking fact that U.S. mortality rates for all causes of death, and not just heart disease, are consistently higher at all ages for divorced, single, and widowed individuals of both sexes and all races. Some of the increased death rates in unmarried individuals rise as high as ten times the rates for married individuals of comparable ages.

Corporations, and especially insurance companies, which gamble their money on their ability to evaluate health risks, have long recognized that a person's marital status is one of the best statistical predictors of longevity. More than four decades ago, Drs. Kraus and Lillienfeld, at The Johns Hopkins Medical School, were among the first to recognize this relationship.[75] In 1956, they summarized as follows the medical data available at that time:

"Married people experienced a lower mortality rate from all causes than did single persons, the widowed, and the divorced for every specific age group in each sex and color. For both sexes and colors combined, the ratios of the age-adjusted death rates in these three not-married groups to the age-adjusted rate in the married group were 1.47, 1.46 and 1.84, respectively.... The relative excess mortality in the not-married categories compared to the married group was greater at the younger ages.... The relative excess mortality in the not-married categories was consistently greater in males than in females." [76]

Forty years later, in 1998, the Center for Disease Control reported very similar data, with one notable difference. The relative disparity in life span for the married and non-married had grown even larger! While longevity appeared to be increasing modestly for the general population, such was not the case for those statistically more likely to be living alone. In its report, the Center stated:

"An examination of the age-adjusted death rates reveals that those never married have the highest death rate, followed by those who are widowed, divorced, and married. The never married have an age-adjusted death rate 79 percent higher than the ever married, and 2.2 times the rate of the currently married. Age adjusted death rates for the widowed and divorced were 86 percent and 78 percent higher, respectively, than for those who were currently married at the time of death.

"For all groups 15 years and over, death rates for married persons were much lower than those for never married persons. For ages 25-34, and 35-44 years, widowed persons had the highest death rates; but beginning at age 45, those who never married had the highest death rates.

Percent of Increased Mortality Risk for U.S. Citizens Relative to Married Persons

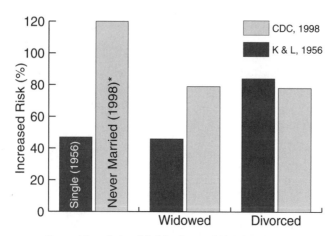

*In recent times, the term "single" no longer reliably indicated that one was "never married." As can be seen here in the difference between Kraus's 1956 study and the CDC 1998 report, current surveys frequently adjust this marital status question to obtain more accurate data.

SOURCE: Kraus & Lillienfeld, 1956; CDC, 1998

"For each marital status group, males have higher age-adjusted death rates than females, ranging from 76 to 94 percent greater. Black persons in each marital status group are more likely to die than white persons, with rates ranging from 13 to 50 percent greater." [77]

All three aspects of the original Kraus and Lillienfeld review, as well as the 1998 Center for Disease Control report, deserve special emphasis:

(1) **All causes of death were higher in the non-married groups.**
(2) **The differences were greatest at the younger ages.**
(3) **The differences were far more apparent in males and in minority populations.**

One additional trend also deserves emphasis, since it directly answers one of the questions raised by a business executive in Dr. Aaron Katcher's class at the University of Pennsylvania, as quoted in this book's initial chapter. He had asked whether future generations might get so accustomed to social isolation and loneliness that they might develop immunity to its consequences. As the medical data suggest, however, far from developing an immunity to the problem, the difference in survival rates between those who are married versus those living alone appears to be greater now than it was forty years ago. Efforts to develop some sort of immunization against the effects of human loneliness do not seem to be working, and in spite of personal denial, the problem is growing more prevalent in our culture.

THE TOLL OF LONELINESS

While the overall death rate for divorced individuals in the United States is almost double that of married individuals, a closer inspection of mortality figures reveals that the differences are far greater than might be initially deduced from these overall statistical assessments.

In their book *Marriage and Divorce: A Social and Economic Study*, Hugh Carter and Paul Glick reported overall increased death rates very similar to those just described.[78] Their text, however, provides additional valuable insights into the large number of diseases that contribute to the excess mortality. They classified death rates per 100,000 population according to marital status, sex, race, and cause of death. For every listed cause of death, the single, widowed, and divorced had significantly higher death rates than did married people, both white and nonwhite, and of both sexes.

Increased Risk of Premature Mortality for Unmarried Men and Women in the United States (Compared to Married Samples)*

MALES

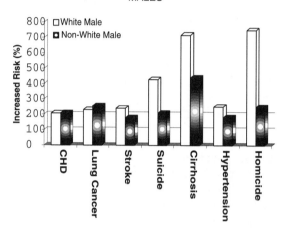

FEMALES

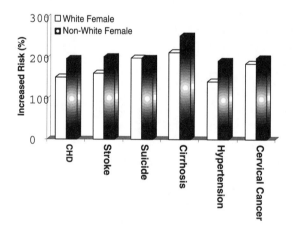

*For example, according to this research, unmarried white males have approximately a 200 percent increased risk for premature death due to CHD than married males.

SOURCE: Carter & Glick, 1970

Representative comparisons help illustrate not only the magnitude but also the consistency of this phenomenon. The following Table shows that for every major cause of death, the rates for divorced males ranged anywhere from two to six times higher than their married counterparts. Single and widowed males showed similarly high death rates when compared to those who were married.

Death Rates of Divorced & Married Men per 100,000 Population
  Ages 15-64 in the United States, 1959-1961

CAUSE OF DEATH	White Males		Nonwhite Males	
	Married	Divorced	Married	Divorced
Heart disease	176	362	142	298
Vehic. accidents	35	128	43	81
Lung Cancer	28	65	29	75
Digest Cancer	27	48	42	88
Stroke	24	58	73	132
Suicide	17	73	10	21
Cirrhosis of liver	11	79	12	53
Hypertension	8	20	49	90
Pneumonia	6	44	22	69
Homicide	4	30	51	129
Tuberculosis	3	30	15	54

Heart disease was by far the leading cause of death for U.S. males. While there were significantly higher death rates for divorced males, there were also important differences in death rate patterns according to race. Deaths caused by strokes and hypertension were significantly higher in the non-white population, although again significantly altered by marital status. Unfortunately, however, U.S. census data, until very recently, grouped all non-white races together, including Orientals, blacks, and Native Americans, so that it was impossible to sort out the relative manner in which these different groups contributed to the non-white death rates when these data were first published.

This problem is particularly important because it is well known that hypertension and stroke afflict blacks significantly more than whites. Since blacks in 1960 comprised roughly 85 percent of the total U.S. non-white population, it would be reasonable to assume that they contributed to the bulk of the deaths attributed to non-white males. This point is especially critical in light of the assumption made by many that the greatly elevated rates of hypertensive heart disease and stroke among blacks reflect some sort of genetic predisposition to these diseases.

And yet, as is made clear by these data, the incidence of hypertension is also significantly affected by marital status, strongly suggesting the possibility that environmental and psychological factors also influence both the development and the incidence of this disease.

Similar changes in death rate patterns by marital status can be seen in women. In order to show the general influence of marital status, the death rate patterns of widowed women can be compared to those of married women.

DEATH RATES of WIDOWED and MARRIED FEMALES per 100,000
Population, Ages 15-64 in the United States, 1959-1961

Cause of Death	White Females		Non-white Females	
	Married	Widowed	Married	Widowed
Heart disease	44	67	83	165
Beast Cancer	21	21	19	28
Digestive Cancer	20	24	25	41
Stroke	19	31	72	147
Vehicular accidents	11	47	10	25
Hypertension	7	10	50	97
Cervical Cancer	7	13	17	34
Cirrhosis	7	15	9	23
Suicide	6	12	3	6
Accidental fires	1	6	4	11

The overall death rate before age 65 for women was significantly lower than for men. As was true with men, marital status significantly influenced the death rates, with married men always having lower rates. Again, there were important racial differences. Stroke and hypertensive heart diseases were much higher among non-white females, but, as usual, the rate was double for widows.

In 1973, Kitagawa and Hauser attempted to correct for statistical factors that might have influenced the higher death rates routinely reported for the non-married. In their book, *Differential Mortality in the United States*, they estimated that divorced white males between the ages of 35 and 64 had a death rate more than double that of their married counterparts (130 percent higher). They pointed out that the greatest increases in death rates occurred among divorced white males and widowed non-white males, with cardiovascular disease in all cases being the leading cause of death.[79]

Thus, for virtually every major cause of premature death, those who lived alone—the single, widowed, separated, and divorced—had significantly higher death rates from virtually every cause of death. And in every case, cardiovascular disease (including stroke and hypertension) was listed for men and women, white and non-white, as the major cause of premature death.

The data also suggest that marital status also significantly influences the general life-style of individuals in these varied conditions. The seven-fold increase in premature death rates from cirrhosis of the liver among divorced white males and the general increase in death rates from this disease among all non-married groups suggest, among other possibilities, that unmarried individuals may abuse alcohol.

The marked increases in mortality also raise questions about the nature of this particular problem. One could well imagine that excessive drinking leads in many cases to divorce, and then to death, while in other instances divorce itself might lead to an increase in excessive drinking, and then subsequently to premature death. Yet, the increase in mortality is so great for divorced individuals that even if it occurred both ways, the result is so dramatic that it scarcely makes any difference.

There are, as well, significant increases in death rates due to motor vehicle accidents and "accidental fires," with widowed men and women having four- to seven-fold increases in death rates from these causes. Suicide increases five-fold in the widowed white male population and four-fold in the widowed non-white male and white female population, while death by homicide also increases dramatically. The doubling of cancer of the respiratory system and the ten-fold rise in tuberculosis among divorced white males led Carter and Glick to suggest that differential patterns of cigarette smoking had influenced these results.

MARITAL STATUS AND CANCER

Of all the varied causes of death other than heart disease, cancer is perhaps the most interesting. Not only is it the second leading cause of death, but it is also commonly thought of as a disease unambiguously physical in nature. And yet, as discussed earlier in this chapter, and as is shown in the following Table, almost every type of cancer appears to be significantly influenced by marital status, with widowed, divorced, and single individuals almost always having significantly higher death rates.

As shown in the following Table, the 4.10 ratio for white males for buccal cavity and pharyngeal cancer means that divorced white males died from this type of cancer 4.10 times more frequently than did married men. What is remarkable about these figures, excerpted from Lillienfeld, Levin, and Kessler's text, *Cancer in the United States*, is that every type of terminal cancer struck down divorced individuals of both sexes, white and non-white, more frequently than it did people who were married.[80]

Ratios of Cancer Death Rates for Divorced to Married Persons* for Persons of Age 15 and over, by elected sites or groups of sites, color, and sex, 1959-1961

PRIMARY SITE	Divorced Male		Divorced Female	
	White	Nonwhite	White	Nonwhite
Buccal cavity and pharynx	4.10	3.14	1.67	1.44
Digestive organs and peritoneum	1.53	1.78	1.15	1.42
Lungs	2.11	2.46	1.49	1.89
Breast	2.50	2.00	1.13	1.42
Cervix uterine			2.38	1.60
Female genital organs except cervix			1.24	1.45
Prostate	1.30	1.45		
Male genital except prostate	1.79	2.69		
All urinary organs	1.52	1.83	1.40	1.70
Unspecified sites	1.70	1.95	1.22	1.37
Lymphatic and hemotapoietic	1.21	1.65	1.05	1.71

*It is important to note that the ratio for married individuals would be 1.00 in all cases.

"A DELICATE STATISTICAL DECISION"

Even something as obvious as the relationship between cigarette smoking and health is not so clear-cut as one might think. This was alluded to earlier, when it was pointed out that Japanese men and women residing in Japan live longer than those who emigrated to America, in spite of the fact that they smoked cigarettes more frequently.

Dr. Harold Morowitz, a professor of biophysics at Yale University, also called attention to similar intriguing data he found buried among the masses of health statistics in the *Hammond Report*. [81] The *Hammond Report*, first published in 1963, was the study that followed the smoking habits of about a half million American men. It led, ultimately, to the warning printed on every cigarette package that "smoking is dangerous to your health." Without quarreling with the overwhelming mass of data supporting that conclusion, Dr. Morowitz pointed out that the relationship is not a simple one. For example, he extracted the following table from *The Hammond Report* on the relationship between marital status, smoking, and premature death:

Age-Standardized Death Rates   Per 100,000 Men, Ages 40-69

	Non-Smoker	Smoke 20+ Cigarettes per day
Married	796	1,560
Single	1,074	2,567
Widowed	1,396	2,570
Divorced	1,420	2,675

The overall influence of marital status on premature mortality closely resembles the ratios cited earlier. Men who were single, widowed, or divorced had overall death rates more than double those of married men. Moreover, it is fascinating to note, as Dr. Morowitz pointed out, that "being divorced and a non-smoker is slightly less dangerous than smoking a pack or more a day and staying married." He added with tongue in cheek that "if a man's marriage is driving him to heavy smoking, he has a delicate statistical decision to make." [82]

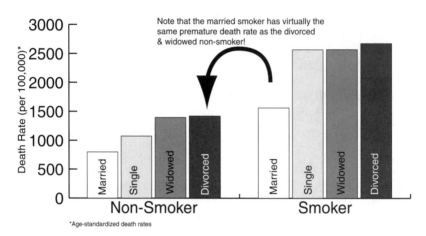

Marital Status, Smoking, and Premature Death in U.S. Males, Age 40-69

By no means should these data be misconstrued as minimizing the very real dangers of cigarette smoking. What these data also reveal, however, is that the ultimate medical consequences of behavioral variables like smoking must be examined in the larger context of a person's total social existence. Of even greater significance, these data suggest that it is possible statistically to sort out the comparative influence of both smoking and marital status.

NARROWING THE FOCUS TO HEART DISEASE

Even the most cursory examination of cardiovascular death rates quickly reveals the potent influence of marital status on the incidence of this disease. The marked increase in cardiovascular mortality linked to marital status was first discussed in detail by Drs. Moriyama, Krueger, and Stamler in their book, *Cardiovascular Disease in the United States.* [83] The following Table, excerpted from their book, shows the ratios of deaths from coronary heart disease for single, widowed, divorced, and married individuals in the United States from 1959 to 1961.

This Table shows that the cardiac death rates for single, divorced, and widowed individuals during that time period were significantly greater than the rates for married individuals. This is true for both sexes and for both whites and non-whites. The magnitudes of some of the increases in death rates in the non-married groups are quite impressive, sometimes exceeding the married death rates by as much as five-fold. The differences are greatest at younger ages and tend to diminish somewhat with age. But never do the death rates of the unmarried groups ever equal or fall below those for married groups.

Ratio of Death Rates of Single, Widowed, and Divorced to Married Persons, for Coronary Heart Disease, United States, 1959-1961

Age	Male			Female		
	Single	Widowed	Divorced	Single	Widowed	Divorced
White 15 and over,						
Age adjusted	1.34.	1.51	1.79.	1.22	1.45	1.32
25-34	1.52	1.98	2.83	3.17	5.17.	2.28
35-44	1.47	1.84	2.47	2.08	2.34	2.14
45-54	1.39	1.66	2.16	1.33	1.69	1.60
55-64	1.28	1.55	1.92	1.03	1.48 .	1.30
65-74	1.37	1.45	1.67	1.05	1.35	1.20
75-84	1.35	1.39	1.56	1.26	1.35	1.32
85 and above	1.27	1.35	1.37	1.63	1.56	1.40
Nonwhite 15 and over,						
age-adjusted	1.53	2.07	1.88	1.39	1.94	1.37
25-34	2.24	4.24	2.64	1.61	2.37	1.26
35-44	2.04	2.61	2.42	1.83	2.42	1.35
45 54	1.77	2.65	2.32	1.39	2.15	1.40
55-64	1.33	2.24	1.91	1.15	2.08	1.39
65-74	1.46	1.83	1.79	1.40	1.87	1.39
75-84	1.55	1.59	1.49	1.39	1.56	1.33
85	1.42	1.58	1.73	1.91	1.91	1.29

(The ratios for married individuals would be 1.00 in all cases).

All other types of cardiovascular disease show the same significant rise in death rates for non-married groups. In addition to coronary heart disease, deaths attributed to hypertensive disease, cerebrovascular disease, rheumatic fever, chronic rheumatic heart disease, and cardiovascular renal disease all show the same pattern. At all ages, for both sexes, and for all races in the United States, the non-married always have higher death rates from these various forms of heart disease, sometimes as much as five times higher than those of married individuals.

The effects of marital status on hypertensive heart disease are especially interesting because of the well-known fact that blacks are much more prone to this disease in young adulthood and middle age than are whites. As discussed earlier, investigators for years have thought this racial difference in hypertension supported the theory of genetic predisposition to the disease. And yet, in the critical ages between 25 and 50, non-white men and women who are divorced or widowed die from hypertensive heart disease at a rate more than double that of married individuals of comparable ages. This fact, combined with similar data for educational status, would seem to suggest a strong interpersonal influence on the disease of hypertension.

Since the original reports linking marital status to the risk of heart disease back in the 1960s and 1970s, a large number of studies have both confirmed, as well as amplified, these observations.

UNIVERSITY STUDIES OF SOCIAL SUPPORT

In 1992, Dr. Case and his colleagues at the Columbia University College of Surgeons examined 1,234 patients between the ages of 24 to 75 years of age who had been hospitalized for a heart attack. They then followed these patients for one-to-four years after their hospital discharge and found that the group of patients who lived alone were at twice the risk of having a recurrent "cardiac" event (e.g., another heart attack) than those who did not live alone.[84]

Similarly, in 1992, Dr. Lisa Berkman and her colleagues at Yale University reported their findings on 194 older men and women (65 years of age and older) who had been hospitalized for a myocardial infarction. Of these 194 patients, 76 (39 percent) died in the first six months after release from the hospital. After carefully controlling for all the usual physiological factors that could influence the risk of sudden death, they observed that when every other variable was controlled, those patients who lacked "social support" (lack of friends, emotional ties, or living alone) were almost three times more likely to die than other patients with identical medical conditions who had social support.[85]

Dying Within Six Months After a Heart Attack: The Effects of Age, Gender, and Number of Sources of Emotional Support for Elderly Patients

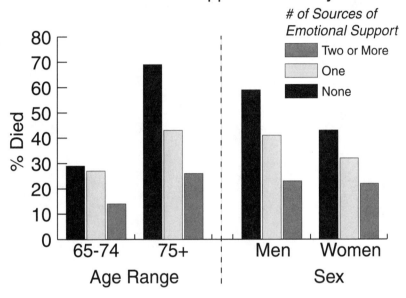

SOURCE: Berkman, Leo-Summers, & Horwitz, 1992

In 1995, medical scientists at the University of London reported the findings of the British Regional Heart Study. This study followed the health of 7,735 men between the ages of 40-59, who were recruited from 24 different towns throughout England and Scotland. They then followed these men for over 11 years, and found that single men (even when controlling for all known cardiac risk factors) still had an increased risk of dying 1.5 times greater than married men. Recently divorced men in this same cohort had an increased risk of dying suddenly from a heart attack that was double that of married men. In what I would label British understatement, these scientists concluded: "It is possible that social support offered by marriage exerts a protective effect for some men."[86]

Swedish cardiologists reported equally intriguing findings in 1998. They gave 1,290 heart patients about to undergo coronary bypass surgery a standardized questionnaire, and followed all of them for five years. Those patients who reported feeling "lonely," the cardiologists noted,

Marriage, Confiding Friends, and Survival After a Heart Attack

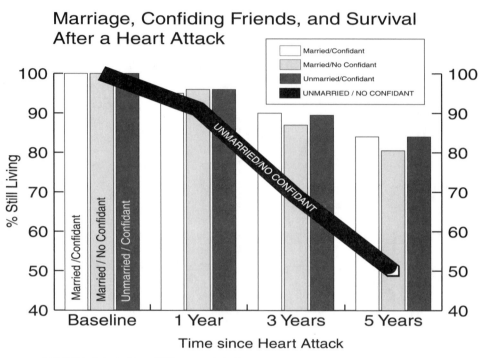

SOURCE: Adapted from Williams et al, 1992

Five years after a heart attack, half of the patients who were both unmarried and reported no confiding friends were dead. This number is strikingly greater than the 80-85 percent survival rate seen after five years in the three groups reporting some measure of support in their lives.

were far more likely to die within a six-month period. This increased mortality occurred even when all other medical factors that might have influenced their outcome were controlled.[87]

In 1998, Swedish scientists also reported the results of studying 131 women between the ages of 30-65 who had been hospitalized for an acute coronary event. Again, after controlling for all known medical conditions and risk factors, they found that women who lacked social support were 2 ½ times more likely to have severe coronary artery disease than women who were married or reported good social support.[88]

In 1992, Dr. Redford Williams and his colleagues at Duke University Medical Center reported their findings on 1,368 patients with documented coronary heart disease whom they followed for a number of years. Similar to other studies, they observed that married patients had a far better chance of surviving long-term than unmarried patients. They then divided

their unmarried group into two categories: those having a "confidant," or friend, and those who did not.

They found that those unmarried patients who lacked a confidant or friend had the lowest survival rates. The differences in survival rates were striking. "Those unmarried patients without a confidant had more than a three-fold increase in the risk of death within five years compared to patients who were either married or who had a confidant."[89]

In many ways, the study by Dr. Williams helps clarify that the key ingredient is not, as the *Chicago Tribune* once asserted, "one is better off wed than dead." It is not marriage per se that is the major health factor. Rather, it is the lack of a confidant, the lack of friends or other source of social support. The data in the accompanying figure illustrating Dr. Williams' findings are quite revealing.

MARITAL DISSATISFACTION AND HEART DISEASE

In what is a mirror image of Dr. Williams' findings, Drs. Theorell and Rahe cite the work of Dr. J. H. Medalie, who screened 10,000 Israeli adult males before any symptoms of coronary heart disease had appeared. During five years of observation, Dr. Medalie noted that those men who later had a myocardial infarction reported far more frequent dissatisfaction with their marital life. For example, men who said they felt a lack of emotional support from their wives were far more likely to become heart attack victims.[90]

On the other hand, Drs. Medalie and Goldbourt found in this same population—men who were at high risk for heart disease—that a wife's love and support were an important balancing factor, reducing the risk of angina pectoris even in the presence of high risk factors for such problems.[91] Conversely, investigators at the University of Iowa found that male patients who had heart attacks and who also concealed their worries from their wives tended to do more poorly over time.[92] Dr. Stewart Wolf and his colleagues also found that patients with coronary heart disease reported a greater number of marital problems than did a control sample. A series of additional recent reports has concluded that the occurrence of marital problems and a sense of interpersonal rejection pre-date a surprising number of heart attacks.[93]

Dr. J. J. Groen at the University of Leiden similarly linked marital status and the lack of love to the development of coronary heart disease. He observed: "It appears that the individuals who are supported by love and secure family and community bonds can cope much better with stressful psychological situations than individuals who are deprived of such support."[94]

While additional research is needed before all of the relationships between marital dissatisfaction and vulnerability to heart disease can be completely understood, sufficient evidence is now available to be certain of a connection between marital discord and the development of coronary heart disease and premature death. This does not mean that marital discord or loneliness causes every myocardial infarction. Such a position would clearly be absurd. And yet, in a surprising number of cases of premature coronary heart disease and premature death, interpersonal unhappiness, the lack of love, the lack of social support, and human loneliness seem to be a hidden underlying contributor to the physical problems.

CURTAINS IN THE WIND

Sometimes an actual case gives one a better sense of the terrible stress one endures after the loss of a loved one. At 72 years of age, Harold was devastated, struggling to bear up under the pain, loneliness, and sense of loss that touch all of us at one time or another in our lives. Several months earlier, he had lost his wife to cancer after 47 years of marriage.

Like many other men, Harold thought he would be the first to die, and had prepared his financial affairs accordingly. His wife was just too full of life, too vibrant, too engaged in activities, to suddenly succumb to cancer. Like so many other couples, he and his wife had struggled most of their married life to raise their children and to help their grandchildren. Only in their last decade together had life gotten easier. Only then did they have the time to spend with each other, traveling, and simply enjoying each other's company. And then suddenly, without warning, it was over.

"Little observations" and "little incidents" sometimes help to encapsulate grief that otherwise is difficult to describe. During one of our sessions, Harold alluded to his struggles with depression, describing how he had been unable to sleep very well in the three months since his wife's death. He told me that the previous evening he had experienced a "curious event in the middle of the night."

With the arrival of autumn, he had shut off his air conditioner and opened his windows. "Strange," he remarked, "but while laying in bed in the silence of the night, a soft autumn breeze began to drift through the curtains in my bedroom. They swayed back and forth, as if they were dancing to some unheard music from the heavens, as if my wife was directing their graceful movements from some far away place in eternity. She had put up the curtains just two weeks before she died. And as they swayed back and forth in the wind, I kept thinking that she was there in those curtains. And yet she was not there. She was gone. All that was left were her curtains blowing in the wind."

Struggling to keep himself from breaking down in tears, he then asked: "Do you think grief is harder to endure now than it was for our parents and grandparents? I mean, when I walk around my village in the middle of the afternoon, I never see a soul. Everyone seems to be away working. Even when I walk in the evenings, I still never meet a soul. And it is the same in the shopping malls and supermarkets. No one seems to know you, or to see you. People seem to look right through you, or even more frequently right past you. Thank God for my church group. They seem to be the only people alive who really care!" And then he added: "I know I am still alive, but it's almost as if I am like those curtains blowing in the wind—here, but not here."

THE BROKEN HEART AND SUDDEN DEATH

In the case of single and divorced individuals, it is often difficult to sort out the specific links between cardiac disease and the lack of human companionship, social isolation, and loneliness. Many divorced and single people who contribute to the marked increase in heart disease death rates not only lack human companionship but also alter their life-styles in a number of ways that contribute to cardiac disease. In other cases, divorced individuals quickly remarry and are therefore listed on statistical tables as married. Many other single and divorced individuals live with other human beings and therefore need not lack either human companionship or love.

Furthermore, many individuals listed as married on statistical tables are married in name only. Through excessive dedication to their jobs or life-styles, many individuals live in a state of complete "psychological divorce" from their mates. Their lives are essentially devoid of love.

From a "scientific" point of view, therefore, the widow or widower who suddenly loses a loved one presents a far less ambiguous picture than single and divorced individuals, or even certain married ones. The sudden loss of a loved one abruptly removes human companionship and a source of love from one's life. Loneliness and grief often overwhelm bereaved individuals, and it is in this situation that the toll taken on the heart can be seen most clearly. As the mortality statistics indicate, this is no myth or romantic fairy tale—all available evidence suggests that people do indeed die of broken hearts.

In his book *Bereavement*, Colin Parkes pointed out that the real cost of a deep personal love for another human being can only be seen in the shattering loss experienced when that love is suddenly and permanently taken away.[95] The idea is not particularly new. A few hundred years ago, "grief" was openly recognized as a cause of death. Today, however, a "broken heart" would never be listed as a cause of death in any U.S. hospital. We have grown far too "medically wise" to tolerate such an ill-defined diagnosis. Patients now die of coronary arteriosclerosis, ventricular fibrillation, or congestive heart failure brought on by age, damaged hearts and arteries, or poor eating habits.

Adding empirical evidence to this intuitive perception, Drs. Kraus and Lillienfeld were among the first to call attention to the abrupt rise in mortality among widows and widowers. [96] They were especially struck by the rise in mortality among the young widowed group. They observed that "the excess risk in the widowed under age 35, compared to the married, was greater than ten-fold for at least one of the specific age-sex groups, involving several leading causes of death, including arteriosclerotic heart disease and vascular lesions of the nervous system." [97]

Arteriosclerosis is generally thought of as a degenerative disease that can begin in childhood and then usually progresses slowly through life. In light of the observations of Drs. Kraus and Lillienfeld, one must wonder what it is about bereavement that seems to hasten a process that usually develops slowly, even imperceptibly, over a span of decades.

Dr. Colin Parkes pointed out that the increased mortality among the bereaved is especially high during the first six months after the loss of a loved one. This finding is especially important because it clearly implies that the increase in mortality in widows and widowers is not due to the fact that these individuals are simply too sick to remarry. Most of the increase in sudden deaths occurs before there would have been sufficient time to remarry. In 75 percent of the cases Parkes studied, the cause of death in bereaved individuals was coronary thrombosis or arteriosclerosis. [98]

ENGLISH AND WELSH STUDIES OF BEREAVEMENT

Parkes cites the work of Michael Young and his colleagues in England who studied 4,486 bereaved males over the age of 54. They found that death rates increased over 40 percent during the first six months of bereavement, and then began to decline back to the death rates for married men of the same age. Parkes also cites the work of Rees and Lutkins, who studied a rural community in Wales. These investigators studied 903 close relatives of 371 residents who died between 1960 and 1965. Of these relatives, almost 5 percent died within one year of being bereaved, compared to a death rate of 0.7 percent for non-bereaved individuals of the same age living in the same community.

THE FINNISH STUDIES OF BEREAVEMENT

In one of the largest epidemiological studies ever conducted, Finnish scientists at the University of Helsinki reported in 1996 the results of a major study on the effects of bereavement. They gathered their data from an enormous pool of 1,580,000 Finnish citizens, whom they carefully followed from 1986 to 1991.

Among those individuals who lost a mate, they found that the incidence of death in the surviving mate rose sharply within the first six months of bereavement. The death rates rose anywhere from 50-150 percent above the norm for accidental, violent, and alcohol-related deaths, while deaths from heart disease rose 20-35 percent. As in all previous studies, far higher increases in mortality were observed among men than among bereaved women.[99]

In addition to the large-scale studies reviewed in this chapter, there are hundreds of similar studies that have been published throughout the world since 1975. Studies involving hundreds of thousands of individuals confirm the links between social support, loneliness, and physical health. For those readers who might want additional confirmatory evidence, I have included brief descriptions of dozens of these studies on my web site (www.lifecarehealth.com). Large-scale studies have been conducted in Evans County, Georgia; Tecumseh, Michigan; Massachusetts; Seattle, Washington; Japan; England; Sweden; Finland; and dozens of other locations.

And all of these studies arrive at the same conclusions. Those individuals lacking social support, those who live alone, those who struggle with chronic loneliness, those who lose a loved one, all exhibit sharply increased risks of dying prematurely. In a similar manner, study after study has revealed that unmarried individuals are vastly over-represented in institutional settings, including mental hospitals and prisons.

In 1998, commenting on the explosion in knowledge since *The Broken Heart* was first published, Dr. Dean Ornish asserted that love and interpersonal relationships were critical to health: "I am not aware of any other factor—not diet, not smoking, not exercise, not stress, not genetics, not drugs, not surgery—that has a greater impact on our quality of life,

Prospective Research Linking Decreased Social Support to Increased Mortality*

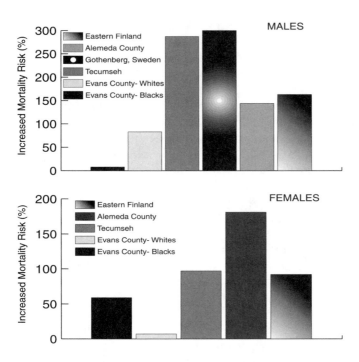

*Rates are based on comparisons of individuals reporting high and low amounts of social support/integration. All rates were statistically adjusted for age (age-adjusted mortality rates).

SOURCE: Adapted from House, Landis & Umberson, 1988
Social Relationships and Health, *Science, 241*, 540-545

incidence of illness, and premature death from all causes."[100] By the end of the twentieth century, there was no longer any doubt about the medical consequences of loneliness. The question had evolved to one of mechanisms: how does this excess in mortality occur?

SCHOOL FAILURE, CHILDHOOD LONELINESS, AND LINKS TO HEART DISEASE AND PREMATURE DEATH

AN OVERVIEW

"A child's mind is a precious thing, don't waste it"
to which I would add
A child's heart is a precious thing, don't break it.

The evidence presented so far has focused primarily on the links between loneliness and premature death in adult populations. In several instances, however, evidence was also cited indicating that loneliness in childhood also has a significant impact on the incidence of serious disease and premature death decades later in adulthood. In prospective studies of graduate students at the The Johns Hopkins Medical School, The University of Pennsylvania Medical School, and Harvard University, investigators consistently observed that even though individuals had achieved high levels of professional success, they were vulnerable to an increased risk of serious disease and premature death because of socially isolating experiences that occurred decades earlier in childhood. Family situations that were emotionally sterile, and those characterized by parental aloofness, appeared to put children at increased risk decades later.

In the next two chapters, I expand on these findings. I present evidence making it crystal clear: childhood experiences that lead to increased levels of social isolation and loneliness have a major effect on the amount of time one spends here on this earth.

The very words, "loneliness" and "premature death," however, usually conjure up images of isolated adults, people who lack friends and social support, the elderly warehoused in old-age homes or other institutions, or people down on their luck in skid row, but almost never children in the prime of their lives. While everyone is aware that children will sometimes get sick and die prematurely, it is generally assumed that such problems are caused by genetic abnormalities, cancers, virulent infectious diseases, or tragic accidents. It is very difficult to imagine that another type of "disease," a communicative disease, which fosters loneliness in childhood, can slowly but surely erode health and lead to premature death decades later. It is even more difficult to imagine that this type of disease will exact a far greater toll than all other causes of infant and childhood mortality combined, and is one of the leading causes of premature death in adulthood!

Though it is difficult to imagine, it is in childhood that the linkages between loneliness and the risk of premature death can be seen most clearly. And nowhere do these relationships appear with greater clarity than in school failure. It may be the single most important and objectively identifiable human experience that helps destroy a person's capacity to engage others in dialogue without undue physiological stress. Educational failure is an experience that increases the risk of social isolation, loneliness, and premature death. It does so in every industrialized nation on this earth. It is also one of the major risk factors contributing to the development of premature heart disease and sudden cardiac death.

As the health data in the next two chapters describe, marked increases in premature death rates, especially from heart disease, can be directly linked to school failure. The excess mortality is quite large, it spans a spectrum of diseases, and is due neither to the lack of income nor the lack of adequate medical treatment. It stems instead from the destruction of a person's capacity to engage in everyday dialogue without experiencing terrible physiological stress.

My hypothesis is that repetitive early experiences with "toxic talk"— those childhood experiences that poison the child's capacity to expect or hope that language can be used in an effective manner to reach others, or developmental experiences that shatter a child's sense of self-worth— make all subsequent communications throughout life physiologically taxing. It leads to a bodily state I have labeled the *"physiology of exclusion"*—a reaction to communicative stress that heightens loneliness, and increases the risk of premature death. It leads as well to what I have identified as the *"disembodiment of dialogue,"* a type of language one speaks outside of one's own body, and outside of one's feelings, which amounts to language literally spoken "*by* nobody *to* nobody."

Clinical hints about communicative problems of this sort have been described in hundreds of major university studies. In 1999, for example, the Center for Addiction and Substance Abuse at Columbia University suggested that teenagers who had trouble communicating with their fathers were far more likely to use cigarettes, alcohol, and illegal drugs, than those whose families had two supportive and understanding parents. [101] Data of this sort are unfortunately but the tip of an enormous interpersonal iceberg, one that leads millions of children to be excluded from the experience of healthy dialogue and healthy relationships with their fellow man. And it produces far more than an increase in drug abuse among adolescents. It sharply curtails the number of years they ultimately spend on this earth.

In their seminal book, *The Hidden Injuries of Class*, Drs. Richard Sennet and Jonathan Cobb also alluded to this "fatal wounding of self esteem," and to the deep-seated form of hopelessness about communication it engenders.[102] It is a type of wounding, a hidden injury of being in the "lower class," that makes it difficult to communicate with anyone other than those who are similarly wounded.

Unable to relate to the larger society in which they live, forced, like social outcasts, into exile on an uncharted island of social alienation, and unable to use language in an optimistic fashion, these children are exposed to a lifetime of loneliness, and an increased risk of premature death. Many of these children eventually opt to narcotize themselves against their own pain with illicit drugs or alcohol, or in some cases explode in violence against others. "The Hidden Injuries of Class" are not just economic in nature, but emerge from the "classroom" itself, including the classroom of early life experiences.

In the next two chapters, I outline the evidence linking school failure and the resultant increase in social isolation and loneliness to premature death. As in the previous chapters, I focus on heart disease since it is the leading cause of death and is generally assumed to have little to do with childhood experiences.

Subsequently, I move beyond the mortality data to introduce some of the physiological processes that help explain how and why this increase in premature death occurs. There, I describe mechanisms common to all sorts of sources of loneliness in both childhood and adulthood. Whether it stems from parental neglect, educational failure, divorce, or bereavement, common to all is a communicative disease that ultimately has the power to break the human heart.

Chapter Five

EDUCATING FOR LIFE AND DEATH

"In terms of such characteristics as the proportion of working mothers, number of adults in the home, single-parent families, or children born out of wedlock, the middle-class family of today increasingly resembles the low-income family of the early 1960s."
— Urie Brofenbrenner, Ph.D., Cornell University

A DROPOUT'S HEART

Perhaps nowhere in life do the experiences of childhood seem more removed from the issues of adult health than in a hospital coronary care unit. Yet, one can see and hear there the linkages patients themselves make as they reveal bodies and hearts that are living repositories of pained memories from the distant past—pained memories etched in their hearts and never forgotten. That surely was the case with Charlotte. Neither her cardiac medications nor dozens of other prescriptive remedies had been able to slow down the rapid deterioration in her physical health. She linked her immediate health struggles to events that had occurred decades earlier.

One brief paragraph in the pages of her hospital medical records alluded to the complex problems her doctors faced as they struggled to keep her alive. Written by her attending cardiologist at the University of Maryland Coronary Care Unit, the note hinted at the likelihood that her rapidly deteriorating cardiovascular health was not going to be reversed for very long by any of the standard medical remedies. A decade of hypertension and diabetes, and her recent heart attack, had taken their toll. Yet, there was another "disease" that threatened her life as well, one that was seldom mentioned in medical charts. Her cardiologist wrote:

"She has a very low opinion of herself, and sees herself as unworthy of attention and care. She has had leg pain since childhood related with intermittent hyperventilation and tremulousness. It is highly likely that many of her symptoms are at least exacerbated, if not caused, by her earlier struggles."

The heart monitor behind Charlotte's bed beeped softly but rapidly as she talked with a coronary care nurse. Charlotte was but one of hundreds of coronary care patients my colleagues and I had been interviewing in order to clarify the links between loneliness and heart disease. Though the details of her story were unique, the pained themes of loneliness, low self-esteem, educational failure, and social isolation had an all-too-familiar ring.

A white, married, 68-year-old woman, Charlotte had been hospitalized in the university coronary care unit because of a recent heart attack. Her immediate problems were further compounded by other physical problems, including periods of acute asthma since adolescence, peptic ulcers, and degenerative arthritis. She had suffered with physical pain for most of her adult life.

In spite of all of her medical problems, including the fact that her heart was pumping quite rapidly (105 beats per minute), she appeared relaxed, smiling continuously as she outlined the pained tapestry of her life. She recounted to the nurse how her mother had died of pneumonia when she was four, and then added: "My father was alcoholic, and so after my mother died, I was sent to live in several foster homes. I was finally adopted when I was six."

Struck by Charlotte's pleasant demeanor, the coronary nurse asked whether she ever got "down on herself." Sighing deeply, while smiling as if trying to erase the pain of her own message, she responded:

"You know what really hurts? It was my schooling. Losing my mother and father was bad, but somehow I was able to cope...perhaps because I felt it wasn't my fault. But school was something else. I wasn't as smart as the other kids, and so my foster parents just stopped sending me after the eighth grade. It was probably because of the long bus ride....It was a long way to high school, you know, so I just didn't go. They had two other children—my foster parents that is—and it kind of made me feel bad that both of them graduated from high school and college.

"I really got down on myself after that. I felt kind of funny and peculiar with other people as I got older...You know the way it is. It was really bad in my twenties and thirties...like I was dumber than everyone else.... I...I...just felt strange and uncomfortable around people."

Struggling to maintain her composure, Charlotte interrupted her train of thought momentarily, and then added:

"Well, anyhow, it went away, sort of, in my late thirties. They say that time heals everything, and that's true. You kind of forget as you get older, or at least the hurt doesn't feel so bad."

Even the briefest appraisal of Charlotte's life makes it easy to concur with her cardiologist's conclusions that many of her symptoms were either exacerbated, if not directly caused, by her earlier setbacks. Her lifelong struggle with loneliness, caused by the early loss of her mother, the alcohol-induced abandonment of her father, and the social isolation that followed her dropping out of school in the eighth grade—these events, piled on top of each other, would have been sufficient to crush any human being.

Charlotte's school failure hurt. She said it hurt! Even near death in a coronary care unit, decades after the fact, she still listed it as the greatest hurt of her life. As she talked about her struggles in school a half century earlier, the monitor behind her bed began to beep ever faster, a stark reminder that her clogged arteries could, at any moment, cut off the oxygen desperately needed by her own heart.

Yet, from a scientific perspective, questions about heart disease always involve issues of mechanisms. How does one go in childhood from social isolation and loneliness, parental loss or abandonment, or low educational attainment, to an increased risk of heart disease and premature death in adulthood? As noted earlier, the process leading to the premature development of heart disease can be indirect, involving an increase in the types of risks known to be linked to heart disease. Or the process can be more direct, as suggested in the studies linking depression to an increase in the incidence of fatal arrhythmias that cause sudden death.

There can be, as well, yet another set of mechanisms—those involving what I have labeled communicative disease. This latter source of her problems was implicit in Charlotte's suggestion that school failure had made her "feel strange and uncomfortable around other people." Her own analysis suggested that a pervasive sense of communicative disease, secondary to dropping out of school, made it difficult for her to talk to or relate to others without constant physiological stress.

TRACKING THE SOURCE
OF HEART DISEASE BACK TO CHILDHOOD

In a sense, attempting to understand the childhood origins of communication problems and loneliness, or the origins of the links between loneliness and a medical problem such as heart disease, is like trying to understand the origins of a great river like the Mississippi. The flood of water that flows into the Gulf of Mexico is the end result of contributions from thousands of small streams from all over the midsection of the United States. While the Mississippi's headwaters can be traced back to Lake Itasca in Minnesota, the Missouri and Ohio rivers bring water from as far away as the Rocky and Appalachian Mountains. Spring storms in the heartland of the United States also add to the flood of water pouring into the Gulf.

If coronary heart disease is like a river, its headwaters—how, when, and where they begin—remain ill defined. Similarly, the manner in which various life events contribute to the buildup of this disease is not known precisely. The search for the sources of heart disease has been further complicated by the long span of time that intervenes between the initial stages of this disease and the appearance of visibly detectable symptoms decades later.

And as was made clear in the original Framingham Heart Studies (whose youngest volunteers were 30 years of age when the study began), it was originally assumed that coronary heart disease began somewhere in mid-life, and then progressed slowly over time, until blockage appeared in one of the arteries sometime after the age of fifty.

Gradually, this point-of-view began to shift with mounting evidence that signs and symptoms of heart disease could begin at a much earlier age, perhaps even in childhood. Autopsies performed on U.S. servicemen killed on the battlefield during World War II and the Korean War, for example, revealed that a significant number of these young men, mostly in their early twenties, already had developed significant signs of heart disease. The coronary arteries of some of these young men resembled those usually seen in men more than 60 years of age.[103]

By 1999, a new and quite different view of coronary heart disease began to gain wider acceptance. Once thought to be a slowly developing, and progressive disease, investigators began to suspect that coronary atherosclerosis might develop more episodically, sometimes advancing rapidly, and then entering a quiescent stage, before developing rapidly again. Scientists also began to suspect that some unknown and poorly understood event or events triggered those periods when the disease was more active, and when it was quiescent.

THE BOGALUSA HEART STUDIES

Any doubts about the importance of childhood links to the development of coronary heart disease were erased when the Bogalusa

Heart Studies confirmed the observations made by coroners on the battlefields of Korea. In 1998, the *New England Journal of Medicine* published the first major findings form the "Bogalusa Heart Studies." [104]

Modeled after the Framingham Studies, this long-term prospective study, conducted in the Washington Parish of Louisiana, was designed to evaluate the effects of risk factors for heart disease from birth through the age of 38 years in a biracial population 65 percent white and 35 percent black. In seven cross-sectional surveys conducted since 1973, each including 3,500 children, the investigators measured all of the well-known risk factors for heart disease discovered at Framingham.

By 1999, they had gathered data on 14,000 children, and as was true with the Framingham heart studies, it was now a process of waiting for several decades to ascertain whether the existence of any of these risk factors would increase the likelihood of the development of heart disease. The first hints of the potentially serious links between the increased incidence of risk factors in childhood and the development of premature heart disease emerged from autopsies performed on a number of study volunteers who died suddenly from accidental traumas, either in adolescence or in their early twenties.

In 1999, the *New England Journal of Medicine* published a study by medical investigators at Tulane University Medical School who performed autopsies on 204 young people between the ages of two and 39. Most of the young people had died from various unanticipated traumas, most notably accidents or homicide in the Washington Parish of Louisiana. In the total group, the coroners discovered in these youngsters an unsettlingly high incidence of significant scarring of the coronary arteries and aorta vessels. Such scarring is correlated with the high likelihood of an eventual development of coronary atherosclerosis, heart attacks, and sudden death.

Quite by chance, 93 of those autopsied were also part of the Bogalusa Risk Factors Heart Study. In all the victims, risk factors such as smoking, elevations in blood pressure, elevations in serum cholesterol, body mass, etc., had been regularly monitored before their sudden deaths. And those autopsies confirmed the findings of the Framingham investigators. The only difference was that these autopsies were performed on young men and women. As was true in Framingham, the medical investigators discovered that, as the number of cardiac risk factors observed in these young people increased (i.e., increased body-mass, cigarette smoking, elevated serum cholesterol, and elevated blood pressure), the greater the fatty streaks and scarring discovered in their coronary and aortic arteries. They reported:

"Subjects with 0, 1, 2, 3 or 4 risk factors had respectively 19.1 percent, 30.3 percent, 37.9 percent, and 35 percent of the intimal surface covered with fatty streaks in the aorta. Comparable figures for the coronary arteries were 1.3 percent, 2.5 percent, 7.9 percent, and 11 percent respectively for fatty streaks."

Thus, a surprising percentage of children and young people had significant signs of cardiovascular disease at very young ages. The scarring observed was proportional to the number of pre-existing risk factors, and was predictive of who was likely to develop premature coronary heart disease.

Yet, while the investigators were able to track the signs of heart disease back to an increase in these pre-existing risk factors, they did not determine or report why these particular youngsters ranked so high on these risk factors. They did not clarify why these young men engaged in such risk-taking activities in the first place. Why were they overweight and hypertensive? Why did they smoke? And why was their serum cholesterol elevated?

The same question asked about the Framingham Heart Studies must be raised once again: *Were there hidden risks behind these risks?* Suffice it to note here that an ever-growing series of research studies indicate that all of the "risk factors" observed in the Bogalusa Heart Study increase in direct proportion to educational failure, increased social isolation, and family fragmentation.

And most important in this regard is the phenomenon of sudden death from trauma itself. The increased risk for sudden death from "accidental traumas" is strongly linked to the hidden emotional scarring of educational failure. In that sense, although it was not reported in the Bogalusa Heart Studies, I suspect that it was loneliness and social isolation that were the real "hidden risks"—the real scars—that put these youngsters at increased risk. I believe that there was a risk behind these risks that was the true silent killer. I suspect that it was family upheaval, social isolation, educational failure, and communicative stress that led some of the children to have excess body mass, increased levels of blood pressure, elevated serum cholesterol readings, etc. I also suspect that it was these hidden risks that contributed to their sudden deaths from "accidental traumas."

Again, I must hasten to add, these suspicions and hypotheses should not be read as a criticism of the Bogalusa Heart Studies. These investigators provided very useful information. They made it unequivocally clear that signs and symptoms of coronary heart disease can begin at a very young age, and that these signs and symptoms would eventually lead to premature death.

As was true in Framingham, unfortunately, the risk factors linked to the development of premature heart disease in the Bogalusa youngsters were reported as if the scientists were weighing these items on a highly sensitive one-sided scale. The more risk factors added to the scales, the greater the risk of premature heart disease.

But was that a complete picture? Was there in fact a two-sided scale, with the hidden risks of family fragmentation, educational failure, communicative disease, social isolation, and loneliness on the other side of the scale? All available data suggest that as one adds these risks to one side of the scale, the conventional cardiac risk factors quickly pile up on the other side. It is the sheer weight on both sides of the scale that inexorably breaks the human heart.

THE PSYCHOLOGICAL AND PHYSICAL IMPACT OF EARLY LOSS

It is encouraging, however, to observe that long-term prospective studies of heart disease are now being extended back into infancy and childhood. For it is no exaggeration to assert that the importance of childhood experiences in shaping adult personality has been the core dogma of both psychiatry and psychology since the founding of these fields at the beginning of the twentieth century. Prospective studies like those conducted at Bogalusa, Louisiana offer the hope that there will be, at long last, a merging of data accumulated in disciplines that have historically developed on parallel tracks. It will inevitably help foster medical understandings about the causes of disease that have eluded public awareness.

The psychological literature pointing out the vital connections between certain early childhood experiences and subsequent physical and emotional disturbance is very large, and only a few studies will be cited here. Lytt Gardner has described a series of studies showing that children raised in emotionally deprived environments can suffer serious physical and emotional damage, including the permanent stunting of their physical growth. [105]

In a report entitled "Deprivation Dwarfism," Gardner retold the legendary story of Frederick II, ruler of Sicily in the thirteenth century. Frederick believed that all men were born with a common language, which he suspected must have been an ancient one, such as Hebrew. In order to test his theory, he took newborn infants away from their natural mothers at birth, gave them to foster mothers, and ordered the foster mothers to physically care for the babies but never to speak to them, so that he might learn what language the children would naturally speak. The experiment was, however, a failure—all of the children died. "For they could not live without petting and the joyful faces and loving words of their foster mothers." [106]

At the beginning of the twentieth century, Sigmund Freud wrote eloquently about the importance of childhood experiences.[107] He described in marvelous detail the manner in which interactions between a child and its parents contribute to personality development in adulthood. The psychiatric research that followed his pioneering investigations has repeatedly shown that childhood experiences such as divorce, sudden loss of love, lack of love, and chronic human loneliness have a major impact on both childhood and adult development.

Psychiatric investigators from Freud onward have recognized that early parental loss is directly related to a wide variety of childhood, adolescent, and adult psychological problems. The scientific data in this field owes much to the classic research of Dr. John Bowlby, who investigated the relationship between maternal care and mental health for the World Health Organization in 1950. He documented the extensive physical, emotional, and intellectual damage that can result when a child is separated from its parents (especially from the mother) for extended periods of time, particularly if this separation occurs in the first few years of life.[108]

Ten years later, Dr. Rene Spitz also described the "marasmus," or physical wasting away, of infants who suddenly lost their mothers. Some infants who suddenly lost their parents, Spitz observed, would refuse to eat and would eventually die even when force-fed.[109]

In one study, conducted with Katherine Wolf, Dr. Spitz followed 91 infants raised in foundling homes in the United States and Canada. Despite being well cared for physically, most of the infants appeared very depressed and quite anxious. They did not grow as rapidly as other infants. They did not gain weight, and some even lost weight. Of the 91 infants studied, "34 died in spite of good food and meticulous medical care." The last trimester of the infants' first year of life seemed to be of special significance, because most of the deaths occurred during this period. But even among those who survived, almost all showed varying degrees of physical and emotional retardation.

Observations such as these fortunately led to important changes in the way orphanages and foundling homes cared for children. Hospitals also became more enlightened. Mothers visiting their sick children are no longer seen as administrative nuisances, but instead are encouraged to live-in with their infants during critical periods, so that serious physical illness need not be compounded by emotional disturbance.

Similarly, Dr. Nelson Ordway and his colleagues at the University of Oklahoma reviewed the cases of three infants hospitalized for a variety of physical problems. All had been deprived of parental love, and all initially "failed to thrive" while in the hospital. All were wasting away until the physicians provided them with warm interpersonal support, given exclusively by one or two nurses (mother surrogates). All three infants improved dramatically after this nurturing care was introduced. Ordway and his associates noted that the infants deprived of parental love "failed to develop strong attachments to people. Their lack of interest extended also to objects.... They did not show anxiety in the presence of strangers or distress when a person or toy was removed." [110]

It is, unfortunately, rather easy to dismiss the research showing the destructive effects of social deprivation as irrelevant to most human situations. After all, few children in the United States are raised in total isolation. The kinds of cases described by Spitz or Ordway are highly unusual, even extreme. Nevertheless, they hint at the potential effects of a subtle kind of social deprivation that appears to be growing with each passing day in our society.

Most infants and children are not raised in total social isolation. On the other hand, ever-increasing numbers are being raised in homes that could easily become socially deprived environments. Not only are there now significantly fewer children in each home (and consequently less dialogue between siblings), but there is also an overall diminution of social interaction in many homes.

As noted earlier, the number of children raised in single parent households in the United States has grown rapidly in the past twenty years. Coupled with this trend is the fact that an ever-growing number of mothers are forced to hold jobs outside the home. The vast majority of adults in single-parent households are undoubtedly forced to work for their economic survival. Many parents do not want to leave their children in the care of others, but they simply have no other choice. Economic necessity dictates their behavior.

An entirely new form of loneliness is embedded in the phrase "latch-key" children—a phrase used to describe the growing number of children who come home from school to an empty house. These situations create environments where something has to give. Something has to be sacrificed. Most parents who work all day and then come home to cook a meal and care for a house will be both physically and emotionally drained. After a full's day exertion in the workplace, it takes a concerted effort by parents to give their full attention to children after their return home.

Time, personal, and emotional pressures will naturally tend to compress the quantity of dialogue. It is not a question of whether parents want to attend to their children. Rather, it is a question of time and personal and emotional exhaustion. More and more, the vital function of interacting with infants and children is left by default to schools, day-care centers, nurseries, baby-sitters, and television, which may be very poor surrogate parents.

A wide variety of adolescent and adult psychiatric disorders have now been linked to the lack of parental contact during infancy. Hundreds of studies have shown that the lack of parental contact or the early loss of parents can seriously undermine the emotional stability of children. Severe adult depression, dependency, psychosis, various neuroses, and suicide have all been frequently reported among individuals who suffered early parental loss. C. N. Wahl, for example, studied 392 male schizophrenics who had been in the U.S. Navy. He found that 40 percent of his total group had lost a parent by death, divorce, or separation before 15 years of age, compared to only 11 percent in the general naval population.[111]

Dr. Roslyn Seligman and her colleagues at the University of Cincinnati College of Medicine examined 85 adolescents who had been referred for psychiatric evaluation from a general adolescent population in their hospital. They found that 36.4 percent of these adolescents had experienced early parental loss (through either death or permanent separation), with the loss of a father reported twice as frequently as the loss of a mother. At the time of the study, the relative incidence of similar parental loss in the general adolescent school population was 11.6 percent.[112]

Dr. Glueck in the United States [113]and Dr. Greer in Australia[114] have shown that adult sociopathy occurs significantly more often in individuals who have experienced early parental loss. Gregory's exhaustive study of almost 12,000 ninth-graders from all geographic and socioeconomic sectors of the state of Minnesota showed that adolescent delinquency rates and school dropout rates were much higher for children who had lost a parent through death or divorce.[115]

Perhaps the most direct link between early psychological trauma, including the loss of one's parents, and subsequent physical illness can be drawn from the fact that adult psychopathology itself leads to serious problems in interpersonal relationships. Individuals who experience serious difficulty or who are unable to form close personal ties in adulthood are the very same individuals most likely to appear in the mortality tables described in the last two chapters. That is, they would be over-represented in the single and divorced categories, and would generally lack social support.

Evidence supporting this proposition can be gleaned from a large number of sources. For example, Drs. George Engel, William Greene, and Arthur Schmale at the University of Rochester Medical School have found out that a strong relationship exists between early parental loss and the subsequent development of various physical diseases. When Dr. Schmale, for example, examined the relationship between separation and depression and the development of physical disease (such as cardiovascular disease), he found that a significant number of adult patients in the hospital with physical disease had suffered the early loss of one or both parents. Confronted again as adults with some new loss or the threat of such a loss, these patients tended to become very depressed and developed various physical diseases, including cardiac disorders. [116]

Dr. Claus Bahnson in Philadelphia made similar observations. He studied early child-parent relationships and the subsequent development of coronary heart disease and cancer. He observed that a significant number of fathers of coronary patients had died prematurely, usually when the son was between the ages of 5 and 17. While usually considered to be evidence of genetic vulnerability, Bahnson demonstrated that it was the loss itself, rather than genetics, that contributed to this problem.[117]

In one of the more extraordinary retrospective studies identifying early predictors of disease and premature death, Dr. Ralph Paffenbarger and his colleagues examined the records of up to 50,000 former students of Harvard University and the University of Pennsylvania who were in college between 1921 through 1950. They examined the college records of the first 590 male students who had died of coronary heart disease and contrasted them with 1,180 randomly chosen classmates of equivalent age known to be alive.

Nine factors distinguished the coronary heart disease victims—heavy cigarette smoking, higher levels of blood pressure, increased body weight, shortness of body height, early parental death, absence of siblings, nonparticipation in sports, a general college style of secretiveness and social isolation, and scarlet fever in childhood.

One obvious and frequently proposed explanation for the relationship between early parental death and subsequent coronary heart disease is genetic predisposition. But Paffenbarger and his colleagues also examined the incidence of suicide (which is not generally thought of as a genetically determined phenomenon) in a sample population of 40,000 students, and found that 225 of the former University of Pennsylvania students had committed suicide in the years following graduation. He compared these suicide cases with a large number of randomly selected students. He found that those who committed suicide were likely to have come from families where the father had a professional status (frequently a physician), the parents were college trained, the parents had separated, or the father had died early.

Other distinguishing characteristics were exactly the same as for death by coronary heart disease: heavy cigarette smoking, nonparticipation in extracurricular sports, secretiveness, and social isolation. Paffenbarger speculated that lack of participation in extra-curricular activities reflected an increased sense of loneliness, fear, hostility, and frustration. He also suggested that the father's wealth or success may have had an adverse influence on the son through paternal absence, deprivation of companionship and counsel, overbearing demand for emulation and perfection, or possible lack of interest or lack of need for individual success or effort in their sons. [118]

In sum, the picture that emerges from these fascinating studies of students graduating from elite universities involves very similar physical factors, personality traits, and life histories. The early loss of a parent, social isolation, and loneliness were highly predictive of both suicide and premature death from heart disease. Paffenbarger and his colleagues summarized their findings as follows:

"Students who later died of coronary heart disease were more likely than their controls to be without siblings, and also were more likely to have lost one or both parents before entering college. It seems, however, that only-child status and early death of a parent were independent precursors of coronary death.... Any of these circumstances might have psychological significance, since feelings of lassitude and anxiety were reported more frequently by the future coronary decedents. The insecurities commonly noted on separation from home to enter college may have been enhanced by overly possessive or protective family ties often associated with loss of a parent or with the status of only child." [119]

Beyond the medical consequences already described, there is another childhood experience that has major consequences for long-term health. And unlike data gathered from family situations, these health data can be examined in a far more objective fashion. As was true with marital statistics in adulthood, so too the educational system provides an invaluable window into objective statistical data of vital significance in childhood. Although educational institutions are not usually associated with loneliness and social isolation, nor linked to problems such as heart disease and premature death, the objective data describe a very different reality.

EDUCATING FOR LIFE OR DEATH

In 1968, two scientists at the University of Chicago, Drs. Evelyn Kitagawa and Philip Hauser, published the first scientific analysis of the effects of education on mortality in the United States. They subsequently refined and expanded their analysis in a book entitled, *Differential Mortality in the United States.*[120] Their analysis of Vital Statistics from the 1960 census led to the first realization that there was a striking inverse relationship between mortality and level of educational attainment.

They noted that virtually every cause of death increased the less education one had. They discovered that premature mortality in white females with less than eight years of school was 105 percent higher than that observed in college-educated women of identical age! For men, the overall death rate was 64 percent higher! This increased mortality also held true at all ages over 25.

Kitagawa and Hauser concluded that if the overall death rates exhibited by college educated individuals had been matched by comparable rates from those with less education, almost a quarter million fewer white American citizens would have died in 1960 and every year thereafter.[121]

Though the overall death rate for those with less education was higher at all ages, particularly revealing was the excessively high rates between the ages of 25-64. For that specific age group in 1960, cardiovascular-renal disease and various cancers accounted for approximately 70 percent of all premature deaths reported in the 1960 census. White women with the lowest levels of education had a death rate from heart disease almost triple that of women who had gone to college for one or more years!

As shown on the following graph, men with less education had a death rate from hypertension 1.8 times that of college educated men, while the mortality rate from this disease in women was almost triple. Similarly sharp rises in mortality were found for cardiovascular-renal diseases, with the overall death rate almost double for less educated men and women.

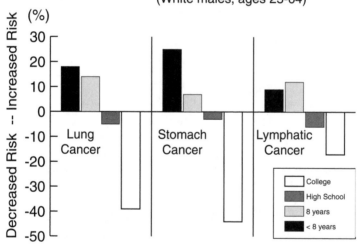

Education Level and Cancer Mortality Risk*
(White males, ages 25-64)

*Risk relative to that of average
population risk for white males, 25-64

Similar trends were evident in deaths caused by cancer. The least educated men had premature death rates from lung, bronchus, and tracheal cancers almost double those of the college educated. A comparable doubling of the death rate could be seen for stomach cancer, while death rates from intestinal and rectal cancer were 22 percent higher. For women, uterine cancer death rates were 2.1 times higher for the least educated, as were higher death rates for intestinal and stomach cancers. (The only cancer that showed an opposite pattern was breast cancer, where the incidence was 22 percent lower in the least educated women. Apparently the best explanation for this finding is the lower incidence of child-bearing and failure to breast feed in the better educated women.)

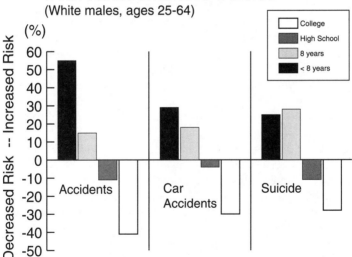

Education Level & Mortality Risk from Accidents and Suicide*
(White males, ages 25-64)

*Risk relative to that of average
population risk for white males, 25-64

For those major causes of premature death that could be directly linked to human behavior, the influence of education was equally striking. Among the least educated males, the mortality rate from accidents (other than motor vehicles) was 2.3 times greater than that found in the more educated. The death rates for motor vehicle accidents were 2.5 times greater, and the suicide rate was double.

Examining these data from yet another perspective, Kitagawa and Hauser estimated the life expectancy of all women who had reached the age of 25 in the 1960 census. They concluded that those with one or more years of college could expect to live almost 10 years longer than females of a comparable age with less than five years of school.

As striking as these statistical findings may be, however, it was clear that the relationship of low education to increased risk of premature death was not a phenomenon operating in isolation. Any number of factors could have entered into the equations to help account for this relationship. Those factors ranged from the more obvious influence of various behavioral factors—such as excessive smoking, alcohol consumption, and overweight—to more chronic socioeconomic stressors, such as unemployment and poverty.

Increases in the incidence of conventional risk factors are one explanation. There is a highly significant correlation between certain maladaptive behaviors, such as cigarette smoking, excessive weight, and level of education. As level of education increases, the incidence of various risk factors decreases. Those with less education tend to engage in a wide variety of maladaptive behaviors conducive to poor health. Yet, even when these factors are controlled and made equal, low education itself has a significant influence on premature death.

Perhaps the most intriguing covariate with education, at least in terms of identifying more precisely what it is about the low level of educational attainment that leads to increased risk of premature death, is economic status. Statistics readily confirm a strong link between education and income. The higher one's education, the greater one's annual income. Statistical data also clearly reveal a significant increase in mortality for those in the lower income brackets. Thus, the question naturally arises as to whether the relationship between education and increased risk of death might be due to some third factor such as a person's economic status.

To help evaluate this problem, Drs. Kitagawa and Hauser performed what is technically known as a "co-variate analysis" on a sample of people from the 1960 Census. That is, they examined death rates in a large group of people in whom age and income levels were held constant, while educational levels were varied. As shown in the following chart, even when income was statistically equalized, there still was a significant increase in mortality for those with less education! Those with high income, but low education levels, still had significantly increased death rates.

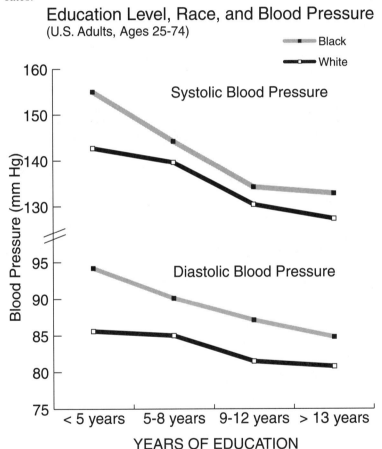

Education Level, Race, and Blood Pressure
(U.S. Adults, Ages 25-74)

NOTE: Current convention holds that the diagnosis of hypertension is considered when blood pressures of 140+ SBP and/or 90+ DBP are found.

Commenting on these consistent findings, Kitagawa and Hauser noted that "persons with both high education and high income have lower mortality, on the average, than persons high on education but low on income, or than persons high on income but low on education. Clearly both education and income have important independent associations with mortality." [122]

A PLAGUE UPON THE LAND

By no means are these findings peculiar to the 1960 census, or unique to the type of medical data uncovered by Drs. Kitagawa and Hauser then. Quite the contrary. A large number of subsequent surveys have demonstrated similar trends. In 1981, for example, the National Center for Health Statistics examined the incidence of hypertension (high blood pressure) in American adults between the ages of 25-74.

Long considered to be a significant contributor to heart disease and strokes, hypertension, according to the American Heart Association, ranks as the nation's number one "silent killer"—"silent" because individuals suffering from this disease frequently do not detect elevations in blood pressure, even elevations up to clinically dangerous levels, and "the number one killer" because it contributes in a significant way to all of the major cardiovascular diseases. Today, it is generally agreed, hypertension is the single most important health problem in modern industrialized countries, with an estimated 50-60 million adult Americans suffering from this disease in 1990.

In a major screening survey conducted on hundreds of thousands of Americans between 1971 and 1975, the National Center for Health Statistics discovered that educational level was one of the strongest factors influencing blood pressure levels in the United States. [123] For males and females of all ages, both black and white, there was a consistent and highly significant inverse relationship between education and blood pressure. As educational levels increased, blood pressure levels decreased. Similar findings have been confirmed in dozens of similar and more recent national surveys. [124]

For blacks—in whom hypertension occurs far more frequently than it does in whites—investigators have found a 13 millimeter difference in systolic pressure and a 10 millimeter difference in diastolic pressure from the best educated to the least educated groups. The average blood pressure readings for all blacks with less than five years education was found to be at levels considered diagnostic for hypertension! Their average resting blood pressure of 155/94 was found to be at a level considered indicative

of hypertension. The entire group was at considerable risk of eventually succumbing from any number of problems caused by the "silent killer" of high blood pressure.

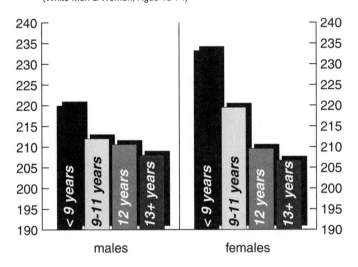

Years of Education, Gender, and Serum Cholesterol Levels
(White Men & Women, Ages 18-74)

males — females

SOURCE: Health Census Survey, 1980

For both blacks and whites, there was a consistent relationship between blood pressure and education. The relationship held true for both men and women, and at every age level. The average systolic blood pressure was almost 12 millimeters of mercury lower among women with the highest educational levels and 8 millimeters lower for men than among those with the lowest educational levels.

Nearly every other health indicator reflects similar trends. Based on a number of national surveys conducted since 1970, the data overwhelmingly confirm that educational level has a major effect on virtually every index of human health. Whether one examines height, excessive weight, smoking, frequency of visits to doctors, annual number of acute hospitalizations, chronic health conditions, cholesterol levels, automobile death rates, murders, or cancer mortality, the picture is always the same—as education level increases, so also do health, general well-being, and long term survival.[125]

Take, for example, average serum cholesterol levels reported in 1980 by the U.S. Department of Health, Education and Welfare for average Americans. Elevations in serum cholesterol have long been suspected to be a significant contributor to atherosclerosis, and a prime contributor to heart attacks. Lowering cholesterol through medications is now a multibillion dollar enterprise for pharmaceutical industries. Measuring serum cholesterol in tens of thousands of individuals throughout the United States, investigators found that educational level made a significant difference. For white Americans between the ages of 18-74, the average levels of serum cholesterol were significantly lower in those with the highest levels of education.[126][127]

EDUCATIONAL LEVELS & SERUM CHOLESTEROL IN U.S. WHITE MEN AND WOMEN BETWEEN THE AGES OF 18-74, 1980 HEALTH CENSUS SURVEY

EDUCATIONAL LEVEL	MALES	FEMALES
Less than 9 years	219.9	233.2
9-11 years	212.0	219.5
12 years	210.6	209.6
13 years or more	208.0	206.7

In 1978, the National Bureau of Vital Statistics conducted a particularly intriguing survey that allows one to grasp the enormity of these health problems. A team of health scientists asked tens of thousands of Americans to assess their own health. A number of comparable self-assessment surveys in the past had demonstrated that a person's assessment of his or her own health was closely correlated with actual health status, as well as with utilization of health services. Earlier surveys, for example, had shown that persons who judged themselves to be in excellent health spent, on the average, three days a year in bed due to illness, and visited doctors 2.5 times a year. Persons who judged themselves to be in poor health spent, on the average, 64 days a year in bed and visited doctors 15 times each year! [128]

Years of education had a highly significant impact on a person's assessment of his or her general well-being. Between the ages of 45 to 54, for example, men and women with no education were nine times more likely to adjudge themselves suffering from poor health than those with 16 or more years of education. Almost half the entire group with no education in the United States were in poor health during what ought to have been the prime of their lives.

Years of Education, Age Group, and Health Status, 1978

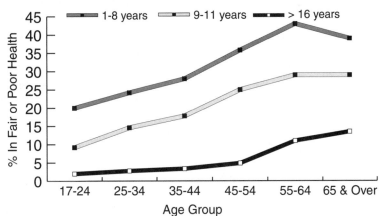

SOURCE: CDC/National Center for Health Statistics

Years of Education, Age Group, and Health Status, 1988-90

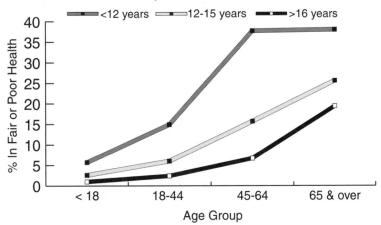

SOURCE: CDC/National Center for Health Statistics

This finding was by no means restricted to the persons aged 45 to 54. On the contrary, these differences held true at all ages, and were equally consistent for both sexes and all races. As educational levels decreased, general indices of health also decreased.

It is important to add that, in this same survey, two other factors showed similar trends. Persons with lower income levels and persons living alone also reported that they were in poor health. These three factors not only interact often with one another, but they also combine in ways feeding a fundamental and shared problem. Indeed, it was an increased incidence in reports of chronic loneliness among those with less education that originally led us to begin searching for a third factor they had in common. That factor, as we have already asserted, is an inability to engage in dialogue with others without undue physiological stress. Social isolation, withdrawal from dialogue, and loneliness are the result.

Hints of the linkage between loneliness, low education, and low self-esteem can be seen in a revealing survey published by the United States Office of Health Research in 1980. This survey analyzed the incidence of depressive symptoms in the average citizen in the United States. Based on a sophisticated measure of depression called the "Epidemiologic Studies-Depression Scale," the investigators set out to analyze symptoms such as feelings of guilt, worthlessness, helplessness, and hopelessness, plus sleep disturbance and weight loss in the United States population-at-large.

Dozens of recent studies have indicated that increases in depression not only put a person at higher risk for sudden cardiac death, but can exacerbate abnormal heart rhythms that have been linked to sudden death. In assessing the impact of depression, the best estimate is that it leads to a four-fold increase in both the incidence of heart disease as well as a four-fold increase in the incidence of sudden death.

The investigators found that three factors had a major impact on these symptoms—marital status, economic status, and education. Those who lived alone, who were low in socioeconomic status, and who had low education, were by far the most depressed. While each factor had its own independent influence, the combination of all three proved to be particularly devastating. At all ages, for both sexes, and in all races, there was a consistent inverse relationship between education and depression. Those with the lowest education had more than double the levels of depression found in college graduates.[129]

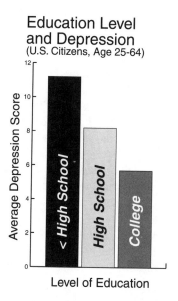

Education Level
and Depression
(U.S. Citizens, Age 25-64)

Thus, whether one examines indices of disease, poor health, psychological suffering, or mortality itself, the results are consistent. In every instance, increasing levels of education are accompanied by increasing levels of mental and physical well-being. Increased visits to physicians, amount of time spent in hospitals, vulnerability to a variety of chronic diseases, increased vulnerability to catastrophic medical problems, and sharply increased risk of premature death—all show the same trends.[130] In light of the epidemic of school dropouts, which in many urban areas now exceeds 50 percent of enrollment, these medical statistics appear to foreshadow even greater economic, psychological, social, and health problems in the future.

They also point to the growth of a problem that will not only threaten to overwhelm the health care delivery system in the United States, but increase the economic burdens of health care for the impoverished, feeding a cycle of poverty that will inexorably doom successive generations. What little money the less educated have, by necessity, will be spent on the increased burdens of chronic ill-health that appear to stem from low education. The costs stagger the imagination. They currently run into the tens of billions of dollars annually and consume an enormous portion of the national health budget. The personal, social, and political costs are simply incalculable, and may, in the future, bankrupt the nation.

AN APPRAISAL

Though the statistical data described in this chapter are highly consistent, by no means do they make certain the precise causal links between low education and increased vulnerability to disease and premature death. Indeed, the obvious relationship of education to various socio-economic factors is but one of a number of considerations that have made it all too easy to discount and ignore the lethal impact of school failure itself. Instead, it has been automatically assumed that any lethal effects of education, almost necessarily, would be due to a variety of intervening factors such as poverty and unemployment, rather than be the result of educational experiences alone.

In this chapter, I began to present evidence to suggest that this commonly held assumption is both misleading and incorrect. Even when factors such as income levels are held constant, educational attainment still has a highly significant influence on longevity itself. In the next chapter, I address this concern directly by discussing the linkages between low-educational attainment and the increased risk of premature death from heart disease in populations where income levels have been equalized and thus ruled out as a potential explanation.

The statistical evidence described thus far, however, does not isolate the specific factor that makes education such a potent influence on long-term survival. In fact, it is extremely difficult to isolate such causal factors from correlational data alone. If taken at face value and isolated from other considerations, such data can be quite misleading.

It is not inconceivable, for example, that a correlation might be found between the temperature of the pavement in New York City and the birth rate in the Fiji Islands. Still another correlation might be noted between the same pavement temperature and the number of robins in Central Park. While the first correlation would most likely have occurred by statistical chance alone, the number of robins in Central Park would likely share a third factor in common with the pavement temperature—namely, seasonal variations in New York City weather.

In spite of the limitations of correlational data, the variety, consistency, and sheer volume of the medical data described in this chapter nevertheless make it highly unlikely that the relationship between education and various health indices is one that exists by pure chance alone. It is unlikely that phenomena as varied as cervical cancer, hypertension, heart disease, lymphatic cancer, suicide, murder, alcoholism, drug addiction, elevations in serum cholesterol levels, and automobile accidents could all show the same type of links to education without sharing something powerful in common.

Yet, even though we presume that the health statistics point toward some common underlying factor, they don't pinpoint with certainty just what that factor or factors might be. I have hypothesized the major culprits to be the increased risk of communicative disease and the disembodiment of human dialogue, both of which stem from crushing shame, humiliation, and resultant human loneliness. But these complex hypotheses cannot be proven by correlational data alone.

Indeed, one could cogently argue quite an opposite point-of-view. One could propose, for example, that these health data indicate that the modern American school system is a remarkably sensitive filtering system that bears awesome testimonial to the wisdom of Darwin's theory about the "survival of the fittest." Although it might be stretching the limits of credibility somewhat, one could use these data to argue, in effect, that school dropouts are less fit in every respect, whether intellectual, emotional, or physical. It could be true that those who are overweight, smoke, abuse alcohol and other narcotics, do not exercise, or who are prone to accidents, are simply less intelligent. It could likewise be true that school dropouts are obese precisely because they are burdened by a low I.Q., which is the common cause of both problems.

While I by no means believe either of those statements is true, one could assert even more bluntly that perhaps school dropouts are too stupid to know how to take care of themselves properly. Perhaps one's IQ or SAT score is a remarkably sensitive indicator of longevity precisely because intelligence, school performance, and survival are all causally interrelated.

By no means do I intend to imply that the foregoing statistical data are not useful or meaningful. Quite the opposite. It is precisely the type of information that forces one to probe deeper. The very consistency of the links between educational level and longevity demands that the phenomenon be investigated further.

In a sense, the overall health trends reviewed in this chapter are reminiscent of the once controversial linkages between cigarette smoking and increased risk of heart disease and lung cancer. The links between smoking, cancer, and heart disease were recognized long before the precise causal linkages were understood. In fact, it was recognition of these relationships that first led scientists to sound the alarm.

Yet, the possibility that such relationships existed by pure chance, that smoking was just incidental to some third factor as yet not isolated, allowed the tobacco industry to continue advertising and promoting cigarette usage long after tobacco's health dangers were recognized. It also allowed the U.S. government to pour billions of dollars into farm subsidies to encourage the planting and harvesting of tobacco, while simultaneously spending tens of billions of dollars to fight heart disease and cancer. Specific carcinogenic and cardiotoxic agents in cigarette smoke had to be identified in order for the causal links to be proven scientifically.

The limitations inherent in correlational data are further compounded by certain unique qualitative issues raised by our hypothesis about the nature of these relationships. Unlike specific carcinogenic and cardiotoxic agents in cigarette smoke, school experiences that shatter the ability to communicate with one's fellow man are not likely to be reduced to any specific causative agent analogous to a chemical compound. No matter how refined the scientific analyses, the lethal ingredient that comprises the essential nature of disembodied dialogue and human loneliness is not likely to be isolated in any specific chemical compound. Nor is the solution to the problem likely to involve recommendations as simple as the prescriptive advice to "stop smoking."

In light of these quantitative and qualitative problems, the scope of the analysis must be narrowed somewhat. Rather than scanning the entire panoramic scene of health indices linked to education, I now focus on one specific class of health problems—namely, the various forms of cardiovascular disease. In addition, the type of studies I review are also quite different. Rather than examining mortality data obtained from census statistics, or health information gathered from various screening surveys, I review studies that have used quite a different approach.

Though it might be easier to document my central theses about the destruction of human communication, survival, and education if I focused on health problems where these are well recognized factors—e.g., in depression, anxiety, or suicide—I nevertheless focus on heart disease for several reasons.

First and foremost is the fact that heart disease, hypertension, and stroke are the most important health problems in the United States—they account for 50 percent of all deaths. Second, it is widely assumed that vulnerability to these health problems is largely due to genetic predisposition or lack of physical fitness. Yet, as I show in the next chapter, recent studies help to pinpoint the feeder streams flowing into the central river of human identity and self-worth in a way that makes unmistakable their links to the heart of our communicative life.

Chapter Six

ISOLATING EDUCATION

"Though some may not admit it, a teacher nowadays meets the school-age child with the distinct idea that he is a little animal, and that he must develop this little animal just a little further than Nature has done hitherto. He will feel differently if he says to himself: here is man, and he has connections to the whole universe; and what I do with every growing child, the way I work with him, has significance for the whole universe. Pedagogy must not be a science, it must be an art. And where is the art that can be learned without dwelling constantly in the feelings? But the feelings in which we must live in order to practice the great art of life, the art of education, are only kindled by contemplation of the great universe and its relationship with man."
—Rudolph Steiner, *Study of Man*, 1919

HEALTHY WORKERS AND STRESSED EXECUTIVES: THE KING WHO HAS NO CLOTHES

In the moss-covered ruins of ancient monasteries that dot the Inishowen Peninsula hills of Ireland's Northern Donegal, one can still sense the devotion to learning that permeated the Celtic people a thousand years ago. The monasteries united the parishes of the "Isle of Owen," joining them to a common cultural, economic, commercial, and religious purpose. Though the majority of people received little formal education, they nevertheless shared with their monks a reverence for learning and scholarship as a means of attaining a clearer vision of the Divine. Successive waves of invading Vikings, Norsemen, and Saxons ended this way of life, and by 1700 A.D. all that remained were stone ruins bearing mute testimony to a theocratic vision no longer deemed relevant.

As a young school child, I was well aware of the fact that my forebears—including my Irish immigrant parents and their parents' parents—had had little formal education going back at least five centuries. Though memories of the monastic traditions had somehow survived to create a genuine reverence for learning, no apology was needed nor felt by my parents for their lack of formal education. It was understood to be the price one paid for centuries of foreign domination. Speaking "beautiful English" was regarded more with suspicion than pride.

"The strangers came and tried to teach us their ways" was a sentiment that echoed in the Irish folk music we sang as children, one full of remorse and rebellion. An education based on the abolition of the Gaelic language and traditions was seen for what it was—tribal and cultural murder. To participate was suicidal, but there did not seem to be a viable alternative.

I do not mean to burden the reader with the legacy of my own personal past. Rather, I recite this history only to emphasize that the links between education, self-esteem, communication, social alienation, isolation, and premature death have a great deal to do with the cultural context, philosophic orientation, and the specific era one is examining. In my youth, education assumed a role quite different than it had for my parents. There was no longer any suspicion that schools might be propaganda outlets of an alien government seeking to establish its control and domination.

Instead, American education was seen as a highly legitimate enterprise, a noble endeavor to be taken seriously. At the same time, American education involved far more than learning the three Rs. Pluralistic education was viewed as a cornerstone of American democracy, and it was well understood that different types of schools taught unique and different attitudes. We were sent to Catholic grammar schools in Boston with the explicit understanding that the teacher who taught us reading also taught us something else far more important— namely values.

"Why did God make you?" asked the nun daily, and with an ascetic seriousness that made answering all other academic questions a joyous relief. "Quid est ad aeternetatum?" ("What is all of this compared to eternity?") was a weighty enough problem to occupy the minds of contemplative monks with time to think about such serious matters. But when asked of third graders who were bungling through their multiplication tables, it was enough to make eternity seem a reasonable alternative. In heaven, you'd either know all that stuff automatically, or it just wouldn't matter. "What was seven times six?" would never be a problem in a place run by the Holy Ghost.

Mixed in with these last vestiges of the monastic traditions, however, was a new belief system that had crept unnoticed into our parochial schools. It was the type of belief that made "7x6" important enough to occasionally make our palms drip with sweat. Though piety, heaven, and God were all considered very important, it was also made clear to us that success in schools—that is, academic success—was the only way to move up in American society. In the industrial cities near Boston that we called home in the post-war era, education was looked upon as a way to break away from the traditions of peasant labor that had been part and parcel of our family tradition since the monasteries crumbled more than two hundred years befoore.

And while my immigrant parents struggled to come to terms with the conflicting crosscurrents of an educational philosophy radically changing our lives, something else was changing as well. Schools were deeply influencing our perceptions of physical labor and our "place" in American society. Perhaps it was part of the national euphoria and optimism that followed America's emergence as a global power in the post-World War II era. While it is difficult to ascertain with certainty, the fact is that, in our youth, nothing seemed impossible or out of reach—if only one did well in school.

Without any conscious awareness on our part, we were caught up in the paradoxes of an educational revolution that swept over our lives as youngsters. On the one hand, hard physical labor was not belittled. The immigrants who worked for the railroads, shipyards, and electrical companies were fiercely proud of their jobs. They had shaken off the shackles of poverty and the enforced idleness of the Great Depression. They had also helped to win World War II. They seemed to be a living embodiment of images we read about in our schoolbooks. Longfellow's Village Blacksmith seemed quite real to us, there to be seen in the blacksmith shops closing in our neighborhoods at the end of World War II.

> "Under the spreading chestnut tree
> The village smithy stands;
> The smith, a mighty man is he,
> With large and sinewy hands;
> And the muscles of his brawny arms
> Are strong as iron bands
> His hair is crisp, and black, and long
> His face is like the tan;
> His brow is wet with honest sweat,
> He earns whate'er he can,
> And looks the whole world in the face,
> For he owes not any man."

Proud, honorable, and in marvelously good physical shape—that was true of many of the workers we saw then on a daily basis. There was, to be sure, a dark side as well. There was still widespread poverty and insecurity, and some workers were unable to keep their Friday paychecks away from the local tavern. In the midst of these conflicting societal norms, one message stood out clearly to us: "Go to school, get an education, and better yourselves."

We knew that other city kids, mostly from public schools, who did not do well in grammar schools, would end up in trade schools or "Voc Techs." We also knew it was a fate worse than death—a sign that you just "couldn't cut the mustard." Everyone knew that the next generation of factory workers would come from the ranks of kids not smart enough to make it in "real" schools. And the next step down the ladder was unimaginable. Dropping out of school meant dropping out of life altogether.

Signs of the changing times were all around us. We knew the village blacksmith was part of a dying breed, while we silently dreamt about a future filled with jet airplanes and rockets hurtling into space, witnessing with wide-eyed astonishment the awesome power of a science that had obliterated Hiroshima and Nagasaki with atomic bombs. Though we did not know his name, it was clear that Charles Darwin had met the scholastic monks of the Middle Ages and given us a new answer to the nuns' question—"Why did God make us?" It was implicit in the structure of our evolving parochial schools. Clearly, God had made us to succeed.

While almost no one noticed, the temporal began to replace the eternal. The three R's began to acquire a new purpose, as our Catholic schools took on the role of gatekeepers to economic success. "Survival of the fittest" demanded brains, not brawn. Brilliance began to supplant the beatitudes in our parochial schools even as our young minds sought to understand the meaning behind the grotesque mounds of human victims from strange sounding places like Auschwitz, Dachau, and Bergen-Belsen. Somehow the Nazi concept of "Untermenschen" seemed uncomfortably similar to our notion of "stupid," and it made even the most laggard of us work all the harder at school.

Though the seeds of a new type of American society were planted in the compulsory education of the post-World War II period, it is difficult to comprehend how quickly everything has changed. In 1975, part of that revolution was made vividly clear to me one broodingly cold, wet November day. I happened to be outside the vast industrial complex of the Bethlehem Steel and Bethlehem Shipyards in East Baltimore. It was four o'clock in the afternoon and thousands of workers were filing silently out of the Sparrows Point complex. Dr. Aaron Katcher, a psychiatrist at the

University of Pennsylvania Medical School, was visiting this industrial complex with me. Caught in traffic by the change in shifts, we sat in our car watching silently as a muted stream of working humanity filed past us.

Suddenly, Aaron remarked in a voice that crackled with astonishment, "Good God, look at these men! Every other one seems to be in terrible physical shape!"

He was right, and the specter was stunning. Many workers were overweight and bloated. Though I could not tell for certain, many also looked stressed, depressed, and defeated. They seemed to form a gray column of ambulatory risk factors waiting for their heart attacks, defeated men marching inexorably toward their premature demise.

It was clear that Longfellow's blacksmith, with large and powerful hands and muscles as strong as iron bands, was no longer to be found in the steelyards and shipyards of industrial America. New types of celluloid heroes with sinewy muscles were taking his place. Arnold Schwartznegger and Rambo were waiting in the wings to emerge as the new American blacksmiths.

Yet, old myths die slowly. Many in our society still believe that less educated workers who engage in physically demanding jobs are in good physical shape. The fact that the Village Blacksmith was strong, not just because he hammered on an anvil, but more importantly because he shared communal values, including spiritual depth, pride, and self-respect, has been completely overlooked.

The images of that industrial scene were still fresh in my mind a few days later when I happened to notice a television commercial. It was one of a genre I had seen and heard hundreds of times in the past. With the sound of a human heart beating ominously in the background, the blurred figure of a graying executive walked down a leaf-strewn country lane holding the hand of his carefree five-year-old son. Gradually, their images grew clearer as the commentator noted soberly: "In the past two years, over one million Americans died of heart disease. High blood pressure is a problem that contributed to many of these deaths. It is our nation's number one silent killer. But it can be treated. If you have hypertension, see your doctor. We're fighting for your life...A message from the American Heart Association."

The essential message implicit in these commercials was widely accepted in our society. The highly successful but stressed business executive, pushing himself beyond the limits of human endurance, was destined to die prematurely from hypertension or heart disease, unless he ate right, exercised, avoided undue stress, and kept in touch with his doctor.

And pity that poor executive. How could he avoid the modern analogue of the bubonic plague? How could he avoid the stress of executive responsibility that cruelly threatened to take away everything he had worked so hard to attain? How could he keep his blood pressure down when a thousand stressors were continuously driving it up?

To the overwhelming majority of Americans, commercials of this sort still make perfect sense. To them, it makes perfect sense that executives are in worse physical shape than workers. To them, it makes perfect sense that executives experience more stress, and that they die prematurely in greater numbers from heart disease. It all makes sense, except for the simple fact that it is almost entirely a myth. Yet, like the image of the eternally happy, dull-witted, tap-dancing Negro of yesteryear, the myth persists in spite of all the evidence to the contrary.

In the context of the American Heart Association's commercials, it is difficult to think of workers with relatively low educational levels, stuck in jobs of unending monotonous drudgery, with little control over their economic lives, as chronically stressed, out-of shape, hypertensive individuals prone to premature death. It is difficult to conceive of the medical reality that their lack of pride and self-respect, shattered self-esteem, and dissolving communities will terminate their lives prematurely. We are, instead, exposed to quite a different health perspective, one that makes it difficult to grasp the powerful influence that these social and psychological forces exert over our individual health and well-being.

No television commercial has ever shown, nor could one ever show, a depressed, unemployed, undereducated steel worker holding his downcast son's hand on a rain-swept East Baltimore street, and then add simplistically—"If you have hypertension, see your doctor...We're fighting for your life." That message might ring a bit hollow. It might even drive more than a few of these men to the barricades instead of to their "doctors."

Perhaps the single greatest and cruelest myth permeating the health consciousness of modern America is the image of millions of happily ignorant, healthy workers employed by highly stressed business executives who sacrifice their lives on the altar of success. And the myth is reinforced by a variety of correlative beliefs. It is not, for example, one's community, sense of self-worth, and family life that are the major arbiters of life and death. Instead, mechanical factors, such as cholesterol, overweight, high blood pressure, and fatty diets are seen as the main culprits.

The fact is that both successful business executives *and* "happily ignorant workers" can suffer from chronic stress that will indeed put them at increased risk of dying prematurely from heart disease. Both are vulnerable to the types of ego assaults that occur in childhood, particularly as they relate to educational attainment. Both are vulnerable to the childhood stresses that can destroy one's potential to engage in real human dialogue. The only difference is that these types of problems occur at far greater rates among workers than among executives, and thus their death rates are commensurately higher.

HEALTH AND EDUCATION IN INDUSTRIAL AMERICA

The last chapter introduced data documenting the links between low educational attainment and an increased risk of disease and premature death. Among the myriad of health risks discussed, one of the more important was the increased vulnerability to cardiovascular disease, including heart attacks, hypertension, and stroke. In addition to the medical data itself, I alluded to the fact that there is also an increased risk of factors known to be associated with heart disease, including elevations in blood pressure and serum cholesterol, excessive weight, lack of exercise, and cigarette smoking. I also discussed those risk factors that co-vary with education, plus other social, economic, and psychological stressors that add "variance" to the equations. Any of these single factors could contribute to heart disease. Poverty and unemployment increasingly could rank as the most important.

Thus, it is obvious that identification of the precise linkages between low education and an increased risk of cardiovascular disease would have to take into account all of the extraneous factors that intervene between low education and the appearance of these diseases decades later. Indeed, I suggested that the very complexity of the linkages between education and premature death has made the discovery of "the crucial" underlying variables of shattered self-esteem, destruction of human dialogue, and increased loneliness quite difficult.

To help find the needles of loneliness and communicative disease in the middle of this multi-factorial haystack, additional studies need to be described. These include data on almost half a million men and women in major industrial settings. The people under investigation were all gainfully employed, many in high paying jobs, and all were in good health when the studies began.

As such, these studies help address many of the crucial questions about the links between educational attainment and vulnerability to premature death. They explicitly rule out the negative health consequences of factors that frequently co-vary with low education, such as unemployment, poverty, chronic disease, and pre-existing illness, because they involve populations where these factors either were not relevant or were precisely identified and controlled. They also implicitly control for other hidden factors, such as mental illness, severe disturbances in behavior, and chronic alcoholism that also co-vary with education, since the individuals under investigation were all functioning in jobs that would preclude these problems, or at least preclude severe manifestations of such problems.

These studies all lead to the same inescapable conclusion: In industrial settings where all of the risk factors that potentially interact with education are controlled, low educational attainment itself, linked to increased social isolation and loneliness, emerges as the single most important contributor to a person's vulnerability to heart disease and premature death.

In order to appreciate these prospective industrial studies, however, it might be helpful to briefly consider the historic antecedents that made them possible in the first place.

PROSPECTING FOR HEALTH IN MID-CENTURY AMERICA: THE INSURANCE MAN COMETH

In an age of sophisticated tax-deferred annuities, individual retirement accounts, and home computer modems that link one's financial portfolio to complex trading programs on Wall Street, the weekly home visits of the neighborhood insurance agent might seem like a quaint anachronism. Yet, in the industrial cities of my childhood, that agent was an institutionalized fixture. Each week, he faithfully came to our house (as well as to most of the other homes in the neighborhood) to collect 50 cents from my parents. Though in retrospect such visits might seem a bit macabre, the agent was insuring our parents against the catastrophic possibility that one of us might die. Nothing was deemed more terrible or dishonorable than to be faced with the death of a child without having the funds for a proper burial. Insuring children's lives was considered far more important than insuring adults.

Burial insurance was one of the legacies of the Great Depression, as well as an offshoot of realities about life and death among the working class before World War II. In large working class families, it was quite likely that one or more children would die before their parents.

In the post-war period, concerns about having money to bury children began to disappear, in large part because health scientists successfully eliminated the scourge of infectious and communicable diseases that once snuffed out youngsters' lives. The death of children became an increasingly rare event. In addition, the poverty of the Great Depression began to disappear, as World War II transformed the industrial cities into a golden age of abundant work. With faith and confidence restored, once defeated workers heaved a collective sigh of relief, and vowed to never be so vulnerable again. The workers began to unionize. In railroad yards, electrical shops, and dockyards, they organized to fight for what they considered fundamental human rights—a decent wage, an adequate pension, and health benefits for their families.

Rather than paying an agent 50 cents a week for burial insurance, these workers and their unions fought to create insurance packages that would become an integral part of their employment. Faced with catastrophic illness or sudden death, they wanted their families protected. Gradually, a new industrial alliance emerged, one in which workers and industrial managers came to share a common concern about workers' health.

Out of the poverty of the Great Depression, despair about ill health, and lack of money to pay for medical care, a new health insurance industry was born. Blue Cross and Blue Shield and other third party payers began to flourish. Yet, when corporate America began to sign on, they were forced to consider the health problems of their workers from a perspective quite different from that of the unions. For the first time in history, the costs of a worker's illnesses had to be factored into the costs of overall production. Concern about workers' health grew in importance because their illnesses and premature deaths became major cost items. Keeping workers healthy became less expensive than ignoring their illnesses.

The emergence of this new industrial health alliance prompted some of the more remarkable medical surveys ever conducted. Once corporate America began to share the economic burdens of their employees' health, it became vitally important to know more about the factors contributing to their catastrophic illnesses. In terms of major debilitating problems, such as cardiovascular disease, where the costs could rapidly escalate into tens of thousands of dollars for just one employee, it became essential to learn what could be done to reduce the incidence of such illnesses.

Large-scale industrial health screening surveys sprang up all across the United States, designed to ascertain what factors contributed to an employee's increased risk of disease and premature death. Particular emphasis was placed on cardiovascular disease, in part because this disease was one of the most costly, as well as the leading, cause of premature death.

These industrial surveys are particularly illuminating because they all involve large-scale prospective surveys of heart disease. They were conducted in widely varying geographic and industrial sectors all across the United States. In addition, the studies were conducted not by corporations, but by independent, university-based research teams. Since they include a wide spectrum of industrialized settings, they help to provide a representative picture of the links between education and health in mainstream corporate America.

"REACH OUT AND TOUCH SOMEONE"

Few corporations acted earlier, or in a more enlightened manner, than the American Telephone & Telegraph Company. AT&T helped lead the shift in corporate health consciousness, and pioneered many of the innovative health insurance programs offered to workers. It was, therefore, no historical accident that AT&T was one of the first major corporations in the United States to underwrite the costs of a major prospective study to evaluate the health of all its employees. Functioning at that time in a dual capacity as a quasi-private and quasi-governmentally sponsored public utility, AT&T was particularly sensitive to health and social trends within American society as a whole.

Before U.S. federal courts ordered the breakup of AT&T in 1984, "Ma Bell" was one of the largest corporations in the United States. Widely respected by the public-at-large for its efficiency, it was also highly regarded by its workers. Job turnover was relatively low and employer-employee relationships were a model that other corporations tried to imitate. For decades, the company operated without labor strife, with excellent job security, fringe benefits, and notable worker-management harmony. It also pioneered one of the more enlightened corporate medical service plans in the United States. Long before other corporations expressed concern for the health of their workers, AT&T executives acted on the assumption that protecting the health and safety of its employees was in the best interests of the corporation itself.

In a very real sense, the health problems of Ma Bell's workers mirrored the health problems of the nation as a whole. The corporation drew its employees from every state in the nation, and its work force represented a real cross-section of Main Street, U.S.A.

Indeed, by the late 1950s, Bell System executives were well aware that heart disease had emerged as the single most important health problem faced by company employees, now that various infectious and communicable diseases had been successfully controlled, and it had made intense efforts to curtail job-related accidents. Thousands of its employees were succumbing to heart disease in the prime of life, and the loss of the talents of these highly skilled, dedicated employees placed an enormous economic burden on the corporation. Premature heart disease and the appearance of crippling chronic diseases, such as debilitating stroke, began to drain the disability and health insurance programs established by the corporation.

By 1960, AT&T corporate executives knew that certain risk factors put a person at increased risk to develop coronary heart disease. Though the type of information published by Kitagawa and Hauser linking levels of educational attainment to heart disease was not yet available, numerous medical studies had identified other risk factors that appeared to increase a person's vulnerability to this disease.

Of all of the risk factors that troubled the directors of the corporation, however, none was more unsettling than a link between job stress and disease. By mid-century, a number of studies had suggested that employees who were competitive, hard working, or forced to work under unremitting pressure in order to accomplish corporate goals were particularly vulnerable to heart disease. These findings were especially worrisome because they implied that the very same traits that helped to make AT&T successful were also placing its employees at increased risk for debilitating health problems and even premature death.

When they first confronted this problem in 1962, AT&T's medical directors knew that the overall incidence of heart disease among its employees was no different than it was in the United States as a whole. Their primary concern, therefore, was not the discovery of some unusual lethal influence that could be attributed to corporate life inside AT&T itself. Rather, they hoped to identify specific physical, social, economic, or corporate stressors that might compound the health problems of its employees. Their goal was to identify these factors so that they might set up preventative programs to ameliorate the situation.

To help achieve this goal, the corporation enlisted the aid of medical investigators at the Cornell University Medical School. In cooperation with Bell System health officers, the Cornell medical team began to systematically examine the records of all 270,000 male employees of AT&T throughout the entire United States. Most of these employees had been hired in their early twenties and had spent their entire adult lives working for the Bell System. All had been in good health when they were originally hired, and all had been covered by comparable health benefits throughout their careers.

For several decades prior to this study, the Bell System had kept careful records on all of its employees, including detailed medical histories, social backgrounds, and positions within the company. Using this information as their initial database, the health team began to track the incidence of heart disease and premature death within the company. For five years, between 1962 and 1966, they monitored the health of all workers in the entire corporation, cross-correlating the incidence of heart disease and death with every known physical, social, and corporate variable that might be remotely linked to this problem. Among the hundreds of variables they tabulated was each employee's level of educational attainment.

In terms of educational attainment, the AT&T population they studied included three general groups:

Group 1: *183,000* men *without college degrees* who were hired as skilled workers, and remained so throughout their careers.

Group 2: *65,000* men *without college degrees* who, though first hired as skilled workers, nevertheless advanced to levels of management. Most advanced to foreman or supervisor, though some advanced to the highest management levels.

Group 3: *22,000* men *with college degrees* who were hired in their early twenties fully expecting to become managers. Many of these men had the same managerial responsibilities as those in Group 2. A larger percentage of this group, however, eventually reached the upper levels of management.

The investigators identified 6,347 employees who, between 1963 and 1965, had developed coronary heart disease that led either to total disability or to death. They found no relationship between many of the well-known psychological stressors that they had assumed might be linked to an increased risk of heart disease. They found no relationship, for example, between corporate mobility and an increased risk of heart disease. Those competitively striving workers who experienced the greatest number of job transfers and promotions actually had fewer cardiovascular problems than those individuals who stayed in the same job category throughout their careers.

Managing without a College Education:
College Education and Rates of Disabling CHD Events
in Bell System Mangement (Men, Aged 30-59)*

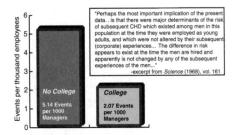

"Perhaps the most important implication of the present data. . is that there were major determinants of the risk of subsequent CHD which existed among men in this population at the time they were employed as young adults, and which were not altered by their subsequent (corporate) experiences... The difference in risk appears to exist at the time the men are hired and apparently is not changed by any of the subsequent experiences of the men..."
          -excerpt from *Science* (1968), vol. 161

*Age standardized to U.S. population, white males, aged 30-59; data representive of Bell System General Area Managers, 1963-65.

College Education and Rates of Disabling CHD
Events in Bell System Employees

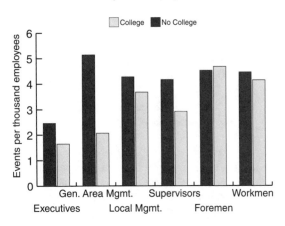

*Age standardized to U.S. population, white males, aged 30-59; data representive of Bell System male employees, 1963-65.

In contrast to the purported influence of the more conventional risk factors, the medical team uncovered a surprisingly strong influence— education. When all employees were grouped together, the investigators discovered significantly higher rates of heart disease at the lower echelons of the corporation. The lower down the corporate ladder, the greater the incidence of heart disease. When all events of disabling coronary heart disease were combined for the entire corporate population, the data were unequivocal. The higher a person moved up the corporate ladder, the lower the incidence of heart disease and sudden death. In general, workmen and foremen suffered from heart disease at a rate more than double that of executives.

Yet, when the data were analyzed further, it became clear that it really wasn't one's position in the company that really mattered. Rather, as shown in the following Table, it was one's level of educational attainment that seemed to be the lethal ingredient. When employees were categorized according to whether they went to college or not, a highly revealing pattern emerged. Education, rather than one's specific job in the company, emerged as the single most important risk factor contributing to overall disease patterns.

FIRST EVENTS OF DISABLING CORONARY HEART DISEASE AMONG BELL SYSTEM MEN AGED 30 TO 59; RATE PER THOUSAND, 1963-1965*

Corporate Function	All Men	No College	College
Executives	1.85*	2.46	1.65
General Area Mgers	2.85	5.14	2.07
Local Area Mgers	3.91	4.28	3.68
Supervisors	3.91	4.17	2.92
Foremen	4.52	4.53	4.68
Workmen	4.33	4.46	4.15

*Age standardized to U.S. population, white males, aged 30 to 59 (*Science,* vol 161, July 1968, p 241).

*1.85 for executives means that the incidence of coronary disease was 1.85 per thousand men. Thus, workmen, with a rate of 4.3, had more than double the rate of heart disease as executives.

The coronary disease rates for workmen (4.3 per thousand) was more than double the rate for executives (1.85). Yet, when these same individuals were divided into those who went to college and those who did not, a striking reversal of these trends was uncovered. General Area Managers who did not go to college had the greatest rates of heart disease in the entire company (5.14 per thousand). Though they ranked second highest in the company and were among the best paid of all employees, their disease rates ranked among the highest! Managers with the exact same salaries and job classifications who went to college had a coronary disease rate less than half that exhibited by General Area Managers who did not go to college.

The health effects of education held true for all ages and throughout all sections of the corporation. Both the incidence of death, as well as the first signs of heart disease (angina or heart attacks), were consistently higher for those men who did not go to college.

Disability and Death from Coronary Heart Disease: Relationships with Education Level and Age*

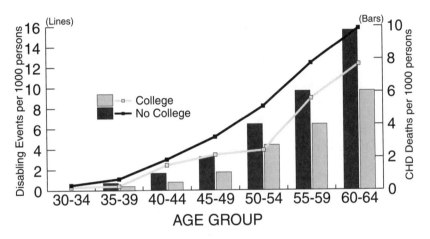

*Bell System - male employees

The health team was particularly struck by the extremely high death rates for some of the company's best-paid employees. These were their top executives, men who differed from other executives in the same job classifications by educational attainment alone. As noted earlier, the psychological stress associated with increased managerial responsibility did not lead to increased risk of heart disease. Quite the contrary. The Cornell medical team found significantly less heart disease as managerial responsibility increased.

What made the crucial health difference inside the corporate boardroom was education. The top executives with less education were clearly as bright and as capable as those who had gone to college. The corporation simply could not afford to promote men to jobs of executive responsibility who were incompetent. If not differences in native intelligence, then what was it about lower levels of educational attainment that put these executives at greater risk? The health survey authors could not come up with a definite answer. They did sense, however, that the central problem had to be very deep and of a long-standing nature, one that troubled these men to such an extent that success later in life did not seem to matter. There was something about lower levels of educational attainment that had lethal consequences far beyond what anyone could have possibly imagined.

Unable to identify the specific lethal ingredient, they concluded their pioneering study with a more general warning:

"Perhaps the most important implication of the present data from the Bell System is that there were major determinants of the risk of subsequent coronary heart disease which existed among the men in this population at the time they were employed as young adults, and which were not greatly altered by their subsequent (corporate) experiences...The difference in risk appears to exist at the time the men are hired and apparently is not greatly changed by any of the subsequent experiences of the men."

THE CHICAGO HEART STUDIES

At almost the same time AT&T began its studies, a number of other major U.S. corporations similarly became concerned about the health of their employees. Like the Bell System, these corporations also were increasingly aware of the importance of heart disease at mid-century. Three huge, major, but separate industrial studies were undertaken in the Chicago area in the 1950's and 1960's:

1. The Chicago Peoples Gas Company
2. The Western Electric Study: The Hawthorne Works
3. The Chicago Heart Association Detection Project in Industry

Though each of these studies differed in certain respects, they all arrived at similar conclusions: Each found a significant inverse relationship between educational attainment and vulnerability to cardiovascular disease and sudden cardiac death. In studies that involved almost 100,000 employed individuals who were followed for decades, the medical investigators discovered that the death rates from heart disease of workers who did not graduate from high school were more than double those of college graduates. All of the standard risk factors known to predispose a person to heart disease—including smoking, increased weight, elevated blood pressure, and electrocardiographic abnormalities—

were also inversely related to education. As education declined, the incidence of these risk factors increased. Yet, the most revealing of all findings was the fact that even when all of these other risk factors were controlled statistically and made equal across all groups, educational level, by itself, still had a powerful, independent influence in determining who lived and who died.

Typical of this group of studies is the one conducted by the Northwestern Medical School health team. Involving more than 100 firms in the Chicago area, it was called the Chicago Heart Association Detection Project in Industry. For five years, between 1967 and early 1973, the research team recruited almost 40,000 young adult and middle-aged men and women, both white and black, from industries all around the greater Chicago area. After collecting all of the normal risk factor data for heart disease, these investigators also divided their volunteers into four groups:

— Not a high school graduate
— High school graduate
— Some college
— College graduate

Again, educational level was correlated with a consistent and highly significant difference in all the standard risk factors for heart disease, even before their studies began. Those people with less education, for example, smoked more, were heavier, and showed far more electrocardiographic abnormalities and higher blood pressure readings than those with higher levels of education.

The next Table shows the percentage of volunteers whose blood pressure exceeded the criteria for hypertension at the beginning of the study. None of these men and women was taking any medicines for high blood pressure when these measurements were first recorded.

PERCENT WITH HIGH BLOOD PRESSURE (SBP>160 OR DBP>95) BY LEVEL OF EDUCATION - WHITES AND BLACKS - CHICAGO HEART ASSOCIATION DETECTION PROJECT IN INDUSTRY - 1967-1973 - (EXCLUDING HYPERTENSIVES ON DRUG TREATMENTS)

| | WHITE | | BLACK | |
	MALES	FEMALES	MALES	FEMALES
AGES 25-44				
EDUCATION				
1+	18.4	8.8	23.7	10.5
2+	14.5	6.0	17.7	6.7
3+	12.8	4.1	14.4	6.0
4+	10.5	3.7	12.8	7.9
AGES 45-64				
EDUCATION				
1	32.9	23.7	44.6	29.4
2	31.2	19.8	40.8	31.5
3	26.9	15.1	31.6	22.9
4	19.7	15.1	29.4	26.7

1 = not a high school graduate; 2 = high school graduate;
3 = some college; 4 = college graduate.

As was the case in virtually every other study, men had higher blood pressure readings than women, older workers had higher pressures than those who were younger, and blacks had higher levels of blood pressure than whites. Yet, even when the usual "co-variates" of blood pressure, such as relative weight, age, and heart rate, were statistically eliminated from the equations (and thus made equal for all different educational levels), there were still highly significant differences in blood pressure due specifically to educational levels alone.

More revealing was the incidence of mortality when this population was re-examined in 1978, five years later. There was a strong relationship between education and mortality from coronary heart disease, cardiovascular disease, and all other causes of death. Men with the least education had death rates two to three times higher than those with the most education.

Attempting to make sense out of this stunning influence of education on the cardiovascular health, the medical team at Northwestern concluded:

"One implication of these findings is that progressive improvement in educational and socioeconomic level of the population can contribute to control of the contemporary epidemic of hypertensive and atherosclerotic cardiovascular diseases. This inference for the modern period in the industrialized countries is in keeping with lessons learned in regard to control of earlier epidemics of nutritional and infectious diseases."[131]

HEART DISEASE IN THE
IRISH INDUSTRIAL WORKPLACE

Similar links between level of educational attainment and heart disease in employed individuals have been confirmed in England, Germany, France, Italy, and Japan, as well as in Scandinavian countries. To show the universality of the influence of educational level on the incidence of heart disease in virtually all industrialized societies, I should at least make brief mention of two studies that have uncovered findings similar to those observed in the United States.

One was coordinated by a group of Irish cardiologists, and reported in the *Irish Medical Journal* in 1984. Like their American colleagues, these medical scientists screened a large number of men (1,583) working in two major commercial enterprises in the Republic of Ireland. Unlike the working population in the United States, the Irish workers shared a common cultural and ethnic heritage. In addition, the wage differentials and living standards of the workers, regardless of educational levels, were not nearly as great in Ireland as they were in the United States. Steeply rising graduated income tax rates and a variety of nationally funded social services, including a national health service, create similar living conditions for persons of different educational levels in Ireland.[132]

As was true in the American studies, when the Irish investigators began their study in 1978, they gathered a large amount of medical and social data on workers at two major industrial work sites. They then subdivided the 1,583 men involved in their study into three distinct educational groups:

Group 1: 537 men who had completed primary education only.
Group 2: 821 men who had completed secondary education (high school).
Group 3: 202 men who had completed university or higher technical education.

As was true in the U.S. surveys, virtually every risk factor that could potentially contribute to heart disease showed a graded inverse relationship to education. As educational level decreased, the incidence of cigarette smoking, high blood pressure, overweight, and elevated plasma cholesterol increased. As in the findings of the Chicago heart studies, there was also a marked increase in electrocardiographic abnormalities as educational level decreased.

More intriguing was the fact that these sharp increases persisted even after all of the other risk factors that initially differentiated the groups (e.g., smoking, weight, blood pressure, etc) were statistically controlled. They still found double the incidence of heart disease in men with the least education. In essence, the Irish medical team had uncovered the same influence of educational level as their American colleagues, even when all other known risk factors were eliminated from the equations.

Yet, these investigators went one step further. They uncovered the fact that educational level had as great an impact on the incidence of heart disease as did all the other risk factors combined! The following figure shows that when those workers with the least education were compared to those who were university graduates, they had almost four times the amount of cardiovascular disease. In the *Irish Medical Journal*, the medical team summarized their findings as follows:

"The results confirm a strong association between education and cardiovascular disease which is not entirely explained by differences in age, cigarette smoking, diastolic blood pressure, weight, or plasma cholesterol. Indeed, on the basis of the logistic analysis, the independent effect of education on cardiovascular disease is as strong as the effects of smoking, blood pressure, weight, and cholesterol combined." (emphasis added) [133]

Perhaps one last international study might suffice to emphasize the universality of these relationships. In 1999, Sarah Wamlala of the Karolinska Institute, along with a number of Swedish and American colleagues, reported that women with low educational attainment in virtually all industrialized countries were twice as likely to develop coronary heart disease as women with a college education. The investigators noted that women with low levels of education tended to exhibit higher levels of job stress, were more socially isolated, and engaged in life style behaviors such as smoking, lack of exercise, increased weight, and higher levels of serum cholesterol.

Wamala suggested that the doubling of the incidence of coronary heart disease might be due to either the increased incidence of risk factors, or even more intriguingly, to the fact that increased psychological stress might influence physiological systems, putting these women at increased risk regardless of their health behaviors.

EDUCATION AND THE HIGH-TECH
MISSISSIPPI OF MODERN LIFE

At this juncture, more than a few readers no doubt will be growing weary of health statistics, in spite of the fact that only the minimum of data has been provided to prove the direct relationship between school failure and premature death from heart disease. And at risk of eliciting a few additional groans, more health statistics remain to be added to make the bridging links between communicative disease and educational failure, social isolation, and premature death. Still, some readers might be tempted to sympathize with the skepticism expressed by Mark Twain a century ago, when he said: "There are lies, damned lies, and then there are statistics."

Yet, I have a sneaking suspicion that the magnitude and consistency of the health statistics reviewed thus far would have jarred even Mark Twain. He was, after all, no admirer of the American school system. He freed his beloved Huck Finn from the shackles of the Hannibal school system in order to have him set sail on the mighty Mississippi.

Although there were life-threatening dangers around every river bend, Mark Twain obviously believed that it was the Hannibal classroom that threatened to constrict and suffocate Huck's life. It was the Mississippi River that offered him freedom, allowing him to grow and breathe and learn. Dropping out of school was a way to enrich and save Huck's life, not terminate it prematurely. Far from socially isolating and humiliating him, dropping out of school permitted Huck to develop friendships and embrace life in a way not possible within the Hannibal school system itself.

It is somewhat sad to reflect on the fact that Mark Twain could no longer tell his story of Huck Finn within the context of modern life. The statistics linking low educational attainment to major increases in the risk of premature death is a stark reminder of just how much has changed since Huck set sail on the Mississippi a century ago. The statistics help make it clear that the high-tech Mississippi's of modern life now exact a terrible toll on school dropouts. It is one that will become even more lethal for twenty-first century Huck Finns who seek to escape the confinement of their classrooms. They will not have Huck's option—to live and work and enjoy life within a labor-intensive society that did not rely on technology and advanced education.

HEART DISEASE IN COAL MINE HOLLOW

To demonstrate how much has changed since Huck Finn set sail on the Mississippi a century earlier, I cite a three-part series that appeared in the mid-April 1999 editions of the *Baltimore Sun*—a lengthy report on the life and work of a Nobel laureate, just retired from The Johns Hopkins Medical School, who had won the Nobel prize for his work on splicing the gene. The series focused not only on his brilliant research career, but on the emotional struggles his children had endured, and this physician's courageous efforts to make amends and begin the painful process of real dialogue with his family. The article noted in part:

No chasm in "their" family was wider than that between the Nobel laureate father and his oldest son, now 37, a stocky man with flowing brown hair and a gallery of tattoos. When this son was a teenager, getting in trouble and dropping out of school, his father banished him from the house. He seemed to swerve as sharply as he could from the intellectual path his father had chosen, working first as a landscaper, then in a slaughterhouse. Today, this son lives far from any neighbors, in an old school-house he restored in the shadow of Virginia's Blue Ridge mountains.

Three years ago while helping his father move a heavy springhouse door, the son clutched his chest. "I feel faint," he said. "I've got to sit down." The father saw immediately that his son was having a heart attack. It was the first of three heart attacks within a brief period of time. Chronically ill, he can't do strenuous work or hold a regular job. Instead, he does occasional chores or yard work for family members.

Now when he visits his son's farm in Coal Mine Hollow, the father goes fishing with his son, or works on his house, or helps pick beans from the garden. The son once ignored his father's accomplishments, but now takes pride in them. By degrees, the years have taught them both forgiveness. "We get along great now," the son says. "We're doing all the stuff now that I wished we had done when I was a kid."

All of the elements are there: lack of dialogue in childhood, educational failure in spite of obvious high intelligence, social isolation, low self-esteem, loneliness, chronic illness, increased cardiac risk factors, and serious premature heart disease. Coal Mine Hollow in the Blue Ridge Mountains was clearly a lonely reflection of the high-tech Mississippi's of modern life. It exacted a toll that Huck Finn never had to pay when he escaped to his beloved river a century earlier.

THE LUNCH BOX THAT CARRIES
A MIND TO THE CLASSROOM

To the casual observer of the educational scene, it sometimes seems as if both medicine and education view a child's body as little more than a lunch box that carries a mind to the classroom. Virtually every educator has absorbed the lessons implicitly and explicitly taught by modern medicine and modern psychiatry. In the American school, the "mind"—the fountainhead of all human "intelligence"—is exercised in the classroom. The body is exercised in the school gymnasium and on the playground.

And so it goes. Everything that occurs in the classroom, including talking, is seen as an attribute of the mind, while everything that occurs on the playground is designed to exercise the body. Virtually every educator has accepted the fundamental division between body and mind first enunciated by Rene Descartes in the 16th century. Virtually every educator uncritically assumes that the mind and the body are two separate and distinct entities, which co-exist, sometimes peacefully and sometimes not so peacefully, within the confines of the same skin. IQ scores, SAT scores, California Achievement scores—all seem to have nothing to do with the beating of the human heart. The heart is a pump, it's believed, and a part of the body-machine, while SAT scores and IQ are attributes of one's "mental abilities."

Without recognizing it, most educators and physicians share the assumptions that human beings are made up of two separate and distinct components—the Cartesian split that led to what I label the birth of *heartless minds and mindless hearts.* Within this philosophical framework, human dialogue is assumed to be an attribute of the human mind, and therefore is assumed to have little to do with success or failure in school itself. It leaves the educational system ill-equipped to adequately respond to children who come to school already struggling to engage in meaningful, heartfelt dialogue. It leaves the educational system blind as well to the ultimate heartbreaking consequences of failure within the system itself.

The interval between one's experiences in school and the appearance of overt signs of heart disease—two, three, four, or five decades later—does little to alter these general perceptions. "Minds" and "hearts" appear to have little in common. Human dialogue appears to be "mental," and thus seems to have little to do with the functioning of the human heart.

To help clarify these linkages, however, several additional medical studies need to be reviewed. In a very real sense, these studies form a conceptual bridge that permits one to cross over to a very different world—from a medical and educational world that believes in mindless hearts and heartless minds, to a new educational system—one that understands and speaks the language of the human heart.

TYPE A BEHAVIOR:
THE WESTERN COLLABORATIVE
GROUP HEART STUDIES

While many of the studies described in the last two chapters probably would not be familiar to this book's average reader, such is not the case for a long-term study with the imposing title, "The Western Collaborative Group Heart Study." For that study added a new phrase to everyday discourse, the "Type A" behavior pattern. "I'm just a Type A personality" is now commonly used in everyday conversations by patients who see me in cardiac rehabilitation. The "Western Collaborative Study" first suggested that a specific behavioral pattern, labeled as "Type A Behavior," could be linked to an increased risk of coronary heart disease. Popularized by the 1974 book, *Type A Behavior and Your Heart*, written by two San Francisco cardiologists, Meyer Friedman and Ray Rosenman, the concept seems to make a great deal of intuitive sense to patients suffering from heart disease.

In the mid-1950's, Drs. Friedman and Rosenman were treating patients with heart disease in the San Francisco area. As relatively young cardiologists, they wondered whether the feelings and thoughts of their heart patients had any bearing on the development of coronary heart disease. Their concerns were first awakened when they monitored the dietary habits of a small group of executive men and their wives. They hoped to find out whether differences in diet could account for the men's vulnerability to heart disease. During their studies, they discovered that the amount of cholesterol consumed by the men was almost identical to that of their wives. Yet, the men were far more vulnerable to heart disease. Differences in diet could not account for this peculiar vulnerability.

Surprised by this finding, the investigators were jarred even further when one of the wives commented at the end of their study: "If you really want to know what is going to give our husbands heart attacks, I'll tell you. It's stress....the stress they have to face in their businesses, day in, day out. Why, when my husband comes home at night, it takes at least one martini just to unclench his jaws." [134]

After hearing comments of this sort, Drs. Friedman and Rosenman started paying closer attention to the role of stress in heart disease. They began to observe that a certain cluster of behavioral traits, including excessive competitive drive, a sense of time urgency, repressed hostility, and rapid and forceful speech patterns, all seemed to be linked to increased vulnerability to heart disease. They coined the term Type A to describe these traits. Type A persons were contrasted with Type B individuals, who tended to be more relaxed and less hurried, who spoke in a more relaxed manner, and who were far less likely to develop heart disease.

Based on their observations of clinic patients, Drs. Friedman and Rosenman launched a long-term prospective study on heart disease in 1960. They hoped to ascertain whether the various stresses and behavioral factors they had observed in their clinic patients, including Type A behavior, could be linked to a person's risk of developing heart disease. To carry out this study, they recruited a large group of men (3,524) between the ages of 39-59 then working in eleven major industrial settings on the West Coast. Each participant was initially healthy and free of heart disease. All were given exhaustive physical and psychosocial evaluations and then re-examined annually.

Two features differentiated this study from other prospective studies. The first was the emphasis placed on more carefully analyzing various blood chemistry factors known to be linked to heart disease (e.g., lipoprotein, serum levels of cholesterol, triglycerides, and B-lipoproteins). The second was a detailed examination of various behavioral factors that the researchers suspected might be linked to this disease.

For more than twenty years, Drs. Friedman and Rosenman coordinated the efforts of a group of research scientists who tracked these men. As with all the other prospective studies, more and more men began to succumb to heart disease as time passed. And as was true in other studies, all those men who smoked at the beginning of the study, or who had elevated blood pressure and elevations in various blood factors, were found to be at greater risk for developing heart disease.

Yet, what catapulted these studies into the international limelight was Dr. Rosenman's and Friedman's convincing documentation that the Type A behavior pattern was also linked to the development of heart disease. These links could not be explained by any of the other conventional risk factors, and thus appeared to have an independent influence on a person's vulnerability to heart disease. Two decades later, after additional research, a panel of experts assembled by the National Heart, Lung and Blood

Institute in 1977 accepted the importance of Type A behavior as an independent risk factor in heart disease.[135]

Unfortunately, when the Type A behavior pattern first came to the attention of the public, the automatic assumption was made that it characterized well-educated but stressed business executives. It seemed unlikely that those with less education would be "aggressive, ambitious, competitive, or senselessly driven to accomplish more and more in less time."

Instead, the behavioral descriptions of Type A seemed to fit the public's stereotypical image of stressed business executives sacrificing their lives to the gods of economic success. Aggressive, ambitious, competitive, and bound-up by an overwhelming sense of time urgency— the behavioral pattern hardly seemed to fit the stereotypical images usually conjured up for those with less education. The executives Drs. Friedman and Rosenman saw in their clinical practice reinforced this perception and served to further obscure one of the most important factors contributing to this behavioral pattern.

Dr. Friedman's and Rosenman's prospective data did not indicate that successful college-educated business executives were the majority of Type A people suffering from heart disease. Quite the contrary. For as was true of all the other prospective studies on heart disease, the Western Collaborative Study readily confirmed that educational level played a central role.

In 1975, fifteen years after their studies began, Dr. Rosenman and his colleagues alluded to this reality when they reported that education had a highly significant inverse effect on vulnerability to heart disease. Those workers with high school degrees or less had a significantly greater incidence of heart disease than college graduates. Men who were 39-49 years of age when their study began, and had a high school education or less, had a rate of heart disease per thousand of 9.4, compared to a rate of 6.0 per thousand for college graduates. For those who were originally between the ages of 50-59, the comparative rates were 16.8 and 9.1 respectively.

After fifteen years of continuous study, the investigators found that the rates of heart disease were actually 50 percent lower for college graduates, most of whom were in managerial positions. These facts failed to support the common opinion that executives were more likely than workers to exhibit Type A behavioral patterns.[136]

In an intriguing article written in 1997 entitled "Social Support: The Supreme Stress Stopper," Dr. Paul Rosch, editor of *Health and Stress:*

The Newsletter of The American Institute of Stress, quoted Dr. Rosenman as follows:

"After 40 years of observing and treating thousands of patients, and doing all of the studies, I believe that what's underneath the inappropriate competitiveness of Type A's is a deep-seated insecurity. I never would have said that before, but I keep coming back to it. It's different from anxiety in the usual sense, because Type A's are not people who retreat. They constantly compete because it helps them suppress the insecurity they're afraid others will sense. 'If I felt this way, how would I cover it up? I'd distract myself, go faster and faster, and win over everybody else. I'd look at everyone as a threat, because they might expose me.' " (p. 7)

TYPE A BEHAVIOR AND LOW SELF-ESTEEM

Of all the aspects of Type A behavior, none was more important than the speech patterns of these individuals. Pressured, intense, rapid, and breathless speech patterns, as well as the habit of interrupting others in dialogue, were the chief indicators of Type A behavior. The speech patterns were also the strongest predictor of vulnerability to coronary heart disease. And, as already noted, while such patterns were exhibited in some business executives, they occurred far more frequently in individuals with less educational attainment. There was something about the combination of low educational attainment and increased risk of Type A behavior that put a person at high risk of developing premature heart disease.

As the years went by, the California medical team began to address a new concern. Though their research efforts were initially geared toward proving that the Type A behavioral pattern was linked to increased risk of heart disease, Drs. Friedman's and Rosenman's interests began to shift toward a new concern. Could Type A types be treated? Could people learn to modify their behavior and thus reduce the risk of developing coronary heart disease?

The answer was soon apparent. Studies confirmed that people could learn to modify this behavioral pattern—by altering, in particular, the way they spoke to others. Studies also confirmed that the modifications could significantly reduce the risk of coronary heart disease.

As efforts to modify Type A behavioral patterns intensified, questions about the origins of the problem also came into sharper focus. In 1985, Dr. Friedman addressed this problem explicitly when he asked:

"Why do Type A persons struggle so ceaselessly and so senselessly to accomplish more and more things or involve themselves in more and more events? Sometimes it is because their position truly demands superhuman efforts, but rarely. Usually they struggle because they suffer from a hidden lack of self-esteem....It may in itself be largely responsible for other aspects of Type A behavior." [137]

Though these cardiologists tended to downplay the interlocking connection of low educational attainment and an increase in Type A behavior, they readily acknowledged that a person's school experiences had something to do with the origins of Type A behavior. They noted, for example, that the educational system was structured to encourage Type A behavior, as well as to endanger a person's self-worth. In their book, *Treating Type A Behavior and Your Heart*, Dr. Friedman and Diane Ulmer asserted: [138]

"This (academic competition) begins when a child enters secondary school and is forced to judge himself against others. 'Why can't I get A's too?' such a child begins to ask, thus beginning a secret self-flagellation that may continue for the rest of his life. It is probable that this practice is the most common cause of damage to self-esteem that male Type A's can suffer at secondary school, college, or graduate school... It seems clear that relative inferiority in mental activities is far more damaging than relative inferiority in athletic matters." [139]

In summary, after decades of painstaking research on coronary heart disease, physicians conducting the Western Collaborative Study arrived at conclusions quite similar to other investigators. Education made a huge difference in a person's long-term cardiovascular health. The studies went beyond this general finding, however, when they linked vulnerability to coronary heart disease to a specific behavioral pattern they called Type A. Certain people behaved in ways that significantly increased their risk of developing heart disease.

Implicit in their findings was the added reality that Type A behavior patterns were usually established in childhood, and that the behavioral pattern itself was fueled by a pervasive sense of low self-esteem. Experiences a person had in school decades before the appearance of heart problems seemed to be particularly formative for the Type A person.

THE SEARING OF THE HUMAN SOUL

In many ways, Clarence F would be the last person in the world who would fit the public's stereotypical image of the Type A personality. Far from being a stressed business executive, Clarence was at the bottom of the economic ladder, and down on his luck.

A six-foot, 240-pound, 36-year-old black male, Clarence had been referred to our clinic by a neurosurgeon after an operation (lumbar laminectomy and disc excision) failed to relieve severe lower back pain caused by several crushed and ruptured discs. He first felt severe back pain while lifting heavy metal castings onto a tray at a local steel foundry. Prior to this accident, he reported that he had been relatively healthy, except, as he noted rather matter-of-factly, "for his diabetes, which flared up from time to time."

Clarence had been employed for 15 years at the same steel mill, virtually without missing a day of work, before becoming totally disabled with pain. A corporate review of his disability claim, however, led to the determination that his medical problems were not work-related, and thus it was ruled that he was ineligible for compensation. After 15 years of steady employment at the steel mill, he had to drastically scale down his standard of living, reduced as he was to financial dependency on a monthly welfare check.

We saw Clarence in our clinic each week for more than seven months, not only to help him learn ways to cope with his pain, but also to control severe hypertension, which was first discovered while he was at our facility. Efforts were also made to help him lower his weight and to curtail his consumption of alcohol (reported as two-to-three beers each day), both of which were seriously compounding his problems with diabetes and hypertension. Though a standard drug regimen had lowered his blood pressure, Clarence periodically stopped taking his medicines, complaining that they interfered with his sex life and made him feel sluggish and depressed.

His parents had separated when he was 10, and he had lived with his father and brother ever since. He described his brother as an "alcoholic who would never live past forty." Several months after he began therapy, his 64-year-old father died after a prolonged struggle with heart disease. "Worked all his life at a chemical factory and he died just before retirement," Clarence noted with a slight smile that muted the grieved anguish of his message: "So maybe my back is the only smart part of me. What's the sense of working yourself to death?"

In an effort to train for a job that would require less physical exertion, Clarence followed our advice and enrolled in an evening program at an electronics school. He had been particularly proud of the fact that he was the first one in his family to ever graduate from high school and he thought electronics would be an interesting field—one that he could work at in spite of his back pain. He greeted our suggestions enthusiastically, though he was anxious about the difficulties he might experience in a technical school.

During one particular session with us, his blood pressure was found to be significantly elevated. He had abruptly stopped taking his blood pressure medications several days earlier, and his heart was beating over 90 beats per minute. Clarence seemed more depressed and agitated than usual and he spoke even more rapidly, intensely and breathlessly than usual. During the course of therapy, the nurse practitioner had repeatedly pointed out to him that his habit of speaking rapidly and breathlessly contributed to the marked surges in his blood pressure when he talked.

Several years before Clarence came to our clinic, we had observed that whenever a person speaks, there is usually an immediate and significant rise in blood pressure and heart rate. Subsequent studies had led us to observe that the rapid, and breathless, speech patterns of patients like Clarence caused significantly greater elevations in blood pressure than slower rates of speech. Slowing down the rate of speech and teaching patients to breathe deeply while talking could help them lower blood pressure dramatically, especially when it was elevated into hypertensive ranges.

These observations were intriguing because they helped clarify Dr. Friedman's and Dr. Rosenman's earlier findings that had linked Type A behavior patterns to sharply increased risks for coronary atherosclerosis and heart attacks. Type A people tend to speak rapidly and intensely and they frequently interrupt others during conversation. Without the aid of the new computer technology when they began their studies, Drs. Friedman and Rosenman were unable to detect the powerful links between talking and blood pressure reactivity. They assumed that speech patterns were part of a behavior pattern linked to increased risk of heart disease, but not hypertension. Our subsequent findings of major blood pressure changes during rapid speech led us to suspect that this trait might be the primary cause of cardiovascular difficulties, rather than merely one of many behavioral traits linked to heart disease.

When reminded to speak more slowly and to breathe regularly, Clarence would usually comply by self-consciously gulping a deep breath of air before reverting to his usual pattern of speech. Showing him minute-to-minute computer displays of his own blood pressure had long ago convinced him, at least intellectually, of the links between his speech patterns and dangerous elevations in his blood pressure. During this session, however, he talked incessantly, in spite of numerous reminders to breathe.

It had been a particularly trying month for him. On top of all his other problems, Clarence was unfortunately floundering badly in school, in spite of his efforts to keep up. What had started out as a well-intentioned effort to open up new career opportunities had unfortunately backfired. In spite of his obvious intelligence, Clarence had reacted to his difficulties at school with a great deal of self-recrimination and humiliation.

"My past schooling was a joke," he noted while bending his head in shame and looking away from the nurse. "Most people in the class ate that test up last night—I just never had the math in school to cope with all these formulas, and I don't have a prayer of passing."

He had taken his first mid-term in electronics the previous night, and his blood-shot eyes suggested that the experience had been particularly devastating. As he rambled on about his sense of intellectual inferiority, the nurse again reminded him to speak more slowly and to breathe deeply. Again, Clarence resisted her advice, and this time angrily blurted out echoes of the torment he had felt all his life.

"What are you trying to do to me, anyhow? Get me to talk like a dumb nigger? Everyone knows that folks that talk slow ain't very smart. Shit, I may be down, but I'm not a dumb nigger and I'm not going to talk like one."

Clarence's blood pressure skyrocketed as he bared his soul, ashamed and overwhelmed by the terror of his own self-doubt and the fear that he might no longer be able to cope. He had been seared so deeply with a sense of intellectual inferiority that he had acquainted rapid speech with intelligence! It was his deepest cry of anguish from the language of a broken-hearted soul. Trapped in a black body, in a world that had taught him that the color of his skin had a great deal to do with intelligence, Clarence had been totally convinced: "Only dumb niggers talk slow."

THE HEALTH INSURANCE PLAN
OF GREATER NEW YORK

Of all the long term prospective studies linking heart disease to education, none are more remarkable than the one conducted by a research team working for the Health Insurance Plan of Greater New York. Since 1961, a health team, directed by Drs. William Ruberman, Eve Weinblatt, and Judith Goldberg has been tracking and systematically documenting the relationships between low educational attainment, social isolation, and increased vulnerability to sudden cardiac death.

Team members inadvertently came upon these relationships while evaluating certain puzzling health trends in the survival rates of coronary care patients insured by their corporation. When they compared survival rates in the 1960's with comparable data for similar populations in the 1970's, they discovered the disconcerting fact that there had been little improvement in the chances of long-term survival after a person had suffered a heart attack.

In spite of vast expenditures of research funds and tremendous advances in the understanding of heart disease between 1960 and 1970, a patient's chances of long-term survival after a heart attack had not improved significantly. Though major technical advances had been made in hospital coronary care and cardiovascular surgery, these developments had not contributed to a significant overall improvement in a patient's chances for long-term survival once released from the hospital.

If a patient was fortunate enough to survive a heart attack until he reached the hospital, then his or her chances of surviving while in the hospital were quite good. In-hospital survival rates of heart patients had risen dramatically after the introduction of specialized coronary care units in the early 1960s. What had not changed, however, was the chance of surviving after release from the hospital. Patients with heart attacks were still dying at rates far in excess of anything that seemed clinically reasonable.

In light of the strides that had been made in the development of medicines to help regulate heartbeat and blood pressure, and the increase in knowledge about heart disease, this lack of improvement in survival rates was troubling. In 1961, the New York medical team began to examine the causes of this problem, setting out on a research journey that was to last more than two decades.

Drs. Ruberman and his colleagues first raised questions about the long-term survival of heart patients while analyzing the health patterns of 120,000 men, 35 to 74 years of age, who were members of a prepaid health insurance plan called The Health Insurance Plan (HIP) of Greater New York. The men in the HIP of New York were by no means socio-economic dropouts at the bottom of society. Rather, these men were all participants of a prepaid health insurance plan and therefore had the economic means to support such insurance. Similar to other prospective studies, all the men were healthy when they first joined the plan. Over the years, however, as was true of other prospective studies, some of the members of this population succumbed to serious medical problems that included heart disease.

The investigators were particularly intrigued by the multitude of health problems associated with heart disease. As was true throughout the United States, heart disease was the single most important health problem faced by the members of their insurance plan. The economic costs of certain catastrophic side-effects of heart disease, including stroke, total disability, secondary organ damage, and sudden death, had created an enormous economic strain on the prepaid health plan.

They were initially interested in obtaining more information about the types of decisions coronary care patients in the HIP program made after surviving a heart attack. It seemed quite likely that such decisions might influence the course of their recovery as well as their chances for long-term survival. Did men who decided to return to work, for example, have a better chance of surviving long-term than those who opted to take early retirement? Did certain psychological responses to a heart attack, such as depression, make men more vulnerable to a recurrent heart attack, and thus put them at increased risk for debilitating chronic diseases or even sudden death? Answers to questions of this sort were particularly urgent since the long-term health of all the participant members determined the economic viability of the prepaid Insurance Plan.

Though the investigators initially focused their attention on the well-known risk factors linked to long-term survival, they quickly uncovered a curious phenomenon they had not anticipated. It was not depression, nor decisions about work, nor any of a large number of conventional psychological and social factors that seemed to influence survival after a heart attack. Other than the extent of physical damage to the heart muscle itself, the strongest predictor of a person's long-term survival after a heart attack was the patient's educational level. They discovered that educational level—quite independent of all other well-known physical risk factors for heart disease—had a powerful influence in determining who lived and who died in the five years following a heart attack.

They compared two groups of men with different levels of education who suffered comparable damage to their hearts and found that there was a significant difference in the incidence of sudden cardiac death. *Death rates for men with less education were triple* those who had attained higher levels of education. Frankly surprised by this finding, the HIP research team probed deeper.

Between 1972 and 1975, they identified 1,739 men in the prepaid health insurance program who had had a confirmed heart attack and been fortunate enough to survive it. They conducted in-depth interviews with each of these men soon after they were released from the hospital. They also performed detailed physical examinations and ordered comprehensive laboratory examinations on each of the survivors. As part of their medical evaluation, each patient was given a standard electrocardiographic examination, and was monitored continuously for an hour to check for abnormal heart rhythms. Of the 1,739 heart patients included in the study, 462 had exhibited abnormal heart beats during their one-hour monitoring period.

In 1976, the team reported their findings in the *New England Journal of Medicine*. Two hundred and eight (208) deaths had occurred among the 1,739 men they had been following. Of these, 85 were classified as sudden cardiac deaths. During a three-year follow-up period, the incidence of sudden death among the men exhibiting these abnormal heart beats was more than triple those without abnormal heart beats. This observation confirmed what cardiologists had already suspected. The existence of abnormal heart rhythms after a heart attack was a significant risk factor for sudden death. Yet, something else quite unexpectedly showed up in their statistics. The simultaneous existence of low education, along with the occurrence of these abnormal heart rhythms, proved to be a <u>particularly lethal combination.</u>

In order to evaluate the unexpected association between the appearance of these abnormal heart rhythms and educational levels, the research team exhaustively examined every factor that could have influenced these findings. Race, religion, physical status, marital status, place of birth, work status, occupation, alcohol and/or coffee consumption, smoking, and height-to-weight ratios, were all examined. None of these factors, <u>with the sole exception of education</u>, helped to identify the men at high risk for sudden death.

The relationship was so striking that it was initially quite difficult to believe. Men with less than eight years of education, who exhibited abnormal heart beats, had a *three-times greater risk* of dying from sudden coronary death than men with more education who exhibited the exact same abnormal heart beats! The effect of low educational levels appeared almost immediately after the heart patients were released from the hospital. Men with low educational levels were dying at unusually high rates as soon as they were released from the hospital, and the difference grew more apparent the longer the study continued. Summarizing the results of their study, Dr. Ruberman and his colleagues noted:

"Among those demonstrating the complex beats, the sudden coronary mortality of the low education men is much higher than the better educated regardless of whether their disease is severe or mild, whether their last myocardial infarction is recent or more remote, whether conditions such as diabetes or hypertension are present, whether or not they have experienced congestive heart failure, whether or not they are taking digitalis or diuretics or anti-arrhythmic drugs, whether or not they smoke cigarettes, and whether or not they are employed."

All 1,739 men had survived a heart attack, all were under constant medical care, and all were given whatever medicines their cardiologists deemed necessary. Thus, the influence of educational experiences 30, 40 or 50 years earlier was particularly perplexing. What was it about low educational attainment that could make such a difference? Was it some unknown stress inherent in the life-style of the least educated men, or something about their coping style to various life stresses? Were they unable to cope with stress in a way comparable to more educated men? Were they more depressed or psychologically unstable?

LOW EDUCATION, SOCIAL ISOLATION, AND SUDDEN CARDIAC DEATH: THE NATIONAL BETA-BLOCKER HEART TRIALS

These findings prompted the HIP team to pursue their investigations still further. In what turned out to be a highly fortuitous situation, the data from their research became available just as the National Heart, Lung and Blood Institute of the National Institutes of Health (NIH) in Washington was planning to undertake a major study of heart patients. This nationwide survey was designed to evaluate the clinical effectiveness of a specific drug, called a beta-blocker, which had shown promising results in treating heart patients. NIH scientists were interested in ascertaining whether this drug could be used to lower the risk of sudden cardiac death in patients who had survived a heart attack.

The NIH enlisted the cooperation of major university clinics all across the United States. By pooling data on large numbers of heart patients, the scientists hoped to find out once and for all whether this drug's regular administration would have any significant effect on saving the lives of post-heart attack patients.

Each of these centers agreed to administer the beta-blocker medication to patients who had survived a heart attack. In the cooperating centers, every heart patient was given a detailed medical examination, and an exhaustive range of medical and demographic information was gathered. The overall plan of the survey was straightforward. Once all the information on each patient had been gathered, the beta-blocker medicine would be administered, with strict research controls applied. The investigators would then track each patient for a two-to-four year period. If beta-blocker medications made a difference in long-term survival, then it would most likely show up statistically within this time period.

The sheer scale of the study, and the scientific controls built into the research design, provided a golden opportunity for Dr. Ruberman's research team. They had the chance to simply "plug into" this study and pursue their own questions about the effects of education on long-term survival. They could find out what it was about heart attack victims with low education levels that made them particularly vulnerable to sudden death. Based on impressions they had gleaned from their original studies, four general factors seemed like potential candidates. The relatively small number of patients in their original studies made it difficult to statistically evaluate their impressions, but it appeared as if men with low educational levels suffered more frequently from the following problems:[140]

1. Relatively high levels of life stress (e.g., those caused by divorce, crime, involuntary retirement, or financial difficulties)

2. Relatively high levels of social isolation (e.g., not being a member of any club, church, synagogue, or fraternal organization; not visiting relatives, or having few friends; being reluctant to talk to medical personnel about problems)

3. Relatively strong Type A behavior patterns

4. Relatively depressed

Thousands of heart patients were involved in the Beta-blocker Heart Attack Studies. The HIP team asked them all, while still in the hospital, if they would consent to interviews after recovering from their heart attacks. The interview itself would be scheduled six weeks later, after the patient had been released from the hospital. Men and women between the ages of 30-69 were included in the survey. In all, 2,320 male heart attack victims agreed to cooperate.

As had been true in their original findings, most of the standard risk factors typically linked to heart disease did not differentiate the more educated from less educated patients. Yet, at the same time, those with less education (less than 10 years schooling) had a far greater chance of dying suddenly than those with relatively more education (more than 12 years of schooling).

Three years into the National Beta Blocker Heart Studies, those with less education had a death rate from recurrent heart attacks nearly four times greater than those with more than 12 years of education. These different death rates were occurring in spite of the fact that all of the patients were being carefully followed in a heart study funded by the Federal government. All patients had equal access to the best possible health care available in the United States. All were treated by university-trained cardiologists, and all were given physical examinations.

This time around, however, Dr. Ruberman and his colleagues were prepared to find out what it was about low educational levels that made these patients so vulnerable to sudden death. Two factors in particular—social isolation and life stress—turned out to be crucial. As shown in graphic form, they discovered that those patients with low education who were experiencing either a high degree of life stress or high degree of social isolation had a far greater chance of dying suddenly than those low on either of these factors. When the two factors were combined—that is, when a person experienced both high stress and high social isolation—chances of sudden death increased four-fold.

Educational level also significantly influenced the relative incidence of these two major stressors. Thirty-five percent of the men with low education experienced both high levels of stress and a great degree of social isolation. By contrast, only 13 percent of the better-educated men (or two-thirds fewer) were struggling in a similar way. Conversely, 46 percent of the more highly educated, and only 14 percent of the least educated men, were found to rank low on both these stressors.

Though the HIP medical team began their research studies in an area quite different from the types of investigations conducted by Drs. Friedman and Rosenman, there was a remarkable degree of overlap in their ultimate conclusions. When Drs. Friedman and Rosenman first formulated their original observations of Type A behavior and vulnerability to coronary heart disease, they were forced to consider what factor or factors contributed to this behavioral pattern. After 30 years of painstaking work, they arrived at the conclusion that low self-esteem, which had its origins in childhood, had a great deal to do with the problem. Dr. Friedman found that low self-esteem made it difficult to relate to other human beings, contributing to the Type A's experience of social isolation.

Drs. Friedman and Rosenman found that a lethal combination of factors led to premature death. Low educational levels, low self-esteem, increased Type A behavior, difficulties communicating, increased social isolation, and loneliness—all fed a viciously cycling set of interrelated problems that ultimately broke the human heart.

In a similar way, when Dr. Ruberman's research team began their studies, they too discovered significant links between low education and vulnerability to sudden cardiac death. After decades of painstaking research, they too uncovered a similar group of inter-related problems— low education, increased life stress, increased social isolation, and ultimately an increased vulnerability to heart disease and sudden death.

Social Isolation and Three-Year Mortality Rates in Male Heart Attack Survivors

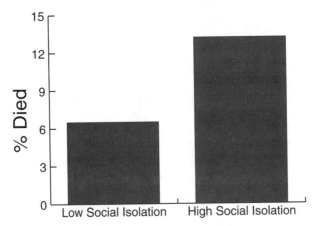

SOURCE: Ruberman, Weinblatt, Goldberg, & Chaudhary, 1984

Dr. Ruberman's research findings highlighted another medical reality as well. All the participants in the National Beta Blocker Heart Studies had survived a heart attack. All had received the same excellent medical care while hospitalized, many in the best university-based health centers in the United States. Yet, in spite of rigorous methodological controls, as well as access to the most advanced health care in the Western World, certain patients died at rates four times higher than others. For these patients, survival was influenced by factors beyond those traditionally assumed to be part of standard medical care. They needed something else to keep them alive.

Dr. Ruberman and his associates alluded to this problem in the *New England Journal of Medicine* when they noted:

"The burdens imposed by the life circumstances that we have defined as being associated with high levels of stress and social isolation are not the conventional risk factors alone. Neither is it possible for most people to determine their way of life completely through personal choice." [141]

SUMMARY

In the slums and ghettoes of urban America, it is easy enough to see widespread family fragmentation, depression, despair, violence, increased incidence of illness, and premature death. Signs of human suffering abound. Alcoholism and drug abuse are but two of the more common ways people try to narcotize themselves against the pain. In many urban ghettoes, school dropout rates can approach or even exceed graduation rates. It has been recently reported (1996) that 25 percent of all children in ghetto schools have admitted to taking a lethal weapon to school to protect themselves from violent physical assaults by fellow students. Sociologists and politicians alike readily speak with alarm about the "growing cycle of poverty and illiteracy," while an army of experts and concerned citizens alike gropes for ways to effectively break a cycle that has damned successive generations.

Though it is seldom explicitly acknowledged as such, when most Americans hear statistics on the disastrous school dropout rates in urban areas, they usually code it as a problem primarily affecting Hispanic-Americans and African-Americans. And while virtually everyone voices concern, few choose to live where these problems exist.

There is, of course, good reason to maintain a healthy distance. Few would be surprised to learn that ghetto environments are not particularly conducive to good health or longevity. A life span for black males in Harlem that is lower than the life span for males in a Third World nation like Bangladesh makes it all too apparent that American ghetto life is not particularly enticing. Indeed, a recent article in *the New England Journal of Medicine* remarked that "Harlem and other inner-city areas with largely black populations have extremely high mortality rates that justify special consideration analogous to that given to natural-disaster areas." [142]

Ironically, this implicit and explicit understanding, coupled with a multitude of health statistics that readily confirm the lethal reality of ghetto life, has allowed virtually everyone to discount or overlook the lethal consequences of low educational attainment itself. The obvious relationship of school failure to the more general cycle of poverty, unemployment, and family fragmentation has led virtually everyone to assume that the health consequences of low educational attainment are due to these latter factors rather than school failure itself. Instead of being seen as part of the overall problem, the educational system is usually seen as just one more victim of it.

In this chapter, I have tried to meet certain aspects of this "implicit understanding" head-on by examining populations far removed from the darkness and despair of ghetto life itself. I focused instead on medical data that examined very different populations. These studies described the cardiovascular health of over one-half million working American adults. Almost all were healthy when the studies began. The majority were white males between the ages of 30-50. All were gainfully employed for decades in industrialized environments noted for their job security. Almost all were well paid, and some held positions of high executive responsibility. Though they did not seem to have very much in common with residents of Harlem or Watts, some, in fact, shared one thing—low education. And this one marker, in spite of all other advantages, seemed to exact a lethal toll not unlike that seen in the heart of the ghetto itself.

Like a hound dog tracking an escapee, the onus of low education seemed to offer little escape for these working men. No matter how hard they worked, or how much money they earned, or how far up the corporate ladder they climbed, they were apparently unable to outrun the baying of their own shattered self-esteem. In the end, their lonely fugitive life exhausted their hearts, and they too were caught by the same hound that has imprisoned the men of Harlem and Watts for generations.

The data indicate that low educational attainment has a powerful, independent, and lethal effect on cardiovascular health, and represents a health problem of enormous significance. The mortality data bear mute testimony to an educational system that continues to reap its own whirlwind. Premature death is the price exacted by a system that assumes "knowledge" can be delivered to human beings, for human beings, and by human beings, possessing mindless hearts and heartless minds. The whirlwind has ironically reaped its devastating toll because, in part, it is its own self-fulfilling prophecy.

In this chapter, I examined issues that move us one step closer to the heart of all communicative life. Rather than focus on the interlocking relationships between education, economic variables, and health, I have presumed that relationships of this sort are generally recognized and readily understood. In a similar fashion, I have presumed that data linking behaviors such as cigarette smoking, obesity, lack of exercise, excessive alcohol consumption, and drug abuse, to low education, and, ultimately, to heart disease, will also be readily understood by the readers of this book. Yet, though these risk factors are linked to heart disease, the fact is that all of these variables combined do not account for the health impact of low education itself.

This issue is raised here again simply to reemphasize that I am attempting to isolate the underlying communicative disease that I believe links all of these factors to heart disease. Educational failure is obviously one of those major life-experiences that isolates people, makes them feel inferior, and makes every communication by them increasingly costly. The destruction of self-esteem inherent in school failure ultimately forces many victims between a "rock and a hard-place." Life in relationship to others can become unbearable. Attempts to escape by isolating oneself, unfortunately, become equally unbearable, forcing those so trapped to pick their own poison or to allow nature to take its own course.

From this perspective, the mortality data outlined in this chapter are particularly sobering. For they suggest that one of the major ways that Nature uses to take its own course is heart disease. In essence, we hypothesize that if a person's sense of self-worth is broken, then his or her heart will be broken as well. Even when all the conventionally recognized direct and indirect risk factors contributing to heart disease are controlled, low education—independent of all these other factors—still makes a huge difference.

Though underlined and repeated several times in this chapter, the overall conclusion is important enough to repeat one final time: "The independent effect of education on cardiovascular disease is as strong as the effects of smoking, blood pressure, weight, and cholesterol combined."

Clearly, the task of repairing human hearts broken by the cumulative effect of low educational attainment, low self-esteem, increased stress, loneliness, and social isolation will not be an easy task. Though I am encouraged that an awareness of these problems will lead to new ways of helping heart patients, it seems clear that the conventional medical procedures will not be sufficient to keep certain of these patients alive.

No pills by themselves—no beta blockers, for instance—can reverse the cumulative, decades' long heartbreak of loneliness and isolation, which stems from shattered self-esteem and communicative disease. Prevention of these problems decades earlier—attacking the problem at its roots by changing early childhood education and early family rearing practices—clearly would be a substantially more efficacious path for us to follow.

BRIDGING THE GAP: LONELINESS AND COMMUNICATIVE DISEASE

The first two sections of this book marshaled health statistics supporting the hypothesis that, for what ostensibly appear to be very disparate life experiences, there is a common explanation and link. The experiences include being divorced, single, widowed, and socially isolated. They also include childhood experiences of school failure, and of growing up with emotionally aloof or dysfunctional parents. It was suggested that all of these varied life experiences share a type of communicative disease that exacts a particularly devastating toll on the human heart.

Still unclear at this juncture, however, are the mechanisms through which this communicative disease and its resultant loneliness are linked to the development of heart disease. How, for example, do these problems cause a person's blood pressure to rise, or lead to the premature hardening of one's coronary arteries? One path was made quite clear. All of the well-known risk factors for heart disease increase with educational failure, as well as for other socially isolating human experiences. In addition, emotional states, such as depression, with its accompanying social withdrawal and loneliness, are also linked both to an increased risk of premature coronary heart disease and to sudden cardiac death. These data all suggest that the absence, breakdown, or lethal poisoning of human dialogue increase the types of risks that lead to premature death.

In order to further clarify the links between communicative disease and premature death, however, it will be necessary to move backward in time, back to when I first began my own research journey more than thirty-five years ago. In the next chapter, I describe the lessons I learned in laboratory experiments about the links between human contact and the functioning of the heart.

This is followed in Chapter 8 with similar lessons drawn from my observations on how human touch affects the hearts of patients in hospital intensive care units. Both the observations made in the laboratory as well as those in clinics indicate that transient human contact has measurable, and at times truly profound, effects on the heart. It was these observations that helped prepare the way for the discoveries that finally permitted me to comprehend how and why human dialogue functions as the elixir of life and why human loneliness is one of the most important sources of premature death.

Chapter Seven

LESSONS TAUGHT BY OUR ANIMAL BRETHREN

"Although the emotion of love is one of the strongest of which the mind is capable, it can hardly be said to have any proper or peculiar means of expression."
—Charles Darwin, *The Expression of the Emotions in Man and Animals,* 1872

"From a distant perspective, in the slanting rays of the sun, we know the vicissitudes of science—and of life; the path leads through dark valleys, over sunlit peaks. The game is unending; we solve one puzzle to see it overlap with the beginning of others. Amid the welter of sights and sounds, we look for harmony and beauty; through the clouds we glimpse the prospects of truth. We hope the work will sometimes help to alleviate suffering and pain and contribute to a more balanced relation with Nature and our Fellowman. So runs my dream."
—W. Horsley Gantt, M.D., *The Johns Hopkins Medical Journal,* 1980

FRUIT FLIES AND LOVE

"There are certain aspects of human behavior—love and compassion and things like that—that you're not going to get out of a fly." So cautioned MIT's Dr. Thomas Quinn while commenting recently on the frenetic attempts to unravel the complete genetic code of the fruit fly. But, he added, "If you want to understand how a nervous system works, and what genes are important in learning and behavior patterns and various human diseases, it's a really cheap way to get a foot in the door." [143]

An explosion in genetic research in the latter part of the 20th century had prompted the professor's comments about Drosophila Melanogaster, the common fruit fly. This lowly creature had emerged as a major player in a remarkable race between the Celera Genomics Corporation, headed by Drs. J. Craig Venter and Hamilton Smith, and the United States Genome Project, directed by the National Institutes of Health. In spite of the lop-sided financial odds favoring NIH, it appeared as if Drs. Venter and Smith just might win. And it was a winner-take-all race, with patent rights and the future control of a vast storehouse of biological information—something between 50 and 90 percent of the entire human gene pool—at stake.

Fruit flies are by no means the only animal of interest to medical research. For the past 350 years, scientists have used all sorts of species of animals to help generate the basic biological information upon which modern medicine is based. The information attained through animal research has helped prevent disease and alleviated an enormous amount of human suffering. Without the assistance of our animal brethren, we would still be living in terror of the bubonic plague, diphtheria, and cholera, and be vulnerable to such lethal diseases as tuberculosis, pneumonia, and polio. The contributions made by animals to medical progress can scarcely be overestimated.

Yet, in spite of all of its medical benefits, reliance on animal research has exacted a hidden cost of significant proportions. There are, as Dr. Quinn hinted, certain unique attributes of human beings that can never be understood by studying animals alone. And among those unique attributes, none is more important than the fact that only human beings talk. The ability to use language to communicate with one another is unique to human beings.

And yet, in spite of this crucial difference, the overwhelming use of non-speaking animals to construct the research edifice upon which modern medical thinking is based has led physicians and informed citizens alike to vastly underestimate the powerful links between human dialogue and physical health. It has also served to obscure certain unique medical problems that emerge from the simple and inescapable fact that human beings, and only human beings, speak!

At the ebb tide of the twentieth century, the issue had at long last been joined. According to an MIT scientist, fruit flies didn't love! Or do they? Are they lonely? Can a fruit fly die of a broken heart? Can fruit flies die prematurely if they fail to learn or get divorced? Is their self-esteem shattered if they drop out of fruit-fly school prematurely? Can educational failure alter the fruit fly's capacity to communicate? Or are all of these struggles uniquely human? Will the mapping of the fruit fly's 165 million chemicals (called "nucleotide bases") help to clarify issues of central concern to this book? Or will "love" and "loneliness" be understood by unraveling the additional 165 million chemical "nucleotide bases," the other 50 percent of the gene pool, found higher up the evolutionary ladder?

Begging to differ with the MIT professor, I must question whether issues of love really involve something we "get out of behavior"— something that a few more hundred million "nucleotide bases" could provide. I suggest that love extends far beyond "behavior."

Indeed, I believe that love is a felt word, spoken in our flesh and blood, which can only have meaning in the interpersonal context of human dialogue. It is not a rational or objectively quantifiable construct whose essential meaning can be gleaned from a dictionary, learned on the Internet, or observed in a microscope. It is, instead, a word first taught to us by others in dialogue, which helps to bind separate bodies together in shared dialogue.

Concepts such as self-esteem, love, and loneliness will never be found in the "nucleotide bases" of an isolated body, for these concepts, to have any meaning whatsoever, require two things: the existence of others, *and* the capacity to communicate in our flesh and blood by using language. The fact is that the interpersonal nature of human dialogue alters the genetic and medical landscapes in fundamental ways that both biological scientists and physicians have failed to fully appreciate.

Has any fruit fly ever taught another fruit fly the meaning of the word "love?" I think not. For love is first and foremost a word, taught to us by other human beings in shared dialogue. One cannot contemplate one's belly button and suddenly awaken understanding the meaning of love. Even more to the point are the limitations imposed by the very use of the word "understanding." "Understanding" that if we put our hand on a hot stove, it will hurt, is clearly not the same as the sensation that is felt by actually putting our hand on a hot stove. There is a world of difference between "understanding" feelings and feeling feelings. The feeling of love is not an affair that occurs in a solitary interchange between one's mind and one's body, or one's mind and one's heart.

Love is first and foremost a *word* that requires a speaker and an object, a person who can use the word to communicate and another who can detect the emotion and share the meaning of that word with us. In the lessons I discuss in this chapter, perhaps none are more important than those that help us bridge this important gap. This bridge, it's hoped, will help delineate what we share in common with our animal brethren, and what we experience in a fundamentally unique manner because we human beings speak and use language to communicate with one another.

This chapter focuses on our non-speaking brethren and examines data garnered from animal research, to help illustrate the power of human contact and human touch. It draws on a vast and highly sophisticated body of evidence that helps both to reinforce and explain the powerful effects of companionship and human touch on the heart. It will also help to delineate what we have in common with our animal brethren as well as clarify the unique nature of human dialogue.

"THE LAND OF SERENDIP"

We owe to an eighteenth century Persian poet the marvelous concept of "serendipity." It is a word born in the delightful Persian tale entitled "The Three Princes of Serendip." *Webster's Dictionary* defines "serendipity" as "the faculty or phenomenon of finding valuable things not sought for." It represents a type of "accidental sagacity; the faculty of making fortunate discoveries of things you were not looking for."

Serendipity is the only word that can adequately describe the confluence of events that surrounded my meeting W. Horsley Gantt, M.D., in 1962. Little did I know at the time that, for the next 18 years, until his death in 1980 at the age of 88, he would be my teacher and mentor. And serendipity is the only word that can adequately describe all that was contained in several of his research concepts that came to serve as the structural underpinnings of this book. Three such concepts are especially important:

The Effect of Person: Research studies demonstrating the effects that human contact can exert on the cardiovascular system of both men and animals. [144]

The Orienting Reflex: Research studies showing that focusing attention outside of oneself elicits immediate reductions in heart rate and blood pressure. [145]

Schizokinesis: Research revealing the splitting off of external appearance from what occurs internally in the autonomic nervous system. [146]

Each of these complex research concepts embodies seminal ideas crucial to the overall perspective of this book. Together, they provide a platform that helps to facilitate an understanding of the hidden links between human loneliness and heart disease, as well as clarify some of the key factors that enhance human dialogue and promote good health.

Serendipity surely was in the winds in 1962 when, as a young graduate student in psychology, I accepted a pre-doctoral fellowship at the Veterans Hospital in Perry Point, Maryland, located at the mouth of the Susquehanna River where it flows into the Chesapeake Bay. I chose this assignment solely because it was the closest research facility I could find to Boston. It made weekend commuting to visit my fiancée in New England at least marginally feasible. The links between loneliness and heart disease were of absolutely no concern to me then. My primary interests centered on simply surviving graduate school and earning a living so that I could get married. That seemed more than enough to deal with at the time.

Yet, in hindsight, this remote setting provided the ideal place for the "serendip" characterizing life in that mythical, ancient kingdom of Persia. At the northern reaches of the Chesapeake Bay, the fog-shrouded autumn and spring mornings provided winter's quarters to hundreds upon thousands of Canadian Geese. In that setting, it was easy to envision W. Horsely Gantt, M.D. as one of the "Three Princes of Serindip," and his white, three-storied laboratory building at the Veterans Hospital as one of its castles.

He had come to the Perry Point Veterans Hospital several years earlier to develop an extension of his Pavlovian Laboratory, first opened in 1929 at The Johns Hopkins Medical School in Baltimore. Already 70 years old, he was "semi-retired" as a professor emeritus from the medical school. Yet, the largesse of the National Heart Institute and the Veterans Administration, inspired in no small measure by the Russians' orbiting of a tiny sphere called "*Sputnik,*" had changed everything. Serendipity had smiled on Dr. Gantt's research career late in life in ways he never anticipated.

Beeping its way around the globe, Sputnik had given Russian science a new-found cachet in the West. The space race had been born, and the challenge of beating the Russians to the moon accepted by American technology. In the U.S., Dr. Gantt was one of only a handful of physicians who knew about Russian medicine and who could fluently speak the Russian language. During his long and distinguished research career, he had been awarded a number of prizes, including the prestigious "Lasker Award in Medicine" and a "Distinguished Service Award" by the American Heart Association. Yet, it was only in Sputnik's aftermath that he found the financial support that had eluded him for most of his working life. At long last, he had attained his dream—developing a second laboratory in the Maryland countryside.

In 1922, as a young resident in internal medicine, Dr. Gantt had answered Herbert Hoover's call for medical volunteers willing to go to Russia. Physicians were needed, Hoover said, to help ease the disastrous suffering brought on by a terrible famine sweeping over that beleaguered nation following the Bolshevik revolution. His personal experiences in Russia eventually led Dr. Gantt to write a book, now widely regarded as a medical classic, describing the famine and all its attendant medical problems.

Dr. Gantt was assigned to the Leningrad sector of the relief effort, where serendipity entered his own life. He accidentally met up with the first Russian to ever win the Nobel Prize, Ivan Petrovich Pavlov. So captivated was he by Pavlov's personality, and by his rigorous application of scientific methods in studying the "conditional reflex," that he decided to stay in Leningrad and study with him for the next seven years. In spite of the terrible poverty, miserable living conditions, and meager research support existing in Russia at the time, Dr. Gantt remained there until 1929, and for several lonely and economically desperate years, he was the only American living in Leningrad.

Returning to America in 1929, Dr. Gantt opened his own "Pavlovian Laboratory" at The Johns Hopkins Medical School and translated his beloved teacher's research findings into English. For the next thirty-five years, all with very meager financial support, he and a large number of research colleagues systematically extended Pavlov's original research.[147]

Their particular interest centered on proving that the cardiovascular system of dogs could be conditioned to respond in much the same way Pavlov's dogs had learned to salivate to a bell signaling food. They hoped that this model would provide a new way to understand the links between stress and heart disease, and especially clarify the links between stress and chronic hypertension. If an animal model could be developed that reliably demonstrated how stress contributed to hypertension, then it was assumed that various experimental drugs could be tested to help treat this disease.

While most readers of this book will know the outlines of Pavlov's central experiment—a dog salivating all alone in an isolation chamber to the sound of a bell signaling the delivery of food—it is far more difficult to fully appreciate the revolutionary scope of his vision. It was the larger context of this research world that I accidentally stumbled onto in 1962. It was a living, vibrant world of cardiovascular research, and Dr. Gantt himself the embodiment of a long tradition stretching back, via Pavlov, to the middle of the nineteenth century. Working in his laboratory truly felt as if one were living in the "Land of Serendip," a throwback to some distant, romantic, eighteenth-century world of poetry. Dr. Gantt made it seem as if men like Ivan Pavlov, Sigmund Freud, Rene Descartes, Charles Darwin, Walter Cannon, and Hans Selye were literally looking over your shoulder.

"To know the work of these scientists, it is important to know the men behind the science," he would occasionally remark with a hearty laugh at "tea" each morning in his laboratory. "Serendipity" marked all conversations at these hour-long affairs, and his "Effect of Person" began to provide a research perspective that altered my life.

Paradoxically, it was the very model Pavlov had used to study classical conditioning that made Dr. Gantt's observations on the "Effect of Person" so intriguing. The fact that the dogs were isolated, all alone, in soundproof chambers is what inadvertently created the perfect setting to observe the power of human contact on the heart. The isolation itself amplified the importance of human contact when people entered these chambers, as if fate had intervened to emphasize what otherwise would have been overlooked.

Dr. Gantt and his research colleagues just happened to study the cardiovascular system of dogs by isolating them in Pavlovian chambers. They continuously monitored the heart rate and blood pressure of these animals. By 1962, he and his staff were well aware that entering the isolation chamber and merely petting a dog could cause an immediate reduction in the dog's heart rate and blood pressure of 50 percent.[148]

It seems ironic to reflect back forty years later and to consider that it was this simple demonstration of the "Effect of Person" that eventually led me to think about the links between human loneliness and heart disease. Strange, too, that the seeds for grasping the health implications of social support were first germinated in the social isolation of a Pavlovian chamber. Equally strange was the fact that Pavlov had originally designed these isolation chambers to study "conditioning," or what we now call "learning." How ironic, then, that three decades later, I would come to realize that one of the unfortunate byproducts of such learning—the failure to learn in school—could crush the human heart. It was indeed the Land of Serendip.

The following is a typical example of the type of heart reactions to human contact that Dr. Gantt was documenting when I was first assigned to his laboratory.[149]

"When alone [in the Pavlovian chamber] the dog's heart rate was quite rapid, varying from 120-160 beats per minute. Immediately after the person entered the room, the heart rate would decrease 20-30 beats per minute, and with the approach of the person would fall even more. During petting, the heart rate fell to the lowest value during the entire session, which was, in many experiments, in the neighborhood of 40-50 beats per minute.

Another procedure used at times involved the person entering the room and sitting next to the dog throughout the rest of the session. Then the person would pet the dog at 2-3 minute intervals for 60 seconds each trial, 5 to 10 trials per session. On these occasions [the dog's] heart rate was remarkably lower and less variable while the person was in the chamber than when the dog was alone, and during petting the heart rate would go as low as 20 to 30 beats per minute. On several occasions, when blood pressure was measured, it fell from 140 mm HG systolic while the dog was alone, to around 75 mm HG systolic during petting."

To my knowledge, cardiac changes of this magnitude are among the most marked ever reported for a dog under any conditions (short of seriously injuring or killing the animal). And while this particular dog repeatedly exhibited these responses to human contact, it nevertheless lived for 14 years in the laboratory.

The manner in which the dogs reacted to human contact encouraged further study of this phenomenon. In a lengthy series of research investigations, Dr. Gantt and his colleagues began to observe that two of the most ordinary aspects of human contact—the simple presence of a human being, and human petting—had a potent effect on the dog's heart. He labeled the phenomenon the "Effect of Person." He found that a person's entrance into the experimental room was usually followed by increases in the dog's heart rate averaging 20-60 beats per minute. Human petting, on the other hand, prompted sudden and marked *decreases* in heart rate from the usual resting rate—a 10-60 beat-per-minute decrease. As already noted, individual dogs varied considerably in their cardiac reactions to human contact.

During the intervening years, the types of cardiovascular reactions that could be monitored grew ever more sophisticated. It was eventually noted, for example, that human contact could have a significant influence on coronary blood flow in dogs. The coronary arteries are the vessels that supply blood to the heart muscles themselves and are vital to the healthy functioning of the heart. While evaluating the effects of eating and exercise on coronary blood flow, Drs. Joseph Newton and R. Walter Ehrlich at The Johns Hopkins Medical School noticed that human contact could dramatically influence the flow of blood through the dog's coronary arteries. Coronary blood flow in dogs seemed to respond to human contact even more than heart rate or blood pressure. The investigators commented on their observations as follows:

"During experiments on the effects of eating and exercise on coronary blood flow, we were surprised to find such large coronary flow increases due to a person entering the room. Indeed, in some dogs the person was almost as potent a stimulus to coronary flow as violent exercise on the treadmill, despite the small increase in motor activity caused by the person." [150]

This observation naturally led us to wonder whether human contact had similar effects on coronary flow in humans. Three decades later, the answer to that question became apparent when my colleagues and I observed that everyday human dialogue could produce in heart patients far greater increases in blood pressure than even the most vigorous exercise!

These general findings about the "Effect of Person" provided a simple yet powerful technique for studying some of the emotional concomitants of human contact. They also prompted a variety of questions about how these heart reactions first develop and what environmental and genetic factors might modify these responses.

When I first joined Dr. Gantt's laboratory staff in 1962, an impressive research project demonstrating the power of human contact was being carried out. A dog was given a modestly painful electric shock to its forelimb without any warning signal, and the degree of heart rate increase to the shock measured. After obtaining consistent heart reactions to this painful stimulus over a period of days, a person then entered the room and petted the dog during the electric shock. I was certain that the dog would bite his human visitor when it was shocked, but much to my surprise, the petting made the pain of the shock far less severe. The heart rate increase resulting from the electric shock was, in fact, half as great during petting as when the dog was alone in the room. [151]

(To the many readers who might be disturbed by discussions of experiments in which dogs are given a painful electric shock, it is important to point out that every effort was made to treat these animals as humanely as possible. A cardinal rule of the laboratory was to care for the animals. Indeed, as already noted, some of the dogs lived for fourteen years in the laboratory, during which every effort was made to provide the best living situation possible for them. Unfortunately, in order to study the links between stress and various cardiovascular problems, including hypertension and coronary heart disease, and to develop appropriate remedies, it was necessary to develop an objective way to measure stress.)

This particular study, begun in 1962, was then repeated with modifications by first pairing the painful electric shock with a tone that warned the dog 10 seconds in advance that it was to be shocked. After a number of training trials, the dog's heart rate usually accelerated about 50-100 beats per minute when the tone was sounded. This necessarily unpleasant situation allowed us to evaluate whether human contact could alter the dog's heart rate in response to both the conditioned or learned fear, as well as alter the cardiac response to the pain of the shock itself.

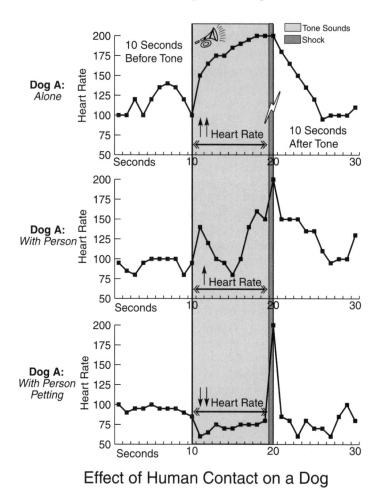

Effect of Human Contact on a Dog

NOTE: The effect of three experimental condtions on a classically conditioned heart rate response to a tone followed by shock. When alone, this particular dog's heart rate increased from a rate of 100 beats per minute up to 200 during the tone and shock. However, when a person petted the dog, the heart rate decreased from 100 beats per minute to 60. Thus, the same tone, signaling the same electrical shock, caused a heart rate difference of up to 140 bpm depending on whether the dog was alone or a person petted him. Human petting had the powerful effect of eliminating the usual cardiac indicators of both fear and pain as well as eliminating the usual behavioral rations to painful shock.

What was observed, however, was at first quite difficult to believe. If the person petted the dog during both the tone and the shock, the usual marked increase in heart rate was either eliminated or became a decrease in heart rate! When petted, some of these dogs did not even give the usual flexion response to the shock. And this effect was just as marked on the sixth day of the experiment as it was on the first.[152]

As shown in the accompanying figure, the heart rate of this particular dog, when left alone, increased from 100 beats per minute up to 200 during the tone and shock. However, when the person petted the dog, the heart rate decreased from 100 beats per minute to 60! Thus, the same tone, signaling the same electrical shock and given at five-minute intervals, caused a heart rate difference of up to 140 beats per minute, depending on whether the dog was alone or whether a person petted him. Human petting had the powerful effect of eliminating the usual cardiac indicators of both fear and pain, as well as eliminating the dog's usual behavioral reactions to a painful shock. While alone, the animal gave the usual flexion response, and, when petted, did not react at all! Human contact had made an enormous difference.

If Darwin was correct in asserting that contact with and petting of animals represent one manifestation of their expression of love, then we were witnessing a remarkable example of its power. Human contact so influenced these dogs that the exact same tone-shock was in one case extremely upsetting to the animal (as measured by heart rate changes) and in the other of no physical consequence whatsoever. And although initially we were startled by these results, perhaps we should have been less surprised. For at the human level, this phenomenon can be seen routinely in everyday life, when, for example, a mother picks up her frightened or injured child and quickly abolishes both the fear and the physical response to a painful injury.

Most people have observed the intense bond of attachment that develops between a mother and her child—a bond that enables a mother to pick up her hurt or frightened child and rapidly eliminate all external signs of pain and fear. Dr. Howard Liddell of Cornell University showed that similar maternal capacities exist in animals such as sheep and goats. He observed that if a kid or lamb was subjected to a stressful environment (such as shock) in the presence of its mother, the kid or lamb could readily resist this stress, while if these same stresses were applied to their twin siblings without the mother's presence, the stresses would rapidly and sometimes permanently disturb these animals. How an animal tolerated these early traumatic experiences also appeared to make a huge difference in how the animal tolerated stress in later life.[153]

Viewed through the eyes of the dog, the question could be asked: What did a person signify? To analyze this question, the same person entered an experimental chamber for three successive weeks, and each time his entry would be followed by one of three different events:

— the dog was petted,
— the dog received a moderate electric shock to his paw, or
— the person simply exited, without petting the dog and without any shock being given to the dog.

Each day, the person entered the experimental chamber ten times during an hour. The same reinforcement—petting, shock, or nothing—was given consistently for one week and then switched. The same person's entry on three successive weeks thus signified three very different types of events or experiments. The largest cardiac increases occurred, not surprisingly, when a person's entry was followed by a shock, and the smallest heart rate change when petting followed the person's entry.

In addition to these different cardiac responses, the dog's behavior indicated that his response to human contact was in part dictated by the events associated with that contact. For instance, during the person-shock sequence, the dog, after a few trials, would draw away from the individual, flex its paw through which it was being shocked when the person entered the room, and keep it flexed until the person left. In one of these dogs, the foot flexion response was so well established that even when that person would enter the animal's kennel, the dog would flex his paw, although it did not flex its paw to other people who entered the kennel. The person elicited cardiac, respiratory, and motor responses from the dog dependent on the reinforcement associated with that individual.[154]

These experiments helped to illustrate a fact about human contact discussed in an earlier chapter: human beings, while a potent source of comfort, can also become signals that elicit extreme anxiety and pain. Aversive, or toxic, language, such as that used by parents, can similarly lead a child to draw away in fear.

In much the same way, educational failure can condition a child, so that the classroom itself can become a conditional signal that triggers fight/flight reactivity. To see human contact as either exclusively "good" or exclusively "bad" would fly in the face of reality. Although this book has emphasized the biological power and therapeutic benefits of human companionship, it does not mean that human relationships cannot be modified by life experiences and become a source of lethal distress. The net effects of human contact on the heart depend on a number of factors, not the least of which is previous experience with human beings.

Different ways of responding to fear and pain are not restricted to animals. Dr. Aaron Katcher and his colleagues at the University of Pennsylvania have shown that about 50 percent of all children placed in the "stressful environment" of a dental chair do not exhibit overt signs of fear. That is, when they are placed in dental chairs, or when they are given a topical anesthetic, or even when they are given a local anesthetic injection, they do not move around or struggle. Of special interest, however, is that if children showed no bodily movements, then no heart rate changes were observed. Only when they moved in their chairs or struggled with the dental assistant did these children show heart rate changes. Like the puppies in the isolation chamber, their anxiety or fear was expressed simultaneously in both their behavior and their hearts. This is in marked contrast to adults, who often show striking cardiovascular changes in threatening environments without exhibiting any overt behavioral movements.[155]

SCHIZOKINESIS AND CLASSICALLY CONDITIONED LANGUAGE

In some adults, there is a marked split between what they exhibit behaviorally and what is exhibited in their hearts. Dr. Gantt was the first to analyze this phenomenon systematically. He labeled the phenomenon *"schizokinesis."* Conditioned fear reactions, as reflected internally in blood pressure and heart rate, might well differ from visible, overt behavioral reactions. It was this split, this divergence, that Dr. Gantt believed might be one of the sources of the development of heart disease, for he believed that the heart itself was rarely fooled.

The research model used to demonstrate this phenomenon was simple enough. Dogs were first conditioned to hear a tone signaling electric shock to their forepaw. After a few pairings of the tone with the shock, the animal would begin to flex its paw during the tone. After several sessions of this training, the tone was no longer paired with the shock. The animal would then quickly learn to stop flexing its paw to the tone, as if it had forgotten this linkage.

Yet, as internally measured by heart rate increases and blood pressure changes, the animal continued to react with major increases in blood pressure and heart rate. Even if this type of "conditioned extinction" was continued for hundreds of sessions, the animal kept reacting internally, even though externally it appeared to have forgotten the paired association. It was as if the animal's foot had forgotten, but its heart continued to remember. [156]

This *schizokinesis*—this splitting of learned memories, in a manner where the cardiovascular system continued to react, but external appearances signaled a different reality—would soon become apparent in the observation of major blood pressure increases in heart patients when they spoke of pained memories from their childhood. Virtually none of the patients was aware of any autonomic arousal when they spoke of memories from long ago, reporting instead that they felt fine and asserting that the discussion of these memories did not upset them. Nor were they are aware of the manner in which earlier use of language triggered a conditioned sense of hopelessness about using language to share their feelings, and highly significant increases in their blood pressure. There was a distinct split between appearance and internal physiological reality.

In Pavlov's view, human beings shared with higher animals a primary signaling system. A tone could be paired, for example, with pain or an electric shock, and both non-speaking and speaking animals would learn how to respond by the repetitive paired associations. Pavlov understood that language was a unique attribute of being human. He postulated that words at times could be just as effective in conditioning human behavior when also paired with either pain or shock. He called this type of conditioning the second signaling system.

All children learn words, grammar, and rhetoric from their parents and other teachers. These words, and especially the rhetoric of words, can condition autonomic reactions of hope and optimism, or fear, hopelessness, and dread. For example, if children, from their parents, learn the words "I love you" while being simultaneously abused, hurt, or punished, they will be conditioned to respond automatically with fear or helplessness when others subsequently utter words such as "love."

This conditioned response to language occurs over time, and especially when language is taught in a repetitive fashion. From it, the child develops an automatic defense that prepares him to engage life primarily in a fight/flight mode—that is, he is largely regulated by the physiology of exclusion. Language, especially felt language, becomes a cry that goes unheard.

Pavlov was attempting to demonstrate that language itself is a phenomenon taught in childhood in a manner that involves the classical conditioning of the autonomic nervous system.[157] He asserted that what language *signals or signifies* is learned or conditioned early in life. One of the most elementary components of this secondary signaling system is the "wiring"—the classical conditioning—of the "communicative physiology of inclusion and the communicative physiology of exclusion." By "wiring," he was referring to those aspects of language that are conditioned early in life, and then involve reflex autonomic reactivity throughout a person's life.

While language involves words, grammar, and rhetoric, the most important aspect of language in childhood is rhetoric. If a child learns that language is used to abuse, control, or hurt—its rhetoric, in effect— then a conditioned reflex is established in which the autonomic nervous system components of language taught in this fashion will be evoked throughout a person's life. These autonomic changes usually occur outside of a person's awareness, and as suggested by Gantt's observations of schizokinesis, are very difficult to extinguish once they are established.

I am suggesting that the communicative physiology of exclusion, once conditioned, is very difficult to extinguish, in part, because the reactions occur outside of the person's awareness. The first step in addressing this problem is the necessity to make the child and/or adult aware of this automatic reflex. One simply cannot change, or recondition, an automatic reaction, which is outside of the person's awareness, until the person is made aware of the process.

While Pavlov's and Gantt's research focused on interactions between dogs and humans, cardiac changes to human contact are by no means peculiar to the canine species. This point was reinforced one evening quite by chance. While attending a dinner at the home of one of my colleagues, a guest asked me, "Have you ever studied the reactions of cats to human contact? I've often heard that Siamese cats are so attached to their owners that if you must leave them with a veterinarian or board them when you travel, some will get so upset they will refuse to eat! You know you ought to look into that phenomenon."

A second guest countered: "Cats and dogs can't even begin to compete with horses in the way they react to human contact. Why doesn't someone study how the horse's heart reacts to human contact?" While a number of studies had shown that the cardiac systems of many species of animals, including monkeys, guinea pigs, rats, rabbits, and cats, respond to human handling, I was unaware of any similar studies with horses.

The question seemed intriguing. One of my colleagues quickly volunteered his horses for study. Knowing nothing about the cardiac system of the horse, or even how we would go about measuring a horse's heart rate, we were fortunate to meet Dr. Fred Fregin, an equine cardiologist at the University of Pennsylvania Veterinary School. Dr. Fregin had already developed all the techniques needed to monitor the cardiac systems of horses, even horses galloping full speed around a racetrack. The results were clear: Horses not only reacted to human petting in a way every bit as striking as dogs, but their heart rates slowed dramatically while being petted, in a fashion reminiscent of the reactions seen earlier in some dogs.[158] As we noted earlier, human petting on several occasions produced cardiac arrest for as long as eight seconds in a dog otherwise quite healthy—and who ultimately lived in the lab to the ripe old age of 14.

TRANSIENT CONTACT AND ENDURING RELATIONSHIPS

What is the relationship between these transient interactions and the more enduring, chronic social experiences of animals, and how do these relate to human health? Among the wide variety of experimental approaches emerging in the past few decades to examine these questions, one of the more interesting was pioneered by the late Dr. Harry Harlow at the University of Wisconsin. His research provided one of the more clear-cut and convincing demonstrations of the biological importance of early social contact.

Dr. Harlow took infant monkeys away from their mothers at birth and placed them in environments where they were totally isolated from all other living creatures. At the same time, he carefully tended to all their other needs, even ingeniously creating a variety of lifeless surrogate mothers, akin to the mannequins seen in department store windows. These he placed in the monkeys' cages. The surrogate mothers conformed to the bodily size of the infants' biological mothers. Some were made of wire on which the infant monkey could climb to get food. Other surrogates were covered with soft terry-cloth.[159]

Harlow's research revealed the importance of "contact comfort" for infant animals. He observed that the isolated infant monkeys maintained continual contact with the soft terry-cloth surrogate mothers. With their biological mothers removed from their lives, the infant monkeys would cling desperately to the soft terry-cloth "surrogate mothers" rather than go to "wire mothers," where they could receive food. So powerful was the need for contact comfort that these infant monkeys became terrified if the terry-cloth surrogate was removed from their cages.

And yet, even the continual presence of the terry-cloth surrogate mother was not sufficient for these infant monkeys. Irrespective of what type of surrogate was used, the social isolation ultimately destroyed them emotionally. When they matured, they refused to breed, and some killed their own offspring when impregnated, convincingly demonstrating the biological importance of early social contact.

The physical and emotional destructiveness of this type of early social deprivation was clear. Psychologically, the monkeys reared with surrogate mothers or in social isolation exhibited severe depression that usually remained long after they were removed from isolation. They remained emotionally scarred for the remainder of their lives.

Dr. Reite and his colleagues at the University of Colorado Medical Center repeated aspects of these studies and noted, as Harlow had earlier, that infant monkeys separated from their mothers for varying periods of time exhibited profound signs of emotional disturbance, including acute depression. Apart from the behavioral signs of depression, Dr. Reite added the interesting observation that the infant monkey's heart rate at rest was significantly lower after separation from its mother than that observed in normal infants.[160] Thus, the link between the absence of maternal contact, depression, and altered cardiac status, reminiscent of that observed by Drs. Greene and Schmale in hospitalized patients in Rochester, could be reproduced in isolated monkeys as well.

In addition to these studies of social deprivation, hundreds of studies have demonstrated that the early social experiences of various animal species routinely used in medical research significantly influence their ability to resist experimentally-induced diseases. Resistance to diseases as varied as cancer, malaria, and tuberculosis has been shown to change significantly by early social experience. For example, the manner in which a rat or mouse is handled, and the numbers placed in each cage, significantly influence the animal's ability to resist experimentally-induced infectious diseases. For those interested in these studies, additional information on them can be found at the web site www.lifecarehealth.com.

From all of these animal studies, a number of summary comments can be made:

- It is readily apparent that while behavioral observations can reveal certain features of an animal's social interactions with humans, the cardiac responses frequently reveal a far more powerful reality.

- The heart exhibits a wide range of responsiveness to human contact, dependent to some extent on the particular circumstances of the experiment. But in general, social interactions with man can have noticeable, and at times profound, effects on the cardiac systems of animals.
- Human contact can alter and even eliminate the usual cardiac responses to fear and physical pain.
- Early experience, subsequent learning, and genetic predisposition all play significant roles in determining the pattern and degree of cardiac response elicited by human contact. All these factors interact in a highly complex fashion to determine an animal's emotional responsiveness to human contact.
- Early in life, humans can be conditioned to respond autonomically to language. Their reaction can either embrace the physiology of exclusion or the physiology of inclusion.

In the next chapter, I describe the research that led to an extension of these early animal studies on the "Effect of Person" to similar studies with patients in various intensive care hospital environments. And it was these hospital-based observations that finally led to an entirely new understanding as to how and why human dialogue serves as the elixir of life, and loneliness functions as a lethal poison.

Chapter Eight

LESSONS FROM THE CLINIC

"How many persons we meet in houses, whom we scarcely speak to, whom yet we know, and who know us! How many we see in the street, or sit with in church, whom though silently, we warmly rejoice to be with! Read the language of these wandering eye-beams. The heart knoweth."
— Ralph Waldo Emerson, *Essays on Friendship*, 1841

"A man wholly solitary would be either a god or a brute."
— Aristotle, 384-322 B.C.

"THE EFFECT OF PERSON" AT THE HOUR OF DEATH

There are those rare moments in life when a single event can encompass a lifetime of research questions while simultaneously generating a sense that some questions may elude objective analysis forever. And sometimes an intense experience can bring one to a point in life where you sense that something is occurring that will change your life forever.

Those thoughts and feelings were present in 1976, the day I watched a 54-year-old man die in the Shock-Trauma Unit of the University of Maryland Hospital. For fourteen days, I had been observing this badly injured man as he lay motionless and comatose in a hospital bed. We never spoke, our eyes never met, and I knew very little about him. For fourteen days, he lay alone, without emitting even so much as a soft groan to reflect the pain endured by his badly shattered body. For fourteen days, not a single friend visited his bedside to comfort him. He apparently had no wife, no children, and no friends. It was almost as if fate had conspired to etch his loneliness in the starkest terms possible to help contrast it with the constant care of the surgeons and nurses who struggled in vain to keep him alive.

From my research on the effect of person, with dogs isolated in Pavlovian Chambers, to the study of patients semi-isolated in intensive care units of a major university hospital, it had been a long and unanticipated journey. Yet, on this particular afternoon, I watched with a sense of semi-paralyzed amazement as this man's heart rate and heart rhythm changed just as soon as a nurse began to hold his hand shortly before his death. She quietly comforted him shortly after the decision had been made to withdraw his life support. Though he was in a deep coma, she softly stroked his hand and told him that she would stay by his side—that he should not be afraid. Not only was he comatose, but every muscle in his body had been paralyzed by a drug known as d-tubocurarine (curare), and he had been able to breathe only with the help of machine-regulated artificial respiration. And yet, in spite of, or perhaps because of, his acute condition, his heart rate and heart rhythm changed the moment the nurse began to comfort him.[161]

A decade of research studying animals isolated in Pavlovian Chambers, coupled with extensive studies of patients in Coronary Care and Shock Trauma Units, had led me to this crossroad in my life. The question could no longer be avoided: If transient human contact had such measurable effects on the heart rate and heart rhythm of both animals and human beings, what in the world were the consequences when such contact was chronically absent? What *were* the medical consequences of loneliness, and the chronic type of isolation that seemed to have characterized the life of this comatose patient?

The question haunted me that Friday afternoon after he finally died. Though not a single friend ever came to his bedside to comfort him, the gentle stroking of an unknown nurse seemed to have made a measurable difference. Questions about human relationships, loneliness, and its medical consequences have occupied my attention ever since.

When the struggle between life and death finally ended, the medical "cause" of his death was succinctly summarized: ventricular fibrillation, ruptured aneurysm, and extensive bodily trauma. There was, of course, page upon page of medical records meticulously charting his demise, and in the end, it seemed remarkably easy to diagnose and summarize the "cause" of his death. There was a great deal about this man that no one in the hospital really knew, but the medical personnel no doubt felt that the missing information had little to do with the immediate treatment of his life-threatening traumas. But still one had to wonder: What was the true cause of his death? Was it really ventricular fibrillation? Technically, there could be no doubt about that assessment. Yet, his medical charts did mention a history of chronic alcoholism, and there were other hints that his life had not been a particularly happy one.

During the fourteen days that he struggled in the hospital, he was, in a very real sense, completely alone in a world surrounded by strangers and strange technologies. It was unsettling to think that I had watched him for so long and yet I did not know who he really was, what he had experienced in his life, or what gave his life meaning. The questions were unanswerable, and perhaps it was more reassuring to simply conclude that the cause of death was ventricular fibrillation. But were his joys and his sorrows related to his premature demise? Was his life filled with love, or with loneliness? Did he, like so many other alcoholics, eventually end up totally alone and isolated? And was his loneliness related to his medical problems? Somehow, these questions seemed out of place. How could one ever hope to repair the damage created by a lifetime of loneliness, compounded by alcoholism and other types of self-destructive behavior?

And yet, I could not ignore one simple fact: the heart of this comatose patient did respond to the quiet comforting of a nurse. In that sense, he shared much in common with the majority of patients in coronary care and shock trauma units. What *were* the medical consequences of loneliness? Fourteen days of lonely suffering in a shock trauma unit had given these questions a new sense of urgency. A man I never engaged in dialogue, and never really knew or understood, had raised questions I could no longer ignore.

HUMAN COMPANIONSHIP IN CONTEXT

Long before scientists began to catalogue the various ways that human contact can alter the human heart, physicians were already well aware of its influence. In his book *The Story of Heart Disease*, Terrence East described how the Greek physician Erasistratus, head of the medical school in Alexandria in 250 B.C., used patients' heart rate reactions to human contact to advance his own medical career.[162]

"Antiochus [the First] had fallen in love with his stepmother, Stratonice, and had really become ill. Erasistratus diagnosed the disorder by observing the patient's pulse-change when the lady of his affections entered the room. Marriage cured him, and established the doctor's fame and fortune."

Similarly, Aulus Cornelius Celsus, perhaps the most famous Roman medical scribe during the era when Christ was born, recognized the power of human contact on the heart. To physicians, he gave the following advice on bedside manner in his text *De Medicina*:[163]

"Bathing, exercise, fear and anger, and any other state of mind, may often be apt to excite the pulse, so that when the medical man first comes, the anxiety of the patient, who is in doubt as to what he may seem to him to have, may upset the pulse. For this reason it is not the part of an experienced doctor that he seize the arm with his hand at once; but first of all sit down with a cheerful expression, and inquire how he feels, and if there is any fear of him, to calm the patient with agreeable talk; and then at last, lay his hand on the patient's body. How easily a thousand things may disturb the pulse which even the sight of a doctor may upset." [164]

These reactions described so long ago by Erasistratus and Celsus describe immediate cardiac responses to brief and transient types of human interactions. In trying to understand the influence of human companionship on the heart, it is important to distinguish between these types of brief interactions and the more enduring social milieu or social life-style of an individual.

Transient human interactions themselves occur within several very important contexts. While many human interactions are fleeting, they nevertheless occur within a far larger cultural and interpersonal setting. A brief handshake with a friend seen weekly is very different from a handshake with a friend not seen in years. The acute loneliness resulting from the sudden loss of a loved one is very different from the chronic loneliness experienced by someone who has spent his or her childhood or adult years in social isolation. The chronic loneliness experienced by school dropouts is different from the loneliness experienced by someone recently divorced or bereaved. The impact of transient human contact on the heart in these varied conditions obviously can differ greatly. In order to understand the effects of any single episode of human contact on the heart, it is necessary to have at least some understanding of the more global life of the individual.

An additional distinction must be made between the effects of transient human interactions on individuals who have healthy hearts and on individuals who already suffer from heart disease. While the emotional reactions might be the same in both, the physiological consequences can be very different. In the first case, the changes usually have no immediate clinical consequences, while in the second case the changes can very well be lethal.

TRANSIENT HUMAN CONTACT IN INDIVIDUALS WITHOUT HEART DISEASE

To the readers of this book, there are, perhaps, no bodily reactions more familiar than the feelings of apprehension experienced when visiting one's family physician. When the physician measures blood pressure, for example, you may feel a bit anxious and even be aware that your heart is beating faster. Physicians routinely measure blood pressure several times in order to get a "true reading," since they are quite cognizant that the interaction itself can elevate a patient's blood pressure. This well-known phenomenon has been labeled "white-coat hypertension."

Before the late 1970s, and the advent of computer technology that permitted one to monitor blood pressure automatically, medical investigators relied on the continuous recording of heart rate to give them some idea of the influence of human interactions. The method historically used to measure blood pressure required silence from both the doctor and patient, since the doctor needed quiet in order to hear the pulse beating in the patient's brachial artery.

This method served to reinforce the notion that blood pressure functioned somewhat like oil pressure in an automobile engine, and that the reactivity known as "white coat hypertension" was little more than a medical curiosity that could be abolished with a few minutes of quiet rest. The silence built into the measurement of blood pressure also served to minimize the importance of talking and human communication.

From an historic perspective, therefore, the continuous monitoring of heart rate was available long before scientists were able to continuously monitor blood pressure. This historic reality is important to note here because only later were I and others able to appreciate the fact that blood pressure is far more reactive to human dialogue than heart rate. Yet, investigators have long recognized the power of transient human contact to influence heart rate.

Drs. Arthur Moss and Bruce Wynar at the University of Rochester, for example, demonstrated that the average heart rate of 10 healthy medical residents (average age: 26 years) increased from 73 beats per minute up to 154 beats per minute while they were presenting medical cases to their senior physician-teachers! While virtually no physical exertion was required to produce these results, such increases were approximately 80 percent of the maximal heart rate change that could be obtained under any condition in this age group. The magnitude of this reaction was greater than the largest heart rate increases observed in skiers of comparable age during vigorous cross-country competition. Clearly, their teachers—all senior medical colleagues—had an amazing capacity to influence the heart rate of their students.[165]

Heart rate responses to transient human interactions have also been examined during psychotherapy. Dr. Milton Greenblatt and colleagues at Harvard University Medical School, for example, recorded the heart rates of both patients and psychiatrist-interviewers. In those sessions where the psychiatrist felt least disturbed and believed that he and the patient had communicated very effectively, their cardiac relationship (the concomitant changes in their two heart rates) was closest. In those therapy sessions where the psychiatrist reported the most disturbance—because he was preoccupied either with something other than his patient's communication or with certain aspects of what the patient had said—the relationship between their heart rate changes was distant. [166]

Drs. Stanek, Hahn, and Mayer at Heidelberg University, in Germany, also observed similar heart rate changes in patients in therapy. During psychoanalytic interviews, they monitored patients who were specifically fearful of having a heart attack, even though they exhibited no detectable cardiac pathology. The most crucial moments in the interviews (as judged by independent observers) were accompanied by the largest changes in the heart rates of both the therapist *and* the patient.[167]

Dr. Kaplan and his colleagues at Baylor University Medical School suggested that the common waxing and waning of bodily changes, such as heart rate, might provide an objective index of the degree of rapport that occurs between a therapist and his patient. They found that cardiac interactions were much more likely to occur between two individuals who either liked or disliked each other than between individuals who had neutral attitudes toward each other or were uninvolved with each other.[168]

Even the menstrual cycle appears to be influenced by relationships. It has been reported, for instance, that the menstrual cycles of close friends and roommates in a college dormitory appear to be related, while randomly selected girls on the same campus showed no such correspondence. [169]

Dr. John Mason at the Walter Reed Army Institute observed that the blood chemistries of three crewmen working closely on a lengthy B-52 flight reached similar elevated levels of 17 hydroxycorticosteroids (involved in stress reactions) at the same time of the same day.

Similar findings were also seen in two all-female groups of college-age volunteers placed on a research ward. The blood chemistries of these two groups of women began to change in similar fashion during the day. A mixed-sex ward of volunteers showed no such correlations, even after five weeks of measurements. The investigators pointed out that "something" other than common exposure to a similar environment seemed to influence blood chemistry. That "something" appeared to be companionship.[170]

HUMAN COMPANIONSHIP IN TIMES OF STRESS

Twenty-eight years after the end of World War II, the Office of the Surgeon General finally completed a thorough analysis of American casualties during the war. In the volume on neuro-psychiatric casualties, the medical staff of the Surgeon General's Office summarized the main lesson learned from World War II as follows:[171]

"Perhaps the most significant contribution of World War II military psychiatry was recognition of the sustaining influence of the small combat group or particular members thereof, variously termed "group identification," "group cohesiveness," "the buddy system," and "leadership." This was also operative in non-combat situations. Repeated observations indicated that the absence or inadequacy of such sustaining influences or their disruption during combat was mainly responsible for psychiatric breakdown in battle. These group or relationship phenomena explained marked differences in the psychiatric casualty rates of various units who were exposed to a similar intensity of battle stress."

In the book *Air War and Emotional Stress*, similar conclusions were reached. Dr. Irving Janis showed that a soldier's willingness to endure the severe stresses of combat was primarily dependent on his identification with, and the cohesiveness of, his combat unit. [172] Other studies have demonstrated that wartime stresses and natural disasters greatly increase people's needs to be with one another, and that people can reduce their feelings of stress and anxiety by seeking out each other's company. Certainly those were the feelings reported by Allyn Leavey, when he described how his friend in Stalag 17 had saved his life.

Dr. Stanley Schachter at Columbia University demonstrated that individuals facing danger instinctively seek out the comfort of human companionship. In a clinical experiment, he threatened a group of volunteer subjects with a series of either mild or painful electric shocks, and then gave them the choice of waiting alone or in the presence of other subjects. Schachter observed that subjects who were threatened with "painful shock" showed a stronger preference for waiting with others than those who were threatened with a "mild" shock. [173] He concluded that "people do serve a direct anxiety-reducing function for one another, they comfort and support, they reassure one another and attempt to bolster courage. There can be little doubt that the state of anxiety leads to the arrival of affiliative tendencies." [174]

Apart from physical torture and death, solitary confinement has long been recognized as one of the most dreaded of human experiences. And those who endure unusually harsh prison environments frequently credit their survival to strength derived from their fellow men. Psychiatrists like Dr. Joe Dimsdale have conducted extensive interviews with survivors of Nazi concentration camps. According to many of these survivors, the strength obtained from their fellow prisoners was the most significant factor in their continued will to live. On the other hand, many victims who were suddenly torn away from their loved ones succumbed to a syndrome labeled "musselmann" by their fellow inmates. Unable to relate to others in the camps, they often gave way to profound despair, lost hope, and perished.[175]

Dr. Bogdonoff and his colleagues at the Duke University School of Medicine demonstrated a relationship between heart rate changes and elevations in free fatty acids (which have been linked to the development of coronary heart disease) in pairs of human beings. In an experiment, one partner simply listened, while the other was forced to answer highly personal questions. After the experiment, individuals who had been told merely to listen passively reported that they felt very personally involved in their partners' answers. And their bodily changes closely mirrored the types of changes exhibited by their partners who were under direct stress. The Duke University investigators also observed that free fatty acids were significantly higher in subjects recruited individually for an experiment than in pairs of recruits who had been prior acquaintances.[176]

Dr. William Schottstaedt and his colleagues at a specialized metabolic ward at the Oklahoma Medical School Hospital observed that various ward stresses could significantly alter hormonal levels, and consequently alter the outcome of treatment. Interestingly, these investigators observed:[177]

"Interpersonal difficulties were the most common source of stress to be associated with metabolic deviations. These accounted for twenty-eight of the forty-six stressful situations associated with such deviations. In general, they seemed to center on the most significant relationships. Interpersonal stresses arising between individuals without strong ties were less often associated with significant repercussions in the metabolic data."

Drs. Stewart Wolf, Schottstaedt, and others then used this metabolic ward to study whether human interactions might alter levels of serum cholesterol in patients suffering from heart disease in an environment where diet and exercise could be rigidly controlled. Reassuring and supportive types of relationships, their findings indicated, could significantly lower the levels of serum cholesterol of patients in an intensive-care environment, while stressful human interactions could significantly elevate cholesterol levels even when diet was rigidly controlled. Within the hospital setting, the patients' serum cholesterol levels changed according to the nature of the human interactions they experienced. Perhaps one case they relate will help describe their general findings.[178]

The patient was a 49-year-old man who had had several previous heart attacks and a history of disrupted human relationships. During hospitalization, they reported, the patient seemed happy and reasonably relaxed, although very eager to please during the first few days of the study while receiving daily visits from a new female friend. When she left town for a few days without telling him, however, he became anxious. Serum cholesterol concentration rose somewhat until she returned, revisited, and reassured him. During this outside-the-hospital visit, however, she had met another man whom she preferred. Her daily visits to the patient fell off and on November 13, 1957, she told him that she had abandoned plans to marry him and would not see him again. He became intensely depressed. Again his serum cholesterol readings rose significantly, and the following day he had a recurrent myocardial infarction. Four days later, he died. (p. 384)

TRANSIENT HUMAN CONTACT IN PATIENTS WITH HEART DISEASE

Transient heart rate changes that occur in individuals who have had a heart attack or who are experiencing other types of cardiac difficulties pose special problems that need not be of particular concern to healthy individuals. After a heart attack, for example, many transient cardiac changes can threaten a patient's life. The importance of human contact in such circumstances ought not to be minimized: human contact can serve as one of the primary healing agents for the injured heart, or it can be the source of lethal distress!

Physicians have long recognized that transient human contact can influence the cardiovascular system of individuals suffering from heart disease. The noted eighteenth-century English physician, John Hunter, who himself suffered from angina pectoris, once remarked that his "life was in the hands of any rascal who chose to annoy and tease him." Ironically, he predicted the precise circumstances of his own death. One day at a medical board meeting, Hunter got into an argument with a colleague who had contradicted him. He became so enraged that he ceased speaking, stormed out of the room, and immediately dropped dead.[179]

Sir William Osler, one of the foremost pioneers of medicine at The Johns Hopkins Medical School and one of America's most eminent physicians, once remarked that "palpitation of the heart in a medical student may be the result of a lobster salad the night before or the girl left behind." While this statement suggests a clinical cavalierness about cardiac disturbances in a healthy young student, Osler realized that "the girl left behind" could cause cardiac arrhythmias even in a healthy medical student. He also recognized the influence of human contact on patients suffering either from cardiac disorders or from a wide range of other serious medical problems.[180]

Osler became the twentieth century's chief spokesman for the medical importance of bedside manner and the crucial role of human companionship in physical well-being. He recognized the connection between angina pectoris, sudden death, and the interpersonal and emotional life-style of his patients. In his famous "Lumleian Lectures on Angina Pectoris," delivered at Oxford University in 1910, he noted:

In a group of 20 men, everyone of whom I know personally, the outstanding feature was the incessant treadmill of practice; and yet if hard work—that "badge of all our tribe"—was alone responsible, would there not be a great many more cases? Every one of these men had an additional factor, worry; in not a single case under 50 years of age was this feature absent.... Listen to some of the comments which I jotted down of the circumstances connected with the onset of attacks: "A man of great mental and bodily energy, working early and late in a practice, involved in speculations in land," "domestic infelicities," "worries in the Faculty of Medicine," "troubles with the trustees of his institution," "lawsuits," "domestic worries," and so on through the list. [181]

A large scientific literature has confirmed the clinical impressions of physicians like Osler. Patients who have recovered from a myocardial infarction are but one example. Dr. Stewart Wolf and his colleagues published a paper that has since become the model for virtually all subsequent investigations in this field. Working at Cornell University Medical School, he and fellow physicians randomly selected 12 patients with previous cardiac difficulties who had come to the hospital complaining of "chest palpitation." They took exhaustive life histories on all 12, and then interviewed them repeatedly while continuously recording their electrocardiograms.

The authors found that anxiety was a prominent feature in 11 of the 12 patients examined. All had experienced a lack of parental love in childhood, had not married, had encountered serious marital problems, or were divorced. In every case, the onset of the patient's cardiac problems could be traced to a specific traumatic interpersonal event in the patient's life. Furthermore, while being interviewed by these physicians, 8 of the 12 patients exhibited marked heart rate increases. When interviewed on topics they were known to be sensitive about, these patients began to develop cardiac arrhythmias not previously present. Here is a typical case:[182]

"A 45-year-old housewife came to the hospital with complaints of palpitations both at rest and upon exertion, which she had had for four years....For almost 20 years prior to the onset of her symptoms, the patient had wavered in her attachment to two men. One she had loved, but feeling unsure of him, she had married the other, who appeared to be stronger but proved to be also unkind. As her husband increasingly mal-treated her, she finally resolved to divorce him. In the setting of this decision, she became aware of marked tension and anxiety and noted the onset of her symptoms.

"These continued as her conflict was prolonged by her inability to detach herself from her husband [following the divorce] and marry the second man. Anxiety was joined by resentment when she blamed both men for her unhappiness [an exercise tolerance test at the height of her anxiety showed a marked inability of the heart to tolerate standard exercise tests in the laboratory].... Following this the patient came to the clinic over a 7-month period during which she ventilated and discussed her conflicts and the origins of her emotional disturbance. During this period she gradually became more relaxed and all her symptoms greatly improved."

This case is particularly interesting because it shows the way in which emotional problems interact with physical factors to influence the heart. It suggests that even the ability to engage in physical exercise is not determined strictly by one's physical condition, but is also affected by emotional tension. Dr. Stewart Wolf similarly documented that clinically serious abnormal heart reactions, including atrial fibrillation and ventricular tachycardia, could occur even in individuals with apparently normal hearts when they discussed topics emotionally stressful to them.

Likewise, Drs. Weiner, Singer, and Reiser observed that the cardiac systems of young healthy subjects changed far more during an experiment in which they were asked to tell a story about a series of ambiguous pictures than comparable subjects suffering from hypertension. They noted, however, that individuals suffering from hypertension uniformly remained distant, uninvolved, and socially isolated from the experimenter, while healthy individuals readily and even eagerly interacted with the experimenter:[183]

"There is clinical evidence to suggest that hypertensive patients are sensitive (both in the direction of, amelioration, and worsening of the medical status) to the vicissitudes of emotional interchange with physicians with whom they have established long-standing close emotional relationships. The insulating device we describe here and elsewhere may be looked upon as a sort of protection erected by these patients against their vulnerability to close relationships." [184]

Dr. Weiner and his colleagues described a cyclical pattern of behavior in the life-style of patients suffering from hypertension. Given their propensity to show exaggerated cardiac changes during various social interactions, such individuals, they suggested, would try to protect themselves from excessive cardiac reactivity by socially insulating themselves. They speculated that such individuals might very well try to remain detached and aloof in social situations, a strategy that could protect them from social "over-involvement," with exaggerated blood pressure elevations, whenever they interacted with others.

Several decades later, with the added advantage of computer technology that automatically measured blood pressure, I would come to appreciate the remarkable clinical wisdom involved in these observations. In the next chapter, I describe studies that have subsequently confirmed that rapid elevations in blood pressure are hypertensive individuals' common response to everyday dialogue. Such cardiovascular over-reactivity inexorably places such individuals between a proverbial rock and a hard place. They can either withdraw from such social situations and increase their loneliness, or engage others while their blood pressure rises to dangerous levels.

This vascular wiring, part of what I call "the physiology of exclusion," can be altered by an alternative approach, one that can help hypertensive patients control their blood pressure surges by learning to develop an interpersonal orientation that fosters the "physiology of inclusion." Through this process, patients can be taught to modulate cardiovascular over-reactivity, and learn to include others in dialogue without undue stress.

THE STRAW THAT BREAKS THE CAMEL'S BACK

That emotional stress is a frequent precipitating factor in the development of congestive heart failure has been shown in a number of studies. Drs. Chambers and Reiser found that in 24 of 25 consecutive cases of congestive heart failure they examined at the Cincinnati General Hospital, the onset of the crises had been precipitated by severe emotional upset.

Of even greater interest is the list of precipitating causes of the "emotional stress." Sudden death of a son, desertion by a wife, desertion by a husband, rejection by a husband—the emotional events all seemed to involve the loss of some type of human love or the loss of security gained from human contact. In almost every case, the emotional crises involved interpersonal losses. Chambers and Reiser noted that the interpersonal life histories of these patients were most likely of major significance in predisposing them to develop heart disease. The following are the factors they were able to identify as precipitating the onset of congestive heart failure:[185]

FACTORS LEADING TO CONGESTIVE HEART FAILURE

1. Desertion by relative
2. Relatives' refusal to care for patient
3. Sudden death of son
4. Desertion by one son and landlady; serious accident to other son
5. Illness of mother; argument with wife
6. Desertion by wife
7. Sudden death of husband
8. Husband's death; rejection by relatives
9. Rejection by husband and son
10. Marriage of daughter; wife's leg amputated
11. Desertion by husband
12. Rejection by children
13. Desertion by brother and sister-in-law
14. Rejection by employer
15. Rejection by husband
16. Rejection by employer
17. Eviction from home of 18 years
18. Eviction from home of 17 years
19. Loss of pseudo-masculine defenses

Drs. Chambers and Reiser suggested that lack of social support, coupled with a variety of interpersonal stresses, led to total circulatory collapse. The lack of love or sudden loss of love, they pointed out, acted like "the straw that breaks the camel's back." One typical case cited by these investigators is included here to underscore the similarity of these life histories:

Patient #3, a 66-year-old black man, was diagnosed as having, among other medical problems, chronic bronchial asthma, pulmonary emphysema, chronic alcoholism, and chronic progressive congestive heart failure of a year's duration.

BACKGROUND
The patient reported that he had been separated from his wife for 15 years and that he had been living alone for this period without maintaining much, if any, direct contact with any of his five children. His life story was characterized by mild pseudo-masculine denial of dependency and chronic alcoholism. Life relationships had been tenuous; his work record was sporadic. He was extremely reluctant to discuss his children, stating that they were all failures and that they did not "figure" in his life situation. He was obviously depressed and talked repeatedly of his aloneness and the fact that there was no one to help him.

PRECIPITATING FACTOR
The sudden death of a son (age 33) who had been living with the patient for many years. Although the patient had not mentioned the fact of his son's death or talked of his relationship with him, it was learned through social service contacts that there had been an extremely close relationship between them. They had been living together, and the patient had been quite dependent upon him. Following the son's death, mild congestive failure developed. On hospitalization, digitalis intoxication was found to be present. [186]

HUMAN CONTACT AND THE RECOVERY PROCESS

This clinical vignette is but a small part of a large series of studies indicating that interpersonal situations can produce dangerous and even lethal cardiac changes, especially in individuals suffering from significant heart disease. But the reverse is also true. If the lack of human love or the memory of earlier personal traumas can disturb the heart, then just as clearly the presence of human love may serve as a powerful therapeutic force, helping the heart to restore itself.

Nowhere is the power of human contact more readily apparent than in the period of emotional crisis that follows the sudden occurrence of a heart attack. As Osler points out, warm, interpersonal support is a critical element in the recovery process of such patients. This therapeutic power begins immediately after a heart attack, in the form of the bedside manner of those who first come in medical contact with the patient, and continues thereafter in the loving support given by the patient's family.[187]

Dr. Gunnar Biorck, for example, examined 223 cardiac patients in the town of Malmo, Sweden. He found that all of the patients who encountered the most serious medical problems after they left the hospital reported the lack of social support as crucial. Having regained their physical and psychological strength in the hospital, many felt deserted and very lonely when they returned to their homes. [188] A special problem in convalescence and in cases of chronic disability, he noted, "is the lack of contact with friends and neighbors—sometimes also with children. The intervals between visits become stretched and finally the contact ceases entirely. Time gets long, and feelings of loneliness and being deserted may present themselves."

It has been estimated that about 50 percent of all patients hospitalized for heart disease show moderate to severe depression, with the most severe depression usually accompanying the more serious disease. In addition, it has been estimated that up to one-third of all patients who have had a heart attack fail to return to work not because of physical problems, but because of psychological problems. This failure to return to work can, in turn, lead to increased social isolation, loneliness, and depression—all of which are quite certain to affect the heart adversely. The problems caused by this new type of loneliness may also be lethal.[189]

HUMAN CONTACT IN A CORONARY CARE UNIT: THE UNIVERSITY OF MARYLAND HOSPITAL STUDIES

While virtually everyone would agree that human relationships are critical to survival, it is not at all clear just what it is about the presence of another human being that is so important, especially in life-threatening environments. It is this lack of clarity about a phenomenon universally recognized as important, coupled with our previous research experiences with animals, that first led us to examine two environments in which sudden death is an ever-present danger: coronary care units and hospital shock-trauma units. In an especially intimate way, we studied the effects of human contact by monitoring the hearts of patients whose lives were in mortal peril. We became interested in studying these critically ill patients when evidence suggested that human interactions could alter heart rhythms in highly significant ways.

Coronary care units were developed as specialized treatment facilities over the past four decades. The units came into being when it was recognized that many patients who entered hospitals after suffering a heart attack were needlessly dying because of the lack of immediate medical care. Of special concern was the fact that many of these patients appeared well on the road to recovery. Not infrequently, nurses would check on these patients, report that they looked quite healthy, and then return a few minutes later, only to find them dead.

These sudden deaths in the hospital, it was determined, were due to electrical disturbances in their heart rhythms. The patients needed to be placed in special units and monitored continuously for a few days after a heart attack. If recurrent cardiac complications did occur during this period, then the medical personnel could at least take immediate measures to aid the patient.

Complications stem from the fact that there is a marked rise in the incidence of abnormal heartbeats in the first 24 to 72 hours after a heart attack. These abnormal beats have the potential to seriously disrupt the normal rhythm of the heart and can lead to ventricular fibrillation and sudden death. The occurrence of these abnormal heart rhythms make it imperative for a person to be taken to a hospital as soon as possible after a heart attack. During this crucial period, even if a patient reports feeling better and the heart pain diminished, their lives still hang in the balance. After the development of these specialized units, the incidence of sudden death while in the hospital dropped by 35 to 40 percent.

The continuous monitoring of the patient's heartbeat in coronary care units enabled my colleagues and I to observe the effects of human interactions in a way previously impossible. Before the development of such units, records on the effects of human companionship in times of distress depended either upon observations of how people behaved in such situations or upon anecdotal reports as to how they felt during these experiences. A person's cardiac reactions could not be directly linked to any physical changes because no means existed for continuously recording those changes.

Paradoxically, many of the coronary care medical personnel seemed to know the answer to our questions even before we began our studies. "Of course human contact affects the human cardiovascular system," a nurse commented after asking what we were studying. "Everyone knows that you have to measure a patient's blood pressure several times in order to get an accurate reading."

"Everyone realizes that sometimes patients are frightened and anxious when a doctor first examines them," commented a medical resident. "That's why bedside manner is so important!"

The answers to our questions seemed, at first glance, to be so grounded in "common sense" that a rather bewildering state of affairs gradually became apparent. Everyone was so certain that human interactions, such as pulse-taking, could affect patients' hearts that no one in this unit, or indeed in any coronary care unit, had ever systematically analyzed it. There were no scientific data about a phenomenon first recognized by Celsus 2,000 years ago and which everyone had subsequently assumed was "common sense." Nor did it take us very long to realize why there had been no systematic investigations in this area. The search for scientific answers to this common-sense question had to be conducted in an uncommon fashion.

In studying this phenomenon, a paramount consideration was the fact that the patients were very sick human beings. Given this reality, it was clearly impossible to do anything not part of their routine clinical care. Our experimental observations, therefore, had to be made in an environment in which nothing was scientifically controlled. This was a dimension of human contact that scientists usually avoid—contact that is unpredictable, with large number of events occurring in a world where each patient can choose to respond to all or none of the stimuli occurring around his or her bedside.

On the other hand, the heartbeat of each patient could be observed from a distance, without the patient's awareness. Physicians and nurses could also be observed interacting with patients, and neither the patients nor the medical personnel had to be consciously aware of the fact that they were being watched. Thus, at least theoretically, it was possible to determine whether these interactions affected the hearts of patients.

Several studies had suggested that human relationships are an important part of coronary care. Dr. Klein and his colleagues at the Duke University Medical Center studied 14 patients transferred from their coronary care unit to an ordinary medical ward, where their heart activity was no longer continuously monitored. The first seven patients were moved abruptly, without advance notice and without having the coronary care nurse or personal coronary care physician visit them after their transfer.

Of these seven patients, five suffered serious recurrent cardiovascular complications while still in the hospital. They complained of being lonely and depressed and felt they had been abandoned by the coronary care team, which had previously cared for them. The next seven coronary care patients transferred out of this same unit were prepared in advance for the move, and one of the coronary care nurses and the same physician followed them through the remainder of their hospital stays. While these seven patients also experienced emotional reactions, none had any recurrent cardiovascular complications. When the relationship with the familiar medical team was not abruptly terminated, these patients experienced no cardiac difficulties upon transfer.[190]

In order to begin assessing the effects of human contact in the coronary care unit, we randomly selected 20 patients for study. These patients had all been admitted to the coronary care unit at least 24 hours prior to our observations, in order to allow them to adjust to the unit and to recover somewhat from the initial shock of major cardiovascular difficulties. Each patient's heart rate was continuously recorded for an eight-hour period, and only one patient was monitored at a time. All events that occurred in the unit (e.g., alarms, noises, crises, and deaths) were marked on the polygraph immediately as they happened.

In addition, all personal contacts with the patient, including physicians' visits, nursing interactions, and family visits, were immediately marked and coded on the patient's heart rate record. Nurses assigned the exclusive task of observing the patients logged the nature of these interactions. Since nurses were routinely assigned observational functions in the coronary care unit, it was easy to blend this type of activity into the unit routine without arousing the attention of the unit's patients.[191]

Since our chief concern was to study the heart reactions of patients in the typical coronary care setting without either the patient or the medical staff being aware of it, no attempt was made to control any of the interactions experienced by the patients. Many of the interactions were quite complex. For example, a nurse might come to the patient's bedside while a physician was examining the patient. We focused our attention, therefore, on interactions that were less complex, such as pulse-taking by a nurse, measurement of blood pressure, visits of relatives, and so on. When changes in heart rhythm were observed during such interactions, the entire context of these interactions had to be examined.

The criteria for what constituted a less complex interaction included two stipulations: that the patient rest quietly, and be alone, for a minimum of three minutes before and after any interaction; and that the environment be quiet during this period. These criteria were necessary in order to allow us to assess reactions to events such as pulse palpation within the larger context of the patient's usual heart rate and rhythm.[192]

A CASE STUDY

The first patient we monitored, a 72-year-old woman, was in the coronary care unit because she had what is known as 2:1 heart block. That is, the electrical impulse controlling her heart beat failed to activate the enntire heart.

Our initial human interactions with her—and their effects—are shown in the following graphs. The first event was a routine pulse-taking by a nurse, before and after which the patient rested quietly in bed for three minutes. During the pulse-taking, the patient's heart rate began to vary back and forth from its pattern of 2:1 block. In essence, her heart began to change from 30 up to 60 beats per minute while the nurse took her pulse.

During the day, there were two other episodes of pulse-taking and one episode of blood pressure measurement where very similar cardiac reactions occurred. While this patient was still in heart block, however, one other pulse-taking episode occurred during which no heart rate or heart rhythm changes were recorded. For three minutes before a nurse came to this patient's bedside simply to give her a pill, the patient's heart rate had been a regular 2:1 heart block, with a rate of 35 beats per minute. But during the entire one minute the nurse was at her bedside, the patient's heart rate abruptly changed, becoming 70-75 beats per minute. It then changed back abruptly to a rate of 35 beats per minute and 2:1 heart block for the three minutes after the nurse left the patient's bedside. A similar reaction occurred when the nurse brought this patient lunch.

Later that same day, the medicine the cardiologist had prescribed (atropine) took effect, and the patient was no longer in continuous 2:1 block. During this period, we again monitored the pulse-taking. This time the beat-to-beat heart rate both before and after pulse-taking was approximately 70-75 beats per minute, with only periodic episodes of heart block occurring. However, when the nurse took the patient's pulse, the heart rate was slightly elevated, the beat became quite rhythmic, and the periodic pattern of heart block was completely abolished.

This particular pulse-taking produced an inverted mirror image of the cardiac reaction to pulse-taking that this same patient had shown earlier in the day.

It was relatively easy to understand the changes in the patient's nervous system that were producing these reactions. Understanding those physiological mechanisms, however, did not help us understand why the nurses had these effects on the patient's heart.

We began to see similar types of heart rhythm changes in other patients, and occasional changes in the frequency of abnormal heartbeats when people were at a patient's bedside. Sometimes, the frequency of these abnormal beats would increase. More often, they would decrease. And sometimes, there were no apparent changes, leading us to wonder whether these changes in arrhythmia were spontaneous fluctuations that would have occurred whether a person came to the bedside or not. [193]

The complex nature of these heart reactions made it clear to us that to continue measuring every heartbeat, and then analyzing mile upon mile of records, would be an overwhelming task. Considering the numerous factors that might influence heart rate and heart rhythm, the many types of cardiac pathologies, the various patient personalities, and the variety of human interactions, we had to enlarge our sample of patients. The trade-off was to restrict the amount of time spent observing any one patient.

What we needed to do was to concentrate on some type of human contact that was relatively simple, yet experienced by all patients in the unit. Pulse palpation seemed to best fit this requirement. Every patient in the coronary care unit routinely had his or her pulse taken by a nurse every four hours, day or night, waking or sleeping. Furthermore, this was a human interaction that involved touch, was discrete and of relatively short duration, required no conversation, and demanded no physical exertion by the patient.

We then examined the effects of pulse palpation on the heart rate and rhythm of over 300 coronary care patients, both during daylight hours and during the night when the patients were sleeping. Each pulse-taking was examined only if the patient was resting alone for three minutes before and three minutes afterward.

After examining these patients, it was statistically clear that even the routine event of pulse palpation could alter the frequency of cardiac arrhythmia in coronary care patients. In some of the patients, the simple act of pulse-taking had the power to completely suppress any arrhythmia that had been occurring. In other patients with high frequencies of ventricular arrhythmia (the type of rhythm disturbance that can lead to sudden death), a nurse's incidental touch while taking their pulse significantly reduced the incidence of these dangerous types of arrhythmia.[194]

The medical implications of these studies need not detain us here, except to point out that human touch could have important influences on a patient's heart rate and rhythm. These observations did, however, raise many questions. Did pulse-taking frighten the patients? After all, they were in coronary care units and undoubtedly concerned with the status of their hearts. Or, conversely, did the pulse-taking serve to comfort and reassure them that they were under continuous care? And what specifically led to the changes in the frequency of arrhythmia? Did the patients move physically in bed or change their manner of breathing in ways not noticed? Or was it an emotional response that influenced these heart rhythms? Any of these factors could have produced the heart reactions we were observing.

An even larger question began to be of concern: was it only patients with cardiac pathology that reacted to human touch, or did patients without heart problems react similarly? These questions led us to shift our studies temporarily from the coronary care unit to one of the most acute clinical areas in any modern hospital—the shock-trauma unit.

HUMAN CONTACT IN THE SHOCK-TRAUMA UNIT

In the mid-1960s, at The University of Maryland Hospital, Dr. R. Adams Cowley developed the nation's first shock-trauma unit. Eventually, it became a prototype for similar units that now exist in most large metropolitan areas in the United States. The highly specialized Maryland Shock-Trauma Center was developed to handle life-threatening medical emergencies, usually involving a patient who had suddenly experienced severe trauma and often had lapsed into a state of circulatory shock and coma. About 60 percent of the victims treated annually in this unit were flown in by a state-operated helicopter medical service. Typical patients included victims of serious automobile accidents, industrial accidents, or gunshot wounds. Most patients flown to this unit were in acute danger of death if multiple medical and surgical procedures were not immediately performed.

The shock-trauma unit itself was far more complex than a coronary care unit. The unit had 12 beds in an open rectangular area, in the center of which was a central monitoring station. Each bed unit was completely autonomous, with its own medical and patient care supplies: refrigerator, sink, running water, respirator, wall suction, wall air and oxygen, equipment for continuously monitoring the patient's electrocardiograms and blood pressure, and so forth. Each bed unit was equipped with all the facilities necessary to conduct almost every emergency medical procedure. At the central desk, all patients' electrocardiograms, as well as a number of other bodily changes, were continuously monitored. A computer constantly scanned each bed, hourly printing out each patient's heart rate, blood pressure, temperature, respiration, and any other physiological data desired by the attending medical teams.

The possibility of monitoring the effects of human contact in the shock-trauma unit was of keen interest to us because, unlike the patients in the coronary care unit, many of these patients were younger, and most had no heart disease. Treatment for many of these patients involved the use of certain extreme medical procedures. One was the use of d-tubocurarine, a drug originally developed centuries ago by the Amazon Indians. The Indians placed the drug, curare, on arrow tips because it had the capacity to paralyze and immediately kill wild animals.

In its modern medical use, d-tubocurarine paralyzes every muscle in a patient's body, so that the patient cannot move, speak, open his eyes, or even breathe on his own without access to an artificial respirator. Yet, curare still leaves a person perfectly aware of what is occurring. If conscious, therefore, the patient can hear and feel the world around him, but cannot move any muscles. In the shock-trauma unit, the drug was occasionally administered when patients had uncontrollable seizures, or when they were delirious or violently struggling against medical procedures employed to save their lives.

The use of curare allowed the exploration of certain basic questions raised by our observations with coronary care patients. Would patients' hearts react to human contact when the patients themselves could no longer move or change their breathing pattern, or when the patients had no discernible cardiac disease? In extreme cases, would these patients react to human touch even if they were delirious or in deep comas?

We decided to study two types of human interactions with shock-trauma patients. The first consisted of relatively simple spontaneous clinical interactions, such as a doctor's visit, in which neither patient nor staff was aware of being observed. The second type involved planned interactions in which nurses, aware of the study's purpose, took the patient's pulse, held the patient's hand, or touched his arm and verbally comforted him with the following type of statement:

[First name of patient], my name is [First name of nurse] and I am a nurse. I know you can't answer me when I talk to you even though you can hear me. That's because of your medication. You're receiving a drug called curare which has temporarily paralyzed you so that you are unable to respond in any way. The drug has also blocked your respiration, so there is a machine at your bedside breathing for you, which you may be able to hear. This medicine is an unpleasant but very necessary part of your therapy, so please try to relax and bear with it. The effect of the drug will only be temporary, and once the drug is discontinued, you will be able to move as before. We will try to anticipate your needs, since we know that you are at present unable to communicate them to us. There is always a doctor or nurse at your bedside, so please try not to worry.

This statement was neither memorized nor delivered verbatim from notes. Rather, the nurse reacted to each patient in an individualized manner. Whenever possible, we required three-minute resting periods prior to and following both types of interactions.

Although a nurse holding a patient's hand and comforting him was among the simplest human interactions we could analyze, even this most elementary aspect of human contact proved to be quite difficult to study within the context of the shock-trauma environment. Various clinical personnel were almost always at the patient's bedside, and the presence of as many as seven or eight physicians and four or five nurses was not uncommon. Then there were the telephones at the central station, which were constantly ringing.

This complex array of stimuli frequently made it necessary to watch patients for as long as four to six hours before a period would occur in which the patient was left alone for as much as seven minutes. This was the minimum time period required to evaluate patient reactions to human touch. Since patients were curarized for various periods of time, there was no precise way of determining whether they were conscious during the interactions. The research team relied on the attending physician's general assessment of mental state during periods when another drug in use reversed curare's effects. However, one of the patients was studied immediately after he was given d-tubocurarine. Since he was talking with the physician just before he was given this drug, it is reasonable to assume that he was conscious during these observations.

In spite of the large number of stimuli bombarding each patient, the most elementary types of human contact, including simple human touch, appeared to produce dramatic changes in the patient's heart rate. For example, the following Figure shows the heart rate of one 31-year-old woman critically injured in an automobile accident. Her heart rate slowed almost 20 beats per minute when a nurse quietly took her pulse. When the episode was recorded, this patient had been in a coma for two days.[195]

A similar change in heart rate was observed in a 30-year-old man who had suffered severe chest injuries in an accident. The nurse in this instance held his hand and quietly comforted him.

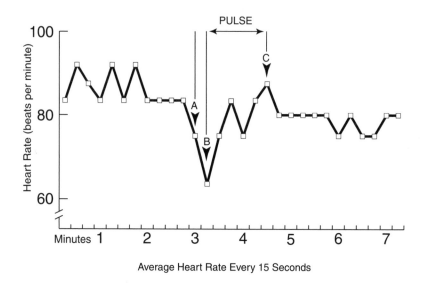

Average Heart Rate Every 15 Seconds

Effect of Pulse Taking on Curarized Woman

Patient's heart rate averaged every 15 seconds before, during, and after pulse taking by nurse. Note decrease in heart rate during pulse taking.
KEY: (A) Nurse Enters, (B) Nurse Takes Pulse, (C) Nurse Stops and Leaves.

Later in that same day, while we were monitoring this patient, seven doctors on medical rounds came to his bedside to discuss his case. After a few minutes, they left. Several minutes later, another physician came in to perform tracheal suction on the patient. This uncomfortable procedure requires the physician to periodically and briefly turn off the patient's respirator, during which the patient is unable to breathe. It is difficult to imagine a more psychologically frightening or physically distressing sensation, and we may assume that the resulting heart rate increase, as the data very clearly indicated to us, was about as great as could be elicited under these extremely traumatic conditions. It is therefore of great interest to note that the heart rate increase was almost as great (although nowhere near as sustained) while the seven doctors chatted about this patient as during a period in which no such drastic procedures were performed.

Finally, the same heart rate changes were observed in an 11-year-old girl when a nurse quietly held her hand. This young girl had been struck by a car, sustaining a skull fracture and multiple pelvis fractures. She was in a coma when first brought to the shock-trauma unit and gradually recovered during the next eight days. When she suddenly became restless, confused, and in great respiratory distress, she was given d-turbo curare.

For the three minutes before the nurse approached her bedside, the girl's heart rate was cycling rather rhythmically from a maximum of 125 beats per minute to a low of 105 beats per minute. No unusual change in heart rate was observed during most of the period that the nurse quietly held her hand. However, just as the nurse let go of the girl's hand, her heart rate increased to a peak rate of 136 beats per minute and then fell to about 95 beats per minute before cycling back into the previous pattern. During the entire seven-minute period, the highest and lowest heart rates occurred within 30 seconds after the nurse let go of the patient's hand.

These observations—especially of the two patients in deep comas (one died shortly after our observations)—push us to the very limits of scientific knowledge. It can never be established with 100 percent certainty, for example, that these heart rate changes would not have occurred by chance, and there is no way to repeat these observations to conclusively resolve that question. All of these shock-trauma observations were of unique and poignant human interactions, and, from a scientific point of view, this uniqueness must be recognized as both a strength and an unavoidable weakness. The events monitored in this study can never be replicated within the precise context of their occurrence. They were simply unique human interactions in a trauma unit where physicians and nurses were caring for patients in immediate danger of death.

The shock-trauma heart rate data did show that the changes seen in the coronary care unit were not unique to human beings with heart problems. They also convinced us that the effects of holding a patient's hand could be seen even in the most intense of clinical environments. If anything, the reaction of the heart rate to human contact seemed to increase under these extreme conditions.

The magnitude of these reactions must also be viewed in the context of the acute clinical environment in which they occurred. The patients, especially those in the shock-trauma unit, were bombarded by a wide array of changing environmental stimuli, any one of which could easily have had a greater impact on heart rate than the touch of a single human hand. The "control periods" just before the human contact were by no means periods of quiet relaxation for the patients.

It is also important to reemphasize that these patients varied from the very young to the very old and that they varied in terms of their cardiovascular conditions, physical status, and the types of medicines they were being given. The fact that the effects of something as routine as human touch or of quiet comforting could still be observed, despite all the factors that could potentially mask their influence, serves to underscore the vital importance they have for human hearts.

From spending many hours observing doctors and nurses in these acute clinical areas, we have also come to recognize that while these individuals spend an extraordinary amount of time with their patients, very little of it is spent talking with them. Almost everything physicians and nurses do is, of necessity, concerned with the patient's condition rather than with the patient himself.

So, even though a great deal of human contact takes place, some patients still feel socially isolated and lonely. It is only speculation, but perhaps it is this peculiar aspect of social interactions in intensive-care units that makes the hearts of so many patients so sensitive to human contact. Dr. Gunnar Biorck, a Swedish cardiologist, reiterated Sir William Osler's advice on bedside manner when he wrote in the *American Heart Journal*:[196]

"Physicians should be careful of their own attitudes, from the time of the first contact with the patient, in taking the history and in making the physical and other examinations, because the first contact will, to a great extent, determine the future interrelationship between the patient and his physician. An optimistic attitude is essential.... In dealing with cardiac patients, much may be learned by listening to their heart with the stethoscope, but it may be even more important to listen to the patient himself without a stethoscope."

AN APPRAISAL

Fifteen years spent observing these powerful cardiovascular reactions to human contact, in both animals and in human beings, inevitably led us to wonder about the opposite reality. The question literally cried out for an answer: If transient human contact had such a potent impact on the heart, what would be the medical consequences if human companionship were chronically absent? Would social isolation or chronic loneliness have a harmful impact on cardiovascular health?

The statistics described in earlier chapters emerged from this basic question. Those who lived alone or were socially isolated were far more likely to die prematurely from heart disease. The single, the widowed, the divorced, and those isolated by childhood traumas or educational failure, were all vulnerable to an increased risk of disease and premature death from literally every cause.

While it was clear that nature had at its disposal an almost limitless number of ways to terminate the lives of the lonely, one of its major weapons was the development of premature heart disease. Yet, while the statistics are overwhelming, it is not certain how it all takes place.

Knowing that school failure, bereavement, and divorce contribute to a pervasive sense of loneliness that increases the risk of premature development of hypertension, coronary heart disease, and stroke, does not clarify how it all takes place. How, for example, does chronic loneliness force one's blood pressure up into hypertensive ranges, or speed up the process of coronary heart disease? And, even more to the point, what can one do, other than use medications, to help patients overcome their vulnerability and avoid paying the ultimate cost?

After *The Broken Heart* was published in 1977, two major directives became clear. The first was to conduct larger epidemiological studies in which we could begin to isolate specific social variables that might be involved in this process. The second was to develop new ways to help people at risk to control their blood pressure and thus avoid the debilitating consequences of long-term sustained elevations.

"THE EFFECT OF PERSON" STOOD UPSIDE DOWN: COMPANION ANIMALS AND HEALTH

One of the very first long-term epidemiological studies we launched after *The Broken Heart*'s publication was an examination of the links between loneliness and survival following a heart attack. At that time, we tried to assess what determined long-term survival after patients were released from the university's coronary care unit. In essence, we tried to weigh the effects of loneliness in what is technically known as a complex variance equation. In post-heart attack survival, we assessed how important loneliness was compared to all of the other well-known risk factors.

While we could not anticipate the outcome of this large-scale study, the results helped in an unexpected way to broaden our focus. We recruited 96 heart patients about to be released from the University of Maryland Hospital coronary care unit, and asked permission to contact them on a monthly basis for at least one year. We recorded every medical, pharmaceutical, social, and economic variable that could possibly influence their long-term survival after their hospital release.[197]

At that time, my colleague, Dr. Aaron Katcher, had become curious about the effects of companion animals on human health. We knew that companion animals helped alleviate human loneliness, but we did not know whether such companionship had any impact on heart patients' survival after they were released from the hospital.

Not surprisingly, we discovered that the strongest predictor of sudden death one year after release from a coronary care unit was the extent of damage suffered by the heart muscle during the heart attack itself. The second strongest predictor, however, came as a complete shock. It was the presence, or absence, of pet companionship. During the two-year period in which we conducted these studies, 96 coronary care patients were interviewed just prior to their release from the hospital. Each patient agreed that we could contact him or her once each month, for at least one year. Twenty-nine (29) of these patients were women and 67 were men. Our question about pet-ownership was just one of a hundred different questions we asked participating patients.

The overall one-year survival rate after release from the hospital was 84 percent—78 of the 92 patients lived for at least one year after their release from the hospital, while 14 had died. A total of 58 percent of all patients reported having one or more pets, while 42 percent had none. One year after release, 28 of the patients without pets were still alive, while 11 of the petless patients had died! Of those *with* pets, fifty were still alive, and only three had died. This mortality pattern stunned us. Almost four times more petless patients had died in that first year, even though they represented only 42 percent of the sample population.

The "Effect of Person" first observed in the isolation of a Pavlovian Chamber had come full circle two decades later. We had begun our journey studying the effects of human beings on the cardiovascular system of animals. Now, it had been turned upside down. Instead of observing that human petting could lower a dog's blood pressure by 50 percent, we were now observing that the presence of a dog could be linked to saving a person's life! The therapeutic benefits of animal companions on human health began to become more apparent, as did the crushing lethality of chronic human loneliness.

Equally interesting was the manner in which these studies began to put us in touch with the lives of patients outside of the coronary care unit. Some of the patients we interviewed had had heart attacks within six months of the deaths of their lifelong mates. They seemed totally overcome by the sudden loss and the subsequent involuntary experience of living alone.

One 50-year-old single woman mentioned that she didn't know the first name of anyone in the neighborhood she had lived in for 45 years. A 44-year-old woman widowed for four years wrote after being released from the intensive-care unit: "I was just filling out one of the folding envelopes [our means of keeping in monthly contact with patients] two days before I received your letter [if a patient did not send a letter back promptly each month, we inquired about his or her health]. It makes me feel very good to know someone is concerned about me."

A 50-year-old single man who survived his heart attack told us he could not recognize a single person on his street. While he claimed to be only slightly lonely, he could list only one person we could contact in case he suddenly moved (a question we added to check on a person's health status). He didn't seem to know anyone else who would be even remotely interested in him.

We began to suspect that those medical scientists like William Osler who had spoken about the will to live were quite right: there *is* a will to live, and that will is fueled by human concern, by human and animal companionship, and by our relationship to the rest of the natural living world. The patient who felt very good knowing someone was concerned about her probably expressed the source of the will to live most eloquently.

One final note: During 1975 and 1976, we were able to take detailed social histories on 154 heart patients in the University of Maryland Coronary Care Unit. Eighty-eight of these patients were between the ages of 45 and 65, while 17 were younger than 45. The population studied was approximately 50 percent white and 50 percent black. Among the more surprising findings was the fact that only 57 percent of these patients were married. Forty-three percent were single, widowed, or divorced.

We were at first somewhat startled by this statistic, and certain that our patient sample was very different from the community at large. It came, therefore, as quite a surprise to discover that for similar age, sex, and race ranges in the Baltimore metropolitan region, 45 percent of a similar adult population was not married. Baltimore in 1976 clearly was very different from the Framingham of 1948 and even different from the

Reno of 1960, which now, at the beginning of the new millennium, seems by comparison to have been a socially idyllic world.

A POSTSCRIPT

Ideally, clinical cases ought to be juxtaposed with population mortality statistics in the depiction of any relationship as complex as that between companionship and health. Yet, sometimes the gap between individual cases and population statistics is so great that one is left sensing that the health mosaic may be too complex to put together. In this book's earlier chapters, statistics enumerating the mortality ratios of single, divorced, widowed, and school dropouts suggested the possibility that the sharp rise in premature mortality was caused by human loneliness, isolation, anxiety, or depression.

But the statistics can only hint at that possibility, and the very objectivity of the numbers tends to make discussion of loneliness more an abstract curiosity than a real attempt to come to grips with human suffering. How destructive loneliness, human isolation, and bereavement are does not strike home until you look at heartbroken patients "being saved" by medical technology, lying all alone in coronary care units and shock trauma units. While there are many patients whose lives have been filled with love, it is difficult to describe the emptiness and pain that fill some of these other patients' lives, and it is clear that no anti-arrhythmic drug or advanced technological procedures will, by themselves, prolong their lives much longer.

For the patients themselves are not abstract statistics at all. They are old men and women, sometimes even young men and women, whose children have moved far away, or whose loved ones have recently died, or who don't know the names of even one person in their neighborhood, or who don't know who you should notify in case they die, and who lie in hospital beds for weeks without visitors. They are literally brokenhearted—there really is no other term to describe it—and something beyond drugs, heart transplants, coronary bypass operations, or artificial pacemakers is needed to save them.

In my own scientific career, I had been personally brought to a crossroads by the loneliness of that 54 year-old man who died after 14 days of isolation in a shock trauma unit. By 1978, it was clear that I had to do something other than continue to observe and observe and observe.

Chapter Nine

THE HEART OF HUMAN DIALOGUE: DECODING THE LANGUAGE OF THE HEART

Serendipity was there in 1962 the very first time I watched a dog's heart rate and blood pressure drop in half in response to human petting. It was there again in 1968 and 1969 when, in coronary care and shock trauma patients, I began to observe powerful cardiac reactions to human touch. And it was surely there in 1977 when my colleagues and I first discovered the therapeutic power of companion animals in helping coronary care patients survive following their release from the hospital.

But if serendipity was ever a force in my research life, then most assuredly it was there in 1978 when I first met Dr. Maynard (Mike) Ramsey. For it was this chance meeting that eventually led me to conclude that blood pressure was linked to human dialogue in ways we had never dreamt possible. He gave us the technological key to begin decoding the language of the human heart and to recognize that human dialogue had the power to regulate cardiovascular health in ways never before understood.

Shortly after *The Broken Heart* was published, I was invited to give a keynote address to several thousand nurses at the Annual Meeting for Critical Care Nurses in St Louis, Missouri. In order to relax prior to my talk, I sought the diversion of the "Exhibition Hall," where a large number of manufacturers of medical devices and critical care supplies displayed their wares to the few visitors interested.

In the midst of the large commercial exhibitions, one tiny booth featured a small, blue, steel-encased computer box. Hosting that booth was a somewhat reserved and reticent middle-aged physician, Dr. Mike Ramsey. He was there to demonstrate his recent invention, a machine that automatically measured blood pressure and heart rate at fixed intervals, and then displayed those recordings digitally on the front panel of his computerized "blue machine." It caught my immediate attention. To accurately measure blood pressure, I had spent what seemed like an eternity at the time-consuming, painstaking, and frustrating task of inserting catheters into patients' arteries, then unclogging them, then removing them, then flushing them with heparin. A machine that actually could measure blood pressure without requiring the insertion of a catheter into a patient's artery? It seemed too good to be true!

With more than a modicum of impertinence, I began our conversation by asking Dr. Ramsey if his machine worked reliably. "Yes," he responded with quiet politeness. "It correlates very highly with in-dwelling catheterized measures of blood pressure, and is every bit as reliable as, and at times far more reliable than, measurements taken with a stethoscope."

"If it really works, then you'll make a million dollars!" I exclaimed somewhat incredulously, revealing both my unabashed crassness as well as my ignorance about the financial world of medical electronics. Dr. Ramsey smiled, almost as if trying to restrain his amusement, and then informed me that he had already sold the rights to his machine to the Critikon Division of Johnson and Johnson, and that he was now a company vice-president for research and development.[198]

No doubt it was my blissful ignorance that permitted the dialogue to continue. We chatted briefly about my convention address, during which I would discuss the links between loneliness and the increased risk of hypertension and coronary heart disease, and the vital interpersonal role that critical care nurses play in intensive care units. We then talked about how his computer device might help hypertensive patients control their blood pressure without relying exclusively on medications. We chatted as well about the various non-drug therapies then used to control blood pressure, and all their limitations.

Gradually, the topic turned to the field of "biofeedback." We both recognized that investigations in this area had been hampered by a lack of instruments to reliably measure blood pressure without relying on a stethoscope. Without intending to dampen his enthusiasm, I nevertheless threw a bit of cold water on his venture's prospects. I asserted that most of the biofeedback literature had tended to exaggerate its claims of clinical utility, and was conceptually over-simplified, especially when it came to issues of treating hypertension. I added that using his computer during biofeedback would be analogous to my using a computer to control my facial blushing.

The simple fact was that I never blushed in front of a computer, and that it was my impression that the cardiovascular system was remarkably sensitive to interpersonal relationships. "I never blushed in front of a machine when I was an adolescent," I added to emphasize my point. "But I always seemed to blush around adolescent girls. So even if I could learn to control my blood pressure with the help of a computer device, how would that help me control blushing when I asked a girl to dance?" [199] He seemed to understand my point, and with no one else visiting his booth, we continued our free associative dialogue.

Dr. Ramsey mentioned that his marketing efforts to date had yielded very promising results with surgeons and anesthesiologists. Yet, at the same time, he was having great difficulty marketing his computer to general practitioners and family physicians. As for why, which was my next question, he said that when he had demonstrated this device to ordinary physicians, they quickly concluded that the machine was inaccurate because the blood pressure readings visible on the screen changed significantly from minute to minute, sometimes in a highly dramatic manner.

"Blood pressure variability is something ordinary physicians apparently do not observe when they take blood pressure with a stethoscope," he added, "and so they assume that it does not change very quickly. But computer measurements reveal quite a different reality." When I asked what he thought caused such variability, he said he was unsure. "When surgeons and anesthesiologists measure pressure, the patients are usually unconscious and artificially respired, and in that condition, blood pressure remains far more constant. And so my machine has found quicker acceptance in that market."

I could readily understand his frustration with prevailing medical attitudes about blood pressure. My own years of measuring canine and human blood pressure on a continual basis had made it abundantly clear to me that blood pressure was highly reactive and could change significantly on a moment-to-moment basis.

I then returned to a discussion of our current research and our interest in better understanding how loneliness was linked to hypertension and coronary heart disease. How did loneliness cause one's blood pressure to rise, or contribute to the hardening of one's coronary arteries? I told him that we were now trying to answer these questions while also trying to help heart patients regulate their blood pressure. I mentioned that we were limited in our efforts because the measurement of blood pressure with a stethoscope and mercury manometer made it difficult to simultaneously carry on uninterrupted dialogue with patients.

After listening a while longer, Dr. Ramsey agreed to donate several of his "blue machines" to our research endeavors. While this may very well have been his only transaction that day, his blood pressure machines can now be seen in virtually every hospital in the western world. I will always be grateful for his generosity, his patience, and his kindness. Serendipity had smiled on me in a particularly benevolent fashion that day in St. Louis. His "blue machine" was about to change my research interests for the rest of my life.

FIGHT/FLIGHT AND
THE LONELINESS OF HYPERTENSION

The challenge was there long before *The Broken Heart* was published, and long before we were able to measure blood pressure with Dr. Ramsey's "blue machines." The evidence was compelling that loneliness was linked both to the development and exacerbation of cardiovascular disease. The death rates for those who were single, widowed, and divorced were just too impressive and consistent to ignore. Equally intriguing were the observations that human touch had a powerful effect on the hearts of patients in intensive care and shock trauma units.

Coupled with the earlier studies of the "Effect of Person" on animals, we had indeed come full circle when we similarly discovered that the long-term survival of heart patients could be influenced by the presence of companion animals. Companion animals appeared to serve as a powerful antidote to loneliness, sufficient to make a significant difference in survival after patients were released from a hospital coronary care unit. And so with the publication of *The Broken Heart*, a cycle of cardiovascular research had been completed—animals reacting to humans, humans reacting to humans, and humans reacting to animals. In all these varied situations, the heart appeared to be central to all relationships in life. And the lack of relationships and companionship, and its resultant loneliness, appeared to be one of the major plagues of modern life.

Yet, even after we were certain that chronic loneliness could sap one's strength and undermine one's chances for long-term survival, we knew that virtually all treatments of lonely patients with pre-existing heart disease were fraught with a variety of special problems. The first involved issues of prevention. In 1978, it seemed as if it would be far more beneficial to develop treatment protocols to help prevent the development of coronary heart disease in the first place, especially in people already at risk. Since loneliness was a major risk factor, we figured, maximal efforts ought to be expended trying to develop methods to help patients overcome this problem. Initially, it seemed that it would be more useful to focus our efforts on hypertension, a major risk factor contributing to the development of a wide range of medical problems, including coronary heart disease, stroke, and premature death, than to treat patients with coronary heart disease. High blood pressure could be treated and subsequent diseases avoided.

Once the treatment of hypertension became our central focus, however, I was immediately confronted by a series of perplexing problems. Research data of the time indicated that most of the non-drug approaches used to help hypertensive patients, such as biofeedback, yoga, and meditation, yielded only modest reductions in blood pressure. More importantly, the only method that appeared to be effective in addressing issues of loneliness was something analogous to the "talking cure" developed by Sigmund Freud. It hardly seemed possible to help patients address issues of loneliness without talking to them about their emotional struggles.

Yet, an extensive research literature suggested that this was precisely the wrong way to approach the problem. Although psychoanalytic and psychotherapeutic techniques appeared to be wonderful in terms of giving patients insight, research data revealed that this "cathartic approach" frequently caused their blood pressure to rise to dangerous levels. The Freudian "talking cure," it seems, had proven to be worse than the "disease" itself, and sometimes could compromise the patient's health.

Thanks in large measure to the brilliant research conducted by Walter Cannon at Harvard University, most physicians were well aware by the mid-1930s that stress played a significant role in elevating human blood pressure. In exquisite detail, Cannon had shown how the activation of the autonomic nervous system in response to life-threatening situations could lead to rapid and sustained elevations in blood pressure. This cardiovascular component of what he called the "fight/flight response" had been so well documented in animals that by the mid-1930s, few investigators doubted the links between stress and hypertension.[200]

The general impression then was that human beings became hypertensive when they perceived danger, and that these dangerous situations triggered repetitive "fight/flight" activation. Civilization and all of its discontents appeared to pose special problems for the human species. The "lions and tigers" of old—those forces in nature that originally posed a threat to one's life and triggered fight/flight reactions—had been replaced by an entirely new set of "lions and tigers" that were an inherent part of "civilization." These included job stress, marital stress, lack of control over one's livelihood, economic stress, loneliness, and industrialization itself, characterized by the movement of large numbers of people off the land and into crowded cities.

The central problem was that the human body continued to react in a "fight/flight" manner to situations that no longer were truly life threatening, reacting to situations that did not merit either a fight or a flight response. Physiological reactions, previously helpful to human beings in their struggle for survival, had now become maladaptive, leading to heightened responses to perceived dangers, and triggering major bodily reactions in situations where human beings no longer either were able to, or needed to, fight or run away.

Cannon's findings were further reinforced by the studies of Dr. Stewart Wolf and his colleagues at Cornell University Medical School. In 1955, they summarized the results of a decade of brilliant medical research in a book entitled *Life Stress and Essential Hypertension.* [201] What they documented about blood pressure and its links to fight/flight reactions, however, was so surprising that it was difficult for physicians of that era to fully integrate their findings. In addition, they published their results just as the first effective anti-hypertensive medications appeared on the market, and the problem of chronic hypertension at long last appeared to be solvable with medications. Thus, the timing of their research findings almost guaranteed that they would be ignored and overlooked.

They began their investigations in a pre-medication era when the only effective remedy for acute hypertension was a surgical procedure called sympathectomy. In this extreme measure, surgeons severed the sympathetic nerves presumably causing blood pressure to rise as part of the "fight/flight response." While the surgery itself was drastic, the alternative of doing nothing was equally unacceptable, since acute hypertension inexorably led to a variety of dreadful problems, including stroke and sudden death. Because of the severity of their medical conditions, the patients at the Cornell Medical School were monitored on a continual basis while in the hospital awaiting surgery. A number of in-dwelling catheters were inserted into their arteries, kidneys, and other crucial organs, permitting medical investigators to monitor their cardiovascular systems and blood chemistries on a continual basis.

Dr. Wolff and his colleagues first examined these patients as they rested quietly for an hour or more. They then engaged them in a stress interview for approximately thirty to sixty minutes, during which they discussed topics they knew to be of significant emotional concern to the patients. The effects of these interviews were stunning. Blood pressures at rest in one particular patient averaged around 160/100 mm/hg. Yet, during the stress interview, it rose as high as 220/130 mm/hg, and then came back down to pre-interview ranges as soon as the patient once again relaxed quietly. Virtually all of the patients they monitored during stress interviews exhibited similar reactions.

In addition to these marked changes during the stress interviews, there were equally dramatic changes in stroke volume (the amount of blood ejected from the heart with each beat or "stroke" of the heart), in the kidney filtration fraction and blood flow through the kidneys, and in cardiac output, where a marked increase was detected. They also reported data showing that blood viscosity (the thickness of the blood) also significantly increased during these interviews, while clotting time decreased. These data suggested animals were prepared to survive injury and bleeding as part of the "fight/flight" response. Nature had its own mechanisms to minimize blood loss during life-threatening combat—including an increase of blood viscosity, which reduced clotting time.

The implications for human beings, reacting in repetitive "fight/flight" ways to perceived dangers no longer "real threats to life," were equally obvious. Repetitive surges in blood pressure, along with the thickening viscosity of the blood and decreased clotting time, plus a myriad of other physiological components of the fight/flight response, suggested an important link between stress and the development of hypertension and coronary heart disease. Even more intriguing, sympathectomy itself did not block these cardiovascular changes during stress interviews. While this surgical procedure did help patients lower their overall resting blood pressure, the reactivity of the cardiovascular system to fight/flight during the stress interviews did not change.

HYPERTENSION AND PSYCHOTHERAPY

The Cornell Medical team's research findings helped clarify a finding that had perplexed psychiatrists since the mid-1930s. At that time, there were no effective medicines or surgical procedures to help patients lower blood pressure. When a person's blood pressure began to rise into extreme hypertensive ranges, it would frequently prove fatal. The diagnosis of severe hypertension during that era, especially with renal involvement, created as much anxiety as the diagnosis of cancer does today. The outcome was absolutely dreadful, including multiple organ and system failure, and either premature death or a crippling stroke.

With no effective remedies available, a psychoanalyst of the time, Dr. Franz Alexander, began the first of what would prove to be an exhaustive series of studies attempting to use Sigmund Freud's talking cure to try to help patients cope with stress. Based on Walter Cannon's research, Alexander correctly deduced that stress was central to the cause of this disease, especially in situations where there was no identifiable organ involvement. He was aware that Freudian psychotherapy had helped patients suffering a variety of other stress-linked emotional problems, and it seemed likely that it could help patients with this disease as well. His investigations, however, revealed quite an opposite reality. Rather than helping, this form of psychotherapy only seemed to make matters worse. His studies, which were subsequently confirmed by dozens of other investigators, led to several intriguing findings.[202]

Patients struggling with essential hypertension seemed to be affected by a number of childhood issues apparently linked to their adult struggles with hypertension. They appeared especially prone to over-utilization of repressive mechanisms to ward off childhood memories of significant emotional stress. Some patients, for example, reported great emotional distress as children attempting to cope with parental alcoholism. The patients nevertheless appeared to gain significant insight during the course of psychotherapy.

As therapy continued, however, blood pressure continued to rise, frequently to dangerous levels in sessions when there had been a great deal of "catharsis." That is, rather than serving to lower blood pressure, the ventilating of emotional struggles only seemed to drive blood pressure higher.

Investigators who repeated Alexander's findings began to observe a linear relationship between a person's resting blood pressure levels at the beginning of therapy and their propensity to discontinue therapy. The higher the resting pressure at therapy's start, the quicker the patients seemed to terminate therapy. It was almost as if the patients themselves could sense the life-threatening nature of "psychotherapeutic catharsis."

Other investigators observed that hypertensive patients frequently maintained a pleasant demeanor, while simultaneously utilizing various stratagems to reduce their level of "involvement" or "engagement" with others. This "friendly under-involvement" or "disengagement" appeared to be a communicative style that pervaded their general lives. Hypertensive patients maintained a friendly demeanor that masked both their emotional vulnerability and their propensity to remain emotionally distant from others.

These findings had been repeated by so many investigators that by the time we began to probe the links between hypertension and loneliness in 1977, it was well understood that analytic approaches relying on catharsis and insight were not necessarily helpful. Forthrightly delving into long-repressed emotional struggles or encouraging patients to ventilate long-repressed feelings of anger or anxiety only seemed to increase the stress placed on their hearts. Other forms of therapy, more cognitive and non-invasive, were subsequently found to be far more helpful with patients suffering from various forms of heart disease.[203]

THE CHAIRMAN IN LOVE

When I began to examine the links between hypertension and loneliness, I was keenly aware of these prior research findings. I knew that it was best not to engage patients in analytic, or "uncovering," types of psychotherapy that encouraged emotional catharsis. On the other hand, I also knew that alternative non-drug approaches, such as biofeedback, yoga, and transcendental meditation, had produced only marginally beneficial results.

The best alternative at that time was an eclectic approach developed by Dr. Herbert Benson at Harvard University.[204] His "relaxation response" relied primarily on deep breathing and focused attention, with an emphasis on the importance of meditation. It appeared to give patients a sense of control in their lives, and it offered us a way out of our dilemma. Rather than use invasive analytic approaches with patients, we could offer them a non-pharmacological method that appeared to be more useful than other alternative approaches, such as biofeedback.

We also recognized that virtually all of the non-drug approaches that showed clinical promise had built silence, deep breathing, and focused attention into their protocols. Whether it was yoga, or meditation, or biofeedback, emphasis was placed on remaining quiet, even silent, and focusing attention outside of one's self. Dr. Benson's approach seemed to combine these elements in the most naturalistic manner.

In retrospect, it seems as if fate or serendipity again played a major role in determining who would be the first patient referred to our newly-formed "loneliness clinic" (actually called The Psychophysiological Clinic at the University of Maryland Medical School). He was a distinguished department chairman in one of the local universities who easily could have been a poster child for *The Broken Heart*.

At fifty-five years of age, he was single, thirty pounds overweight, and had not dated in over two decades. And yet, he steadfastly denied that he was lonely, and even insisted that his academic and social life involved "too much time with other people." Although there was no strong family history of heart disease, he nevertheless had suffered a heart attack ten years earlier. He was sent to our clinic when he experienced a transient ischemic attack (suggestive of a possible impending stroke) while delivering a lecture to graduate students. His blood pressure was high (around 170/100 mm/hg at rest) and was not well-controlled with conventional medications. Since we had suggested that loneliness was linked to hypertension, his doctors felt that there was "little to lose" by sending him to us for help.

I did not share that conclusion. After all, contributing to the premature demise of a highly respected departmental chairman would hardly have been an auspicious way to launch a new, and at that time, still highly experimental clinic. We took on the Chairman, guided by the time-honored medical maxim to "do no harm," and committed to making sure our "cure" for him would not compound his medical problems. I enlisted the Chairman in his own treatment and reviewed with him all the existing non-drug approaches in the literature. I also discussed the problems posed by emotionally "cathartic alternatives."

He readily agreed that, among the smorgasbord of options, the best one would be my modification of Dr. Benson's relaxation techniques, which might crassly be called a form of "shut up and breathe" therapy. I was determined to not make matters worse by emotionally upsetting him. Thus, whenever the Chairman tried to raise an issue of emotional significance, I simply instructed him to be quiet and to breathe deeply. Every ten minutes or so, one of the nurses would enter the room and take his blood pressure with a stethoscope, and then we would continue our dialogue, trying to maintain our conversations on mostly "surface issues."

Yet, even the best-laid plans of mice and men can easily go astray in clinical situations. In this case, when we met each week for an hour-long session, the Chairman, much to my consternation, refused to "shut up and breathe." Instead, he wanted to talk about an issue that he felt was of major significance in his life. And, in spite of all my protestations, he was determined to talk about this stress and meet it head-on.

Much to my surprise, the Chairman's main concern was a matter of the heart! Soon after our first session, it became quite apparent that the Chairman had been platonically in love with a certain, apparently unavailable woman for almost a decade. Yet, during that period, he had never signaled his feelings to her. He was a deeply ethical, highly religious, and sensitive human being, and it turned out that the object of his affection, a woman named Esther, was already married. Although he had little knowledge beyond that of her private life, it later turned out that she had been unhappily married for almost two decades. One day, she told her silent admirer that she had been so unhappy with her husband that she intended to divorce him soon. Shortly after that revelation, the Chairman had his transient ischemic attack and his blood pressure began to rise into hypertensive ranges.

Dr. Paul Rosch, an internist and Director of The American Institute of Stress in New York, is fond of saying "that one's man's stress is another man's delight." That certainly was true in the Chairman's case. For the major stress confronting him when he first came to our clinic was how to ask Esther to dinner! He was uncomfortable with the prospect of bungling a marvelous opportunity that had come to him rather late in life. While I continued to discourage discussions of stressful issues, he persisted, and with a bit of coaching from one of our older nurses, we began to walk the Chairman through his first dinner date with Esther. Surviving that first social outing appeared to give him precisely the confidence he needed. He began to engage Esther in far more frequent and delightful dinners, and although he denied that he had ever been lonely before, his dinners with Esther seemed to make a significant difference in his physical condition.

And although we did not have the slightest idea as to why it was occurring, the Chairman's blood pressure began to fall dramatically, down and down over the next six months, until it reached normal levels. He then went one step further and began to slowly reduce his medications until he no longer needed them. We had cured the Chairman's hypertension over a six-month period, but did not have the slightest idea how or why. What had we done other than to tell him to "shut up and breathe" whenever he discussed stressful issues, and coached him on how to ask Esther to dinner? Was it our therapy? Or was it simply dinner with Esther that brought his blood pressure back down to normal levels?

Just as we were finishing this encouraging yet unintelligible "cure," Dr. Ramsey's donation of his "blue machine" arrived at our clinic. I could scarcely wait to show it to the Chairman. For the first time, we would be able to monitor his blood pressure without needing to stop our conversations while a nurse took his blood pressure with a stethoscope. Since the "blue machine" monitored his pressure every minute, I would be able to tell immediately whenever his blood pressure rose to dangerous levels. And I could immediately instruct him to be quiet and breathe.

What happened next, however, was completely beyond my wildest imagination. No sooner had my demonstration begun then the "blue machine" appeared to go berserk. When the Chairman was quiet, his blood pressure averaged around 120/60 mm/hg. But as soon as he began to speak, his blood pressure increased more than fifty percent, up to

190/100 mm/hg! And the blood pressure surged to a very high level even though he seemed not to be talking about anything particularly stressful! Nor did he himself feel this sudden and dramatic change in blood pressure. When the pattern repeated itself half a dozen times, I immediately joined the ranks of doubting Thomases about Dr. Ramsey's blue machine. I was convinced that the computer had to be broken! I knew human blood pressure was variable, but it just couldn't change that quickly and that dramatically!

And so I took the "blue machine" over to the University Hospital Cardiac Catheter Laboratory, where patients routinely were diagnosed for coronary artery disease. In-dwelling catheters continuously measured their blood pressure while a physician slowly threaded a tiny catheter up into their coronary arteries. In this laboratory, it was easy to gauge the computer's accuracy. Measured against the in-dwelling catheter readings of blood pressure, Dr. Ramsey's "blue machine" was amazingly accurate.

I then measured the blood pressure of every staff member—nurses, medical residents, and technicians—and of patients, and they all showed the same patterns. Whenever they talked, their blood pressure rose, anywhere from 10-50 percent above levels recorded when they were quiet. The only difference between the staff's blood pressure and that of the hypertensive patients was that the latter's blood pressure rose much higher, even though they were on medications designed to block such reactivity. The higher a person's resting blood pressure, the more it went up when they began to talk. It seemed counterintuitive.

My colleagues and I immediately recognized that those findings called into question all those large-scale studies that had measured blood pressure with a stethoscope. For clearly the pressure that was obtained depended on who was talking just before the measurement was made. The same was true for physicians measuring a patient's blood pressure in clinics. While most physicians intuitively understood the phenomenon of "white coat hypertension," and recognized that stress could cause a patient's blood pressure to rise in a transient fashion, the crucial question remained: How did the doctor think he could help the patient to relax? Did he get the patient to talk and ventilate, and then measure pressure again, or did he talk while leaving the patient quiet? That simple decision could change the next pressure reading over 50 percent!

Two reactions set in that prevented me from initially understanding the importance of this observation. The first was the implicit assumption that there was nothing essentially new in this discovery. Rather, I assumed initially that this new computer technology had revealed essentially the same type of fight/flight phenomenon that Walter Cannon had observed in animals fifty years earlier, and that Dr. Stewart Wolff had witnessed in catheterized patients during his stress interviews at mid-century.

My second response to these new observations was far more personal. Had I been the victim of some cruel Irish joke? After all, I had just published a widely-read book asserting that loneliness was a major contributor to heart disease. And just as the book was being favorably reviewed, I observed that talking drives blood pressure up, sometimes into extreme hypertensive levels. Loneliness kills, but talking can drive your blood pressure up into dangerous levels! The paradox seemed too much to bear. Perhaps I had helped to "cure" the Chairman only when he remained quiet! And what was the clinical advice to be derived from these preliminary observations? Should the Chairman avoid talking while having dinner with Esther? To avoid loneliness without talking, were we all to join contemplative orders or be consigned to some prison where we could beneficially spend our lives in solitary confinement? Questions of this sort came in a flood, and they all seemed to mock my published statements and assumptions about loneliness and heart disease. A major dilemma had been dumped in my lap, and there were no easy answers.

NO LANGUAGE BUT A CRY

Fortunately, just as I was observing the powerful links between talking and blood pressure elevations, my application for a sabbatical from the university was being approved. For several years, I had planned to spend a six-month period in Ireland on the Inishowen Peninsula of Northern Donegal, where my parents and my wife's parents were born. After publishing *The Broken Heart,* I was looking forward to an unencumbered six months in rural Ireland writing my next book. Now, however, my sabbatical began to take on an entirely new meaning. I began to feel that this remote region would not just give me the time I needed to write, but also the space to escape the embarrassing, Banshee-type paradox that had confronted me at the university. Although there was no way to know it at that time, serendipity was about to enter my life once again, just when I needed it the most.

While bewildered by the paradox of communicative blood pressure surges, and how they were linked to loneliness and heart disease, I thought—with just a bit of tribal humor—that the "blue machine" might help me find out why the Irish drank so much. (Well, maybe not all the Irish, but at least a few of my ancestors in Inishowen). My new hypothesis was that the Irish drank in their pubs to eliminate this significant, vascular reflex to talking. Since I was going to be in the country for six months, why not see if I was right?

Once the idea was conceived, the rest was easy. Convert the "blue machine" to European electrical current, go to the local pub in my parents' village, plug it in, and observe the results. A brilliant research idea—until I arrived in the village to discover there was no electrical plug in the pub! While I could have circumvented this technical problem, it did not take long to recognize that there were already far too many other intrusions eroding the Gaelic way of life in this remote peninsula. With American television already undermining the heart and soul of their pastoral lives, the locals scarcely needed the "blue machine" to disturb what was in essence their last bastion of communal life.

And so, for the next five months, I donated the blue machine to two obstetricians in Dublin, who, it turns out, were trying to evaluate the reliability of a German Doppler machine they were using to measure the blood pressure of new-born babies. As they informed me, it was difficult and sometimes impossible to hear the muffled Karotkoff sounds of an infant's pulse as it coursed down the tiny brachial artery of his or her arm. The bargaining was easy enough. I would loan these obstetricians the "blue machine" if they would allow me to come to Dublin once each week to observe what they were doing.

And so it was that I found myself each Friday staring at fat, ruddy-cheeked, newborn Gaels in an Irish nursery while the blue machine took their blood pressure on a minute-to-minute basis. Sometimes these infants would sleep soundly. Sometimes they would stare at me with wide-eyed astonishment. And sometimes they would scream bloody murder. And when they screamed, their blood pressure would quickly rise, frequently doubling from what it had been when they were quiet or asleep. And the longer they cried, the higher their blood pressures would go up. As I had done in America, I initially discounted the importance of this observation. Instead, I simply assumed that the "blue machine" was demonstrating another example of the links between stress and blood pressure.

Sometimes ideas intrude into one's conscious awareness at the oddest moments, and under the most unusual and unlikely circumstances. Certainly that was the case on a dismal, rain-swept Friday evening in late May as I left Dublin for the trip back to my home base on the Inishowen Peninsula. After one long, wet, and cold month in Ireland, I was feeling especially lonely because my wife and three children had not yet joined me. As I reached the border town of Aughnacloy, the last thing on my mind was blood pressure or research.

The isolation, the loneliness, the dank weather, and the British soldiers repeatedly requesting me to "open my boot and bonnet" at Northern Ireland border crossings had gradually taken their toll. Each Friday, I had to make the eight-hour roundtrip journey to and from Dublin. On my return, I would leave Northern Ireland at Derry, and continue northward toward the Insihowen Peninsula, which, while north of Northern Ireland, was part of Southern Ireland.

The cartography was only one aspect of the madness that had engulfed the unfortunate and beleaguered Province of Ulster, whose very name conjured up divisiveness and tragedy. The soldiers' suspicious questions about the "blue machine" sitting in the back seat of my car may have been the catalyst. Perhaps the soldiers thought it was some sophisticated timing device that I intended to use to blow up one of their border crossings.

Whatever it was, after passing through the checkpoint in that driving rainstorm, I began to sink into a well of despair darker than any I had ever felt in my life. Border crossings manned by guards armed with machine-guns; constant threats of violence; historic hatreds that seemed anachronistic and silly; bombed out buildings; desperate poverty; a pervasive sense of foreboding and dread; and always the unending, cold rain—all contributed to my own, ever-deepening sense of loneliness and despair. Over and over again I muttered the words "bonnets and boots," mocking the soldiers' request at Aughnacloy to inspect the "bonnet and boot" of my car. Babies wear bonnets. Even women in Easter parades wear bonnets. But Hillman Hunter automobiles do not wear bonnets. It was, so far as I was concerned, ridiculous use of language by the Queen's best in a God-forsaken country.

In the rainy, cold despair of that evening, the only antidote was to talk to myself. And talk I did as I continued the lengthy drive across the full length of Northern Ireland. Yet, somewhere on that long journey, and somehow without my awareness, those ruminating words—that obsession over "boots and bonnets"—were replaced by an entirely new set of ideas, and an entirely new focus.

Those babies in Dublin were actually doubling their blood pressure when they cried! How could I have ignored that reality? And as the babies' vascular reactivity grew ever clearer, I began to think once again about the observations we had made back at the university just a few weeks earlier. What if the blood pressure changes exhibited by the Chairman when he talked were an adult analogue of a baby's cry? What if we had actually heard his cry and somehow mothered his blood pressure back down to normal levels? The linguistic importance of "boots and bonnets" faded from my consciousness as this new reality and an entirely new set of questions began to occupy my mind.

I recalled my discussions with Dr. Ramsey about human blushing, and began to wonder whether blood pressure elevations while talking were the equivalent of crying, or somewhat akin to blushing. What if the Chairman's pressure rises were more than just a response to talking and more than part of an elaborate fight/flight response? What if his blood pressure increases, recorded while talking, were really a covert form of crying or a hidden form of blushing? What if they were hidden components of human communication that had gone unrecognized, unheard, and unnoticed?

Surely in the case of blushing, the reality of vascular communication was all too apparent. Whenever I blushed, people almost always noticed, and they usually tried to change the topic. They could instantly read the vascular message embodied in my dilated facial blood vessels. They understood that my vasodilatation (the swelling of my facial blood vessels) indicated that I was feeling uncomfortable, and even embarrassed. Perhaps we had inadvertently decoded similar vascular messages with the Chairman. Perhaps, when he began to respond internally, and we told him to be quiet and breathe, we had inadvertently changed the topic! Perhaps we had muted his internal way of blushing and helped him overcome his own discomfort. Perhaps, whenever he began to speak, we had inadvertently heard and understood the vascular message embodied in his blood pressure surges.

As I continued my northward journey, a new word, and a new clinical concept, began to enter my awareness. "Titration!" "Titrating dialogue!" What began to strike me as crucial was how people usually try to make certain a person is not emotionally overwhelmed in a conversation. When a person begins to blush, for example, the other person will usually change the topic. And in changing the topic, usually the blusher finds relief.

And although it was a simplistic comparison, I began to think that just like blushing, one should only engage a person in a dialogue that can be tolerated. One should not engage a person in a dialogue that forces his or her autonomic nervous system to react with acute fight/flight responses. For if a "body" is in full "fight/flight" mode, even while a person ostensibly remains calm on the surface and engaged in the conversation, then the dialogue is a kind of elaborate game—of "let's pretend everything is okay even though I am terrified."

Perhaps by instructing the Chairman to be quiet and to breathe deeply, we had "titrated the dialogue" in a way that had dampened his own cardiovascular reactivity. Perhaps we had tempered and tamed his long-established communicative pattern of "fight/flight" without even being aware that we had done so!

As I continued towards the Inishowen Peninsula, the rain was now accompanied by an intensifying gale that shook the Hillman Hunter and made it increasingly difficult for me to see the road. I began to wonder whether the entire thrust of the seventeenth century philosophy of Rene Descartes had lulled medical scientists into accepting what was ultimately a boring and one-dimensional view of the human body. Perhaps the body was far more than the machine Descartes had depicted. Perhaps the human body was far more than a sophisticated Buick or Cadillac, or even a sophisticated "blue machine." Perhaps the entire human body was an instrument of communication and dialogue. Perhaps there was a *"language of the heart"* that had been overlooked and utterly ignored by medicine.

At the very least, I ruminated aloud, a human heart involved in dialogue was far more interesting than a heart that was little more than a sophisticated water pump. And if the heart's language was not heard or seen, and never understood, then perhaps we had overlooked an important reason why people get sick and die prematurely. People may die of a broken heart because their hearts are neither heard nor understood.

As these ruminations began to echo in the recesses of my obsessive mind, I began to wonder whether the vast panorama of diseases that medical science had examined in a strictly mechanical way might not be the end result of serious disorders in human communication—the end result of dialogue betrayed, dialogue ruptured, or bodily messages neither heard nor understood.

My journey that late May evening unleashed a torrent of ideas that more than matched the deluge washing across my car's windshield wipers. The heart of love that Blaise Pascal had talked about began to take on an entirely new meaning in the face of checkpoints manned by soldiers with machine-guns. The human heart, I thought, could love because it engaged others in dialogue! And perhaps the digital images of blood pressure changing during dialogue with another human being were but one small part of a vast, and largely uncharted, internal universe.

Was it possible that the entire human body—with its trillion cells— were all involved in human dialogue? Was it possible that human bodies were crying out to be heard, longing to share and to be understood? Were a trillion cells engaged in dialogue striving to be understood? Were the machine-guns the end result of a breakdown in that dialogue? Was it a breakdown in dialogue within the larger "communal body" that led not just to violence, but to disease and premature death? Did good health equal good dialogue? Did the lack of dialogue, the loss of dialogue, the isolation and loneliness resulting from a breakdown in dialogue, lead inexorably to complete indifference, one's self-destruction, or the violent destruction of others?

As if these questions weren't enough, I was suddenly overwhelmed by the phrase "I love you" and the possibility that love spoken in dialogue within one's flesh and blood might be biologically infinite. Martin Buber, William James, and others had made it quite apparent that human identity could only occur in dialogue. There was, Buber had asserted in his brilliant book *I-Thou*, no "I" without the "Thou." Following up on his core idea, I was stunned to think that there was a biological "I" with a trillion cells that converted the word "love" into a transitive verb that then crossed over to the other, the "you." And the reciprocal sharing of that word in dialogue, that word spoken in our flesh and blood, the sharing of that love, had to be such that it met in the middle, between two human beings. It was a "felt dialogue" that joined two separate bodies together, and gave human identity its special meaning.

I thought also of Marcel Proust. He was quite right when he asserted in the *Guermantes Way* that a person could lose his identity when he lost his mate or a very dear friend. For Proust understood quite clearly that the "I"—the very core concept of self—could only exist in a dialogue with the other. When one lost a loved one, it was the dialogue that was lost. And in the loss of that dialogue, that part of one's self—shaped and formed by the dialogue—also died. Martin Buber was equally correct when he spoke of I-Thou relationships, as opposed to I-It relationships. The latter, he noted, tended to isolate, erode, and ultimately destroy human identity.

The biological possibilities inherent in heartfelt human dialogue had transformed my feelings of loneliness and despair into a growing awareness that I was not really alone. I could engage in dialogue, not only with my loved ones but with the entire universe! Indeed, the very words I was using to talk to myself in the car had to have been taught to me by someone else. I was never alone!

Far from being a boring machine, as Descartes had asserted, the human body encompassed an internal universe as complex and as vast as the external universe. A trillion cells in flux could speak to another trillion cells! A trillion cells encompassed the word "love" and conveyed those trillion cells of love to another human being, who then added a trillion cells to the equation. The shared meeting of two trillion cells in the middle, in their "in-between," had to be a dance with biological infinity. The orchestra for the dance was dialogue, the rhythm for the dance the human heart, the object of the dance to share love and avoid loneliness. There were no biological limits to the possibilities of love.

Nor, unfortunately, were there biological limits to any other feeling as well. We could be consumed by love, or be destroyed by hatred. And both began as words taught to us by other human beings who either spoke from their own hearts or tragically spoke from outside their own hearts, from, quite literally, "no place." And if they spoke from "no place," then by necessity they also spoke to "no body!" In a monologue masquerading as a dialogue, a person's sense of self, his bodily self, was simply annihilated.

As these weighty thoughts tumbled through my mind, it became more apparent to me how loneliness was linked to hypertension and heart disease. These diseases were inextricably linked to the chronic lack of dialogue, the sudden loss of, or the breakdown or dysfunction in, human dialogue. The very concept of lethal dialogue began to take on a new meaning—the horrifying use of language, not to reach other human beings, but to hurt, control, and humiliate them in a manner that would overwhelm them and ultimately lead to their premature death. It had to be the most horrifying experience a small child could ever endure.

For, as my analytic teacher, Dr. Herbert Gross, so frequently had reminded me, the teaching of language was part of the taming of the infant's cry. Parents taught their children that they did not have to cry to communicate their emotional needs, that they could learn to use language to convey those feelings. Lethal dialogue, as carried on and demonstrated by one's own parents, was surely an annihilating experience because it resulted in the annihilation of one's self. And, by separating us from our fellow man, it was lethal because it caused loneliness, isolation, hopelessness, and eventually premature death. That kind of talk induced feelings of hopelessness. When used in adult life to reach another human being, it had to ignite a bodily storm of terror, the fight/flight required to escape a language used to annihilate one's self earlier in life.

And what if our schools inadvertently did the same thing by teaching certain children that they were stupid? What if the educational system inadvertently taught certain children that every time they opened their mouths to talk, they ran the risk of exposing their own stupidity and shame to others? Could school failure serve to compound the linguistic injuries already inflicted on a child by its own parents? Could the educational system impart its own toxic poison, forcing a child raised by loving parents to accept the fact that he or she was a "failure"?

Branded in an educational and social context, these children might talk to their fellow man in a way that forced them to feel an unbearable sense of shame, humiliation, and rejection. Was the experience of being "kept back" in school, or dropping out of school, or otherwise failing in school, the educational equivalent of learning toxic talk? Did it also foster a life of social exile in which a child, robbed of the possibility of talking with one's fellow man without feeling an overwhelming sense of shame and humiliation, lived a life marked by "fight/flight" over-reactivity?

Indeed, once the lesson had been learned, was the child who "failed" confronted by the very same "hyper-tense" reality faced by adult patients in analytic therapy? Just as adult hypertensive (i.e. hyper-tense) patients dropped out of therapy to escape what was in essence lethal dialogue, did children drop out of school because the communicative experience for them was also increasingly murderous? Did the child actually drop out of school, or succumb to drugs and alcohol, in order to find some relief and attempt to save what was left of their shattered communicative life? And in the context of such a murderous experience, was it any wonder that some of these children would react with violent rage? Fight/flight in dialogue with another was proportional to the actual threat posed. Consider the feelings of shame, humiliation, and powerlessness that such dialogue could elicit in those who had been branded "failures."

And what of "toxic talk" and "lethal dialogue"? Was it the origin of the fight/flight response that we had seen in the Chairman when he talked? Did he possess a beautiful command of the English language to convey his thoughts, while having learned in early childhood that language could not be used to convey his feelings to others? Did the Chairman and the school dropouts share a bodily reality? Did their use of language guarantee that their essential cries, fears, and terrors would go unheard? Was premature death, the loneliest of all loneliness, the only escape from this?

The problem with catharsis and hypertension also became clearer. The central problem was the possibility that blood pressure elevations during catharsis were part of an essential message! These bodily changes were indeed the analogue of an infant's cry. Yet, if the therapist did not hear, see, feel, or sense this essential message, then the patient was left like an infant crying in the night, delivering a bodily message neither heard nor understood. The essential element in catharsis was the sharing of feelings, not the mere discharge of long, pent-up emotions, the "emotere" or chemical perturbations that Descartes had donated to our lexicon. To me, it also grew ever clearer that when a person begins to talk, the over-reaction of the cardiovascular system would create its own form of hidden loneliness. The links between this communicative problem and loneliness became crystal clear.

If conversations were accompanied by rapid increases in blood pressure that were not seen, felt, or understood, then the person experiencing such increases would have no option but to withdraw from the dialogue because it was potentially murderous. And, unfortunately, that withdrawal would only serve to compound the problem and further exacerbate loneliness.

It was not talking per se that was problematic, but the hopelessness felt when engaging in dialogue that was potentially both toxic and lethal! It was language spoken without an awareness of the other person's heart—language that was, in essence, nothing more than a monologue masquerading as dialogue. The paradox between blood pressure elevations while talking and the links between loneliness and premature death were finally obvious. They were heads and tails of the same coin.

As I finally reached the Inishowen Peninsula late that Friday night, the rain had stopped for the first time in weeks. As I crossed over a mountain pass southeast of the town of Moville, the northwestern sky was aglow in what had suddenly turned into a magnificent late-spring sunset. Scattered purple clouds were silently racing in off the still-foaming ocean before bursting upward to the sky, dramatically set against the peaks of the North Donegal mountains.

Perhaps it was the lifting of the weather that accelerated the change in my mood, but I was no longer depressed or in despair. Instead, I began to feel a sense of peace—a quiet sense of reassurance and relief, as if I had at long last arrived home, perhaps for the first time in my life. Except for the ghosts of my ancestors haunting the countryside, there was not a soul on the road as I traveled through the highland moors and peat bogs glistening in the dew-soaked twilight. Slowly wending my way down the stonewalled mountain roadway towards the town of Culdaff, I knew, as I had never known before, that home resided in the human heart, a place where we could share our lives and our feelings with others through heartfelt dialogue. It was a place where one, quite simply, could live— indeed, had to live—a life in dialogue with others.

Chapter Ten

The Heart of Dialogue

The sabbatical I had begun with the hope of writing another book ended six months later without a single sentence put down on paper. While my plans had not turned out as I expected, I returned to the university ready for the new work that needed to be done. My perspective on the links between talking, loneliness, and blood pressure regulation had changed completely in the intervening six months, and a great deal of additional research needed to be done.

For it was clear that human dialogue itself was somewhat akin to a prism. Each time the light passed through a prism, it could be diffracted in a unique way that created a different spectrum of colors. Dialogue and communication were a similar phenomenon, and human identity emerging from the prism of human dialogue and communication was potentially infinite in its potential. In a dialogue that involved the human heart, there was far more at stake than we had ever thought possible. Words spoken in our flesh and blood, words incarnate, opened up entirely new dimensions that needed to be examined.

From the moment of my return from Ireland, we began intense efforts to examine every aspect of the complex prism of dialogue, loneliness, and the cardiovascular system. And even as a large number of research studies were initiated, we also began to refine a unique treatment approach to help patients suffering from certain cardiovascular disorders—hypertension, coronary heart disease, migraine headaches, and vasovagal syncope (a problem where blood pressure drops quite suddenly and can cause a person to faint). Our premise was that these disorders could be the end result of a breakdown, or a pre-existing pattern, of dysfunctional dialogue contributing to an ever-deepening sense of loneliness and emotional isolation. In certain cases, we began to hypothesize that communication problems contributed to the development of these diseases.

In other cases, we began to observe that pre-existing heart disease could exacerbate a person's problems communicating with others. Thus, we began an elaborate series of studies to test whether our new understanding about the involvement of the heart in human dialogue might help patients more effectively deal with these disorders.

Rather than merely assume that hypertension, coronary heart disease, or migraine headaches were the result of mechanical breakdowns in a machine body, we began to perceive that these problems could be the end result and symptom of a more basic disease—the *dis*ease caused by dysfunctional dialogue. And as we formed and shaped this premise, we began to more clearly understand how these diseases were linked to human loneliness.

RESEARCH LINKING DIALOGUE TO THE HEART

In my second book, *The Language of the Heart*, I described our initial research that linked talking to changes in blood pressure, and I outlined steps patients can use to cope with various cardiovascular disease linked to dysfunctional dialogue. I thus describe the results of these research investigations here in only the most general terms.

With simplicity in mind, we designed the research model to examine the links between blood pressure and talking. Initially, we set out to assess blood pressure changes while talking and communicating across the widest range of populations. From infants crying in their bassinettes, to the aged, in both sexes, all races, and in a variety of clinical, laboratory, classroom, and home settings, we observed that blood pressure rose as soon as a person began to communicate. In normal individuals, neurotics, schizophrenics, deaf mutes, people with heart disease, people with heart transplants, those free of heart disease, people on and off cardiac medications, children saying their ABCs, and school children reading books aloud, the approach was basically the same. Blood pressure and heart rate were recorded and monitored while people were quiet for 3-5 minutes, then when they talked or read aloud for 1-3 minutes, and once again when they were quiet.

This Quiet-Talk-Quiet model permitted us to compare cardiovascular changes in a controlled manner across a wide variety of human conditions.

Since that time, thousands of human beings have been measured. Except in schizophrenics, where a drop in blood pressure was observed while talking (whether they were on or off medications), the general pattern is always the same. Within thirty seconds after a person begins to talk, blood pressure rises anywhere from 10-50 percent above pre-talking/resting baselines. And generally blood pressure rises far more rapidly and to a greater degree than heart rate. And since this is a "normal reflex," what was crucial to understand were the factors that determined or influenced the magnitude of the increases.

A blood pressure that increased five to ten percent while talking, for example, was clinically and emotionally far less problematic than a blood pressure that suddenly increased more than 50 percent. And a diastolic pressure, rising from 60 mm/hg to 75 mm/hg in an adolescent child, was certainly far less worrisome than a diastolic pressure in an adult patient with coronary heart disease that suddenly rose from 95 mm/hg to 145 mm/hg!

Our attention to these communicative blood pressure changes was split in two divergent paths almost from the outset. One path led us to study children, and the implications these changes had for the educational system. The other path led us to examine heart patients, and patients with other cardiovascular disease, in order to determine how this information could help in the development of new ways to treat communicative problems linked to heart disease.

EDUCATIONAL DIALOGUE

When we originally monitored school children, we were merely trying to examine the widest range of populations possible in order to determine how their blood pressure rose while talking. By observing blood pressure increases in children, especially those in elementary school grades, however, we were led to re-examine the links between educational failure, increased loneliness, and premature death. It was an unexpected by-product of research initially aimed only at gathering normative data about blood pressure.

Our studies began when we examined blood pressure reactivity in 52 fifth-graders from a Baltimore inner city neighborhood—racially mixed and blue-collar. Twenty-one of these children were black, and 31 were white. When we initiated this study, we were not interested in examining the effects of stress, but in examining the links between vocalizing, the number of words spoken per minute (by having them read a text book), and their blood pressure reactivity. We had no interest in examining any links between educational performance and stress, and so we chose for reading a book two grades below the students' reading level, and had them read individually to a nurse. (The students had volunteered for the study after a nurse gave a classroom lecture and demonstration about the computerized monitoring of blood pressure.)[205]

The children were called two at a time to a quiet corner in the back of the classroom, and one child was recorded while the other sat and observed the procedure. The experimental procedure and setting—a classroom environment that was very familiar to them—were chosen to minimize any apprehension the children might have. None of these children had any problem reading the simple text. Yet, in many of them, their blood pressure while reading aloud was elevated into extreme ranges, as measured against NIH criteria for children of their age. Out of the total of 312 measurements of systolic and diastolic blood pressure, 84 were above the 95th percentile of normal levels for children of their sex and of their age ranges. And the great majority of these extreme readings occurred while they were reading aloud!

Some of the readings were extraordinarily high. For example, one fifth-grade child had an average resting blood pressure in the hypertensive range of 169/105 mm/hg. His blood pressure immediately increased to 174/126 mm/hg while reading, an extraordinarily high level for an eleven-year old child! Another student's blood pressure while resting was 140/86, but it rose to 156/102 while reading. Many of these children exhibited blood pressure elevations into such acute ranges that, wesurmised, they could not possibly recall what they had just read, even though they had no difficulty reading the material. It was almost as if the very task of reading a book aloud had become a potentially lethal threat, and the book itself a significant threat, instead of a "friend."

In general, black male children had significantly higher blood pressures while resting and while reading, explained at least in part by their larger body mass. Because of their increased weight, they also exhibited greater increases in blood pressure while reading aloud. It was apparent that the "coronary risk factor" of increased bodily weight, subsequently observed in children in the Bogulasa Studies, also had important educational ramifications for blood pressure reactivity experienced while performing the most common of all educational tasks—reading a book aloud.

These unanticipated findings eventually led me to wonder about school failure and its links to loneliness and heart disease. It also led me to wonder about the increased risk factors for certain children noted in the Bogalusa Heart Studies, and changes in communicative blood pressure in these very same children.

Following up on these initial school studies, I then turned to a very different population, and with very different "investigators." In the inner city elementary school study, it was possible that the students did not know the nurse recording their blood pressure, which might have increased the children's anxiety. Thus, I recruited teachers in an affluent suburban kindergarten who had known their five-year-old students for an entire year. And rather than ask these children to read a book aloud, I requested that the teachers record the blood pressure of children as they said their ABCs and counted aloud. All of these children appeared to enjoy participating in our "computer game." And yet, as shown in the accompanying graph, the blood pressure of some of these children became elevated to high levels during the recitation of their ABCs.

Blood Pressure Changes in African-American and Caucasian Children While Reading Aloud in School

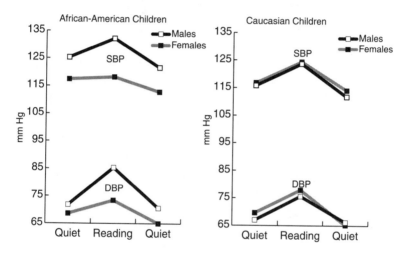

SOURCE: Public Health Reports (1984), Vol, 99 (1) 77-84.

And then, for the first time, I not only heard the end of the ABCs— "Now I've said my ABCs, tell me what you think of me"—but began to see the power of educational dialogue. It was all about identity—human identity—continuously etched and shaped in educational dialogue with one's teachers, peers, and classmates. "Tell me what you think of me" would help shape the children's sense of self, their sense of worth and relative value, and thus would determine to a large extent the repetitive magnitude of the blood pressure excursions that would occur during dialogue with their fellow man for the rest of their lives.

Those who were implicitly informed that they were stupid, inferior, dumb, academically behind, developmental laggards, or otherwise not up to snuff, would suffer the most. Their blood pressure would rise far more when they tried to talk with their fellow man than those who were told that they were "gifted" or "superior" or "intelligent" or "talented." It would not take long to prove that "relative status" in the dialogue had a great deal to do with the magnitude of the blood pressure movements observed while talking. Those who were led to believe that they were inferior would always be in a position of "talking up," and the toll exacted on their hearts would frequently be devastating.

There were ways, as well, to help alleviate the magnitude of these communicative blood pressure rises. When we examined children reading books within a home setting, for example, and introduced a new variable—a pet animal—we were able to observe that the magnitude of the communicative blood pressure surges could be reduced. [206]

For those who were damaged the most—those children who were the most emotionally upset—it was apparent that their non-speaking, non-judgmental animal brethren were a source of great comfort to them. Dr. Aaron Katcher would subsequently show that animal companions could have a major impact on reducing the incidence of violent temper outbursts among adolescent, institutionalized children who could not be handled within normal school settings. To children who had learned that normal dialogue and normal channels of human communication were hopeless, companion animals provided a path back home, back into their own hearts, and back into their own feelings.[207]

SUMMARY FINDINGS

In addition to the blood pressure studies conducted of children, we observed a number of variables that could influence the magnitude of the communicative blood pressure increases. And each of these variables was crucial in developing strategies to help heart patients control and lower the magnitude of these increases whenever they tried to communicate with others. Among the more important variables that influenced the magnitude of blood pressure increases while communicating were the following:

1. **RATE OF SPEECH**. Speaking rapidly increased blood pressure more than slower rates of talking. Thus, the linkages between Type A behavior and vulnerability to coronary heart disease had a potential explanatory cause not observed previously.[208]

2. **BREATHING PATTERNS**. Speaking in a breathless pattern generally led to greater increases in blood pressure than talking with regular, paced, breathing patterns. [209]

3. **STATUS DIFFERENCES**. Talking with someone perceived to be of higher social status produced greater increases in blood pressure than talking to someone of equal or lower status.[210]

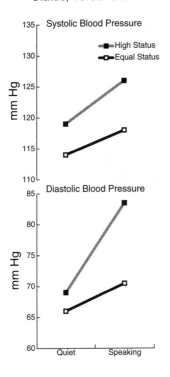

Status, Verbal Communication, and Blood Pressure

SOURCE: Long, Lynch, et al, 1982

4. **SELF-ESTEEM**. Individuals with lower self-esteem experienced greater blood pressure increases while speaking to someone believed to be of higher status or greater importance.[211]

5. **AFFECTIVE CONTENT** In general, talking about emotionally-charged subjects contributed to greater increases in pressure than discussing more neutral topics.[212]

6. **AGE**. The magnitude of blood pressure elevations while talking generally increased with age. This is due at least in part to a decline in

arterial elasticity over time. Thus, the data suggest that the aging process creates unique communication problems that deserve special attention.[213]

7. **THE ACT OF COMMUNICATION**. Deaf mutes using sign language experienced blood pressure increases, just as speaking individuals did, suggesting that it is not talking per se, but rather the act of communicating that leads to pressure increases.[214]

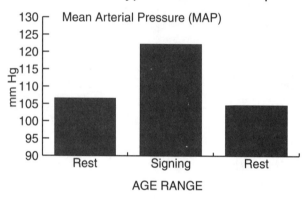

Blood Pressure Levels Pre-, During, and Post-Signing Periods in a Hypertensive Deaf Population

SOURCE: Malinow, Lynch, et al, 1986

8. **CORONARY HEART DISEASE.** Patients with heart disease generally experienced blood pressure increases greater than individuals free of heart disease.[215]

9. **HYPERTENSION.**. The higher one's resting blood pressure, the more blood pressure tended to increase while talking.[216]

10. **MEDICATIONS.** Few, if any, cardiovascular medications effectively blocked blood pressure increases while talking.[217]

11. **ATTENTIONAL MECHANISMS** Blood pressure rises whenever one begins to speak. It drops rapidly below baseline resting levels, however, just as soon as a person begins to listen to another person. Focusing outside of oneself, looking at nature, or watching fish swim in a tank, for example, lead to rapid reductions in blood pressure.[218]

Comparisons of Blood Pressure Levels Pre-, During, and Post-Talking Periods for Three Age Categories

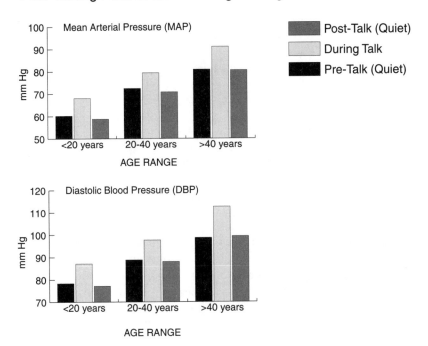

SOURCE: Lynch et al, 1982

In addition to these factors, a variety of studies indicated that there were at least three major physiological mechanisms involved in these blood pressure increases:[219]

Intrapleural Pressure, which is linked to breathing patterns and changes in lung capacity.

Left Ventricular Ejectile Force, which measures how forcefully the heart's left ventricle pumps.

Vasoconstriction: Central and Peripheral Resistance. This mechanism is the most important of all. Basically, during periods of stress, the blood vessels, including the coronary arteries, can narrow (constrict). In addition, there can be an increase in peripheral resistance.

This refers to the action of the arteriolar system—small arteries that take blood from the arteries to the capillaries and then into the venous system.

These function much like the nozzle on a garden hose. If the nozzle is tightened (vasoconstriction), then the water shoots from the hose at a high pressure and the garden hose itself becomes rigid. If, on the other hand, the nozzle is opened (vasodilitation), then more water pours from the hose at a lower pressure, and the hose itself is less rigid.

"HEY GUYS, LOOK UP!"

It was one of those delightful May weekends in the Blue Ridge Mountains, where my wife and I had spent a wonderful time with our oldest son, his wife, and our two young grandsons. Their van was alive with conversation as we slowly wound our way around one particularly sharp S curve in the road. A mountain ridge suddenly towered 600-700 feet above us, ablaze in pastel greenery, purple and white rhododendrons, and pink mountain laurel typical of the early springtime.

Quite suddenly, our four-year-old grandchild, Joseph, reminded us with the clarity seemingly gifted only to children that there was something far more important and wondrous than our idle chatter, and it deserved our immediate attention. "*Hey guys, look up!*" he suddenly exclaimed, focusing our eyes on the extraordinary beauty that we might otherwise have taken for granted. The car grew silent as we followed his instructions, and we collectively looked up and smiled.

Our research with blood pressure and communication had taught us a vital and similar lesson. Whenever we are quiet, whenever we "look up and outside of ourselves," whenever we attend to nature, blood pressure falls significantly below its resting baseline levels. Joseph had instructed us to engage in one of the most relaxing exercises that the human heart can experience. It is nature's tonic for those experiencing cardiovascular difficulties.

Similarly, even while our research revealed highly significant increases in blood pressure when we talk, subsequent discoveries began to reveal that blood pressure also falls rapidly when we listen to others in a non-defensive way, and that it can fall significantly below baseline pressure levels when we look outside of ourselves at others and at nature. "*Hey guys, look up*" was part of what I now call nature's dialogic seesaw—pressure rising when we speak to others, dropping when we listen, and dropping below normal when we look outside of ourselves.

The so-called orienting reflex was a cardiovascular reflex first discovered by the Russian physiologist Y.E. Sokolov, and described in detail in his 1963 book *Perception and the Conditioned Reflex.*[220] Like so many other pioneering efforts, Sokolov conducted his study during an era when it was difficult to measure blood pressure directly. Nevertheless, he was able to observe that when human beings and animals attended to their external world in a non-defensive fashion, their heart rates would suddenly slow, along with changes in circulation.

His reports, and others from Russian laboratories, caught my eye while conducting research at the Pavlovian Laboratory at Johns Hopkins. Virtually everyone has watched animals as they react—in a non-defensive manner—to nearby sounds and sights. This "orienting reflex" can easily be observed in dogs, for example, as they listen attentively to sounds, sights, and smells in their nearby environment. Typically, when a dog hears a sudden soft sound in its immediate surroundings, it will cock its ears, pace its own respiration, stop its tail wagging, and focus all its attention on the source of the stimulus. I first observed this highly reproducible heart rate slowing in animals in 1964, when I confirmed what Russian scientists had previously observed.[221]

Like so many other laboratory observers, however, I failed to fully appreciate the importance of these findings until subsequent research by Dr. Aaron Katcher led me to understand not only the universality of this cardiovascular reflex, but also its importance in assisting patients with heart disease. Observing that pet animals aided hospitalized heart patients in their long-term survival led Dr. Katcher to examine what it was that helped to produce this extraordinary effect.

As part of these efforts, he began to re-examine all of the non-pharmaceutical methods of lowering blood pressure, including yoga, biofeedback, the relaxation response, and deep meditation. He then compared the effectiveness of those methods in lowering blood pressure against the simple expedient of having people watch goldfish in an acquarium. What he discovered was that simply having people focus their attention on fish swimming in a tank lowered blood pressure more than all of the other "relaxation" techniques. In essence, Dr. Katcher reconfirmed the importance of the orienting reflex, but this time in human beings, with a new, blood pressure-related twist. Non-defensive orienting to stimuli in the natural living world has a powerful effect on lowering blood pressure.[222]

It was the focus outside of oneself, and in particular the focus on the natural living environment, that proved to be nature's solution. The folk wisdom to "wake up and smell the roses" had an effect on our hearts that was difficult to appreciate. In the competitive pace of modern life, more and more people appeared to be focused inward on themselves, unable to "look out, look up, and listen to others."

It is an easy matter to demonstrate to heart patients the vascular importance of human dialogue. When they begin talking, their blood pressure quickly rises, sometimes far more than 50 percent above baseline pressures. And conversely, when they are quiet and listen to others in an unthreatened way, their blood pressure immediately falls back to normal levels. As one charts an hour of blood pressure recordings with heart patients, the results frequently appear to depict a repetitive vascular storm, with abrupt elevations and rapid decelerations in blood pressure. We could show patients the difference in pressure reactivity if they *"talked with, rather than at,"* another human being. Talking "with" a person involved looking out into the world in a non-defensive fashion, while talking "at" a person invariably triggered fight/flight reactivity.

The clinical goal was to help patients reduce the magnitude of their blood pressure spikes, and gradually lower their communicative surges. Long-established patterns of communication had to be relearned as patients saw what would happen if, instead of listening, they would think about what they intended to say next. Their blood pressure, rather than fall, would ratchet ever higher the next time they spoke. They could see what would happen if they "talked at, rather than with," someone.

Section Four

HEALING DIALOGUE

Chapter Eleven

HEARTS THAT NEVER FORGET

"Am I my brother's keeper?"
asked Cain, the first born son of Adam

A PERSPECTIVE

In the last chapter, some of the more recent discoveries about human dialogue and the regulation of the cardiovascular system were introduced. In this chapter, the implications of these findings are discussed, primarily within the context of treating patients in what is technically called Phase Two Cardiovascular Rehabilitation. This outpatient phase of cardiac rehabilitation, which is highly recommended by the American Heart Association, is designed to assist patients in their recovery from either a heart attack or bypass surgery.

Here in this chapter, the consequences of toxic talk are laid out in vivid terms. And here, as well, I focus on the links between the recovery from heart disease and the larger communicative context of a person's life. Yet, even as the focus is narrowed to a discussion of the links between human dialogue and the treatment of heart patients, a far broader perspective is introduced. I simultaneously address far more general issues of health and illness within the broader, interpersonal, social, political, and spiritual contexts in which we live our lives.

For, in the end, the question first raised by Cain, and the consequent loneliness and exile he confronted, is the very same problem we all must confront. So I attempt here to show that the answer each of us gives to Cain's question will largely determine the health of the community in which we all must live, including the "heart" that sustains the health of the nation's "body-politic."

THE TEN COMMANDMENTS OF SINAI FITNESS

Friday mornings invariably heighten the contrast, a weekly change of pace that inevitably engenders an uneasy Dickensonian sense of the best—and worst—of medical times. Each week, I leave the comfort of my own Life Care Clinic in suburban north Baltimore to travel a few miles around the Baltimore Beltway to the Sinai-Wellbridge Health Center,[223] where I try to be of assistance to heart patients in Phase Two cardiac rehabilitation.

The Sinai Fitness Center is one of those spanking new multi-purpose health facilities (built in 1997) that helps people in every way possible to achieve maximal physical fitness. Sparkling blue swimming pools, indoor tracks, and basketball courts are but a few of the superb amenities designed to encourage the young, the middle-aged, and the elderly to keep their bodies in tip-top shape. By the hundreds they come, in hourly shifts, many wearing Sony Walkmans to seal themselves off from the external environment, or plugged into headphones to hear televisions mounted into the ceilings in front of their treadmills, bicycles, and rowing machines, as they doggedly try to sweat every ounce of fat from their bodies.

For a few Center members, the quest for fitness appears to be part of a New Age form of bodily narcissism—the heroic, solitary pursuit of physical perfection irrespective of the cost in time, physical exertion, and emotional commitment. For them, bodily images reflected from mirrors appear to be the sole arbiter of worth. For still others, the efforts stem from a desire to have the approval of one's "significant other," or the hope of attracting a "significant other." For the large majority, however, the issue is simply one of personal health. For almost all, the pursuit is solitary, with the exception of mostly middle-aged women dressed in fashionable Spandex, who dance aerobically together in the supervised privacy of side-rooms.

When I arrive at this Center, I am occasionally reminded of the ways technology has so rapidly altered our society. One such transformation has been the elimination of hard physical labor for most of our citizens, making spas of this sort an increasingly important health component of modern life.

And whenever this reality sinks in, I find myself drawn back to the memories of an earlier time, recalling my peasant ancestors and their lives of hard physical labor. And I wonder: What in the world would my Irish fisherman grandfather and my immigrant railroad-worker father have thought of this wondrous display of physical energy expended by so many without any financial compensation? Perhaps their peasant instincts would have led them to consider rigging the treadmills, bicycles, and rowing machines to generators so that at least the energy being generated could be converted to the production of electricity, which would help lower the building's sizeable air-conditioning and heating bills.

Yet, even when consumed in my private musings of times long past, I can still see the stunning results achieved by some of the members.

Occasionally, I even catch myself wondering how long it might take me to arrive, even remotely, at the crafted musculature of these Greek-like gods and goddesses. Thank goodness others look more like me—people in transition somewhere between middle age and retirement, sweating profusely as they try with religious fervor to reduce their bulging "abs and buns," seeming to pursue infomercial images of bodies worthy of the company of sun-drenched beauties on far-away tropical beaches.

Each Friday at 8 A.M., as I depart for the Sinai-Fitness Center, I feel somewhat like my distant cousins must have felt wandering around the other Sinai several thousand years ago. Strange desert-like places—these concrete ribbons we call "Beltways." Tens of thousands of cars moving at 70 miles an hour, a tribe-less army of commuters in solitary exile, each a stranger to the other, seeking at breakneck speed to find whatever new Jerusalem happens to promise them financial security and an escape from loneliness this particular week.

Arrival at the fitness center, and the reality of the heart patients to be seen that day, quickly make it apparent, however, that there will be little time to reflect on the rootlessness of modern life, or to contemplate the spiritual meaning of the historic journey from Sinai to Jerusalem, or even to consider the shape of my own sorrowful "abs and buns." Occasionally, to break the inherent tension that can be involved in assisting patients who have survived very serious heart operations, I will pause to reflect on what I have grown fond of identifying as the "Ten Commandments of Sinai Fitness"—instructional guidelines that represent the collective wisdom of the Framingham investigators and now codified to help people achieve optimal cardiovascular health. And I try to think of these Ten Commandments in the context of our own discoveries linking cardiovascular disease to loneliness, emotional isolation, and dysfunctional communication.

— **Thou shalt not eat saturated fat**
— **Thou shalt lower thy cholesterol**
— **Thou shalt exercise daily**
— **Thou shalt avoid salt**
— **Thou shalt keep blood pressure low**
— **Thou shalt not smoke**
— **Thou shalt drink in moderation**
— **Thou shalt maintain weight within normal guidelines**
— **Thou shalt avoid excessive reliance on caffeine and stimulants**
— **Thou shalt avoid stress whenever possible**

The "Ten Commandments of Sinai Fitness" are admonitions aimed at guiding an individual in the solitary pursuit of physical health. And while they are obviously correct, helpful, and conducive to good health, they are quite different from the original Ten Commandments Moses smashed in a fit of rage in the Sinai wilderness. Those ancient Commandments were directed far more at the tribe's overall health than at the health of a single individual. Etched in stone tablets, they were social and interpersonal in nature, rather than solitary exercises to improve one's individual health. In that sense, they were more akin to our own discoveries about communication and heart disease, hardly enterprises that were solitary in nature. And it was the tribe, after all, and not a rag-tag assembly of rugged individualists, that had to get to the Promised Land.

— **Thou shalt not kill**
— **Thou shalt not commit adultery**
— **Thou shalt not steal**
— **Thou shalt not covet thy neighbor's goods**
— **Thou shalt honor thy father and thy mother**

Occasionally, when I think of these issues, I find myself indulging in a bit of self-pity, feeling somewhat like a Jeremiah crying in the wilderness about the links between heart disease, loneliness, and dialogue, shouting a message to people isolated by headphones, hooked to Sony Walkmans and television screens, and unable to hear. During those periods, I think again about Moses, lost and wandering in the Sinai wilderness—and his yearnings for the Promised Land. I wonder how, if Moses were alive today, he would he react to the mechanized and highly individualized wilderness of this new Sinai. I also wonder whether he would be more than a bit surprised to discover the relative importance attached to these two very different sets of commandments.

For it seems to me that far more is known today about the "Ten Commandments of Sinai Fitness"—those that produce personal health— than about those far older Commandments focusing on the health of the larger tribe. For somewhere in the historic journey from the original Sinai to this new Sinai, we seem to have lost our way, succumbing to an ever-increasing risk of dissolving into a tribe of "I" people without a collective "we."

A personal, unscientific survey of 100 well-educated patients at this Center, half of them Christian and half of them Jewish, was an eye-opener in this regard. Less than 25 percent of those I interviewed could correctly answer my query: "What is the first of the Ten Commandments that God gave to Moses?" When asked, by way of contrast, if they could identify Oprah Winfrey, all 100 percent knew the correct answer. When asked if they could list three or four of the "Ten Commandments of Sinai Fitness"—the well-known risk factors for heart disease—virtually everyone knew the correct answers. Yet, there in the background, seemingly lost in the din of the treadmills and the pursuit of our individual health, was the eternal wisdom inherent in that first of all Commandments.

"I am the Lord thy God ...Thou shalt not have false Gods before me."

In a world where image is increasingly blurred with reality, with an ever-increasing acceptance of disembodied dialogue and the consequent rising tide of human loneliness, this lack of knowledge about the first of the Ten Commandments left me wondering: Is the most important false god we hold up for adoration not the Golden Calf of old, but rather our own narcissistic image of our "separate" and limitless selves? Did this, the most elemental of all false gods, prevent us from recognizing our life within the larger tribe, our dialogue with the communal body, our life within the rest of the living world, and the real dialogue within the Jerusalem of the human heart?

Lost in the wilderness of our highly individualized journeys through the Sinai of modern life, I had to wonder whether the Promised Land that Moses sought in vain for his entire people, the communal body in dialogue with each other, as well as in dialogue with the Land and its Creator, was still as remote as ever.

Each Friday, when I scan their medical charts, I am well aware that the heart patients at Sinai Fitness live in a metropolitan area blessed with some of the best health care facilities in the United States. At centers like The Johns Hopkins Hospital, Sinai Hospital, and others, patients routinely survive heart operations that only a few years ago would have resulted in certain death. For them, it is clearly the best of medical times in which to live.

Yet, within a few blocks of these hospitals, the murder rate of young black men and women, including children hit by stray bullets, ranks among the highest in the nation. The average lifespan for black males living near these hospitals ranks among the worst in the nation. Dr. Christopher Murray of the Harvard University School of Public Health reported that the average black male's life expectancy in Baltimore City was 59.9 years, which is comparable to that found in India, Bolivia, and South Africa.[224] In 1999, epidemiologists at The Johns Hopkins Medical

School warned that Hepatitis C, spread by the sharing of needles among heroin addicts, had reached epidemic proportions in Baltimore neighborhoods surrounding the world-famous Hopkins Hospital. For these addicts, it was the worst of medical times.

Within the hospital itself, stroke patients survived some of the most complex surgical procedures, assisted by some of the best neurosurgeons in the world. For them, it was the best of medical times.

Unfortunately, within a few square miles of The Johns Hopkins Hospital, ranked by *US News & World Report* the number one university medical facility in the United States, the urban school dropout rate far exceeded the graduation rate, and large numbers of children promoted within the school system were functionally illiterate. More than 25 percent of black men in Baltimore were in the criminal justice system— more than the percentage that graduates from college. For them, it was the worst of medical times.

"I may not get there with you," Martin Luther King, Jr. had proclaimed shortly before his death in 1968, "but we, as a people, will get to the Promised Land." Dr. King's haunting promise still seems but a distant dream, not only for the inner city black population of Baltimore, but for all of the other casualties of loneliness described in this book. "We, as a people"—the collective tribe of Americans—appear to be lost in the desert of individual health, without a moral compass or the means to engage in a heartfelt dialogue that would help guide the whole tribe of Americans to the Promised Land of equal health.

SOLITARY MACHINES AND TALKING HEARTS

Irrespective of my own philosophical musings about life and death in the spiritual, communal, and interpersonal deserts of modern life, it is abundantly clear that the Sinai heart patients are not exercising on treadmills to shape their abs and buns. Nor are they doing so because of some fantasized lure of sun-drenched beauties in exotic, warm weather climes. They are there for the shape of their hearts. For them, the exertion, fatigue, sweat, and breathlessness don't represent energy expended to enhance their corporal image, but rather an all-out effort to extend both the quality and quantity of the time left to them on this earth. Many of these patients have survived major surgical battles, coming face-to-face with the fragility and pain of life, and forced to confront the reality of their own mortality.

Powerful impressions have been seared into the consciousness of these heart patients, shocked as they have been by the sight of angiograms showing their coronary or carotid arteries blocked or clogged. They have seen the before and after look, and they know and they feel the difference. First, their arteries were blocked. Then, through angioplasty or bypass surgery, their coronary arteries were opened. Crushing chest pain, bodily weakness, fluid retention, and shortness of breath that once threatened their lives have been banished, offering them new hope and a new lease on life.

Many speak anxiously about their own parents dying prematurely from heart disease, and the work they must do to overcome their genetic bad luck. Their struggles with overwhelming chest pain and flirtations with premature death have made it easy for them to appreciate the delicate genetic nature of their bodies' machinery. Care for it properly, and they increase their chances for a long and healthy life. Abuse or neglect that machinery, and they hasten their inexorable march to the grave.

Like most people in the United States, these heart patients are well aware that what they eat and how they exercise will either improve or diminish their chances for long-term survival. They have no difficulty grasping the fact that physical fitness is vital to the restoration of their cardiovascular health. Three days each week, they come to the center, where their blood pressure, heart rate, and heart rhythm are monitored— both at rest and during exercise. Solicitous cardiac nurses and well-trained exercise physiologists, under the watchful eye of cardiologists, slowly increase their level of exercise to match their increasing capacity for it— all without unduly straining their heart muscles, or overtaxing their cardiovascular systems.

Weight is also monitored, the scales again providing precise and unambiguous guidelines to desirable levels. The dietician adds her expertise, carefully crafting nutritional guidelines to precisely fit the needs of individual patients. Diabetics are given precise instructions. The overweight are given reasonable ways to lose excess pounds. Those with elevated serum cholesterol levels are instructed about foods they need to avoid, and medicines they might need to take to reduce those levels. Patients with high blood pressure are similarly instructed, and encouraged to exercise and alter their diets, while adhering to their cardiologists' prescriptive remedies.

Permeating the consciousness of everyone at the Center—both the heart patients in Phase Two rehabilitation, as well as the younger staff members dedicated to their physical fitness—is the unquestioned and all-encompassing belief that the human body functions like a machine. This

Cartesian belief is embraced with a conviction that borders on religious dogma.

Like the very air the heart patients breathe, this deeply-entrenched belief is implicitly accepted and taken for granted. The surgical procedures they have survived have left little doubt about the "plumbing" of their hearts, and the hydraulic nature of their cardiovascular systems. Clogged coronary arteries are replaced by new ones. Angioplasty opens up arteries in much the same way a rotor-rooter device might unclog a kitchen drainpipe. Heart, leg, arm, and lung muscles are exercised and trimmed so that they will be more physically fit. Hearts are aerobically exercised to increase "stroke volume" so that their "cardiac pumps" can hydraulically eject increasing amounts of blood with each beat of the heart.

Hypertension is viewed as an "it." If necessary, "something"—usually a pill—is prescribed and taken for "it." These patients owe their very lives to the triumph of scientific medicine and they see no reason to question one of its most basic and treasured assumptions—the mechanical nature of their cardiovascular systems.

Similar to the excellent hospital-based care found in Baltimore, the cardiovascular rehabilitation program at Sinai ranks among the best in the nation. Here, there is strict adherence to the guidelines of the American Heart Association and the four major components of cardiac rehabilitation—proper exercise, weight control, diet, and stress reduction. Yet, while certain of these components are easy to comprehend, some aspects of this mandate are more difficult to integrate into the overall mechanical perspective. Dr. Jeffrey Quartner, the Medical Director of Sinai's program, has continuously emphasized—through the many years we have worked together—that the most effective cardiac rehabilitation program possible must work with "real people who live in the real world."

Instructing patients to lose weight in order to save their lives, for example, is fine and dandy in theory, but frequently difficult to implement in "real" life. As can be readily affirmed by anyone who has ever attempted to lose weight, this problem extends far beyond the confines of the Sinai Cardiac Rehabilitation program. Seemingly each week, a new and different diet book pops onto the bestseller list providing a "new and guaranteed" way to lose weight—52 "can't fail" diet books published each and every year. At some point, virtually everyone would get the idea that these "sure-fire" diets are far more "smoke and mirrors" than real solutions to weight loss problems.

"Real solutions to real problems" is even more problematic when trying to address the links between heart disease and stress. While most of these patients and their physicians intuitively sense that excessive stress is not conducive to overall cardiovascular health, there is a great deal of shared confusion about which stresses ought to be of greatest concern.

Most would admit that loneliness can kill, but except for the divorced and the widowed, few heart patients would ever admit that they are lonely or have problems communicating. Most actively resist these notions, frequently categorizing such difficulties as "mental problems" that have little to do with their own personal heart disease. Nor is it easy for them to accept the fact that they could benefit from seeing a psychologist or psychiatrist, since they are utterly convinced that they suffer from cardiac problems, not "mental" ones.

Like structural engineers, most of these patients assume that the real stress of life involves forces that are "out there" rather than forces that are within. In very much the same way that a mechanical engineer might assume that various environmental forces threaten a bridge's structural integrity, so, too, do the majority of patients implicitly assume that various environmental stresses can wear down, and eventually threaten, the mechanical structures of their bodies. Noise and air pollution, automobile traffic, financial pressures, job stress, urban crime, perhaps even their adult children struggling in their own lives—the list of external stresses that potentially victimize and threaten their lives seems endless.

And while they readily acknowledge the potential danger of these "external stresses," it is far more difficult for them to comprehend that the most important source of physical stress is one they usually take for granted. Ironically, this source is not "out there," but is both internal and interpersonal. While it involves the most basic aspect of human life, and plays a crucial role in determining their cardiovascular health, it is a stress almost always overlooked and vastly underestimated. It is rooted in the most elementary of all human attributes—our capacity to use language to communicate with one another. And among the issues that produce the greatest communicative stress, discussing issues of love or talking about the loss of love or the lack of love frequently prove to be the most vexing.

SHIFTING PARADIGMS:
FROM HEART PUMPS TO HEARTFELT DIALOGUE

It is not difficult to understand why patients resist the idea that "communicative stress" and heart disease are linked. My own research journey took a quarter century before I fully understood and grasped these links. As described earlier, I—along with most of my colleagues—went through a lengthy period of denial, followed by a series of conceptual struggles, before we could fully appreciate the implications of what we had discovered. For me, it was extremely hard to change a paradigm fully embedded in my training, let alone change a paradigm that was part and parcel of these patients' lives.

Since the links between loneliness, struggles with communication, and blood pressure reactivity had caused me a great deal of conceptual difficulty, it was easy to understand why patients and their physicians might also struggle grasping the same phenomenon. Even after witnessing major blood pressure increases when they talk about certain issues, it was hard for heart patients to accept the fact that their blood pressure could change in a highly significant manner during even the most ordinary of conversations.

Beyond the phenomenon itself, however, it was even more difficult to integrate this interpersonal and communicative dimension of cardiovascular fitness into the Ten Commandments of Sinai Fitness. For none of these commandments has anything to do with one's interpersonal or communicative life. They are, instead, mandates about the body-machine issued from the Framingham Heart Studies.

Yet, at the same time, the reality of blood pressure surges while talking can scarcely be ignored. The same patients whose hearts, they believe, function in a totally mechanical manner, also communicate in a heartfelt manner. The very same body-machines they exercise on treadmills also talk and communicate with other human beings in and through their hearts and blood vessels. And the magnitude of the physiological changes exhibited by these cardiac patients while talking is truly stunning.

Even more difficult for the patients to understand is the manner in which the regulation of their cardiovascular system—their resting blood pressure levels, for example—is determined by their relationship, their ongoing dialogue, with the world outside the confines of their own flesh and blood. Their dialogue with their loved ones, friends, and neighbors, as well as their dialogue with the living world of nature, of pets and plants, gardens and trees, all has a truly profound influence on the regulation of their own hearts and blood vessels.

"THE LORD OUR GOD, THE LORD IS ONE"

During the past two decades, Peter Hubner's "Medical Resonance Therapy Music" has been demonstrated effective in helping to alleviate

pain, insomnia, anxiety, headaches, and other stress-related complaints in a variety of hospital and outpatient settings. This remarkable German musicologist and classical composer developed a sophisticated, computerized, digital music laboratory to create compositions based on Pythagorean precepts.

Although he is best remembered as a mathematician, Pythagoras was also an accomplished physician, astronomer, and musician. He taught that each of these disciplines, as well as all of nature, were governed by *laws of harmonious proportion* that were interrelated in some concordant fashion. He coined the term "cosmos" to describe this orderly and harmonious universe, where everything could be reduced to mathematical principles. In Pythagoras' day, both music and medicine were considered to be branches of mathematics, as well as an art or science, and pleasing music or good health required maintaining harmonious relationships. Since everything in the cosmos was interrelated, knowledge gained from a greater understanding of mathematical principles in the microcosm of music could be utilized to restore disruptions in balance and harmony that were responsible for different diseases.

In the most general sense, our approach to the treatment of heart patients encompasses a similar view, one in which we attempt to bring patients back to what I believe is a biological state of *"harmony"* with the rest of their living world. This state of harmony is what I have called the *"physiology of inclusion,"* a state in which one's fellow man and the rest of nature are interwoven into the fabric of a person's life. It does not accept a strictly mechanical view of the human body and a strictly mechanical view of the human cardiovascular system, which is always primed to be in a *"fight/flight"* mode of "self-preservation," a body set against the rest of the living world in a ceaseless struggle for individual survival (the *"physiology of exclusion"*).

Our approach essentially believes that no "body," whether human or animal, can live in a healthy condition so long as it is living in physical isolation from the rest of the living world. To the contrary, healthy lives are those lived in harmony with the rest of creation, including harmony with one's fellow man. The aim of our therapy is to bring people back into a life where they live in integral harmony, as *part of and with the rest of the living world, rather than living "apart from Nature."*

And as we have asserted earlier, human beings negotiate their relationship with the rest of the natural world primarily through dialogue. While space precludes a detailed discussion of our therapeutic approach, it generally utilizes cardiovascular changes during human dialogue to gauge the degree of harmony and disharmony a person is experiencing in relationship to the natural world.

It was a similar description of the struggle for harmony, and the struggle for cardiovascular peace, that led one of my patients, Dr. Barry Lever, to proclaim *"Shema Y'Israel, Adonai Elohenu, Adonai Ehad—Hear Oh Israel, The Lord Our God, The Lord Is One."* His eyes beaming with a mixture of reassured joy and confidence, Dr. Lever uttered the central Jewish prayer to summarize the lessons he has learned in our sessions together. At age 64, he is fully aware that his life has been full of personal suffering. But he also knows of his own good fortune, having survived bypass surgery (seven coronary arteries), and three heart attacks—the first in 1985, the second in 1994, and the third in 1997. He was blessed, he realized, to have the expert assistance of physicians who helped keep him alive. A permanent pacemaker helped to compensate for a serious loss of pumping capacity (the so-called ejection fraction) caused by extensive damage to the muscle tissue of his left ventricle.

"Hear Oh Israel" he repeats a second time for emphasis. "Harmony—harmony with self, harmony with others, most importantly harmony with those you love, as well as harmony with Nature." That, as he sees it, is the essence of the therapy, but, he adds, the therapy requires—above all else—the ability to hear.

"For most of my life, I was deaf—partially deaf to those who were close to me, deaf to the power of my own words, and certainly deaf to what my own heart was trying to tell me. Even though I had heard and intoned the prayer *Shema Y'Israel* ten thousand times, I had never heard the essence of that message—*Hear Oh Israel.* I have learned in this therapy that what I say—the words I speak to others, the words I pray—and what I hear, and what I do not hear, are intimately connected to my heart. The blood pressure and heart rate technology you use during the sessions is simply a teaching aid, a marvelous teaching aid, but nonetheless just a tool."

Then, smiling broadly again, he continues, "But in order to hear, you must first be ready to hear. I was not ready to hear, even after my first two heart attacks." *Shema Y'Israel,* he repeats once again, before adding, "there are exercises that can help you to hear. All the great meditative techniques, and all of the major religions, use equivalent techniques, including deep nasal-abdominal breathing prior to engaging in prayer. You must first stop to breathe, breathe deeply, to free yourself of all extraneous worry; breathe deeply in order to take in oxygen, which is the breath of life; watch the way it helps to lower your heart rate and blood pressure.

"And then you are ready to begin the journey, ready to change from a fight/flight approach to life, to one that is far more accepting, far more willing to reach out and to hear one's fellow man." Pausing momentarily once again, he then adds, "It is, of course a journey, a journey that can expand ever outward, but a journey that I feel truly blessed to have begun."

LISTENING TO THE LANGUAGE OF THE HEART

Dr. Lever is quite right. Dr. Ramsey's computer technology is a marvelous adjunct to our treatment of heart patients, and it is a marvelous way to show them that the words they speak do have a powerful effect on their blood pressure and their health. The way they talk, what they talk about, the way they listen or do not listen, as well as their sensitivity or insensitivity to the language of their own hearts, are all lessons that must be learned before fundamental change can occur. Perhaps the most important first lesson is to teach patients the central role that communication plays in their overall cardiovascular health. A recent discovery makes this lesson quite easy to teach.

With 65 heart patients we saw sequentially in Sinai Hospital's cardiac rehabilitation program, I, Dr. Francis Craig, and our colleagues demonstrated that peak increases in blood pressure were significantly greater during an hour-long interview than they were while exercising to maximum capacity on treadmills. And the increases in blood pressure while talking occurred in spite of the fact that most of these patients were taking a variety of heart medicines designed to block their blood pressure reactivity. The patients' blood pressure increases were even greater than the changes observed by their cardiologists during exercise stress-testing prior to surgery.

In stress-tests, heart patients are run on treadmills either to their maximal capacity, or until they exhibit signs of cardiac ischemia (heart pain). Yet, blood pressure surges while talking were greater than those observed while exercising to maximal capacity—even while there was little change in the patients' heart rate. [225] The data suggested that there were literally two aspects to human physiology—one hydraulic in nature and the other communicative. Both the shape of the "machine man" and the shape of the "communicative man" had to be addressed.

Peak Blood Pressure Responses in 60 Recovering Heart Patients

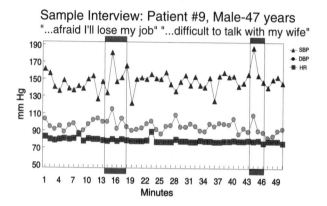

Sample Interview: Patient #9, Male-47 years
"...afraid I'll lose my job" "...difficult to talk with my wife"

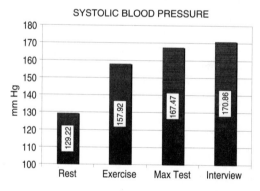

SYSTOLIC BLOOD PRESSURE

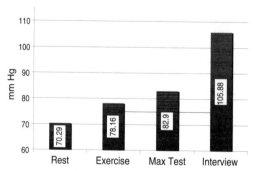

DIASTOLIC BLOOD PRESSURE

Beyond the sheer magnitude of the blood pressure increases, the changing, minute-to-minute variability of blood pressure, and the sensitivity of the vascular system to the ongoing therapeutic dialogue, were equally impressive. The following two figures show the types of blood pressure increases routinely observed in cardiac rehabilitation patients when they talked about various issues.

The first figure shows the blood pressure of a 78-year-old man recovering from quadruple bypass surgery. Three times during this particular session, his blood pressure increased to hypertensive levels when he expressed concern about his daughter.

The second graph shows similar blood pressure surges in a 47-year-old man when he described his difficulties in talking with his wife. His pressure also surged into hypertensive ranges when he expressed fears of losing his job.

THE PROBLEM OF AGING AND BLOOD PRESSURE SURGES WHILE TALKING

Several aspects of these observations, coupled with our earlier findings, immediately caught our attention. From a cross-section of populations tested in previous studies, we had discovered a direct correlation between age and both resting blood pressure and the magnitude of blood pressure increases while talking This also turned out to be the case at the Sinai Cardiac rehabilitation program. And the law is relatively straightforward: Generally, with all else being equal, the older a person is, the larger the increases in blood pressure that can occur while talking.

In spite of the fact that virtually all of these patients were taking medications designed to control their blood pressure, the law generally held constant. The older the patient, the more their blood pressure tended to increase while talking.

Nor is this problem difficult to understand from a physiological perspective. As we age, our arteries generally stiffen, and they tend to expand less during exercise. And as our arteries stiffen, they tend to resist the flow of blood, especially the pulsatile flow in the large arteries near the heart. This resistance is a key factor in the systolic blood pressure that rises with aging.

In addition, the blood ejected with each heart-beat courses down the arteries of the body, until it passes over to the veins, which return the blood to the heart once again. Between the arteries and the veins are very tiny arteries, called aterioles. The arteriolar system functions much like the nozzle on a garden hose. When the nozzle is tightened, the water is ejected at a high pressure, and the hose feels hard. This is analogous to what is called peripheral vasoconstriciton—the narrowing of the arterioles, which are the nozzles, so to speak, of the vascular system. With peripheral vasoconstriction, blood pressure rises.

In the opposite situation, called peripheral vasodilitation, the arteriolar system opens wide, and blood passes through at a relatively lower pressure. While exercising, peripheral vasodilitation occurs, and oxygen-enriched blood pours out to the rest of the body. By contrast, the act of speaking, especially if the communication is stressful or emotionally provocative, causes peripheral vasoconstriction to immediately increase, and blood pressure rises. The mechanisms of vasoconstriction and vasodilitation are generally altered by the aging process. As we age, the entire vascular system begins to lose its arteriolar tone, and our vascular "piping" becomes a bit more rigid. In such a state, changes in vasoconstriction can lead to far greater increases in blood pressure, and a slower recovery time from blood pressure surges.

Put in the broader context of the aging process, this means that everyday dialogue and communication can be physiologically more taxing for older people, especially those with pre-existing heart disease. As seen in the attached figures, there can be marked surges in pressure, which can exacerbate underlying cardiovascular problems. This physiological problem may help explain why at times the aged can be a bit more irritable, and find it more difficult to discuss emotionally upsetting topics.

There are, fortunately, a number of ways to counteract this problem. The aged can be taught to slow down and to pace their rate of speech. They can be taught to breathe more deeply while talking, a mechanism that tends to help block peripheral vasoconstriction. They can learn the value of spending more time pursuing hobbies such as gardening and walking. These quiet-time activities help them "look up and look out," gearing their bodies in a more relaxed manner toward the "physiology of inclusion."

On the other hand, this physiological "problem," especially if it is added to pre-existing communication problems, can trap the elderly in a vise that compounds their own loneliness, especially when they need to talk about issues that can be emotionally upsetting. Trapped in a communicative pattern that is physiologically oppressive, they may have little or no choice but to withdraw or feel misunderstood. This is where the type of "stress reduction" taught in our communicative cardiac rehabilitation program can play a major beneficial role.

THE PARADOX OF PHYSICAL FITNESS
AND COMMUNICATIVE STRESS

In observing that blood pressure increases in cardiac rehabilitation patients are greater while talking than while exercising to maximum capacity during stress tests, we raise an additional problem. In general, physical exercise is geared towards increasing what is technically known as "stroke volume," or the amount of blood ejected with each heart beat. As one improves his or her physical fitness, heart rate tends to slow down because the heart is beating more efficiently and pumping out more blood with each beat. And though such physical fitness has much to recommend it, I have been struck by the number of patients I have seen in the past twenty years who have exercised all their lives, and dieted regularly, who nevertheless have serious premature coronary heart disease.

Perhaps the best-known individual example of this was not a patient of mine. James F. Fixx, preached the gospel that active people live longer, and thus earned the nickname "the guru of running." He wrote a number of best selling books on the topic, including "The Complete Book of Running," which remained a best seller for over a year in 1977 and is widely credited with helping to initiate interest in long distance running in the U.S.

He died while running alone in 1984, at age 52, of a heart attack. An autopsy revealed that two of his coronary arteries were sufficiently blocked to warrant a bypass operation. Several well-known "risk factors" could have contributed to this blockage. The first was a genetic predisposition—his father had died of a heart attack at age 43. In addition, earlier in his life, James Fixx weighed 220 pounds, and smoked two packs of cigarettes daily. He eventually lost 61 pounds, and stopped smoking.

Yet, there are other problems almost never mentioned in connection with James Fixx's untimely death. Perhaps most interesting is the fact that he died while jogging alone on Route 15 in Hardwick, Vermont. He had been alone in Vermont that summer, in part because he had just gone through the second of his two divorces. Equally difficult to ascertain is why Jim Fixx smoked in the first place, and why he had gained weight in his younger years. As suggested earlier, it is not unreasonable to speculate that these problems might have had something to do with pre-existing struggles with low self-esteem, and social isolation not unlike that experienced by school dropouts. The potential communicative difficulties in his two marriages, the premature loss of his father, his possible loneliness and isolation, are "the other side of the scale"—the "hidden risk factors"—that are almost never measured or considered and which went unexamined in Framingham.

There is, in addition, one other hypothetical dimension for James Fixx's coronary heart disease that has never been considered. Blood pressure surges in cardiac rehabilitation patients while talking can be greater than those observed during maximal running on a treadmill. What physiological mechanisms are involved in stressful communication? What happens to a person, like James Fixx, who was in excellent physical shape, yet who might have had a history of increased cardiac risk factors, and who also might have had great difficulty communicating?

Recall that communicative difficulties lead to an immediate increase in peripheral vasoconstriction. By contrast, during vigorous exercise, there is an increase in peripheral vasodilitation (to allow blood to flow out to the muscular system). Exercise in general is designed to increase the heart's "stroke volume"—that is, to get the heart to eject more blood with each beat, and thus lower overall heart rate. Thus, people in good physical shape, but who have difficulites communicating, might find themselves in situations where their hearts are ejecting large amounts of blood against a peripheral system that is constricted. In such situations, marked surges in blood pressure will occur while talking.

Certainly Jim Fixx was a well-known public speaker, and evidence is growing that this type of activity has the potential to place great stress on the heart. And there is mounting evidence that these blood pressure surges can irritate or damage the inner linings of the coronary arteries and put a person at increased risk for heart disease. Although there is no way to know for certain, perhaps this may be why Jim Fixx, the noted author and proponent of cardiac fitness, died prematurely of a heart attack while jogging for his health. He may truly have personified that much-used phrase, "the loneliness of the long distance runner."

In other words, we live in bodies that must accommodate two very different sets of physiological demands—one that is hydraulic in nature and the other that is communicative. Our data suggest that no matter how much you jog, you may not be able to achieve cardiovascular fitness if you continuously fight with your mate, or remain socially and emotionally isolated. Communicative fitness has to be taken every bit as seriously as physical fitness.

SILENT KILLER OR DEAF PATIENTS?

Because of its well-known links to serious cardiac problems, the American Heart Association long ago dubbed high blood pressure, or hypertension, the "silent killer." It was so labeled because of the observation that most patients do not detect or feel significant elevations in their blood pressure. Without being aware of increases in their blood pressure, patients are less likely to take remedial steps, and thus unwittingly put themselves at increased risk. While watching repetitive surges in blood pressure during dialogue, however, we wondered whether high blood pressure was not so much a "silent killer," but the result of an internal dialogue that went unnoticed and was ignored. Was it a really a silent killer, or were some heart patients peculiarly deaf and dumb to their own bodily feelings, especially to pressure increases that occurred during everyday human dialogue?

It is quite possible that these repetitive hidden blood pressure surges during communication might be part of a pattern of dialogue in which people literally talk their way into hypertension and coronary heart disease. That is the bad news. The good news is that, with the new computer technology, we can teach patients how to talk their way back to health.

MENTAL STRESS AND THE PIMI STUDIES

Recent studies by several universities examining the links between mental stress and heart function, as well as follow-up studies known as the PIMI studies (Psychophysiological Investigation of Myocardial Ischemia) add credence to the importance of the communicative blood pressure surges I and my colleagues have been observing since 1978. These medical studies have confirmed the very communicative blood pressure surges we have been observing for two decades, and reinforced the need to take this phenomenon seriously.

Working at university medical centers in Boston, Bethesda, Baltimore, Detroit, St Louis, Birmingham, Gainesville, and Johnson City, research investigators have shown that heart patients with documented coronary artery disease can exhibit exaggerated cardiovascular responses to what has been commonly referred to as "mental stress." These changes include marked blood pressure surges, wall motion abnormalities, increased evidence of myocardial ischemia (suggesting a reduction of oxygen to the heart muscle), and electrical disturbances in heart rhythm. Evidence of excessive reactivity have also been linked to an increased risk of sudden death.

They have also underscored the urgent need to develop effective means to control these problems. In one important sense, these studies are a bit of a misnomer because they purport to study "mental stress" and its effects on patients with heart disease. Yet, they employed two ways to stress patients: require them to do "mental" arithmetic aloud, and engage them in public speaking. Both involve talking aloud.

One group of investigators, led by Dr. Rozanski and his colleagues at the Columbia University College of Physicians, for example, demonstrated that myocardial ischemia (reduction of blood flow to myocardial tissue) could be triggered by the "mental stress" induced by having people do arithmetic aloud—an aspect of talking.[226] (In addition, in 1999, Drs Rozanski, Blumenthal and Kaplan published a comprehensive review of the research linking heart disease to a variety of psychosocial factors. For those wishing more scientific data, this review is highly recommended reading.) [227]

Dr. Steve Manuck and his colleagues at the University of Pittsburgh similarly showed that heart patients' cardiovascular reactivity to the "mental stress" of vocalized arithmetic was predictive of who would be subject to a subsequent reinfarction (have a second heart attack). [228] In a similar way, Drs. Tom Kamarck and his colleagues, also at the University of Pittsburgh, showed that in patients with pre-existing carotid artery disease, exaggerated blood pressure responses to "mental stress"—i.e., doing mathematics aloud—were related to the progression of this life-threatening disease.[229]

Dr. David Sheps and his colleagues at East Tennessee Medical School reported in 1999 that in patients with coronary heart disease, significant blood pressure increases while doing mental arithmetic aloud were predictive of both increased myocardial ischemia as well as sudden death.[230]

Similarly, in late 1999, Drs. Peter Stone, Dr. David Krantz, and their colleagues from a variety of university medical centers noted that this "purported mental stress" could induce myocardial ischemia in 30-60 percent of patients with coronary artery disease. Moreover, they demonstrated that these talking tasks could induce "wall motion abnormalities in the heart muscle," and that these abnormalities were strongly predictive of subsequent "cardiac events" such as sudden death, or additional heart attacks, in 35 percent of the patients they studied. [231]

All of these recent studies unfortunately speak of "mental stress" as if the problem were between one's mind and one's heart, rather than one triggered by the act of speaking. Arithmetic, especially when vocalized aloud, is a form of communication, and a source of "evaluation" by others. Public speaking is obviously interpersonal and triggers evaluation by others. It thus contains the rudiments of stressful dialogue, and a state that elicits the physiology of exclusion. In that sense, these studies independently confirmed our own observations. In short, it is not a great leap to suggest that excessive blood pressure surges during talking can be directly linked to cardiovascular disease, as well as potentially predictive of sudden death.

These data suggest that patients' problems were not "mental" at all, but profoundly interpersonal and communicative in nature. One thing was certain. Talking—everyday talking—was linked in our own heart patients at Sinai cardiac rehabilitation to truly profound increases in blood pressure. The increases were as great as, and frequently far greater than, those seen in the Mental Stress and PIMI studies, and were observed in even the most ordinary of clinical situationsrehabilitation settings where every effort was made to keep the patients calm and relaxed. Indeed, every effort was made to avoid topics that would cause their blood pressure to rise.

HEALTHY DIALOGUE AND THE TREATMENT OF HEART TRANSPLANT PATIENTS

Long before observing communicative blood pressure surges in Sinai Rehabilitation Center patients, Dr. Paul Rosch and I had demonstrated that this information could be utilized for the therapeutic benefit of patients suffering from a variety of cardiovascular problems. We had previously shown, for example, that heart transplant patients—people literally kept alive with hearts that once beat in someone else's body and totally lacking in nervous system enervation—could exhibit rapid increases in blood pressure as soon as they began to speak. The following figures show the types of repetitive surges in blood pressure exhibited in two heart transplant patients as soon as they began to talk.[232]

Even more intriguing, as shown in the accompanying Figure, we were able to use a novel therapy—based on the discovered links between talking and blood pressure regulation—to help these patients lower their blood pressure, as well as lower their heart rate. That is, we could help patients with dennervated hearts to communicate in a fashion that would help them slow down their own heart rate, and lower their blood pressure! In addition, we could help them reduce the high levels of anti-hypertensive medications they were required to take because of the drugs given them to help prevent tissue rejection.

Effects of Talking on Heart Rate (HR) and Mean Arterial
Blood Pressure (MAP) on 44 year-old Heart Transplant
Patient on and off Beta Blockade

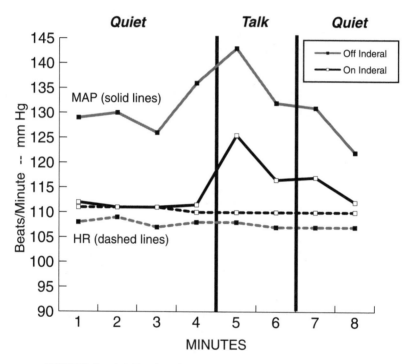

SOURCE: Lynch & Rosch, 1990

A LIFELONG CONTRACT

The "Chairman in Love" may have been the first heart patient I treated to help lower blood pressure. But in some ways, Mrs. E, at 84 years of age, has been equally memorable and equally important in our conceptual thinking, if for no other reason that I have engaged her in therapy and followed her longer than any other patient—continuously now for almost a quarter century. Her family history was literally littered with risk factors for coronary heart disease. Both of her parents, as well as her two sisters and a brother, all had serious problems with coronary heart disease by their mid sixties.

"I don't want to be finished," she said in 1978, at age 63, as I was planning to discharge her from my care after nine months of treatment for hypertension. She had managed to completely control her blood pressure, without any change in her medications. She had been able to lower her blood pressure from acute hypertensive readings back down to normal. "Why can't I come back and see you every month or two just like I see my family physician?" she asked. "Why can't I just keep coming to see you until I die?" she asked, almost as if she wanted to emphasize the serious nature of her request.

Her father had died of heart disease at the age of 52, and her mother haddied of a stroke at age 72 after a prolonged struggle with hypertension. Her only brother had had triple bypass surgery at age 62 and died of a heart attack at age 69. Each of her two sisters—one younger and one older—had had triple bypass surgery, at ages 64 and 69 respectively. One of her sisters also had had a heart attack prior to her bypass surgery.

When I first saw Mrs. E, she had worked as a pharmacist and been on anti-hypertensive medications continuously since 1954, when she was 39 years of age. Recognizing some of the problems inherent in long-term use of these medications, she wanted to find an alternative, non-drug way to control her blood pressure.

Thus began an empirical and clinical odyssey with Mrs. E that continues even as this book goes to print. She had struggled with hypertension for almost three decades before coming to our clinic, and found that medications did not well control her blood pressure. She knew that she was at very high risk of heart disease, and was shocked to observe the way that her blood pressure surged to dangerous levels whenever she began to talk.

I utilized this knowledge to help her control her blood pressure for nearly 20 years, and to help her avoid developing serious coronary heart disease. Indeed, I believe it is safe to assert that, as a byproduct of that good result, I recorded more blood pressure measurements on Mrs. E than have ever been recorded in any clinical situation before. Over the period of 20 years, more than 8,000 individual measurements of her blood pressure and heart rate have been recorded during therapeutic dialogue, a fact that might in itself merit a note in the *Guinness Book of World Records*!

Now at 84 years of age, some twenty years after we began our therapy, she is in good health, and her cardiovascular status is excellent. As shown in the following graph, during the first 18 years of treatment, during which her medications were unchanged, a highly significant reduction in her blood pressure occurred, as well as a significant decrease in her so-called double product. Double product is a measurement derived by multiplying systolic blood pressure by heart rate. This measurement provides an index of the heart's workload. Typically, both blood pressure and double product increase with aging.

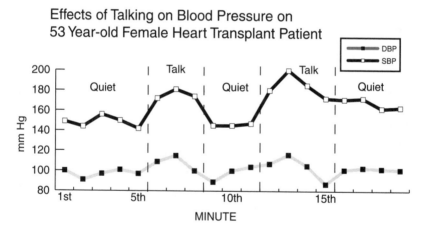

Effects of Talking on Blood Pressure on 53 Year-old Female Heart Transplant Patient

SOURCE: Lynch & Rosch, 1990

While detailed specifics of her treatment are beyond the scope of this book, I focused her attention, as I focus the attention of all my patients, on the links between blood pressure and abnormally large increases in blood pressure when talking. In general, the thrust of my therapy was to focus her attention on the world outside of herself, and to teach her how to breathe properly whenever she spoke, and especially as she began speaking. She was also trained to "look outside herself"—"to look up and look out"—and to focus on other people, rather than wonder how other people were evaluating her. This was accomplished in part by teaching her that the world was not necessarily threatening to her.

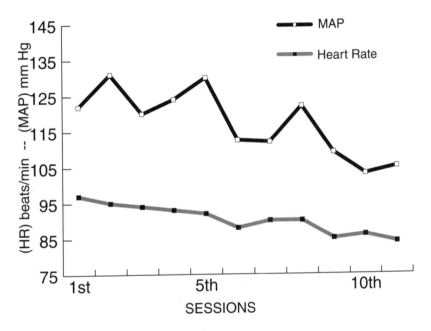

Heart Rate and Blood Pressure Reductions in
53 year-old Female Heart Transplant Patient in Therapy

SOURCE: Lynch & Rosch, 1990

And as was true of many of my patients, she had had a number of early-life experiences that had turned her eyes inward. She described her father as very hard-working, but almost never home. She described her mother as equally hard-working, but somewhat cold and aloof. She was also raised in a rural part of Maryland in an environment that was virulently anti-Semitic, and the name-calling by some of her playmates left a deep and lasting emotional scar. She also alluded to other traumatic experiences, including a first marriage to a person she described as absolutely terrible. She had two daughters in this marriage, and after her divorce, she was the sole source of their support. Later in life, she remarried, and described her second husband as very kind. She worried constantly about her two grown daughters, and her grandchildren.

Utilizing scientific information gathered about speech patterns, blood pressure regulation, and attentional mechanisms (such as gazing at fish swimming in a tank), I directed Mrs. E to focus her attention outside of herself, and back onto living creatures in the natural world. I reinforced the idea that pursuing some of her own loves, like that of gardening, would lead to the lowering of her blood pressure. This concept of focusing "outside of self" was then extended to human dialogue itself. I slowly introduced her to the idea that she could engage in dialogue with others without triggering her own fight/flight reactions and its resultant rapid increases in blood pressure.

Modifying Dr. Herbert Benson's relaxation response, I taught her the importance of deep, relaxed breathing, and the importance of incorporating this habit into her everyday dialogue. Previously, she had talked breathlessly to others. I gradually helped her change this communication style from what I have described previously as the "physiology of exclusion," to one termed the "physiology of inclusion." Instead of "looking at people looking at her" while she talked, she began to learn how to truly look outside herself, and to see and feel the vulnerability of other human beings.

And with this shift in focus, aided by our teaching, her blood pressure began to come down to more normal levels. At age 84, she has an average blood pressure of 130/80, with little evidence of serious coronary heart disease. She is the only one in her family to avoid cardiac surgery for coronary heart disease!

A recent analysis of her echocardiogram by her cardiologist revealed the following assessment:

"The left ventricular cavity size, wall thickness, and global systolic function are normal. There are no regional left ventricular wall abnormalities. The estimated left ventricular wall ejection fraction is in the range of 60-65 percent. The left atrial, right atrial, and right ventricular cavity sizes are normal. The pericardial cavity is normal." (*Excerpt from patient's diagnostic assessment, June 1, 1996*)

One last note: The total cost of seeing Mrs. E monthly and bimonthly for the past two decades has been less than one-third the cost of a single coronary bypass surgery, which every one else in her family underwent, and which she has avoided. Of course, the quality of life enhancement, compared to the health of her two sisters, and the premature death of her brother, cannot be measured in financial terms.

SPEAKING OF THE HOLOCAUST: SPEAKING "FROM NO-PLACE TO NO-BODY"

Perhaps no experience in life has more riveted my attention backwards in time, forced me to think more of the original Ten Commandments, or focused my attention more intensely on the power of human dialogue and the meaning of human health, than my meeting of heart patients with dark blue tattoos on their arms.

Because of its links to Sinai Hospital and Baltimore's large Jewish community, a substantial number of Holocaust survivors with heart disease come to the Sinai Cardiac Rehabilitation program. Now in their mid-to-late seventies and eighties, they appear like ghosts from a long-ago time—haunted and surreal—and always with those unbelievable numbers tattooed on their forearms. From Buchenwald, Bergen-Belsen, Auschwitz, and Dachau, as well as from small Polish and Russian villages where they witnessed scenes of astounding atrocities, they come to the cardiac rehabilitation center.

And as part of their "stress management," they tell their stories to me. It is always the same—blood pressure surges that quickly reach such acute levels that I must interrupt them and tell them to speak more slowly and to breathe deeply. More often than not, I also change the topic in order to permit the patients to speak about these events at some later time.

If there is ever doubt that human dialogue sometimes needs titration, it is erased as they discuss life events, which are both overwhelmingly painful and frequently impossible to speak about. There is, of course, a need to bear witness, to remember the past, but their hearts simply cannot bear the stress of what they try to convey. Many report that, during their lives, they have talked very little of these events. And little wonder! Their cardiovascular reactivity makes it virtually impossible to talk at length without becoming physically overwhelmed. The following figure shows the rapid and dramatic surges in blood pressure in what are typical patterns exhibited by Holocaust survivors when they try to talk about their death camp experiences.

Speaking the Unspeakable:
Talking About Experiences in Concentration Camps

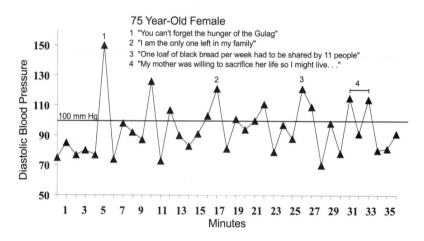

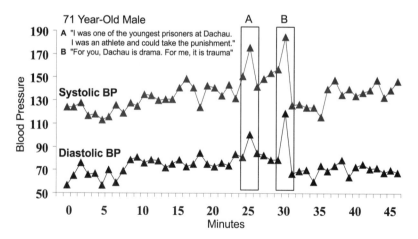

One diminutive 72 year-old woman, of Polish-Jewish ancestry, made me aware of this phenomenon as she quietly described witnessing the machine-gun murder of her mother, father, sister, and two brothers along with many thousands of other human beings in a graveyard in a rural Polish farming village in 1942. She was 16-years-old at the time.

"Good God!" I exclaimed in horror, completely caught off guard, not anticipating the nature of the story she began to tell. "How did you survive witnessing such an event?"

"You mean, how did I survive Auschwitz for three years?" she responded, as if she had misunderstood my reaction.

"No, I mean how did you survive witnessing the murder of your own mother and father and your brothers and sister?"

"You only survive horror one way," she answered as if numbed by pain experienced in her early life, and as her blood pressure skyrocketed to 220/145 mm hg! "You leave your own body. You leave your own heart."

"Where, then, do you live?" I asked while instructing her to breathe, feeling almost too stunned to immediately change the topic.

"You live no place, and you speak from no place, and you speak to no body."

Titration of such dialogue is obviously necessary if patients are to talk without becoming physically overwhelmed. By helping them titrate the emotional intensity of the dialogue, I try to help them talk about their suffering without overwhelming their own hearts. With the focus on graded titration, deep breathing, and slowing the rate of the reports and the rapidity of their speech, many of these patients tell me that they are able to talk about events that they had never been able to share with anyone before in their lives. By slowing the rate of their speech, by instructing them to breathe, and, if necessary, by changing the topic when the discussion's effects become too overwhelming, they appear able to convey far more than if the language of their hearts went unheard or was ignored.

Since *The Broken Heart* was published in 1977, I had come a long way in understanding the relationship between loneliness and heart disease. New technology and breakthroughs in the continual measurement of blood pressure had permitted me to observe the stunning linkages between the simple act of talking and powerful surges in blood pressure. They helped me understand the links between human loneliness, difficulties communicating and sharing feelings, and vulnerability to heart disease in ways that had not been possible when that book was published.

Such understanding also helped me develop an entirely new method to help patients talk about these painful memories—a method that could alleviate the terrible stress which had previously gone undetected and which threatened their health and their very lives. It was this understanding that helped these patients to begin telling their stories in a way that had not been possible before. My approach helped them titrate dialogue so they could modulate the severe and sustained hypertensive elevations that occurred in their blood pressure when they spoke. Now it was possible for them to learn to speak about what had previously been unspeakable.

There are certain lessons learned early in life that are etched in one's heart forever, never to be forgotten. Such memories frequently remain "unspeakable" for the remainder of a person's life. The unspoken suffering embedded in such memories helps elucidate other forms of pain that are equally difficult for the human heart to bear. There are, unfortunately, many other life experiences that are equally difficult for the human heart to endure, and are equally "unspeakable."

Earlier in this book, I described the statistics linking low educational attainment to the sharply increased risk of dying prematurely from heart disease. The statistics, though shocking, are made far more vivid by interviewing heart patients who speak about such experiences. Some of the most dramatic and powerful surges in blood pressure I have ever observed have occurred in heart patients trying to speak to me about school failure earlier in their lives. It seems to represent, in a way, their own personal holocaust, one that destroyed their capacity to engage their fellow man in a carefree dialogue for the remainder of their lives.

SPEAKING THE UNSPEAKABLE: THE TRAGEDY OF SCHOOL FAILURE

Joe W was, in many ways, typical of the patients I see at the Sinai Cardiac Rehabilitation Center. At 70 years of age, he had been fortunate. His myocardial tissue was still intact. The surgical bypass of four of his coronary arteries two months earlier had helped him avoid the more serious consequences of a heart attack. Bypass surgery had abolished the ever-increasing anginal pain that had severely restricted his capacity to exercise, prompting optimism in Joe W that his rehabilitation efforts would soon get him back onto the golf course. Without anginal pain while swinging his golf clubs, or the need to pop a "nitro pill" while walking on the golf course, he hoped to have his score back in the high eighties soon.

Joe W deserved his good fortune, his good medical prognosis, and the marvelous assistance of the heart surgeons and cardiologists who had saved his life. His determination and commitment to hard work had helped him rise to the upper echelons of a large corporation. He was, as well, a genuinely kind human being, quite typical of the patients in the cardiac rehabilitation program—truly wonderful human beings who hardly fit the stereotypical descriptions of men and women filled with anger, or who are depressed, or who are the Type A personalities that the medical literature seemed to repeatedly link to heart disease.

Joe W initially came to me, by referral, after reporting to his cardiac nurse his anxiousness about recent incidents of lightheadedness and dizziness. His symptoms had begun two weeks earlier and, as a result, he said, he was frightened and worried about the possibility of fainting unexpectedly and injuring himself. He was concerned, too, about the cause of these symptoms. His family physician believed that his blood pressure had been set too low by medications, and suggested that perhaps his beta-blocker medications could either be reduced or eliminated. His cardiologist agreed that his pressure might be a bit low, but preferred to wait until Joe W finished his rehabilitation program before making a final determination.

The day I first met Joe W, he was halfway through his rehabilitation program, and had just finished one of his exercise sessions. Throughout our first hour-long therapy session, his blood pressure and heart rate were recorded automatically by a computer each minute we talked. Joe W spoke of his progress in the program, and how pleased he was that bypass surgery had eliminated his anginal pain.

For most of his life, he had exercised regularly and carefully scrutinized his diet, and considered himself fortunate to be in reasonably good physical shape. He was a bit perplexed as to why he had developed severe coronary artery disease in the first place, especially since he had religiously exercised and dieted for most of his life, and did not have any of the well-known risk factors linked to heart disease. He never smoked; he exercised daily; he drank quite moderately; and he was slightly underweight.

For ten or fifteen minutes, we talked about his rehabilitation program, which was progressing nicely, his life in general, and his success as a business executive. Ever so gradually, the conversation turned to more personal issues. He spoke with great fondness about the loving support he had received from his wife throughout their married life. After chatting about the usual struggles faced in raising three children, and his pride about their professional success in adult life, he began to talk about his early life, and his family's struggles with poverty.

His father, he said, had died when he was five years of age. He had no idea as to the cause of his death, except that he died at the beginning of the Great Depression. He spoke of the pain and suffering he, his older sister, and his younger brother had had to endure because of this loss and the ensuing poverty. He added that both of his siblings had died in their early fifties, noting that it would not surprise him if the stress of their childhood had contributed to their premature deaths.

He then talked about the way his mother had tried to cope, and the great shame the family had suffered, when she was forced to accept public assistance. Joe W then added wistfully that "certain images never leave your mind, and certain emotional scars never seem to heal." He described the secret shame he had carried with him all his life. In the wake of his father's death, he had been forced to drop out of school in the ninth grade in order to help take care of his mother and siblings.

Joe W's blood pressure prior to this revelation had averaged around 140/80 mm.hg., shifting up and down minute-to-minute some 10-30 millimeters as we talked. His medications seemed to have his heart rate and blood pressure under reasonable control. Yet, his talk of dropping out of school was followed by a sudden surge in his blood pressure from 130/60 mm hg. all the way up to 230/137 mm hg.!

As soon as this surge in pressure occurred, I instructed him to breathe deeply and to remain silent until his pressure came back down to normal. When his pressure stabilized, I asked him whether he had felt this sudden pressure surge. With a quiet smile, he asserted that he was feeling very relaxed and had not felt any change whatsoever!

Curious as to how high his blood pressure would have to go before he would begin to sense the change, I reminded him to watch the computer readings so that he might learn how to detect these unfelt surges in his blood pressure. In spite of this instruction, Joe W seemed unconcerned, and rather disinterested in the red digital numbers that flashed each minute on the computer screen. Nor did he seem interested in the extreme hypertensive surge that occurred when he talked about dropping out of school. It was almost as if he was living with a total stranger, so totally disconnected was he from the emotional pain so clearly imprinted on his own heart.

After instructing him to continue to breathe deeply, which helped to rapidly bring his blood pressure back down to normal, I asked Joe W: "Who is that person reflected in the digital numbers you see on the computer?" I wanted him to begin his long journey back home, a journey back into his own body and ultimately back in touch with what were his own unfelt feelings. The journey was necessary if he was to become aware of two important things: his physiological vulnerability, and the hidden cost he had paid for attempting to cope with painful feelings outside of his own awareness.

"I don't know," he answered serenely, with a sigh and a sense of fated resignation.

"Do you suppose that these blood pressure changes indicate just how deeply you care about what you are talking about? Do you suppose that this blood pressure surge might reflect the hidden pain of your caring?"

He seemed perplexed by this perspective. I continued, "Do you suppose that your blood pressure is surging up to such high levels because you care so deeply about this topic? Perhaps the hypertensive surge reflects the hidden price of caring and the price you have paid for the difficulties you have experienced when you have tried to share your most intimate feelings with others."

"I don't really know," he quietly responded, adding that his early struggles had helped sensitize him to the suffering of others, and that all his life he had cared deeply about others. He then mentioned that he was very concerned about what others thought of him—that he was, in fact, "way too concerned" about that. He recalled how ironic it was that he had never told anyone, except his wife, that he lacked a high school diploma. He was just too uncomfortable and too ashamed.

Reviewing Joe W's medical charts after the session once again highlighted for me the medical paradoxes. Both his family physician and cardiologist had been concerned that his blood pressure was too low! They simply had not seen the type of extreme hypertensive surges recorded during our dialogue. His blood pressure response to maximal exercise stress-tests in his cardiologist's office, as well as readings recorded by the rehabilitation nurses while he was on the treadmill just prior to our session, confirmed what we already knew.

Virtually all patients exhibit higher blood pressures when they talk about emotionally meaningful topics than when they carry on maximal exercise! Joe W was, in that sense, the rule rather than the exception.

His highest blood pressure, recorded in his cardiologist's office during the stress test's maximal exercise, was 172/80 mm hg, a reading far lower than the 240/139 mm hg. recorded when he spoke about dropping out of school. It was also far lower than the blood pressure recorded during his treadmill exercise in the hour just before we met. This painful memory of personal shame seemed to be etched in his heart and blood vessels, hidden from everyone's view, only bursting into vascular reality when he tried to share that emotional pain and shame with another in dialogue.

"THAT WAS LONG AGO AND THIS IS NOW"

Phyllis G shared with Joe W one crucial experience in what was otherwise a remarkably different life of health behaviors. A black woman who was moderately overweight and out-of-shape, she looked much older than her stated age of 55. Unlike Joe W, she had already suffered two heart attacks, and had come close to death on numerous occasions. She was struggling in her cardiac rehabilitation program to cope with even the most minimal exercise. Her very survival bore witness to the extraordinary skill and competence of her cardiologists. Indeed, "medical miracle" could easily be used to describe the outcome of her harrowing health struggles during the past year. While recovering in the hospital from a second severe heart attack, she had endured eleven different episodes of ventricular fibrillation requiring cardioversion. Eleven times she came close to dying, only to be shocked back to life again with paddles delivering a strong electric stimulus to her heart.

Unfortunately, the pumping capacity of her heart had been seriously impaired by her two heart attacks, and her cardiologists were deeply concerned. The weakened condition of her heart muscles required particular vigilance by the rehabilitation nurses, who were only slowly increasing her exercise regimen.

During our initial session, Phyllis G readily acknowledged that a lifetime of stress, a lifetime of "bad behaviors"—including 30 years of cigarette smoking—and the lack of exercise had finally caught up with her. While discussing all this, her blood pressure, well controlled by a battery of medicines, was quite low.

Halfway through the session, however, she, like Joe W, casually mentioned that she had dropped out of school in the seventh grade. Her blood pressure immediately doubled. Her diastolic pressure, which had been averaging approximately 62 mm/hg for over thirty minutes, abruptly surged to over 130 mm/hg, and remained elevated for two minutes while I instructed her to breathe deeply.

Typical of most heart patients, Phyllis G was entirely unaware of this huge increase, and denied that dropping out of school bothered her. "That was a long time ago and this is now," she remarked as if to reinforce her conviction that the matter no longer troubled her.

"Perhaps the topic does not bother you," I countered in an attempt to help put her in touch with her own bodily feelings, "but it certainly seems to bother your heart!"

In truth, Joe W and Phyllis G were exceptions. Relatively few heart patients in the Sinai cardiac rehabilitation program talk about their struggles in school because few are school dropouts. A wide gamut of problems—from poverty to self-destructive tendencies, all the way to the lack of insurance to pay for such rehabilitation—would practically preclude the dropouts' substantial presence in the program. The majority of school dropouts represent, in that sense, part of a class of people I call the "modern medically disappeared."

The typical stresses cardiac patients first talk about are easy to appreciate—the stress of open heart surgery and chronic pain, their fear of death, their struggles with medical, financial, and retirement concerns, struggles with aging and bereavement, the health of their mates, children, and grandchildren, and the stress of ongoing business ventures, even their common perceptions and concerns about the nation's moral decay.

Yet, it is the pained memories from childhood—feelings of inadequacy, low self-esteem, loneliness, marital stress, emotional neglect, difficulties finding the right words to express their feelings, or difficulties communicating with those who are closest to them—that cause the greatest changes in their blood pressure and heart rate. These are the types of fundamental communicative problems that a number of patients in this rehabilitation program have in common with school dropouts. These are the communicative stresses that need to be identified and discussed in a manner that does not threaten their very lives.

Survivors of concentration camps over 50 years earlier speak of horrific struggles with memories that seem beyond the capacity of the human heart to endure. Discussion of such topics invariably triggers instantaneous, and at times truly stunning, increases in blood pressure, irrespective of what medicines their doctors have prescribed to help control such reactivity. Others speak of struggles that on the surface seem less traumatic. Yet, their blood pressure also surges to extreme hypertensive levels.

As measured by the computer monitor, there appear to be similar heartfelt reactions whether one talks about witnessing the execution of one's parents in a concentration camp or the execution of one's self-worth by parental rejection or by school failure four or five decades earlier. They appear equally difficult for the human heart to endure and equally difficult to forget! And even more to the point, such topics seem to be equally difficult to discuss with others without triggering physiological storms so overwhelming that they can easily threaten a person's life.

Ironically, in spite of their hidden internal storms, these patients usually appear serenely calm when they talk about such matters. Most have a marvelous command of language and are highly articulate. Indeed, the stunning contrast between the quiet, subdued surface calm of their narratives and the concomitant cardiovascular storms occurring underneath creates a serious paradox and communicative dilemma. It is the "language of their hearts" that speaks most eloquently and that cries out to be heard. Memories of long-forgotten childhood struggles seem to be etched in their hearts and blood vessels, erupting as soon as they begin to talk about them. Speaking about the lack of love in childhood, the loss of love early in life, and early emotional traumas, particularly school failure, rank among the topics that elicit the greatest cardiovascular changes.

These heartfelt storms erupt during human dialogue from what appear to be "communicative templates" hard-wired into their beings early in life. Like Konrad Lorenz's goslings, many of these patients appear to be imprinted with a sense of hopelessness, terror, and despair when it comes to the basic human need to communicate one's feelings in a heartfelt manner. Trapped between the Scylla of their own loneliness and the Charybdis-like hopelessness that accompanies attempts to share feelings with others, they live a life of rhetorical exile, struggling daily — albeit outside of their own awareness—to keep their hearts from breaking.

Strangely oblivious to the sensitivity and reactivity of their own hearts, many of these patients appear to be living in exile from their own bodies, in exile from their own feelings, and thus in exile from the feelings of others. Unaware that the lessons learned early in life are etched most deeply in their hearts, they wander in corporal exile, lost in their own fleshless Sinai, and stressed to the limits of human endurance by their own communicative isolation They search relentlessly, to the point of physical exhaustion, and in unfelt loneliness, for their true "homeland"—a place where they might live a life shared with others in the "Jerusalem" of the human heart.

THE JOURNEY FROM A MONOLOGUE IN GALUT
TO A DIALOGUE IN TESHUVA

In this book, I have used Biblical metaphors to discuss the links between human dialogue and heart disease. I have done so for two reasons. The very name of the fitness center that houses the cardiac rehabilitation Center, Sinai Wellbridge, as well as the many Holocaust victims I have met there, create a context in which issues of health and disease can be easily placed within the framework of a larger historical backdrop.

Second, it is my conviction that history has a great deal to teach us about human loneliness and disease, including ways to address this problem with historical wisdom. While at times it seems as if there is an incessant need to be both relevant and "au courant" when giving advice, we are by no means the first human beings to feel the sting of human loneliness. "Nihil novi sub luna" ("nothing new under the moon"), the Roman scribe admonished, and in the case of human loneliness, there is much to be learned from the past. I would hope, therefore, that you might indulge one last foray into Biblical metaphor before ending this chapter.

Earlier, I described a conversation with Dr. Barry Lever, one of the heart patients at Sinai who has shared his heart and soul with me. Like so many other patients, he has taught me a great deal, and I owe to him the essential nature of the story of Cain and Abel as it unfolded in our sessions together, and the insights linking that story to heart disease and modern loneliness.

As related in the Torah and in its translation as the Bible, it has always been a somewhat jarring story. No sooner has paradise been lost than the children of Adam and Eve are set against each other in a way that leads to murder. We are told that Abel becomes a shepherd and Cain a tiller of the ground. And then the story continues:

"After a period of time, Cain brought an offering to God of the fruit of the ground; and as for Abel, he also brought of the firstlings of his flock and from their choicest. God turned to Abel and to his offering, but to Cain and to his offering he did not turn. This annoyed Cain exceedingly, and his countenance fell.

And God said to Cain: "Why are you annoyed, and why has your countenance fallen? Surely, if you improve yourself, you will be forgiven. But if you do not improve yourself, sin rests at the door. Its desire is toward you, yet you can conquer it."

Cain spoke with his brother Abel. And it happened when they were in the field that Cain rose up against his brother Abel and killed him.

God said to Cain, "Where is Abel your brother?"

And he said, "I do not know. Am I my brother's keeper?"

Then God said, "What have you done? The blood of your brother cries out to Me from the ground. Therefore, you are cursed more than the ground, which opened wide its mouth to receive your brother's blood from your hand. When you work the ground, it shall no longer yield its strength to you. You shall become a vagrant and wanderer on earth."

God's punishment for fratricide was to force Cain to live as a wanderer, to live in exile. In Hebrew, the word "exile" is "*Galut.*" For Cain, exile and loneliness are God's ultimate punishment. To this day, the "Mark of Cain" refers to a sentence—a life of loneliness and exile. And as the medical statistics readily verify, there is no greater punishment.

"*Teshuva,*" the opposite of *Galut,* is the great quest to return to "a place," to return home, so to speak.

Exile and return are the two great themes of this book. The "Great Exile" that I have described has been the exile from heartfelt human dialogue, the exile from dialogue within the confines of one's own body, and the exile from one's true self. These dimensions of exile disrupt real human dialogue and make it difficult to share one's heart with another. They help to foster the pandemic loneliness of modern life, and they foster the dialogical *Galut* that inexorably leads to premature death. The return from exile, the return to one's own body, the return to one's own heart, the return to one's "true self"—is to speak with others in heartfelt dialogue. It is life lived in the real *Teshuva,* the Jerusalem of the human heart.

Language spoken from outside our bodies, language spoken outside our hearts, language spoken outside our feelings, is the language of exile. It is the type of language spoken by those who are narcissistically injured. It is a language spoken without any real feelings. Disembodied dialogue is the language spoken in *Galut,* in the "communicative desert" of exile. It is literally spoken outside one's own natural land, one's own heart, and one's true home. The quest for the restoration of a dialogical *Teshuva,* the return to a communicative Eden, is to return language to its rightful place in the human heart—the "real self" in dialogue with others and with the rest of the natural living world.

Earlier in this book, I speculated that the growth of modern electronic technologies is compounding the communicative difficulties many experience. And although it is not generally recognized now, communicative disease will become as important a health threat as communicable disease in the twenty-first century. And just as is the case with the recent development of new drug-resistant strains of bacteria and viruses, so too there seem to be ever-increasing new strains of technologically-induced communicative loneliness that are highly resistant to either easy identification or control.

In a sense, modern technologies that "speak" in a disembodied manner have made it increasingly difficult to recognize the difference between language spoken in the desert of *Galut* and dialogue spoken in Eden. They have made it increasingly difficult to identify the increasing communicative loneliness now sweeping through our lives. Modern technologies that ostensibly speak without the need for the human body, without the need for a human heart, have made it increasingly difficult to recognize the problem.

And that is precisely the challenge that must be faced when trying to give advice to those wishing to return to a communicative Eden. The sources of human loneliness are many and varied. In addition to the confusion created by modern "talking technologies," dialogue can be lost through the loss of a loved one. Dialogue can be ruptured and betrayed through infidelity and divorce. Dialogue can be difficult for those who are single and live alone.

School failure and other major humiliating experiences in life can destroy the capacity to engage one's fellow man in heartfelt dialogue. The elderly can be isolated and crushed by the horrific loneliness felt in nursing homes. Children can be abandoned by their own parents, or learn early in life that dialogue with one's own parents is both impossible and abusive. The mentally ill are frequently unable to use language to convey their feelings to others, and thus become locked in an emotional exile of tragic dimensions.

However different the sources of loneliness, the medical consequences are similar. For that reason, advice on coping with such varied sources of loneliness can never be reduced to a few simplistic formulas, but must be tailored to the specific situations producing the problem. Yet, there are some general principles that can guide us on our way. These can help alleviate one's loneliness, and help ameliorate some of the problems unique to the new millennium. One solution is inherent in the admonition to "look up and look out."

"Am I my brother's keeper?" Cain asked, in a provocative, rheotorical question the *Torah* does not even bother to dignify with an answer. In Paradise, we would naturally be our brother's keeper, as well as the custodians of the entire living world. And the medical data suggest that if we did indeed look after our brothers, if we accepted our roles as custodians of the rest of the living world, if we understood that we cannot live apart from our brothers and the rest of nature because we are part and parcel of nature, then our own health would be much improved.

The cardiovascular data are equally clear. When we look outside ourselves, when we reach out to others, when we act as our brother's keeper, when we love our neighbors as we love ourselves, we help ourselves in the process. Joining organizations that have as their goal assisting one's fellow man invariably helps. Taking part in the activities of a synagogue, church, temple, or mosque involves, by definition, joining communities dedicated to helping others, and thus offers the hope of escaping one's individual loneliness.

Other benevolent organizations, many of which have fallen out of favor in recent times, offer similar outreach programs to benefit the larger communal body. The Moose, The Elks, The Masonic Lodges, The Knights of Columbus, The Heart Association, The Cancer Society, Alcoholics Anonymous, The Sierra Club, The Appalachian Hiking Club, The Delta Society for Animal-Human Bonding—all of these volunteer organizations (and many, many more) perform invaluable outreach services that help alleviate one's own loneliness in the process. For not only do they provide us a community of like-minded members, but they focus our attention on the needs of others, and thus focus our vision outside of our selves. The benefits for one's heart are proportionate to the benefits extended to others.

In a similar manner, pets provide an important, indeed a vital, way of getting outside of one's self and focusing attention on others. And looking at a mountain ridge in the springtime or working in a flower garden will yield similar benefits.

But advice to "look up and look out," "to love your neighbor as yourself," "to be your brother's keeper" has an important limitation—only a "real self" can make use of the advice. And therein resides the central problem that consigns so many to permanent exile in their own communicative desert. For the fact is that those ostensibly the most self-centered, the most unable to reach out to others, the most unable to hear others, have no "real self," but are trapped inside an "image of self."

Few terms are more misunderstood in our culture than the word "narcissist." It is a form of pathology that is spreading within our society of disembodied dialogue. As used in everyday parlance, the term is generally understood to mean "self-centered." But as used by psychiatrists and psychologists, the term actually means "no real self," no "felt self." The language of narcissists, as the holocaust survivor indicated, is a language spoken outside of one's own body, outside of one's own feelings. With no real self, no real feelings, there can be "no real other," and thus the narcissist is unable to see the world outside of himself or herself.

Narcissists are trapped in their own circumscribed world—trapped in their own "narcissistic image." They cannot go outside of themselves, because they have no "real self" capable of making the journey. Narcissists cannot feel the meaning of "I am the Lord thy God, thou shalt not have false Gods before me" because they are consumed and trapped in the mirror of their own false image. Their self-image is indeed its own false god.[233234]

As suggested in the last chapter, parents give their children the very concept of "self," the very birth of the "real self," through real dialogue. The very phrase "I love you" represents the essential message, the guiding principle, that points the way out of *Galut* and back to *Teshuva.* And since it is a phrase spoken in dialogue, it is a journey that can never be made alone. When the love that is spoken is "real," when it is felt within one's heart and in one's flesh, then the journey back home can begin.

Unfortunately, many parents do not possess "real love," and they speak outside the feelings of their own hearts. They speak to their own children in a contradictory, abusive, or humiliating fashion, or they function from a sense of what a "good parent" should be, instead of feeling their own parental hearts.

In those situations, children face the potential annihilation of their emergent "real selves," and are thus forced to exit their own bodies and their own hearts, to escape the pain. Such children grow up speaking outside their own bodies, outside their own hearts, outside their own feelings—in essence, living in and speaking the language of communicative exile. They speak from no place to no body. They speak a language that modern psychiatrists label as narcissistic dialogue, a dialogue that is nothing more than a sophisticated monologue masquerading as dialogue.

Similar problems emerge from school failure, where the injury to one's self-image is so severe that children have to escape the source of the pain—their own bodies and their own hearts—and live instead in a defensive image of self, instead of in their own real selves. Again, the narcissistic injury, the injury to one's real self, is so severe that the child escapes into the world of narcissistic imagery, banished by an educational system that is sworn in principle to uphold their "right to life," but which, in reality, drives them to premature death. School failures are driven into social exile, where they bear the mark of shame, "the Mark of Cain," for the rest of their lives.

Again and again in therapy, I have been struck by the emotional pain expressed either in words, or more powerfully in blood pressure surges, by people who were temporarily held back in school, or who failed to finish school of one level or another. One highly educated nurse waited more than three years of therapy to finally reveal to me that she had been kept back in the third grade. A priest mentioned that even today he is tormented by the fact that he was forced to repeat the first grade. And a self-made millionaire was retained three times in the first grade.

His was perhaps the most graphic story of injury. He recalled hiding once from a truant officer—in a large drainage ditch. At one end of the ditch were several large sewer rats. At the other end, he heard the footsteps of the truant officer threatening to take him back to school. He chose, at the tender and formative age of eight, to escape in the direction of the rats rather than face the shame of his "educational failure" one more time.

There are, of course, remedies—some quite simple—and others far more complex. At the very least, the price in premature death now paid by so many of our citizens ought to give us all pause. Perhaps our leaders could bring us together to discuss the seriousness of the problem and the vital role that the educational system plays in the health of our nation. Perhaps, as our brother's keepers, we could move towards developing school systems that would foster cooperation among and between children—instead of foster competition. Perhaps the educational system could be coaxed into redefining a child's worth, so that all praise, glory, and political rewards would not be heaped on those children who score the highest on the California Achievement Tests.

Perhaps we might even begin to consider rewarding those children and institutions who score high on brotherly love. If one's value were found in places other than high achievement scores, perhaps we would be less surprised when our "educational failures" seek worth outside themselves, anywhere but in dialogue with their fellow human beings. Is it any wonder that children raised to worship high SAT scores, and unable to achieve them, might well search for their worth in high-top tennis shoes, gold necklaces, or money made from selling crack on the street corners to others looking to narcotize themselves from similar pain arising from similar reasons?

Every so often, I wonder whether it wouldn't be useful to dispense altogether with the notion of "IQ," and get on with the task of teaching all children the art of real dialogue, spoken by and with people able to engage their fellow man in a heartfelt way, rather than through hypothetical educational monologues. Perhaps our schools could create an environment where those most at risk could be given the benefit of a loving relationship, and where those more fortunate could help engage these children in the real dialogue of love at a point in life when they are most vulnerable. Perhaps this might help restore educational dialogue to its rightful place in the human heart, restore children to their real nature and their real homes, and restore their real relationship to the rest of the living world.

Those lessons would please all the patients at the Sinai Cardiac Rehabilitation Center. It would please those whose hearts have been broken by the Holocaust. It would please those who have had the courage to share the pain of their educational failure with me. It would please those who have endured terrible losses in their own lives and the haunting loneliness that follows the loss of their loved ones. It would please those heart patients whose children and grandchildren have suffered the pain and loss of failed marriages.

In their own heartfelt pain, the patients at the Sinai Cardiac Rehabilitation Center, with lifetimes of wisdom frequently forged in fires of great suffering, would endorse these three simple, yet truly profound truths:

"We are our brother's keepers."
"Dialogue is the elixir of life."
"Hey guys, look up and look out!"

Chapter Twelve

LIFE AND THE DIALOGUE

And the Lord said, "It is not good that man should be alone.
I will make a helpmate for him."
— Genesis 2:18

What are the answers to the problem of human loneliness?

Surely a profound change in consciousness is the first step that must be taken. This book has tried to aid in that effort by delineating the magnitude of the problem, and the terrible toll loneliness now exacts on our nation. It may very well be our single greatest health threat, and it most assuredly is sapping the vitality of our nation.

Yet, in spite of the mortality data in this book, and the discomfort it will surely engender, there will be obstacles to change. The return to a medicine—and a society—which once again recognizes the healing power of "real human dialogue" and the healing power of human relationships will encounter resistance from a number of important sources. Our view of human relationships and human dialogue, as outlined in this book, represents a radically new prescription for the maintenance of health.

Traditional medical wisdom has viewed human contact largely as a primary source of communicable disease. By ostracizing the afflicted from the community, we controlled leprosy. The spread of smallpox and tuberculosis was restricted through quarantine. In these and other cases, human contact was considered a means of spreading disease and death. Accepting the time-honored medical notion of "communicable disease" makes it difficult to accept the fact that human relationships both cause and prevent disease and death. To repeatedly suggest, as I have, that "communicative disease" will compete with "communicable disease" as the great health threat of the twenty-first century turns this ancient, accepted medical attitude on its head.

Also being reversed is the proposition that the human body is solely a sophisticated biological machine. Suggesting, instead, that the human body is an instrument of dialogue reverses four hundred years of well-entrenched philosophical-medical history. In that context, it is radical to suggest that a biological function like human blood pressure is not only determined by an internal bodily mechanism, but that it also can be regulated by the dialogue between and among human beings. To suggest that the "dialogue" goes beyond the spoken word, to include all sorts of human interactions with the rest of the living world, is to open up an entirely new vista. To assert that "looking up and looking out" can lower one's blood pressure, or to demonstrate that watching fish swimming in a tank can lower that pressure, is to place the regulation of important bodily functions like blood pressure into an entirely new region.

Blood pressure regulated both within and without the human body, blood pressure regulated by dialogue, blood pressure determined by one's perceptions of the living world, is quite a different notion than blood pressure regulated solely by the renal system. To suggest as well that the most ordinary of all human activities—simple human dialogue—can profoundly alter not only the cardiovascular system, but also the entire cellular regulation of the body, is to cast communicative disease into an entirely new and controversial light.

There will be other reasons why the reality of our communicative biology will be denied. A major source of denial resides in the phenomenon itself. The individual frequently does not detect major changes in blood pressure while talking. If a biological process is not felt or sensed, then its reality is relatively easy to deny.

Unfortunately, the fact that people engage in dialogues that elicit major and at times truly stunning increases in blood pressure, without detecting these changes, suggests that the individual, as well as others, are disconnected from the true physiological cost of the ongoing dialogue. That disconnection helps to exacerbate and hasten a journey into what Nietzsche called "the loneliest loneliness." And blood pressure changes are but one dimension of the vast interior changes that occur during human dialogue. For the vascular system interacts with every living cell in the human body, and thus reflects changes occurring in every cell of our bodies.

For almost four hundred years, scientific medicine has been guided by the overarching assumption that the human body is a complex biological machine. Yet, in spite of all the evidence that change is in the winds, there will be fierce resistance to any assumptions to the contrary. One source of it can be readily appreciated by examining the plight of those who fail in school, or the plight of inner city minority groups. It is well known, for example, that black Americans suffer far higher rates of hypertension than white Americans.

In addition, those of all races with low educational attainment have far higher rates of hypertension, and shockingly higher rates of premature cardiovascular disease and premature death. Great psychological comfort is provided, unfortunately, by using a mechanical perspective to explain these "medical problems." If hypertension is assumed to be merely genetic, or dietetic, rather than communicative, then that lets the "corpus majoris," and the larger "body-politic," off the hook and detaches it from the disease.

But what if, as the data indicate, hypertension is at least partly communicative in nature? What if this life-threatening medical problem, as well as many others, could at times be symptomatic of a communicative disease not only between two individuals, but part of a more general breakdown in dialogue between the "corpus majoris" (the larger body) and the "corpus minoris" (the smaller body)? What if average people in the United States had to confront the possibility that they were in fact inextricably linked to the premature death of millions of their fellow citizens? In all those instances, it's far easier to blame hypertension on the kidneys, the arterial system, or other bio-mechanical problems than to accept this alternative perspective.

That's true, too, in dealing with the reality that educational failure is linked to premature death. Denial is a powerful psychological mechanism, and like the plight of inner city blacks afflicted with high levels of hypertension, there is a strong need for educators to view a child's body as little more than a lunch box that carries a mind to the classroom. While grasping an alternative reality could be exhilarating and lead to a fundamental change in educational perspective, the current medical realities linking educational failure to sharp increases in premature death rates are deeply unsettling. For what would happen if teachers came to realize that when they spoke to children in the classroom, they touched their hearts as well? Talking no longer viewed as "mental," but "heartfelt," would elevate educational dialogue and cast it into an entirely new realm.

As asserted earlier, I believe that health expenditures in the United States could be cut in half if problems such as educational failure and the communicative disease it fosters were seen as the primary source of premature death in our nation—if educators, with the help of medical science, could shake off the outmoded notion that the body is solely a machine! If they could come to recognize that academic performance is not just "mental," and that dialogue and talking are not "mental" but heartfelt, they not only might turn their own educational world upside down, but, in the process, help create a new "body-politic," one in which all children would come to understand that they are indeed their brother's keeper. The "body-politic" of our nation would once again get its "body" back.

I believe that no notion has done more to inadvertently cause distress to millions of American school children than the educational acceptance of a "mental faculty" called IQ (intelligent quotient). Originally born out of an altruistic impulse to spare brain-damaged or mentally retarded children the trauma of educational failure in normal classrooms, the concept unfortunately has taken on a life of its own in the twentieth and twenty-first centuries.

In one form or another, the notion of "mental faculties" and IQ that can be quantified and thus made concrete has been implicitly accepted as the primary "explanation" for academic success and academic failure. Just as with human speech that is assumed to be mental, the fact that IQ is assumed to be "mental" in nature has rendered the importance of heartfelt dialogue in the educational process as utterly irrelevant. A new school and a new educational philosophy have replaced Plato's notion of "Dialogue" as the centerpiece of modern education. In the current model, a passive, non-speaking child, is required to sit in a chair and to remain relatively quiet while information is fed into its mind. Politicians have come to believe that computers and the Internet will be the great educational equalizer, as if human contact itself and human dialogue were of minimal importance.

Thus, it is now assumed that a five-year-old child could come from the most communicatively dysfunctional of families and still function well in school. Deemed irrelevant is the fact that the child learned early in his formative years that language was used not to communicate and share feelings, but to hurt, control, humiliate, and destroy.

In spite of this exposure to poisoned language at a child's critical developmental stage, it is still assumed that such children arrive at school with their "mental faculties" and their "intelligence" intact. The notion that education is essentially communicative and an extension of what occurred in the child's home seems almost impossible for many teachers to grasp.

The linguistically-based loneliness of the child's first five years of life can quickly turn, therefore, into an educational nightmare. The original lessons of being unloved and unlovable are compounded by an additional message and a terrible wound, one in which children learn of their "mental inferiority" to fellow classmates. It is a coup de grace delivered on a daily basis across the nation's educational landscape by well-intentioned teachers who hope to assure every child his right to life, liberty, and the pursuit of happiness. Unfortunately, the lethal wound that implodes 10 to 40 years after the "failure" in the classroom is mislabeled heart disease rather than heart *break*.

Nor is this process respectful of economic class, since it is quite clear that children from even the "best families" have parents who use language abusively. These "well-off" children, too, can be primed for failure or rejection within the classroom of well-heeled suburban schools. "Loner" and "social misfit" rather than merely "dumb" are some of the labels applied to these children. Some ultimately employ shotguns, pipe bombs, and high-powered rifles, psychotically responding to the perceived collective murderers of their self-esteem. Most, however, just quietly fade into the background to a self-imposed social exile that leads inexorably to premature death.

There is, as well, a viciously cycling aspect to these problems. At the 1999 meetings of the American Heart Association, it was reported that children whose mothers have higher levels of education have lower blood pressure readings than children whose mothers are less well educated, even when socio-economic levels are made equal. A child could be part of a lower socio-economic group, yet, so long as the mother was better educated, his blood pressure reactivity to stress would be significantly lower. Attempting to understand this trans-generational phenomenon, the American Heart Association quoted Drs. Dawn Wilson and Wendy Kliewer from the Virginia Commonwealth University as explaining: "Children of more educated mothers were more likely to feel that their mothers were available to discuss stressful life events."

One additional note: Teachers, unable to communicate with children who mistrust language used to "educate" them (the word "educate" is derived from the Latin term "e ducere," meaning to lead out of oneself) also pay a price in the process. Teachers who deal with the children most at risk—those children unable to trust language to communicate with others—deserve our utmost support.

If we are to ask these teachers to care for and love the most injured of our children, to communicate on a daily basis with those most isolated, then we must recognize that we are requesting these teachers to give of their selves to others. It can be an emotionally draining and exhausting experience, and one that requires periods for teachers to restore their own depleted selves. An increase in salary will not solve this problem, even though, in light of the health expenditures now draining our nation, it would be money well-spent.

Additional personnel to help reach out to the most needy, while simultaneously reaching out to their parents, would surely help. Simply increasing the salaries of teachers who care for children most at risk will never solve this problem, and can by itself degenerate into little more than a sophisticated form of educational prostitution. Children are quite capable of recognizing those who genuinely care for them. Teaching is far more than a profession. It is a vocation, and one of life's most important callings. It most assuredly determines the future "body-politic," the health of nations, and the political dialogue of all societies.

A new educational perspective is long overdue. The isolation and loneliness of bodies assumed to be separate—the loneliness of hearts assumed to be mere pumps—must be replaced by a new educational and medical perspective recognizing that all real dialogue, including all educational dialogue, is heartfelt.

If only children and their teachers could watch as a vast array of physiological systems inside children's bodies change as they begin to speak. If only they could grasp the fact that a trillion cells are engaged in human dialogue. Then all surface differences—sex, and race, and IQ—would be subsumed under a far more awesome reality. It would involve an educational dialogue more complex than gazing at the galaxies on a crystal clear autumn evening. It would return awe, and respect, and mystery back into an educational dialogue that has degenerated into a Darwinian race to see which school can get the most children into Harvard. It is a Darwinian race where the winners win by necessarily creating losers.

A child's heart is a precious thing. Don't break it.

THE PARADOX OF COMPANIONSHIP

There is an additional basic problem that makes it difficult for the nation to accept a health prescription that "real," heartfelt human dialogue and human relationships must be nurtured. The reality is that all relationships inevitably will be dissolved and broken. The ultimate price exacted for commitment to other human beings rests in the inescapable fact that loss and pain will be experienced when they are gone, even to the point of jeopardizing one's physical health. It is a toll that no one can escape, and a price that everyone will be forced to pay repeatedly.

Like the rise and fall of the ocean tides, disruptions of human relationships and human dialogue occur at regular intervals throughout life. These include the loss of parents, death of a mate, divorce, marital separation, death of family members, children leaving home, death of close friends, the change or disintegration of neighborhoods, and loss of acquaintances to retirement from work. Infancy, adolescence, middle age, old age—all seasons of human life—bring with them human loss.

A prescription to nourish human companionship is, therefore, a unique type of health tonic. Part of the inescapable human dilemma is that the same companionship that keeps people healthy can also seriously threaten their health when it is taken away or lost.

In many cases, unfortunately, the unavoidable dissolution of human bonds is further compounded by an avoidable loneliness that dominates people's lives. Many unnecessarily spend their lives in social isolation or in relationships whose disruption could have been avoided. But, even here, it is obvious that marital disharmony, divorce, and social isolation existed long ago. Cain committed fratricide long before anyone suggested that human dialogue was mental in nature. Man's inhumanity to man dates back to the dawn of creation. Man's brutal mistreatment of man has been as much a constant as mankind's capacity for healing and love. One cannot help but be aware of these problems' continuing nature.

A great deal of social disharmony, moreover, emerges out of serious emotional upheaval that has little to do with any individual belief system. Some people simply cannot live together because they are emotionally disturbed.

The paranoid schizophrenic's inability to get along with his mate, for example, is far less influenced by any subtle social philosophy than it is by the devastating effects of his own psychopathology. The sociopath's disconnectedness, and the narcissist's self-focus, are not likely to be altered by simple prescriptive exhortations to love others. To suggest to the emotionally disturbed that they ought to get along with other human beings for the sake of their health is to offer advice that will ricochet off them more certainly and swiftly than a bullet will deflect away from solid granite.

For many people who live alone, the sad reality is that they have repeatedly tried, but failed, to develop satisfactory human relationships. Bland advice that they should seek to nourish companionship for the sake of their health can be a prescriptive remedy equivalent to a cruel joke. Many who experience the torment of loneliness believe that they have already done everything possible to find companionship. Their past failures have bred a deeply-rooted pessimism, blinding them to the reality that others still desperately need them, and that they still desperately need others.

We must understand the legions of "silent lonely watchers in the night" about whom Thomas Wolfe so eloquently wrote. We must reach out to them. And they can and must reach out to others, if only to recognize that they are not alone in their loneliness.

These dilemmas serve to underscore the complexity of this book's subject matter. The causes of disease are complex. The process of surviving disease is complex. To experience human companionship, love, loneliness, life, and death is complex. This complexity is further compounded by the fact that these experiences must be evaluated on both an individual and a cultural level. Everyone's early childhood experiences, their own experiences with dialogue, their own history of disease, and their own experiences with friendships and love, marriage, interpersonal difficulties, and losses are all unique. And guidelines for nourishing human relationships for the sake of one's health must therefore be fashioned in terms of this unique history. And yet, at the same time, these guidelines must also be fashioned in terms of the society in which we all live.

The mortality statistics cited earlier are the sum total of a large number of individual life histories—statistics which were then grouped together under certain objective categories. But obviously, each person's experience with a social situation like divorce is somewhat different. Some people quickly remarry, others are financially ruined, some find the separation an enormous emotional relief, and still others become deeply embittered. Which of these reactions contributes most to increased mortality rates for divorcees is still far from clear.

In light of this lack of information and the diversity of reactions and adaptations to the same "objective situation"—in this case, divorce—it would be difficult to give specific advice without such counsel becoming a book in itself, and a rather tenuous one at that.

Similarly, it has been established that certain psychological reactions predictably occur after human loss—for example, both increased anxiety and depression—and that such emotional reactions are preceded and followed by well-known biochemical changes that can very well contribute to premature mortality.

For good reason, this important topic has been glossed over here. The fact is that there are many books available on stress, anxiety, grief, and depression. Most of them trace these feelings back to interpersonal difficulties. And all of these feelings have been linked here to an increased risk of heart disease and premature death. Rather than repeat this clinical material, however, I have restricted myself to discussing the more general social context in which such individual emotional reactions occur. That does not mean that emotional reactions like anxiety or depression are any less important. Instead, it reflects my belief that information and guidance are already available for individuals experiencing emotional pain stemming from the disruption of their human relationships.

Earlier, I raised concerns about psychoanalysis that attempts to produce emotional catharsis in patients. And I will reiterate that point one last time. I have never seen a heart patient improve after ranting and raving about his past, or spewing anger or disappointment over the behavior of his parents, children, or mates. Such "catharsis" not only does not provide relief, but it triggers major and at times life-threatening increases in blood pressure and cardiac function.

A large and growing body of research indicates that more supportive, cognitive-based types of therapeutic approaches can be much more helpful. And while I believe that such therapy ideally should include monitoring of heart patients during therapeutic dialogue, dozen of studies have demonstrated that people reduce their risk of recurrent heart attack when therapists titrate emotional dialogue in a way that helps them tolerate the experience. [235]

NEW-AGE LONELINESS

In the most general sense, neither the problem of human loneliness nor its cure is particularly new. Even Adam, wandering about as a solitary creature in the Garden of Eden, was not happy until he had "a companion in his own likeness." The Book of Life barely begins before the Creator of Paradise determines that "it is not good for man to be alone." Paradise itself was imperfect without companionship, God concludes.

Throughout the history of mankind, this point has been readily acknowledged. Over the course of centuries, a large number of elaborate rituals, cultural traditions, and religious ceremonies have been developed to provide general sources of human contact and friendship—to the lonely and those who have suffered human loss. These folk traditions have been a source of comfort for uncounted millions in the past. And yet, in spite of this long historical experience of dealing with loneliness, more and more people no longer seem able to find companionship within our society.

In the 1600s, Rene Descartes made a heroic effort to create a new medicine based on what he called science (with a small "s")—a method rooted in objectivity. Prior to that, science had a capital "S," and was called Scientia, which was based on knowledge both objective and subjective, including a notion that knowledge derived from the Divine. I advocate a return to "Scientia," a medicine based not only on objective science, but on wisdom as well. And it would be a wisdom that would readily understand the healing power of religion, music, the arts, and the living environment, and apply that wisdom to the disease of loneliness now spreading in our midst.

The toll of scientific objectivity on traditional institutions has been far greater than is at first apparent. Thus, in addition to eroding the healing role of religion, the posture of pure objectivity and the mechanization of the human body also challenged religion's social role. By the mid-twentieth century, people had such "purist" viewpoints toward institutions like religion, for example, that they often regarded attendance at a church or temple, for any reason other than worship, as a vacuous or hypocritical gesture. "He's only going to church to fill his social needs" became a common form of condemnation.

And so, the very important social function of religion—structuring a means for regular social contact—was obscured. If it did nothing else, formalized religious services did tend to bring people together on a weekly basis, make them feel like they were part of a community, and reduce their loneliness. Emerson knew this full well when he wrote in 1841: "How many we see in the street, or sit with in church, whom though silently, we warmly rejoice to be with! Read the language of these wandering eyebeams. The heart knoweth." [236]

Religion is by no means the only institution that performs this vital social function. Every institution that brings people together performs this service to some degree. The non-specific but very real social role of many institutions, ostensibly founded for other purposes, should be recognized. For if social institutions are to be downgraded in importance or even eliminated, we must recognize that their disappearance will create a social vacuum not automatically filled by newly created institutions. Social needs are diffuse and non-specific, and can best be summarized as the desire simply to be with other people. The agenda of all groups, irrespective of their reasons for assembling together, includes the satisfaction of people's need simply to be with one another.

Beyond its impact on traditional social institutions, the new objectivity toward human emotions has led many people to adopt a peculiar attitude toward companionship and loneliness. Greater importance has been placed on independence, individualism, and new-found freedom, and correspondingly less on dependency. To need someone else is viewed today as a sign of weakness, a social sin. The "free spirit," it appears, should not interact with someone else out of biological necessity, but only out of choice. Those who lack companionship are inadvertently encouraged to suffer in silence or, in the most subtle manner, to give up their quest for human companionship, accept the status quo, and revel in their aloneness. To be unattached and independent of everyone else is, according to this definition, to be truly free, and truly liberated. In this context, loneliness is currently being packaged in an entirely new way—as the price of freedom.

A second implication also emerges quite forcefully—feelings of loneliness are a sign of weakness. If a person is truly independent, then he or she should be happy, and not suffer from loneliness. The new individualists seemingly rejoice in the knowledge that they are unattached. In many ways, the situation is reminiscent of the "good thinking" of "Newspeak" in George Orwell's *1984*—only in this case, the lonely are not the victims of a malevolent governmental propagandist, but the victims of their own penchant for self-deception.

During the twentieth century, our society gradually refined a response to human loneliness that can best be described as a "cultural pact of ignorance." This is a peculiar type of conspiracy in which some of the victims of loneliness are seen as the perpetrators of their own suffering. The conspiracy involves a subtle denial of certain aspects of loneliness.

As noted previously, many people—in fact, almost all people—recognize that loneliness exists in our society. And yet, in spite of all the talk about loneliness, the word "loneliness" often seems to be completely detached from feelings, and especially detached from the idea that it produces suffering. "If you don't tell me you're suffering from loneliness, then I won't tell you I'm suffering either." With the meanings of words changed or impoverished, the impression is created that loneliness is no longer an issue. No one is suffering, and all are liberated and free to do their own thing. Anyone who wants a "relationship" can have one, and that's "cool." Anyone who wants to meditate alone can do so, and that's "cool," too. In fact, everything is "cool."

Many lonely people do not appear to be lonely at all—they do not look like they are suffering—and so the truly lonely individual is forced to believe that, as the only one suffering, he therefore shouldn't discuss his plight. Everyone believes he or she is the only one who feels lonely, and therefore we are forced to tell ourselves that loneliness must be a mirage. In our society, King Loneliness has no clothes, but we are afraid to acknowledge that fact.

It is increasingly difficult for all of us to share the most basic of all human truths: that we desperately need each other, that we really are dependent on one another. Instead, many people console themselves with cliches such as "I'm O.K so you must be O.K.," while all the while few of us *are* O.K. Or are there other explanations for the communicative difficulties we are experiencing? Perhaps "men are from Mars and women really are from Venus." Feelings of isolation, feelings that real communication is nearly impossible, are massaged with slogans that only serve to make lonely people all the lonelier.

In a conspiracy of silence about their true loneliness, people deceive themselves and each other, and so make loneliness and isolation all the more silent and prevalent. Some even go a step further and begin to kid themselves, telling themselves they are not lonely, that they are self-sufficient, that they don't need anyone. Unlike Adam in Paradise, they can make it alone, they tell themselves, even though our modern world is a far cry from Paradise. This constant indulgence in self-deception eventually makes it very difficult for them to recognize their own suffering.

We deny cultural status to the fact that loneliness causes pain and leads to premature death. The result is that many people no longer feel a need to protect themselves from the ravages of loneliness. Since our mass media now continually suggest that it is good to become independent of other humans, many enthusiastically try to construct a world free of the "tyranny" of human bonds.

Just as the iron-lung machine was quickly discarded once polio was no longer considered a threat to health, so many people have discarded basic social supports that once provided companionship. Indeed, so many traditions, cultural practices, and beliefs, once providing relief from loneliness, have been eroded or eliminated in the past few decades that a person cannot assume human companionship will be available when he or she needs it.

It is now each individual's obligation to find the supports necessary for surviving the cyclical disruptions of human bonds that are an inevitable part of life. This observation may seem bland enough, but it carries with it, in fact, a sweeping mandate. People should consider their investments in human companionship of even greater importance than their investments in a 401-K and other non-financial aspects of their lives. Human companionship is, as we have documented, our most important form of life insurance.

LONELINESS TRAPS

What can individuals do to combat loneliness? Within a society that fosters uprootedness, disconnectedness, disembodied dialogue, alienation, and depersonalization, avoiding loneliness on an individual level is by no means an easy task. Decisions about moving, for example, are often brutally simple from an economic standpoint—either move or lose your job. In many facets of our lives, events seem to be beyond our individual control. Taking stock of our current social network, therefore, requires some recognition of the relationship between alienation and loneliness and a rapidly changing society. Moreover, certain rather abstract ideas about health and human relationships must be incorporated into the practice of medicine before a significant shift can occur in society as a whole.

And yet there are decisions which people can make even now that are quite independent of such broadly based philosophical issues. There are steps that individuals can take to combat loneliness at the individual level.

Even in a social utopia, every individual will experience some type of loneliness during his or her life. Thus, far more problematical than a person's initial experiences with loneliness is his or her response to it. Even in its milder forms, loneliness hurts. It creates an uncomfortable feeling from which people almost immediately try to escape. The problem is that loneliness can be like a spider's web. If a person struggles to escape, he may become all the more enmeshed, until he becomes so entangled that escape is impossible.

Many reactions to loneliness lead inexorably to greater isolation. As already described, one of the more pervasive loneliness traps is woven by those who try to reduce issues of love and loneliness to mere objective problems. Perhaps more than any other impulse, there are those "scientifically-minded folks" who appear to be actively battling against the lack of love in our society, and yet their struggle leads to more loneliness because they equate love with objects. They try to find love through the use of objectivity, an intellectual response that can only lead to greater isolation.

In a similar fashion, those who suggest that modern men and women should be totally self-sufficient and independent have woven an elaborate loneliness trap. Interpersonal freedom is the melody they play, and millions now march in step behind them. These pipers trap people because they make them feel guilty and ashamed for even admitting that they are lonely. They insinuate that it is a sign of weakness to admit publicly that a person really needs someone else. Yet, such an admission to another human being is frequently the catalyst allowing the other person to also admit that he or she is equally lonely.

The search for interpersonal freedom, and the resultant loneliness, manifest themselves in many different forms. One of the more fashionable forms to emerge in the last decade is the "identity crisis," which involves "knowing who you are," "doing your own thing," and "doing it your way." The most important goal is to become a "real person," and this apparently is accomplished by becoming different from everyone else. Great fear is expressed at the thought of being only marginally different—instead, the cleavage between the individual and everybody else must be sharp and total.

The search for one's own identity cannot be found relative to somebody else, or lots of somebody elses. It is a private, solitary, and lonely struggle. It is a quest that is not only futile, but psychologically and biologically absurd. Identity, as we have repeatedly stated, can only be found in a dialogue with another. There can be no "I" unless there is a "you." There can be no "boy" unless there is "girl," and so forth.

Where, then, do people seek their identities, if not with other people? That is the "crisis question," and many resolve it by equating their "identity" with their careers. Careers become their main objective, and all other objectives become secondary. Everything else—from one's spouse, family, friends, relaxation, and aesthetic interests—must play second fiddle to the pursuit of a successful career. In its most acute form, this process leads to the full-blown development of the Type A character described by Drs. Friedman and Rosenman. Driven and work-addicted, the Type A person often ends up in total social isolation—and dies of premature coronary disease.

There are, however, far more subtle loneliness traps in our society. Not every lonely person is trapped by interest in a career, pursuit of independence, or love, based on a scientific love-seeker's belief system. Many lonely people are not particularly trapped by these issues. In fact, many readily admit that they would give anything to find the "right person" with whom they could share their lives. And yet they still find themselves enmeshed in isolation.

Part of the problem is that we have very few formal institutions that deal specifically with problems of human loneliness. This is a particularly glaring weakness when one considers that there are formal institutions for practically every other human problem. Hospitals care for the sick, schools teach the uneducated, Alcoholics Anonymous ministers to the addicted, mastectomy and colostomy groups organize to discuss common physical problems, PTA groups meet to help the schools, and so forth. On closer examination, however, it becomes apparent that the great majority of these organizations have a major hidden prerequisite. Before joining, the person must already have companionship or declare himself sick. These covert requirements make it difficult for those lacking companionship to find legitimate social outlets in existing groups.

For many lonely or isolated individuals, illness itself becomes the only legitimate method for gaining attention. Many lonely people experience very real secondary gains by becoming ill. At least for a brief period during hospitalization, they are flooded with the compassion provided by hospital staffs, nurses, and physicians who care for them, inadvertently providing something that is missing in their lives—human attention.

And the cost for obtaining this secondary type of human companionship soars into uncounted billions of dollars in the United States alone. The typical single, widowed, or divorced individual remains far longer in the hospital for the identical medical problems than do married people. Those who fail in school utilize the medical system far more frequently. And the lonely succumb more often to illness in the first place.

Experience has shown that powerful therapeutic benefits flow from meetings in which people band together to discuss common problems. Alcoholics Anonymous, for example, produces remarkable benefits for individuals who can stand up among their fellow men and admit, "I am an alcoholic." Admitting to others that they have a problem is one major reason they are able to battle it. So, too, with people suffering from obesity. Again, the recognition and admission of a problem to a group similarly afflicted helps reduce the feelings of guilt and shame, thereby producing secondary benefits in overcoming the problem.

The denial of dependence and of feelings of loneliness even lead some people to redefine many of the terms that describe aspects of intimate relationships. Some, for example, confuse sexual intercourse with companionship. So thoroughly confused have these notions become that the word "love" is now frequently used as a code word for sex. "Let's make love." "How's your love-life?" "Do you have a lover?" These comments refer to activities that don't necessarily include love.

While sexual pleasure can be a part of a love relationship, it is clear that sexual pleasure can be achieved without any love, dialogue, or companionship. Prostitutes and gigolos are not the only ones who have demonstrated that fact. Drs. Masters and Johnson convincingly showed that the physiological response and subjective experience of sexual pleasure are similar in both men and women, regardless of whether an orgasm is produced by masturbation or intercourse.

The investigators go even further and assert that in some cases, because of timing or emotional tension, the sexual pleasure and physiological reactions experienced through masturbation can be greater than those produced by intercourse. Clearly, human love involves much more than an orgasm. While this may seem self-evident, read any number of best sellers, or tune into most afternoon television talk shows, and you'll realize that it is not all that obvious to the culture at-large.

The covert, non-specific agenda of sexual intercourse—or for that matter, of any other human relationship—often involves more than sexual pleasure or sexual exploitation. One of the agenda items is companionship—real, live, honest-to-goodness companionship. And often the agenda goes even beyond companionship to include something called love. The "West World" fantasy of the perfect computerized mistress ultimately leaves us cold: it is as unsatisfactory for us as the hand-on-a-stick petting machine is for dogs. Vibrators, brothels, massage parlors, and masturbation all yield pleasure, but they do not provide love or companionship.

These loneliness traps by no means constitute an exhaustive list of the major factors contributing to human isolation in our society. But to list all the potential sources of loneliness is like delineating all the dangers of life. It is impossible, just as it is impossible to predict all future dangers. But beyond that, a preoccupation with danger might prove to be the greatest danger of all, producing an individual with a warped sense of proportion, trapped in a self-fulfilling prophecy. Preoccupation with the dangers of loneliness may, in the long run, be just another loneliness trap.

Obviously, many people are able to avoid loneliness traps even without realizing that such traps exist. Not everyone who lives alone hurdles inexorably into physical or emotional disaster. Not every person with low educational attainment, nor every divorced spouse, bereaved individual, or single person, is lonely. Nor do they all suffer from emotional or physical difficulties. Many lead rewarding and healthy lives, sustained and enriched by many friends and acquaintances.

And, conversely, simply being married or physically living under the same roof with other human beings does not by itself guarantee human companionship or good health. Many married people are far more socially isolated and lonely than those who live alone. Physical living conditions do not seem to be the critical variables. Rather, it appears that the way people respond and interact with other human beings—inside and outside their own homes—is the crucial factor. To be truly worthwhile, living together must involve true dialogue.

PARADISE LOST: THE LOSS OF REAL DIALOGUE

In the latter part of this book, I have offered several Biblical allusions, to some extent because the Bible is one of the great repositories of historical wisdom. Scientists now inform us that the capacity for human speech first arose in human beings some 400,000 years ago. They also believe that the process was evolutionary in nature. Yet, in spite of the objective evidence provided by paleontology regarding the development of language, it might be helpful to consider other dimensions of dialogue. One important alternative perspective can be found in the Bible. Whether one considers the story of our linguistic origins as described in Genesis to be factual, metaphorical, or allegorical is of little consequence here. Irrespective of one's sense of its objective truth, the story of Creation is truly worth considering, if for no other reason that it is the repository of so much intuitive wisdom.

In Genesis, we are told that God created Adam out of the clay of the earth. His very name, "Adama" (from the earth), signifies his humble origins, and his ultimate destination. Springing from dust, he will return to dust. We are informed as well that Adam is created to live in a place called "Paradise," a land of perfection free from all worry, except for the problem of human loneliness. Long before Aristotle remarked that "a man wholly solitary would either be a God or a brute," the Creator had already confronted this particular dilemma, recognizing that Adam would never be "complete," or even completely happy, so long as he remained all alone in Paradise. "It is not good for man to be alone," said God. [237]

And while in Paradise, Adam is assigned one task by God, and one task alone. He is to name all the animals and all the things of nature. Adam is recruited by his Creator to become the first Etymologist, the first Botanist, and the first Zoologist. But why? Why in God's name would a Supreme Being, the Creator of the Heavens and the Earth, ask a human being to codify all the living creatures in Paradise? Indeed, what's so important about naming a tiger a tiger, and a lion a lion, unless it is a task meant to remind Adam that all of creation existed in "God's name"?

This Divine assignment puzzled me for several decades, until suddenly one day an even more basic question welled up in my conscious awareness: Who in the world taught Adam to talk? Based on the Biblical story, there could only be one answer to that question. With no one else on the scene, Adam had to have been taught to talk by God!

As we consider this book's central issues, it might be helpful to reflect briefly on the potential, albeit hypothetical, origin of human speech. Dialogue is the "elixir of life" because it may be Divine in origin! It is, to say the least, a sobering and humbling perspective; certainly one that gives language a far richer and more awesome potential.

Language resides in its biological home within the human body, and emerges as potentially Divine, because it is in fact biologically infinite in its potential. "Love," one of many felt words that describe one's own feelings, is spoken in a trillion cells, and thus understood to be biologically infinite when spoken in dialogue with another human being with his or her own cellular nature. And if that notion appears to be unsettling and a bit mind-boggling, it does help one to understand how language could at least be biologically infinite in its potential, and Divine in its origins!

From this linguistic perspective, the notion of "Paradise Lost" could also be cast in a new light. First, we are informed that the Creator decided "it is not good for man to be alone." With the arrival of Eve, created from Adam's rib, a new, indeed astonishing and potentially self-limiting word would have to have emerged from Adam's lips. For in the creation of Eve, the word "I" would have to be born. Conversing with Eve for the first time, Adam would have been required to recognize the existence of another human being, a "you" that necessarily required an "I" to engage "the other" in dialogue. This "self-concept," first born in Paradise, would have posed a variety of problems. All sorts of "self-concepts" and "self-centered" words were potentially added to Adam's lexicon.

The self-concept of "male" is now given meaning because of the arrival of a "female." "I" is a separate entity, separate from the "you," and thus potentially separate and distinct from the rest of Adam's world in Paradise. "Adama," first assigned the task of naming the animals, suddenly is confronted with the problem of "naming" himself! He is also assigned the task of "naming the creature" taken from his own rib. It was potentially a trap, one that paved the way for "the fall"—"I" alone and now separate from "you," an "I" that is also separate from the rest of Paradise, an "I" quite distinct and different from Eve! It might very well have been the concept of "I" as a separate and distinct entity that led Adam down the slippery path that finally led him and Eve to the gates East of Eden.

The apple loomed in the primeval forest as the "fruit of knowledge," not to be eaten because it awakened one's awareness of "good and evil." Perhaps that awareness was rooted in separateness instead of union—

separateness from God, separateness from the rest of Nature, instead of united with the Creator, and united with the rest of nature. The "I" was waiting to ripen and fall from the core of an apple!

And while focused on the concept of Paradise Lost, there is an additional issue of important metaphorical consequence. When the serpent tempted Eve, why didn't she immediately come running back to Adam in shocked amazement, stunned because she had just met a snake that could actually talk? Stop for a moment and reflect on how you would respond if you met a talking snake in the forest. I suspect that any such encounter would surely be grist and fodder for your analyst.

Yet, "talking serpents" may not have been surprising to either Adam or Eve because the very definition of Paradise included union with all of the rest of Nature. Perhaps in that sense, all of nature "talked" in Paradise because Adam and Eve were united, and not then "separated" from the rest of the living world.

Their "egos," the "I" and the "you," may still have been in perfect union, both with each other, and with the rest of nature. The very definition of Paradise is of a place in which a person lives in perfect union with the rest of the living natural world, as well as with each other. Perhaps "union" with the rest of the living world is the very definition of Paradise—a Paradise so defined because it was devoid of separateness and thus devoid of loneliness.

Perhaps it is we, trapped in lives of varying degrees of separateness, denying our own loneliness, puffed up with our own grandiose notions of self-importance, and feeling distinct and separate in our personal triumphs, who create the communicative equivalent of Paradise Lost. Perhaps as self-centered "ego-centric" creatures, we have wandered far away from our own origins. Perhaps loneliness itself is the measure of how far we have strayed from that perfect union, not only from each other, but from the rest of the living world as well! Even if the story of Adam and Eve, and their fall, is entirely metaphorical, it does help define the journey that we must take.

For it is dialogue that offers the hope of uniting us, not only with one another, but also with the rest of the living world. It is dialogue that unites, and dialogue that ends our separation and isolation, because it links us back to our origins, back to that which is biologically infinite and, if one is so inclined, back to that which is potentially Divine. Dialogue unites—dialogue abolishes the "I" of separateness. Dialogue is the vehicle that takes us back towards the paradise of union with others. It is dialogue, real dialogue, which fuels our journey through life.

On the other hand, consider language that is used in a way that distances; language that is used to hurt; language that is used to manipulate; empty language that is designed to suppress hope; language that is spoken from outside our own hearts. Therein is the path that leads to the loneliness that ultimately kills. It is Paradise Lost—life on earth reduced to a living hell when human dialogue is ruptured, destroyed, or used in an abusive fashion. It leads to both the death of self, and the potential murder of others. It is the language spoken in *Galut,* East of Eden, where Cain, after killing his own brother, asked: "Am I my brother's keeper?" Cain was separate from his own brother, and blind to the lack of fusion, to the lack of dialogue, with him, and therefore missing the obvious answer to his own immortalized question.

As stated earlier, this form of pathological dialogue, this language of disembodied dialogue, appears to be growing as we move into the new millennium. Those who marry such individuals, or experience them as parents, know full well the pain they can inflict. Yet, strange as it may seem, the severity of the toxic talk experienced in childhood frequently blocks such individuals from even recognizing that they have a communicative problem.

Using rational defenses that remove themselves from all bodily feelings, they generally deny what happened to them as children, and instead look outside themselves for the explanation of their own internal problems. "Others are to blame." "Others do not understand." This is what they say, even as they exploit, hurt, injure, and even destroy those who try to love them.

We owe to modern astronomy the intriguing concept of black holes. These super-condensed masses in the middle of the galaxy cannot be seen by the naked eye, or even with powerful telescopes, because they emit no light. Thought to be huge stars that imploded instead of exploding outward, they end up as objects in space with an incredibly dense mass.

From physics, we know that the gravitational pull around large fields, such as the earth, is proportional to the mass of the object. Thus, the gravitational pull on earth is greater than the gravitational pull on the moon, because the moon is of smaller mass. Black holes have the greatest and most condensed mass, and thus their gravitational pull is so great that quite literally nothing can escape their gravitational fields, not even light reflected from afar. Thus, black holes pull everything in, including light, and allow nothing to escape.

I am fond of using a black hole analogy with patients suffering from communicative problems commonly seen in disorders we label as narcissist or sociopath. The mass of the black hole of their "core" personality is proportional to the magnitude of the injuries they experienced in childhood. The greater the injury, the greater the black hole.

Like black holes in space, such individuals absorb all light and all objects around them, while emitting nothing back. Nothing escapes the gravitational pull of their interior emptiness. If love is the light sent in their direction, then it is absorbed inward, and cannot escape outward. Attempts to direct love to others collide with the ferocious gravitational pull of their own inner emptiness. The phrase "I love you," seen in such a context, and directed outward, quickly collides with the gravitational pull of their own internal emptiness, and bends the love back inward towards the black hole of their own injured self. The phrase "I love you" turns back in on its self and becomes "I love me."

Extreme examples of such human black holes can be readily seen in the prisons of our nation. Few people on death row, for example, come from loving and supportive families. These murderers are, instead, men and women who exported to others the linguistic hopelessness, the violence, and the abuse that they experienced as children. The mass of the injury to them was so great that other human beings ceased to exist, and exploiting or destroying others became, for them, a relatively easy matter. With no experience in dialogue, they could never be a real "other," and so they murdered objects, not fellow human beings.

"HEY GUYS, LOOK UP AND LOOK OUT!"

Perhaps, in the end, we can avoid all the various age-old loneliness traps that now engulf our nation with the same simple advice that helps to lower blood pressure and produce good health—"Hey guys, look up and look out!"

"**Hey guys, look up and look out**!" Look out into the world beyond the confines of your own skin to find your real place in the larger world, your real self in dialogue with animals, plants, oceans, mountains, clouds, and wind, with your own biological nature and the communality that you share with the rest of the natural living world. Focusing on a lowly goldfish swimming in an indoor pool can lower blood pressure. Watching the waves ripple in the wind can lower blood pressure. Listening to a bird sing can lower blood pressure. Gazing at the stars can lower blood pressure. Listening to one's fellow man in dialogue can lower blood pressure.

"**Hey guys, look up and look out**!" in order to alter awareness about the plague of loneliness in our midst, to shift our dialogue from the physiology of exclusion to the physiology of inclusion. Reach out to those who are less fortunate. Reach out to those who are suffering the most. Shift your consciousness in a way that will help all of us realize that loneliness is the single greatest health threat now facing our nation.

"**Hey guys, look up and look out!**" Spoken by a child who was loved and in love with his world, this guiding principle can help lead the lonely to look at the loneliness of others. And it can prompt those fortunate enough to have been loved in a way that allowed them as children to "look up and look out," to reach out to others less fortunate— to those whose eyes turn inward, unable to look up and look out. Looking out to one's fellow man, reaching out to those in need, will also lower blood pressure and ensure health.

"**Hey guys, look up and look out**!" can guide teachers as they help children whose eyes have been turned inward by the devastating consequences of toxic talk, and the shame of the intellectual inferiority they are made to feel in school. As a guide, it can help teachers redirect those inward-looking children whose isolation and loneliness will most assuredly lead to premature death unless their gaze, too, can be redirected to "look up and look out." It can help these children become part of the peer group, rather than apart, and isolated, and held in cultural contempt.

"**Hey guys, look up and look out!**"—A guiding principle to help us look out for those who cannot reach out, or look out, or see us. We should reach out to those who are infirm, those abandoned in nursing homes, and those who are emotionally distraught and unable to "look up and look out" themselves.

"**Hey guys, look up and look out!**"—to redirect our gaze not just to NASA's stars in space, but to once again see, as a Pulitzer prize winner instructed us several years ago, "Dante's stars in the heavens." To hear the Pythagorean rippling of the universe, as it pulsates its message of infinite beauty. To change the focus of our gaze, so that our eyes can see beyond objectivity, to the beauty of the human soul that surely resides within our hearts.

"**Hey guys, look up and look out!**"—To realize that we are indeed "our brother's keeper," and that a power far larger than ourselves refused to dignify that question with an answer. The Mark of Cain, the mark of shame, the mark that isolates and destroys, was man-made and thus can be abolished by man as well.

"Hey guys, look up and look out!"—In order to understand that the journey from exile to paradise occurs in real dialogue with others, born of a love that resides within the human heart.

"Hey guys, look up and look out!"—To grasp the biologically infinite potential of all human dialogue, and to recognize that to engage another in the dialogue of love is to speak in a trillion cells, and to dance with infinity and the Infinite.

ENDNOTES

[1] James J. Lynch. The Broken Heart: The Medical Consequences of Loneliness. Basic Books, New York, New York, 1977. Paperback Edition, 1979.

[2] Births to Unmarried Mothers: United States, 1980-1992. Vital and Health Statistics, Centers for Disease Control and Prevention. Series 21, No. 53, U.S. Dept. of Health and Human Services, PHS, DHHS Publication No (PHS) 95-1931, June 1995.

[3] Evelyn M. Kitagawa and Philip M. Hauser, Differential Mortality in the United States: A Study in Socioeconomic Epidemiology, American Public Health Association, Vital and Health Statistics Monographs. Harvard University Press, Cambridge, MA, 1973.

[4] James J. Lynch. The Language of the Heart: The Human Body in Dialogue. Basic Books, New York, NY, 1985.

[5] J. Lynch, K. Lynch and E. Friedman. A Cry Unheard: Sudden reductions in blood pressure while talking about feelings of hopelessness and helplessness. Integrative Physiological and Behavioral Science, 1992; 27: 151-169.

[6] J.Lynch. Decoding the Language of the Heart: Developing a Physiology of Inclusion. Integrative Physiological and Behavioral Science. 1998; 33: 130-136.

[7] Playboy, October 1999.

[8] "Program avoids too easy answers." David Zurawik, Baltimore Sun, January 18, 2000.

[9] Health and Selected Socioeconomic Characteristics of the Family, 1988-1990. Vital and Health Statistics Series 10, no 195, DHHS Publication no 97-1523, Dec. 1996

[10] A National Program to Conquer Heart Disease, Cancer and Stroke, 2 vols. 1965; Government Printing Office, 2:18.

[11] Victor R. Fuchs, Who Shall Live? Health, Economics and Social Choice (New York: Basic Books, 1974).

[12] Health, United States, 1998, With Socioeconomic Status and Health Chartbook Department of Health and Human Services, DHHS Pub. No 98-1232, September 1998.

[13] Morbidity and Mortality: 1996 Chartbook on Cardiovascular, Lung and Blood Diseases National Institute of Health, Heart, Lung and Blood Institute. U.S. Department of Health and Human Services, May 1996.

[14] Births to Unmarried Mothers: United States, 1980-1992. Vital and Health Statistics, Centers for Disease Control and Prevention. Series 21, No. 53, U.S. Dept. of Health and Human Services, PHS, DHHS Publication No (PHS) 95-1931, June 1995.

Marital Status and Living Arrangements: (Update) March 1998; Unmarried-couple Households, by Presence of Children, 1960-1998. U.S. Bureau of Census, Current Population reports, Series p20-514, Jan. 7, 1999. Births to Unmarried Mothers: United States, 1980-1992. Vital and Health Statistics, Centers for Disease Control and Prevention. Series 21, No. 53, U.S. Dept. of Health and Human Services, PHS, DHHS Publication No (PHS) 95-1931, June 1995.

Marital Status and Living Arrangements: (Update) March 1998; Unmarried-couple Households, by Presence of Children, 1960-1998. U.S. Bureau of Census, Current Population reports, Series p20-514, Jan. 7, 1999.14

[15] Colin Harrison: Who Needs Men? Addressing the prospect of a matrilinear millennium: A forum with Barbara Ehrenreich and Lionel Tiger. Harpers Magazine, June, 1999, p. 46.

[16] D.Popenoe & B. Whitehead. The State of our Unions: The Social health of marriage in America. The National Marriage Project, 1999, p. 3. (marriage@rci.rutgers.edu) (http://marriage.rutgers.edu).

[17] Karen S. Peterson. "Marriage losing key role in families" USA TODAY, November 24, 1999.

[18] Deaths: Final Data for 1996. National Vital Statistics Reports, U.S. Dept. of Health and Human Services, Center for Disease Control, vol 47, 9, Nov. 1998. Hugh Carter and Paul C. Glick, Marriage and Divorce: A Social and Economic Study, American Public Health Association, Vital and Health Statistics Monograph (Cambridge: Harvard University Press, 1970).

[19] S. J. Ventura, R.N. Anderson, B.L. Martin. Births and Deaths: Preliminary Data for 1997. National Vital Statistics Report. Vol 47, 4, p. 32., 1989. Hugh Carter and Paul C. Glick, Marriage and Divorce: A Social and Economic Study, American Public Health Association, Vital and Health Statistics Monograph (Cambridge: Harvard University Press, 1970).

[20] Births to Unmarried Mothers: United States, 1980-1992. Vital and Health

Statistics, Centers for Disease Control and Prevention. Series 21, No. 53, U.S. Dept. of Health and Human Services, PHS, DHHS Publication No (PHS) 95-1931, June 1995.

Marital Status and Living Arrangements: (Update) March 1998; Unmarried-couple Households, by Presence of Children, 1960-1998. U.S. Bureau of Census, Current Population reports, Series p. 20-514, Jan. 7, 1999.

[21] Births, Marriages, Divorces and Deaths. Provisional Data for May, 1998 Vol 47, No 9 .pp 1-13. National Center for Health Statistics, Center for Disease Control. (*ref, pg 1)*

[22] Births, Marriages, Divorces and Deaths. Provisional Data for May, 1998 Vol 47, No. 9, pp 1-13. National Center for Health Statistics, Center for Disease Control. D. Popenoe and Barbara Whitehead. et al. The State of our Unions: Social Health of Marriage in America. The National Marriage Project. Rutgers, The State University of New Jersey, 1999. (http://marriage.rutgers.edu)

[23] Births, Marriages, Divorces and Deaths. Provisional Data for May, 1998 Vol 47, No 9 .p 1. National Center for Health Statistics, Center for Disease Control.

[24] Marital Status and Living Arrangements: (Update) March 1998; Unmarried-couple Households, by Presence of Children, 1960-1998. U.S. Bureau of Census, Current Population reports, Series pp. 20-514, Jan. 7, 1999.

[25] Ibid, 21

[26] Philip Slater, The Pursuit of Loneliness (Boston: Beacon Press, 1970).

[27] Dean Ornish. Love and Survival: The Scientific Basis for the Healing Power of Intimacy. Harper Collins, New York, NY, 1997.

[28] A National Program to Conquer Heart Disease, Cancer and Stroke, 2 vols. (Washington, D.C.: U.S. Government Printing Office, 1965).

[29] A National Program to Conquer Heart Disease, Cancer and Stroke, 2 vols. (Washington, D.C.: U.S. Government Printing Office, 1965).

[30] American Heart Association: Office of Communication and Advocacy. Heart Attack, Stroke, and Other Cardiovascular Diseases. www.americanheart.org, 1999

American Heart Association. Economic Costs of Cardiovascular Disease. www.americanheart.org, 2/9/1998

[31] Jennifer Steinhauer. "It's Infectious: Fear That's Out of Proportion," New York Times, Sec. 4, p 16, Oct 10, 1999.

[32] Alternative Medicine: Expanding Medical Horizons, A report to the National Institutes of Health on Alternative Medical Systems and Practices in the United States. NIH Publication, No. 94-066, Dec. 1994.

[33] United States Abridged Life Tables, 1996. National Vital Statistics Report, U.S. Dept of Health and Human Services, Center for Disease Control, vol. 47, 13, Dec. 1998

[34] Health, United States, 1998, With Socioeconomic Status and Health Chartbook Department of Health and Human Services, DHHS Pub. No 98-1232, Sept., 1998.

[35] Paul Recer, AP Science writer. "Good health habits can extend life." Associated Press, Nov. 30, 1999. Washington, D.C.

[36] American Heart Association. Cardiovascular Disease Statistics. www.americanheart.org, Jan. 1999.

[37] American Heart Association. Cardiovascular Disease Statistics. (www.americanheart.org), Jan. 1999.

[38] American Heart Association: Office of Communication and Advocacy. Heart Attack, Stroke, and Other Cardiovascular Diseases. (www.americanheart.org), 1999.

[39] Morbidity and Mortality: 1996 Chartbook on Cardiovascular, Lung and Blood Diseases National Institute of Health, Heart, Lung and Blood Institute. U.S. Department of Health and Human Services, May, 1996.

[40] M.G. Marmot, S.L. Syme, A. Kagan, et al. Epidemiologic studies of coronary heart disease and stroke in Japanese men living in Japan, Hawaii and California: prevalence of coronary and hypertensive heart disease and associated risk factors. American Journal of Epidemiology, 1975, 102 (6): 514-525.

M. G. Marmot and S.L. Syme. Acculturation and coronary heart disease in Japanese-Americans. American Journal of Epidemiology, 1976, 104 (3) 225-247.

[41] J. Brown. Nutritional and epidemiological factors related to heart disease. In World Review of Nutrition and Dietetics, vol 12, ed. Geoffrey Bourne. 1970, Karger, New York, pp 1-42.

[42] U.S. News & World Report, Sept 7, 1998.

[43] In various reports, the actual participants change somewhat, since it was subsequently discovered that only 2,282 men and 2,845 women, or a total of 5,127, were free of heart disease at the beginning of the study.

[44] Tavia Gorden and William B. Kannel, "Section 1: Introduction and General Background," in The Framingham Study: An Epidemiological Investigation of Cardiovascular Disease, Department of Health, Education and Welfare, National Institute of Health (Washington, D.C.: U.S. Government Printing Office, 1968); see also William B. Kannel and Thomas R. Dawber, "Framingham Study Follow-up Reports. Contributors to Coronary Rise: Implications for Prevention and Public Health: The Framingham Study," Heart and Lung I (1972): 797-809; William B. Kannel and Manning Feinleib, Natural History of Angina Pectoris in the Framingham Study," American Journal of Cardiology, 29 (1972): 154-163; William B. Kannel and William P. Castelli, "The Framingham Study of Coronary Disease in Women," Medical Times 10 (1972): 73-184.

[45] Ibid, note #37.

[46] The Framingham Heart Study: Habits and Coronary Heart Disease, Public Health Service Publication no. 1515 (Washington, D.C.: U.S. Government Printing Office, 1966), pp. 227-243.

[47] S. C. B. Thomas and E. A. Murphy, "Further Studies on Cholesterol Levels in The Johns Hopkins Medical Students: Effect of Stress at Examinations," Journal of Chronic Diseases 8 (1958): 661; S. M. Grundy and A. C. Griffin, 44, "Effects of Periodic Mental Stress on Serum Cholesterol Levels," Circulation 19 (1959): 496; P. T. Wertlake et al., "Relationship of Mental and Emotional Stress to Serum Cholesterol Levels" Proceedings of the Society for Experimental Biology and Medicine 97 (1958): 163; M. Friedman and R. Rosenman, "Association of Specific Overt Behavior Pattern with Blood and Cardiovascular Findings," Journal of the American Medical Association 169 (1959): 1286; S. V. Kasl, S. Cobb, and C. W. Brooks "Changes in Serum Uric Acid and Cholesterol Levels in Men Undergoing Job Loss," Journal of the American Medical Association 206 (1968): 150; 1. F. Hammarstein et al., "Serum Cholesterol, Diet and Stress in Patients with Coronary Artery Disease," Journal of Clinical Investigation 36 (1957): 897; W. Raab, "Emotional and Sensory Stress Factors in Myocardial Pathology," American Heart Journal 72 (1966): 538, W. Raab, J. P. Chaplan, and E. Bajusz, "Myocardial Necroses Produced in Domesticated Rats and in Wild Rats by Sensory and Emotional Stress," Proceedings of the Society for Experimental Biology and Medicine 97 (1958): 163.

[48] James P. Henry, John P. Meehan, and Patricia M. Stephens, 'The Use of Psychosocial Stimuli to Induce Prolonged Systolic Hypertension in Mice,"

Psychosomatic Medicine 29 (1967): 408.

[49] Albert J. Stunkard, The Pain of Obesity (Palo Alto, Calif.: Bull Publishing, 1976).

[50] Stewart Wolf and Helen Goodell, Behavioral Science in Clinical Medicine (Springfield, Ill.: Charles C. Thomas, 1976). B. Egolf, J. Lasker, S. Wolf & L. Potvin. Featuring health risks and mortality: the Roseto effect: A 5-year comparison of mortality rates . American Journal of Public Health, 1992, 82 (8): 1089-1092.

S. Wolf. Predictors of myocardial infarction over a span of 30 years in Roseto, Pennsylvania. Intergative Physiological & Behavioral Science, 1992, 27 (3): 246-257.

[51] I am indebted to Mr. L. Timothy Giles of the Fidelity and Guaranty Life Insurance Company, Baltimore, Maryland, for providing me with the comparative figures.

[52] United States Abridged Life Tables, 1996. National Vital Statistics Report, U.S. Dept of Health and Human Services, Center for Disease Control, vol 47, 13, Dec. 1998

[53] Alternative Medicine: Expanding Medical Horizons, A Report to the National Institutes of Health on Alternative Medical Systems. NIH Publication No.94-066, Washington, 1994

[54] C. David Jenkins. Recent evidence supporting psychologic and social risk factors for coronary heart disease (two parts). The New England Journal of Medicine, 294, 1976, pp287-994 and 1033-1038.

[55] Ian C. Wilson and John C. Reece, "Simultaneous Death in Schizo-phrenicTwins," Archives of General Psychiatry 11 (1964): 377-384.

[56] "Depression can break your heart." National Institute of Mental Health. NIH Publication No 99-4592, June 1999.

[57] Pratt, L.A., Ford, D.E., Crum, R.M., Armenian, H.K., Gallo, J.J., Eaton, W.W. Depression, psychotropic medication and risk of myocardial infarction: Prospective data from the Baltimore ECA follow-up. Circulation, 1996, 94:3123-3129.

[58] Everson, S., Goldberg, D.E., Kaplan,G.A.,Cohen, R.D., Pukkala, E., Tuomilehto, J., Salonen, J.T. Hopelessness and risk of mortality and incidence of

myocardial infarction and cancer. Psychosomatic Medicine, 1996; 93: 113-121.

[59] Alexander H. Glassman, and Peter Shapiro. Depression and the course of coronary artery disease. American Journal of Psychiatry, 155,1,1998. pp 4-11.
Dominique L. Musselman, Dwight Evans, & Charles Nemeroff. The relationship of depression to cardiovascular disease. Archives of General Psychiatry. 1998, 55, 580-592.

[60] Pennix, B.W., Van Tilburg, T., Krieggsman, D.M., et al. Effects of social support and personal coping resources on mortality in older age: The Longitudinal Aging Study in Amsterdam. American Journal of Epidemiology, 1997, 146 (6):510-19.

[61] Walter Cannon, "Voodoo Death," Psychosomatic Medicine, 1957, 19:182.

[62] George L. Engel, "Sudden and Rapid Death During Psychological Stress: Folklore or Folk Wisdom?" Annals of Internal Medicine 74 (1971): 771-782.

[63] William A. Greene, Sidney Goldstein, and Arthur J. Moss, "Psychosocial Aspects of Sudden Death: A Preliminary Report," Archives of Internal Medicine 129 (1972) 725-731.

[64] Stewart Wolf, "Psychosocial Forces in Myocardial Infarction and Sudden Death," Circulation (supp. IV) vols 4-40 (1969) 7681.

[65] Thomas, C.B. and Duszynski, K.R. Closeness to parents and the family constellation in a prospective study of five disease states: suicide, mental illness, malignant tumor, hypertension, and coronary heart disease. Johns Hopkins Medical Journal, 1974, 134:251.

[66] L. Russek, S. King, S. Russek & H. Russek. The Harvard mastery of stress study 35 year follow-up: prognostic significance of patterns of psychophysiological arousal and adaptation. Psychosomatic Medicine, 1990, 52: 271-285.
L. Russek and G. Schwartz. Narrative descriptions of parental love and caring predict health status in midlife: A 35 year follow-up of the Harvard mastery of stress study. Alternative Therapies in Health and Medicine. 1996, 2: 55-62.
L. Russek and G. Schwartz. Feelings of parental caring predict health status in midlife: A 35 year follow-up of the Harvard mastery of stress study. Journal of Behavioral Medicine, 1997, 1: 1-13.

[67] Berkman, L.F. and Syme, S.L. Social networks, host resistance, and mortality: a nine year follow-up study of Alameda County residents. American Journal of Epidemiology, 1979, 109 (2):186-204.
Berkman, L.F. The role of social relations in health promotion. Psychosomatic

Medicine, 1995, 57: 245-254.
Berkman, L. & Breslow, L. Health and Ways of Living: The Alameda County Study. New York, Oxford University Press, 1983.

[68] Reynolds, P. and Kaplan, G.A. Social connections and risk for cancer: prospective evidence from the Alameda County Study. Behavioral Medicine, 1990, 16, 3, 101-110.

[69] Marshall, J.R. and Funch, D.P. Social environment and breast cancer. A cohort analysis of patient survival. Cancer, 1983, 52 (8): 1546-1550.

[70] Friedmann, E., Katcher, A., Lynch, J.J., and Thomas, S. Animal companions and one-year survival of patients discharged from a coronary care unit. Public Health Reports, 1980, 95: 307-312.
Katcher, A. H., Friedmann E., Beck, A. and Lynch, J.J. Looking, talking and blood pressure: The physiological conseqeunces of interaction with the living environment. In New Perspectives on Our Lives with Companion Animals., ed. by A. Katcher and A. Beck, Philadelphia, University of Pennsylvania Press, 1983.

[71] Siegel, B., Love, Medicine and Miracles. Harper and Row, New York, 1986.

[72] Perhaps the most helpful overall Web site for individuals with any type of medical problem is one developed by the U.S. Government, www.healthfinder.gov. This marvelous site not only helps explain all that is known about virtually every disease, and permits one to access all the most current scientific literature, but it also helps one find all sorts of support groups via chat rooms in every state and county in the United States.

[73] Siegel, B., Living beyond Limits: New Hope and Help for Facing Life Threatening Illness. Times Books, New York, NY, 1993.

[74] Fawzy, F.I., Fawzy, C.S. Hyun, et al., Malignant melanoma: effects of an early structured psychiatric intervention, coping, and affective state on recurrence and survival six years later. Archives of General Psychiatry, 1993, 50:681-689.

[75] Several statistical concepts referred to in these reports need to be clarified. The first is the concept of age-specific death rates. Within any given age group, a certain percentage of people die. At younger ages, obviously, fewer people die than at older ages. Excessive age-specific death rates, therefore, refer to any increase for a specific age group above the average death rate for that age. Quite often this is expressed in terms of a ratio. Thus, the 1.84 overall age-adjusted death rate for divorced people in the United States means that when the death rate at all ages is averaged together and adjusted for the average death rate at each age, divorced people die 1.84 times more frequently than married people. This is, of

course, calculated from the relative numbers of divorced to married people at each age.

A second statistical concept needing clarification is that of excessive mortality. If, for example, 1 out of every 100 males dies at the age of 30, while 2 out of every 100 30-year-old divorced males die, then the excessive mortality of divorced males is said to be double that of their married counterparts for that specific age. Premature death as a statistical concept refers to deaths occurring before the ages of 75, while age-specific death rates are the death-rate patterns at any and all ages.

Another statistical construct that needs to be understood is the difference between what are called "Prospective Studies" and "Retrospective Studies." Retrospective studies generally involve census data, in which certain phenomena are observed (such as the links between marital status and mortality) and in which one tries to go back in time to figure out why certain relationships occurred. Usually, one formulates hypotheses that are then tested in prospective studies, such as the Framingham Studies, or those done in Alameda County and elsewhere.

Prospective studies are much akin to prospecting for gold. First, you formulate a reasonable hypothesis about where the gold might be located, and then you start digging. The risk involved is clear—the digging might end up as a lot of work for nothing. The reward is equally clear—you might hit pay dirt! Scientists generally consider prospective studies to be more "powerful" because they examine people before they get sick, and thus are better suited to identify more precisely why some people are at increased risk of illness or death. As suggested earlier, however, even the most comprehensive prospective studies can also have their conceptual limitations.

[76] Arthur S. Kraus and Abraham M. Lillienfeld, "Some Epidemiologic Aspects of the High Mortality Rate in the Young Widowed Group," Journal of Chronic Diseases 10 (1959): 207-217.

[77] CDC 1998 report (www.cdc.gov) . Also, Health, United States, 1998. With Socioeconomic status and Health Chartbook. US Dept of health and Human Services. 1998; DHHS Pub No 98-1232.

[78] Hugh Carter and Paul C. Glick, Marriage and Divorce: A Social and Economic Study, American Public Health Association, Vital and Health Statistics Monograph (Cambridge: Harvard University Press, 1970), p. 345

[79] Evelyn M. Kitagawa and Philip M. Hauser, Differential Mortality in the United States: A Study in Socioeonomie Epidemiology, American Public Health Association, Vital and Health Statistics Monograph (Cambridge: Harvard University Press, 1973)

[80] Abraham M. Lillienfeld, Morton L. Levin, and Irving I. Kessler, Cancer in the United States (Cambridge: Harvard University Press, 1972), pp. 126-14. See also David L. Levin et al., Cancer Rates and Risks, 2nd ed, U. S. Department of Health, Education and Welfare (Washington, D.C.: U.S. Government Printing Office, 1974), p SS.

[81] Harold J. Morowitz, "Hiding in the Hammond Report," Hospital Practice, August 1975, pp. 35-39.

[82] Ibid, p. 39.

[83] Iwao Moriyama, Dean E. Krueger, and Jeremiah Stamler, Cardiovascular Diseases in the United States, American Public Health Association, Vital and Health Statistics Monograph (Cambridge: Harvard University Press, 1971), p. 2.

[84] Case, R.B., Moss, A.J., Case, N., et al. Living alone after myocardial infraction. Impact on prognosis. Journal of the American Medical Association, 1992, 267 (4): 515-519.

[85] Berkman, L.F., Leo-Summers, L., and Howwitz, R.I. Emotional support and survival after myocardial infarction. A prospective population-based study of the elderly. Annals of Internal Medicine, 1992, 117 (12):1003-1009.

[86] S. Ebrahim, G. Wannamethee, A. McCallum, M. Walker, & A. Shaper. Marital status, change in marital status, and mortality in middle-aged British men. American Journal of Epidemiology; 1995, 142;8: 834-842.

[87] J. Herlitz, I. Wiklund, K. Caidahl, M. Hartford, M. Haglid, B. Karlsson, H. Sjoland, and T. Karlsson. The feeling of loneliness prior to coronary artery bypass grafting might be a predictor of short-term and long-term postoperative mortality. European Journal of Vascular and Endovascular Surgery, 1998, 2:120-125.

[88] K. Orth-Gomer, M. Horsten, S.P. Wamala, M. Mittleman, R. Kirkeeide, B. Svane, L. Ryden, and K. Schenck-Gustafsson. Social relations and extent and severity of coronary artery disease. The Stockholm female coronary risk study. European Heart Journal, 1998; 19: 1648-1656.

[89] William, R.B., Barefoot, R.M., and Califf, R.M. Prognostic importance of social and economic resources among medically treated patients with angiographically documented coronary heart disease. Journal of the American Medical Association, 1992, 267 (4) 520-524.

[90] J. H. Medalie, Factors Associated with the First Myocardial Infarction: 5 Years

Observation of 10,000 Adult Males, Presented at the Symposium on Epidemiology and Prevention of Coronary Heart Disease, Helsinki, 1972, cited in Life Stress and Illness, p 91.

[91] J. Medalie and U. Goldbourt. Angina pectoris among 10,000 men: II. Psychosocial and other risk factors as evidenced by a multivariate analysis of a five year incidence study. American Journal of Medicine, 1976; 60: 910-921.

[92] J. Suls, P. Greene, G. Rose, P.Lounsbury, and E. Gordon. Hiding worries from one's spouse: associations between coping via protective buffering and distress in male post-myocardial infarction patients and their wives. Journal of Behavioral Medicine, 1997; 4:333-349.

[93] Stewart Wolf, "Psychosocial Forces in Myocardial Infarction and Sudden Death," Circulation (supp. IV) vols 4-40 (1969) 7681.

[94] J. Groen, "Influence of Social and Cultural Patterns on Psychosomatic Diseases," Psychother Psyehosom 18 (1970) 189-213.

[95] Colin Parkes, Bereavement: Studies of Grief in Adult Life (New York: International Universities Press, 1972).

[96] Arthur S. Kraus and Abraham M. Lillienfeld, "Some Epidemiologic Aspects of the High Mortality Rate in the Young Widowed Group," Journal of Chronic Diseases 10 (1959): 207-217.

[97] Ibid, p. 217.

[98] Colin Parkes, Bereavement: Studies of Grief in Adult Life (New York: International Universities Press, 1972).

[99] P. Martikainen, T. Valkonen. Mortality after the death of a spouse: rates and causes of death in a large Finnish cohort. American Journal of Public Health, 1996; 86-1087-1093.

[100] Dean Ornish. Love and Survival: The Scientific Basis for the Healing Power of Intimacy. Harper Collins, New York, NY, 1998.

[101] "Teens who have problems with fathers use drugs more." August 30, 1999. CNN Interactive. Written by Eileen O'Connor and Associated Press.www.cnn.com/US/9908/30/teen.drugs.02.

[102] Richard Sennett and Jonathan Cobb. The Hidden Injuries of Class. W.W. Norton & Co., New York, 1972.

[103] W. F. Enos, R. H. Holmes, and J. C. Beyer, "Pathology of Coronary Arteriosclerosis," American Journal of Cardiology 9 (1962) 343-354; A. R. Moritz and N. Zamcheck, "Sudden and Unexpected Deaths of Young Soldiers: Diseases Responsible for Such Deaths during World War II," Archives of Pathology 42 (1946): 459-494; W. M. Yater et al., "Coronary Artery Disease in Men 18 to 39 Years of Age: Report on 869, 450 with Necropsy Examinations," American Heart Journal 36 (1948), 334-372 481-526, 683-722; M. Newman, "Coronary Occlusion in Young Adults Review of 50 Cases in the Services," Lancet 2 (1946): 409-411.

[104] G. Berenson, S. Srinavasan, W. Bao, et al. Association between multiple risk factors and atherosclerosis in children and young adults. The New England Journal of Medicine, 1999,338 (23), 1650-1656.
L.S. Weber, A. Voors, S. Srinavansan, et al, Occurrence in children of multiple risk factors for coronary artery disease: The Bogalusa Heart Study. Preventative Medicine, 1979:8: 407-418.
G.S. Berenson, W. Wattingey, R. Tracy, et al. Atherosclerosis of the aorta and coronary arteries and cardiovascular risk factors in persons aged 6-30 years and studied at necropsy.(The Bogalusa Heart Study) American Journal of Cardiology, 1992, 70:851-858.

[105] Lytt Gardner, "Deprivation Dwarfism," Scientific American 227 (1972): 76-82.

[106] Ibid, p. 101.

[107] Sigmund Freud, Mourning and Melancholia (1917) in Complete Psychological Works Standard Edition vol. 14, J. Strachey, ed. and trans. (London: Hogarth Press, 1957), pp. 237-260.

[108] John Bowlby, "Maternal Care and Mental Health," World Health Organization Monograph 2 (1951); "Some Pathological Processes Set in Train by Early Mother-Child Separation," Journal of Mental Science 99 (1953): 265; "Pathological Mourning and Childhood Mourning," Journal of the American Psychoanalytic Association 11 (1963): S00; Attachment and Loss, vol. 1, Attachment (New York: Basic Books, 1969).

[109] Rene A. Spitz, "Anxiety in Infancy: A Study of its Manifestations in the First Year of Life," International Journal of Psychoanalysis 31 (1950): 138.

[110] Nelson K. Ordway, M. F. Leonard, and T. Ingles, "Interpersonal Factors in Failure to Thrive," Southern Medical Bulletin 57 (1969): 23-28.

[111] C. W. Wahl, "Some Antecedent Factors in the Family Histories of 392 Schizophrenics," American Journal of Psychiatry 110 (1954): 668.

[112] Roslyn Seligman et al. "The Effect of Earlier Parental Loss in Adolescence," Archives of General Psychiatry 31 (1974): 475-479.

[113] S. Glueck and E. Glueck, Unraveling Juvenile Delinquency (Cambridge: Harvard University Press, 1950).

[114] S. Greer, "Study of Parental Loss in Neurotics and Sociopaths," Archives of General Psychiatry 112 (1964): 177.

[115] I. Gregory, "Anterospective Data Following Childhood Loss of a Parent," Archives of General Psychiatry 13 (1965): 99-120.

[116] Arthur H. Schmale, Jr. "Relationship of Separation and Depression to Disease. I: A Report on a Hospitalized Medical Population," Psychosomatic Medicine 20 (1958): 259-277.

[117] Claus B. Bahnson, "Emotional and Personality Characteristics of Cancer Patients," in Recent Developments in Medical Oncology, Alton Sutnick, ed., (Baltimore, Md.: University Park Press, 1975).

[118] Ralph S. Paffenbarger et al., "Chronic Disease in Former College Students: I: Early Precursors of Fatal Coronary Heart Disease," American Journal of Epidemiology 83 (1966): 328, see also, R. S. Paffenbarger et al., "Chronic Disease in Former College Students. II: Methods of Study and Oberservations on Mortality from Coronary Heart Disease," American Journal of Public Health 56 (1966): 97; R. S. Paffenbarger, M. C. Thome, and A. L. Wing, "Chronic Disease in Former College Students. IX: Characteristics in Youth Predisposing to Hypertension in Later Years," American Journal of Epidemiology 88 (1968): 25; R. S. Paffenbarger, S. H. King, and A. L. Wing, "Chronic Disease in Former College Students. IV: Characteristics in Youth that Predispose to Suicide and Accidental Death in Later Life," American Journal of Public Health 59 (1969): 900.

[119] Ibid, p. 327.

[120] Kitagawa & Hauser, Differential Mortality.

[121] Ibid, 76.

[122] Ibid, p. 26

[123] Hypertension in Adults 25-74 Years of Age. United States, 1971-1975. National Health Survey, Series 11, No 221, DHHS, Publ. 81-1671, 1981.

[124] M. Winkleby, D. Jatulis, E. Frank, & S. Fortmann. Socioeconomic status and health: How education, income and occupation contribute to risk factors for cardiovascular disease. American Journal of Public Health; 82: 816-820.

[125] M. Micozzi. Childhood hypertension and academic standing in the Phillipines. American Journal of Public Health, 1980; 70: 530-532.
M. Mittleman, M. Maclure, M. Nachnani, J. Sherwood, and J. Muller. Educational attainment, anger, and the risk of triggering myocardial infarction onset. Archives of Internal Medicine. 1997; 157:769-775.
J. Roberts. Hypertension in Adults 25-74 years of Age. US 1971-1975. US Department of Health and Human Services, DHHS Publication 81-1671; 1981.
K. Liu, L. Cedres, J. Stamler, et al. Relationship of education to major risk factors and death from coronary heart disease, cardiovascular diseases and all causes: Findings of Three Chicago Epidemiologic Studies. Circulation, 1982; 66: 13081314.
B. Jacobsen and D. Thelle. Risk factors for coronary heart disease and level of education. The Tromso Heart Study. American Journal of Epidemiology. 1988; 127: 923-932.

[126] M. Winkleby, D. Jatulis, E. Frank, and S. Fortmann. American Journal of Public Health; 1992, 82:816-820.
B.K. Jacobsen & D. Thelle. Risk factors for coronary heart disease and level of education. American Journal of Epidemiology, 1988:127:923-932.
US Department of Health, Educationa and Welfare. Lipid research clinics' manual of laboratory operations. Vol 1: Lipid and lipoprotein analysis. Washington, D.C., US Government Printing office, 1974.

[127] Trends in serum cholesterol among US adults aged 20 to 74 years. Data from the National Health and Nutrition examination surveys, 1960 to 1980. National Center for Health Statistics-National Heart, Lung and Blood Institute Collaborative Lipid Group. Journal of the American Medical Association, 1987; 257:937-942.

[128] Health, United States, 1998: With Socioeconomic status and health chartbook. 1998. US Department of Health and Human Services, Center for Disease Control, DHHS Pub.98-1232.

[129] A. Glassman and P. Shapiro. Depression and the course of coronary artery disease. American Journal of Psychiatry; 1998; 155: 4-11.
D. Musselman, D. Evans, and C. Nemeroff. The relationship of depression to cardiovascular disease. Archives of General Psychiatry. 1998;55: 580-592.
B. Jacobsen & D. Thelle. Risk factors for coronary heart disease and level of education. The Tromso Heart Study. American Journal of Epidemiology, 1988, 127: 923-932.

[130] W. Lewis. Marital status and its relation to the use of short-stay hospitals and nursing homes. Public Health reports; 1984; 99: 415-424.

[131] Circulation, 1982, p.1313.

[132] R. Mulcahy, L. Daly, I. Graham, and N. Hickey. Level of education, coronary risk factors and cardiovascular disease. Irish Medical Journal; 77: 316-318.

[133] Ibid, p. 318.

[134] M. Friedman and R. Rosenman. Type A Behavior and Your Heart. 1974; Alfred A. Knopf, New York, NY.

[135] M. Friedman. Type A Behavior: Its Diagnosis and Treatment. 1996, Plenum Publ Corp., New York, New York.

[136] R. Rosenman, R. Brand, C. Jenkins, M. Friedman, R. Straus, and M. Wurm. Coronary heart disease in the Western Collaborative Group Study: final follow-up experience of 8 ½ years. Journal of the American Medical Association, 1975; 233:872-877.
R. Rosenman, R. Brand, R. Scholtz, and M. Friedman. Multivariate prediction of coronary heart disease during 8.5 year follow-up in the Western Collaborative Group Study. American Journal of Cardiology; 1976;37: 903-907.

[137] M. Friedman and D. Ulmer. Treating Type A Behavior and Your Heart. 1985; Fawcett Books, New York, NY.

[138] Ibid, 125.

[139] Ibid, pp. 34-35.

[140] M. Friedman. Type A Behavior: Its diagnosis and treatment. 1996; Plenum Publ. Corp., New York, NY.

[141] Ibid, p. 559.

[142] C. McCord and H. Freeman. Excess mortality in Harlem. The New England Journal of Medicine. 1990, vol 322, 3, pp 173-177.

[143] Baltimore Sun, May 10, 1999.

[144] J. E. O. Newton and Walter W. Ehrlich, "The History of a Catatonic Dog," Conditional Reflex 3 (1968): 45-61; see also W. Horsley Gantt et al., "Effect of

Person," Conditional Reflex 4 (1966): 18-35.

[145] J. Lynch. The cardiac orienting response and its relationship to the cardiac conditional response in dogs. Conditional Reflex, 1967; 2: 138-151.

[146] W. Horsley Gantt, "The Cardiovascular Component of the Conditional Reflex to Pain, Food and Other Stimuli," Physiological Review 40 (1960): 266-291.

[147] Ivan P. Pavlov, Lectures on Conditioned Reflexes, trans. W. H. Gantt (New York: International Publishers, 1928).

[148] J. E. O. Newton and Walter W. Ehrlich, "The History of a Catatonic Dog," Conditional Reflex 3 (1968): 45-61; see also W. Horsley Gantt et al., "Effect of Person," Conditional Reflex 4 (1966): 18-35.

[149] Ibid, 124.

[150] Joseph E. Newton and Walter W. Ehrlich, "Coronary Blood Flow in Dogs: Effect of Person," Conditional Reflex I (1966): 81.

[151] Sandra Anderson and W. Horsley Gantt, "The Effect of Person on Cardiac and Motor Responsivity to Shock in Dogs," Conditional Reflex I (1966): 181-189.

[152] James J. Lynch and J. F. McCarthy, "The Effect of Petting on a Classically Conditioned Emotional Response," Behavioral Research and Therapy 5 (1967): 55-62.

[153] Howard S. Liddell, "Conditioning and Emotions," Scientific American 190 (1954): 48.

[154] . James J. Lynch and J. F. McCarthy, "Social Responding in Dogs: Heart Rate Changes to a Person," Psychophysiology 5 (1969): 389-393.

[155] A. Katcher, H. Segal, and A. Beck. Comparison of contemplation and hypnosis for the reduction of anxiety and discomfort during dental surgery. American Journal of Clinical Hypnosis, 1984; 27:14-21.

[156] W. Horsley Gantt, "The Cardiovascular Component of the Conditional Reflex to Pain, Food and Other Stimuli," Physiological Review 40 (1960): 266-291.

[157] Ivan P. Pavlov, Lectures on Conditioned Reflexes, trans. W. H. Gantt (New York: International Publishers, 1928).

[158] James J. Lynch et al., "Heart Rate Changes in the Horse to Human Contact,"

Psychophysiology 11 (1974): 472-478.

[159] H. F. Harlow, "The Nature of Love," American Psychologist 13 (1958): 673; "The Development of Affectional Patterns in Infant Monkeys," in Determinants of Infant Behavior, ed. B. M. Foss (New York: Wiley 1961), pp. 75-97; "Love in Infant Monkeys," Scientific American 200 (1959) 68; Wm. T. McKinney "Primate Social Isolation: Psychiatric Implications," Archives of General Psychiatry 31 (1974): 422-426.

[160] Martin Reite et al., "Depression in Infant Monkeys: Physiological Correlates," Psychosomatic Medicine 36 (1974) 363-367.

[161] . James J. Lynch et al., "Effects of Human Contact on the Heart Activity of Curarized Patients in a Shock-Trauma Unit," American Heart Journal 88 (1974): 160-169.

[162] C. T. East, The Story of Heart Disease: The Fitzpatrick Lectures for 1956 and 1957, Given Before the Royal College of Physicians of London (London: Dawson and Sons, 1957).

[163] Ibid, as quoted in A. C. Celsus, De Medicina, Liber III, 6 (Circa A.D. 30).

[164] Ibid, page 15.

[165] Arthur J. Moss and Bruce Wynar, "Tachycardia in House Officers Presenting Cases at Grand Rounds," Annals of Internal Medicine 72 (1970).

[166] S. Alberto DiMascio, Richard W. Boyd, and Milton Greenblatt, "Physiological Correlates of Tension and Antagonism During Psychotherapy: A Study of Interpersonal Physiology," Psychosomatic Medicine 19 (1957): 104; Alberto DiMascio et al., "The Psychiatric Interview (A Sociophysiologic Study)," Diseases of the Nervous System 16 (1955): 4; Roy Coleman Milton Greenblatt, and Harry C. Solomon, "Physiological Evidence of Rapport During Psychotherapeutic Interviews," Diseases of the Nervous System 17 (1956): 71, 77.

[167] Brigitte Stanek, P. Hahn, and H. Mayer, "Biometric Findings on Cardiac Neurosis. III: Changes in ECG and Heart Rate in Cardiophobic Patients and Their Doctor During Psychoanalytical Initial Interviews. Topics of Psychosomatic Research, 9th European Conference on Psychosomatic Research, Vienna, 1972," Psychother. Psychosom 22 (1973): 289, H. Mayer, Brigitte Stanek, and P. Hahn, "Biometric Findings of Cardiac Neurosis. II: ECG and Circulation Findings of Cardiophobic Patients During Standardized Examination of the Circulatory System. Topics of Psychosomatic Research, 9th European Conference on Psychosomatic Research Vienna, 1972," Psychother. Psychosom. 22 (1973): 299.

[168] Howard B. Kaplan et al., "Affective Orientation and Physiological Activity (GSR) in Small Peer Groups," Psychosomatic Medicine 25 (1963): 245.

[169] M. McClintock, "Menstrual Synchrony and Suppression," Nature 229 (1971): 229-244.

[170] J. Mason, "Psychological Influences on the Pituitary Adrenal-Cortical System," Recent Progress in Hormone Research 15 (1959): 345.

[171] Medical Department, United States Army, Neuropsychiatry in World War 11, Vol. 2: Overseas Theaters (Washington, D.C.: U.S. Government Printing Office, 1973), p. 995.

[172] Irving L. Ianis, Air War and Emotional Stress: Psychological Studies of Bombing and Civilian Defense (New York: McGraw Hill, 1951).

[173] Stanley Schachter, The Psychology of Affiliation (Stanford, Calif.: Stanford University Press, 1959).

[174] Ibid, p. 133.

[175] Joe W. E. Dimsdale, "The Coping Behavior of Nazi Concentration Camp Survivors," American Journal of Psychiatry 131 (1974): 792-797.

[176] K. W. Back and M. Bogdonoff, "Plasma Lipid Responses to Leadership, Conformity and Deviation," Psychobiological Approaches to Social Behavior, ed. P. H. Leiderman and D. Shapiro (Stanford, Calif.: Stanford University Press, 1964).

[177] William W. Schottstaedt et al., "Sociologic and Metabolic Observations on Patients in the Community of a Metabolic Ward," American Journal of Medicine 25 (1958): 248-257.

[178] Stewart Wolf et al., "Changes in Serum Lipids in Relation to Emotional Stress during Rigid Control of Diet and Exercise," Circulation 26 (1962): 379-387.

[179] E. Home, "A Short Account of the Author's Life: A Treatise on the Blood, Inflammation and Gunshot Wounds, by J. Hunter" (Philadelphia: T. Bradford, 1796).

[180] William Osler, "The Lumleian Lectures on Angina Pectoris: Delivered Before the Royal College of Physicians of London," Lancet I (1910): 839-844.

[181] Ibid, p. 698.

[182] Ian P. Stevenson et al., "Life Situations, Emotions and Extrasystoles," Psychosomatic Medicine 11 (1949): 257.

[183] Herbert Weiner, Margaret T. Singer, and Morton F. Reiser, "Cardiovascular Responses and Their Psychological Correlates I: A Study in Healthy Young Adults and Patients with Peptic Ulcer and Hypertension," Psychosomatic Medicine 24 (1962): 498.

[184] Ibid, p. 494.

[185] William N. Chambers and Morton F. Reiser, "Emotional Stress in the Precipitation of Congestive Heart Failure," Psychosomatic Medicine IS (1953): 38-60.

[186] Ibid, p. 55.

[187] William Osler, "The Lumleian Lectures on Angina Pectoris: Delivered Before the Royal College of Physicians of London," Lancet I (1910): 839-844.

[188] Gunnar Bjorck, "Social and Psychological Problems in Patients with Chronic Cardiac Illness" American Heart Journal, 58 (1959): 414-417.

[189] Z. L. Lipowski "Psychophysiological Cardiovascular Disorders," Comprehensive Textbook of Psychiatry, 2nd ed., eds. A. M. Freedman, H. I. Kaplan, and B. J. Sadock (Baltimore, Md.: Williams and Wilkins, 1974).

[190] Robert F. Klein et al., "Transfer from a Coronary Care Unit: Some Adverse Responses," Archives of Internal Medicine 122 (1968) at 104-108; see also W. Doyle Gentry, Gerard J. Musante, and Thomas Haney, "Anxiety and Urinary Sodium/Potassium as Stress Indicators on Admission to a Coronary Care Unit," Heart and Lung 2 (1973): 875-877.

[191] James J. Lynch et al., "The Effects of Human Contact on Cardiac Arrhythmia in Coronary Care Patients," Journal of Nervous and Mental Disease 158 (1974): 88-91.

[192] James J. Lynch et al., "Human Contact and Cardiac Arrhythmia in a Coronary Care Unit," Psychosomatic Medicine (1977). See also, M. E. Mills et al., "The Effects of Pulse Palpitation on Cardiac Arrhythmia in Coronary Care Patients," Nursing Research 25 (1976): 378-382.

[193] James J. Lynch, D. Paskewitz, K. Gimbel, S. Thomas. "Psychological Aspects

of Cardiac Arrhythmia," American Heart Journal, 1977; 93: 645-657.

[194] Ibid, 164.

[195] James J. Lynch et al., "Effects of Human Contact on the Heart Activity of Curarized Patients in a Shock-Trauma Unit," American Heart Journal 88 (1974): 160-169.

[196] Gunnar Biorck, "Social and Psychological Problems in Patients with Chronic Cardiac Illness," American Heart Journal 58 (1959): 414-417.

[197] E. Friedmann, A. Katcher, J. Lynch, and S.Thomas. Animal companions and one-year survival of patients discharged from a coronary care unit. Public Health Reports, 1980; 307-312.

198 Since that time, the Critikon Company became a separate company from Johnson and Johnson, and Dr. Ramsey retired. He has since moved on to new ventures in medical technology working for the Cardiocommand Corporation in Tampa, Flordia, where he serves as company president.

[199] J. Lynch and D. Paskewitz. On the mechanisms of the feedback control of human brain wave activity. Journal of Nervous and Mental Disease,1971;153:205-217.

[200] W.B.Cannon. Bodily changes in Pain, Hunger, Fear, and Rage.1929, Appleton-Century-Crofts, New York.

[201] S. Wolf, et al. Life Stress and Essential Hypertension. 1955, Williams and Wilkins, Baltimore, MD.

[202] F. Alexander. Psychoanalytic study of a case of essential hypertension. Psychosomatic Medicine, 1939; 1: 139-156.
F. Alexander. Emotional factors in essential hypertension. Psychosomatic Medicine, 1939, 1: 173-175.
F. Alexander. Psychosomatic Medicine: Its Principles and Applications. 1950; W.W. Norton, New York.

[203] W. Linden, C. Stossel, J. Maurice. Psychosocial interventions for patients with coronary artery disease. A meta-analysis. Archives of Internal Medicine,1996; 156:745.752.

[204] H. Benson. The Relaxation Response. 1975, Morrow, New York.
H. Benson. The physiology of meditation, Scientific American, 1972; 226: 84-90.

[205] S. Thomas, J. Lynch, E. Friedmann, M. Suginohara, P. Hall, and C. Peterson. Blood pressure and heart rate changes in children when they read aloud in school. Public Health Reports; 1984; 99: 77-84.

[206] E. Friedmann, A. Katcher, J. Lynch, and P. Messent. Social interaction and blood pressure: Influence of animal companions. Journal of Nervous and Mental Disease.1983; 171: 461-465.
A. Katcher, E. Friedmann, A. Beck & J. Lynch. Looking, talking and blood pressure: The physiological consequences of interaction with the living environment. In New Perspectives on our Lives with Companion Animals, ed. by A. Katcher, and A. Beck. 1983; University of Pennsylvania Press, Philadelphia, PA.

[207] A. Katcher and G. Wilkins. A controlled trial of animal assisted therapy and education in a residential treatment unit. Paper presented to the Sixth Annual Conference on Human Animal Interactions; Sixth International Conference on Human Animal Interactions, 1996, Montreal.

[208] E. Friedmann, S. Thomas, D. Kulick-Ciuffo, J. Lynch, and M. Suginohara. The effects of normal and rapid speech on blood pressure. Psychosomatic Medicine, 1982; 44:545-552.

[209] Ibid, Note # 4.

[210] J. Long, J. Lynch, N. Machiran, S. Thomas, and K. Malinow. The effect of status on blood pressure. Journal of Behavioral Medicine, 1982; 5: 165-172.

[211] Ibid, 180.

[212] Ibid, Note # 5.

[213] F. Craig, J. Lynch, J. Quartner, and P. Rosch. Peak blood pressure and heart rate during maximal stress testing, aerobic exercise and during an interview in Phase Two cardiac rehabilitation patients. Submitted to Psychosomatic Medicine, 2000.

[214] K. Malinow, J. Lynch, P. Foreman, E. Friedmann, and S. Thomas. Blood pressure increases while signing in a deaf population. Psychosomatic Medicine, 1986; 48: 95-101.

[215] Ibid, 183.

[216] J. Lynch, J. Long, S. Thomas, K. Malinow, and A. Katcher. The effect of talking on the blood pressure of hypertensive and normotensive individuals.

Psychosomatic Medicine, 1981; 43: 25-33.

J. Lynch, S. Thomas, J. Long, K. Malinow, E. Friedmann, and A. Katcher. Blood pressure changes while talking. Israeli Journal of Medical Science. 1982; 18: 575-579.

[217] Ibid, 186.

[218] Ibid, 176.

[219] Ibid, Note # 5.

[220] Y. E. Sokolov. Perception and the Conditioned Reflex. Trans. By Stefan W. Waydenfeld. 1963, The MacMillan Co., New York.

[221] J. Lynch. The cardiac orienting response and its relationship to the cardiac conditional response in dogs. Conditional Reflex, 1967, 2:138-152.

[222] Y. E. Sokolov. Perception and the Conditioned Reflex. Trans. By Stefan W. Waydenfeld. 1963, The MacMillan Co., New York, p. 176.

[223] As this book was going to press, Sinai-Wellbridge changed its name to "Lifebridge Health and Fitness Center."

[224] "Health commissioner calls life expectancy study unfair. Comments on study by Dr. Christopher Murray of the Harvard School of Public Health." Baltimore Sun, Dec. 6, 1997, B3.

[225] Y. E. Sokolov. Perception and the Conditioned Reflex. Trans. By Stefan W. Waydenfeld. 1963, The MacMillan Co., New York, p. 183.

[226] A. Rozanski, C. Bairey, D. Krantz, et al. Mental stress and the induction of silent myocardial ischemia in patients with coronary heart artery disease. New England Journal of Medicine, 1988; 318: 1005-1012.

[227] A. Rozanski, J. Blumenthal, and J. Kaplan. Impact of psychological factors on the pathogenesis of cardiovascular disease and implications for therapy. Circulation. 1999, 2192-2217.

[228] T. Kamark, S. Everson, G. Kaplan, S. Mauck, R. Jennings, R. Salonen, and J. Salonen. Exaggerated blood pressure responses during mental stress are associated with enhanced carotid atherosclerosis in middle-aged Finnish men. Circulation, 1997; 96: 3842-3848.

[229] Ibid, 197.

[230] D. Sheps. PIMI (Psychophysiological investigations in myocardial ischemia). Paper presented at the 48th Scientific session of the American College of Cardiology, New Orleans, LA, Clinical Cardiology, 1999; 22: 370.

[231] P. Stone, D. Krantz, R. McMahon, et al. Relationship among mental stress-induced ischemia and ischemia during daily life and during exercise. The Psychophysiological Investigation of Myocardial Ischemia (PIMI) Study. Journal of the American College of Cardiology, 1999; 33:1476-1484.

[232] J. Lynch & P. Rosch. The heart of dialogue: Human communication and cardiovascular health (pp 31-52) in A New Medical Model: A Challenge for Biomedicine. Ed H. Balner. 1990, Swet & Zeitlinger, Amsterdam.

[233] E. Golomb. Trapped in the Mirror: Adult children of narcissists in their struggle for self. 1992. William Morrow Co. New York, NY.

[234] A. Miller. The Drama of the Gifted Child: The Search for the True Self. 1981; Basic Books, New York, NY.

[235] One other feeling has constrained me from giving clinical advice—our society is already saturated with such counsel. There are books on bereavement, divorce, being single, anxiety, depression, etc. Almost every major U.S. newspaper has a daily advice section for interpersonal difficulties. Sometimes, however, such advice can be used as a substitute for personal action. Many bereaved individuals or anxious divorcees do not need advice at all. What they need is human compassion and human friendship; they just need you to be there. Your counsel is often far less important than your mere presence.

[236] It is of interest to note that Comstock and Patridge, in a detailed retrospective study in Maryland, found that men who were frequent attenders of religious services had a coronary mortality rate only 60 percent of those who rarely or never attended church. In women, the rate was 50 percent. In the same article, the authors cited the work of Shamgar and Medalie in Israel who reported similar findings. Comstock and Patridge also noted that they could find no support in their data for an alternative hypothesis that the beginnings of illness reduced the frequency of church attendance in those who died subsequently. [I should add that I am grateful to C. D. Jenkins, who called these intriguing data to my attention in his article published in the New England Journal of Medicine in 1976, entitled "Recent Evidence Supporting Psychologic and Social Risk Factors for Coronary Disease."

[237] I find myself frequently alluding to this story when patients who have been

injured in relationships inform me that they will never again try to relate intimately with another human being. Although the pain they have experienced makes such sentiments understandable, I do remind them that they are attempting to "pull off" what Adam could not accomplish in Paradise, and that they were scarcely leading their own lives in Paradise.

INDEX

Abortion, 37

Accidental death, 103

Adrenaline, 5

African-Americans, 3
  Life expectancy for, 50
  Greater susceptibility to heart disease
  and stroke, 55
  Higher mortality rate compared to
  whites, 99
  Higher mortality from strokes and
  hypertension, 101-02
  Among women, higher mortality from
  strokes and hypertension, 102
  Susceptibility to hypertension and heart
  disease, 107-08
  Hypertension in, 140-41
  Life expectancy for, 189-90, 283-84
  As victims of low educational
  attainment, 324-25

Alcoholics Anonymous, 318

Alexander, Dr. Franz
  Research on psychotherapy and stress,
  249-51

Alternative medicine, 49

American Heart Association, 31, 47, 52, 297,
327
  Public Service Announcements by, 155-
  56

Animals (*Also see Pets* and *Companion
animals*)
  Research on, 195-212

Anti-anxiety drugs, 2

Anti-depressant medication, 2

Anxiety (*Also see Stress* and *Mental Stress*)
  As found in heart patients, 222-23

Appalachian Hiking Club, 318

Aristotle
  Warning about human loneliness, 77

Arteriosclerosis
  Views on causes of, 60

AT&T, 160-166

Autonomic nervous system, 5

Benson, Dr. Herbert
  And "relaxation response," 251, 304

Bereavement
  Studies of, 114-15

Beta-blocker
  Testing effectiveness of, 185-89

Bible
  Value of its lessons on human
  companionship, 315-16
  References to Adam, Eve, and Paradise,
  339-42

Biofeedback
  Limitations of in controlling blood
  pressure, 244

Birth control, 37
Birth rate
  In U.S., 35

Blood pressure
  Normal rises, drops, 3
  Ordinary equipment for measuring, 3-4
  In emergencies, 5
  Emphasis Americans put on readings
  for, 58
  Teachers' impact on students', 217
  Surges as responses to everyday
  dialogue, 224
  Method of getting accurate readings of,
  228-29
  Variability of, 245
  Reasons to doubt usefulness of
  stethoscope readings, 254
  And infants, 256-58
  Surges and impact on social contact, 263
  Studies linking it to talking, 266
  Measurements of children reciting
  ABCs, 267-68
  Changes in children reading aloud, 269
  Reductions through listening, focusing
  on nature, etc, 272
  Increases while talking vs. increases
  during stress tests, 291-92
  And public speaking, 296
  And heart transplant patients, 299-300
  Seen as regulated by the renal system,
  24

LUMINARIES PRAISE JAMES LYNCH'S "A CRY UNHEARD"

"In the field of mind/body medicine, Dr. James Lynch is one of the true pioneers. His classic *The Broken Heart*, one of this field's most important books, was far, far ahead of its time, and helped inspire my own work. This new follow-up to *The Broken Heart* should encourage everyone to begin healing their hearts -- physically, emotionally, and spiritually."
—**DEAN ORNISH, M.D.**, Preventive Medicine Research Institute, University of California Medical School, and author, *Love & Survival* and *Dr. Dean Ornish's Program for Reversing Heart Disease*

"This is a gem of a book that deserves wide readership, because virtually everyone is personally involved in its contents. The author has devoted a great deal of time and highly productive effort to gathering his material and has presented it so well that it makes for very easy reading. I recommend it highly as a valuable and immensely illuminating experience."
—**RAY ROSENMAN, M.D.**, author, *Type A Behavior and Your Heart*

"On the silver anniversary of the publication of *The Broken Heart* comes this major new book, which should be received as an elegant gift of pure gold. Just the chapters on the links between educational failure, its consequent loneliness, and the stunning increased vulnerabilty to premature death decades later are enough to make this must reading for every parent, teacher, and policy maker in our nation."
—**PAUL ROSCH, M.D.**, President of the American Institute of Stress

"A pioneer in the field of mind/body/interpersonal medicine has given us an updated, useful, and wise prescription for better health and well-being."
— **HERBERT BENSON, M.D.**, President, Mind/Body Medical Institute, Harvard University, and author of *The Relaxation Response* and *Timeless Healing*

"In his first book, *The Broken Heart*, James Lynch began a sea change in modern medicine that anticipated the whole holistic therapy movement. His demonstration that friends, family, and community are vital necessities for continuing health and longevity was the catalyst for the rapid growth in knowledge about the health value of companion animals and contact with nature. This book, *A Cry Unheard*, with its wealth of new data, is absolutely required reading for all parents and school teachers, as well as anyone interested in the therapeutic value of contact with animals and nature."

—**AARON H. KATCHER, M.D.** Emeritus Professor, The University of Pennsylvania, and author of "Between Pets and People: The Importance of Animal Companionship" and "New Perspectives on Our Lives with Companion Animals"

"James Lynch is one of the pioneers of the so-called 'humanistic' approach to medicine -- the belief that the human organism is not merely a machine to be repaired but a person to be respected. His *The Broken Heart*, which argued that heart disease and loneliness were intimately correlated, went on to become one of the most important and successful publications of its kind. Now in *A Cry Unheard*, he returns with more evidence that failure and loss have a powerful impact on heart disease and blood pressure, and that the touch of a friendly human hand can have an enormous effect on an ailing patient. In particular, he demonstrates that school failure dooms many to a life of guilt and pain and sickness. American medicine has been forced to take his work and that of similar pioneers seriously. Now, in his second masterpiece, American education will have to listen to him, too."

—**ANDREW M. GREELEY**, best-selling novelist, columnist, and sociologist

"Just when many people expected that high-tech medicine would be our salvation, an avalanche of evidence is showing that our health is highly dependent on our loving connections with others. Love, connectedness, and empathy are not just feel-good issues; they are life-and-death factors for everyone. Dr. James Lynch is THE authority in this field. If we expect to live long, healthy lives, we *must* come to terms with the information in this landmark book. "

—**LARRY DOSSEY, M.D.**, best-selling author of *Reinventing Medicine*, and editor of the medical journal *Alternative Therapies*

ABOUT THE AUTHOR

James J. Lynch, Ph.D., is the author of three books, including his two previous ones, *The Broken Heart* and *The Language of the Heart*. He is a board member of The American Institute of Stress, on the staff of the Cardiovascular Rehabilitation Program at Lifebridge Health, formerly known as the Sinai-WellBridge Center, and the Director of the Life Care Health Center in Baltimore, Maryland. For more than 30 years, he served on the medical school faculties of the Johns Hopkins University, the University of Pennsylvania, and the University of Maryland. He lives in suburban Baltimore with his wife Eileen.

Lynch studied under Dr. W. Horsley Gantt, the last American student of the late, great Pavlov. He began his own teaching as a psychiatry instructor at the Johns Hopkins Medical School in 1966. In 1976, he was made a full professor at the University of Maryland Medical School. From 1976 through 1989, he directed the Center for the Study of Human Psychophysiology at the University of Maryland School of Medicine. Since 1989, he has directed his own clinic and research center at Life Care Health in Baltimore.

More than 10 chapters Lynch has written have been published in medical textbooks. He has also published more than 100 articles in peer-reviewed medical journals. A prominent and active member of the International Pavlovian Society, he based *A Cry Unheard* on 36 years of research and clinical work with heart patients.

Lynch interviews in connection with *The Broken Heart* appeared on or in 19 international/national TV programs, 32 national magazines, three national radio programs, 31 major daily newspapers, 16 national news syndicates, and 17 medical publications. His "60 Minutes" segment documenting the health benefits of pets has been rebroadcast numerous times. It was that appearance that began the movement to bring pets into institutions such as nursing homes and hospitals, to help alleviate loneliness and improve patients' health and overall quality of life.

At his Baltimore office, Lynch can be reached by phone (410) 321-5781; fax (410) 296-0260; or website http://www.lifecarehealth.com, which includes addendum information to *A Cry Unheard*.